Why is nationalism so widespread today? How does the phenomenon arise? How can its negative consequences be controlled? This collection of essays by economists, sociologists, and political scientists from North America and Europe tries to answer these questions at the forefront of contemporary political discussion. The work differs from others in that the authors' responses are not based on avowed ideological perspectives but are rather drawn from rational-choice analysis, the foundation of social science.

Although each of the contributors to *Nationalism and Rationality* takes a distinctive point of view, the collection, as a whole, focuses on three subjects – the origins of nationalism, whether and why it promotes good or evil, and how to deal with its occasional destructive consequences. Readers will find provocative insights into nationalism through the contributors' diverse diagnoses and prescriptions.

Nationalism and rationality

Nationalism and rationality

Edited by
ALBERT BRETON
University of Toronto, Canada

GIANLUIGI GALEOTTI
Università di Roma (La Sapienza), Italy

PIERRE SALMON
Université de Bourgogne, France

RONALD WINTROBE
University of Western Ontario, Canada

CAMBRIDGE
UNIVERSITY PRESS

32 Avenue of the Americas, New York NY 10013-2473, USA

Cambridge University Press is part of the University of Cambridge.

It furthers the University's mission by disseminating knowledge in the pursuit of education, learning and research at the highest international levels of excellence.

www.cambridge.org
Information on this title: www.cambridge.org/9780521480987

© Cambridge University Press 1995

This publication is in copyright. Subject to statutory exception and to the provisions of relevant collective licensing agreements, no reproduction of any part may take place without the written permission of Cambridge University Press.

First published 1995

A catalogue record for this publication is available from the British Library

Library of Congress Cataloguing in Publication data
Nationalism and rationality / edited by Albert Breton ... [et al.].
p. cm.
Papers presented at the 5th Villa Colombella Seminar, held on Sept. 2-4, 1992.
Includes index.
ISBN 0-521-48098-1
1. Nationalism - Congresses. I. Breton, Albert. II. Villa Colombella Seminar (5th : 1992)
JC311.N3225   1995
320.5´4 – dc20   94-47970
                                                                CIP

ISBN 978-0-521-48098-7 Hardback
ISBN 978-0-521-14267-0 Paperback

Cambridge University Press has no responsibility for the persistence or accuracy of URLs for external or third-party internet websites referred to in this publication, and does not guarantee that any content on such websites is, or will remain, accurate or appropriate.

Contents

	List of contributors and discussants	*page* vii
	Introduction	ix
1	Rights, rationality, and nationality *James S. Coleman*	1
2	Self-interest, group identity *Russell Hardin*	14
3	Some economics of ethnic capital formation and conflict *Ronald Wintrobe*	43
4	Ethnic clubs, ethnic conflict, and the rise of ethnic nationalism *Roger D. Congleton*	71
5	Nationalism revisited *Albert Breton & Margot Breton*	98
6	The reemergence of secessionism: Lessons from Quebec *Stéphane Dion*	116
7	Notes on the political economy of nationalism *Ronald Findlay*	143
8	Conservative nationalism and democratic institutions *Jean-Dominique Lafay*	159
9	Can economics explain nationalism? *Ugo Pagano*	173

Contents

10 The economics of socialist nationalism: Evidence and theory 204
Mario Ferrero

11 Regulating nations and ethnic communities 245
Brendan O'Leary & John McGarry

12 Nations conspiring against themselves: An interpretation of European integration 290
Pierre Salmon

Index 313

Contributors and discussants

Albert Breton
Department of Economics
University of Toronto

Margot Breton
Faculty of Social Work
University of Toronto

James S. Coleman
Department of Sociology
University of Chicago

Roger D. Congleton
Center for Study of Public Choice
George Mason University

Stéphane Dion
Département de Science Politique
Université de Montréal

Mario Ferrero
Dipartimento di Economia
Università di Torino

Ronald Findlay
Department of Economics
Columbia University

Gianluca Fiorentini
Dipartimento di Scienze Economiche
Università di Bologna

Gianluigi Galeotti
Istituto di Economia e Finanza
Facoltà di Giurisprudenza
Università di Roma (La Sapienza)

Russell Hardin
New York University - Politics

Manfred Holler
Institute of Economics
University of Hamburg

Jean-Dominique Lafay
Laboratoire d'Économie Publique
Université de Paris I, Panthéon-Sorbonne

Massimo Marelli
Dipartimento di Economia Pubblica
Università di Napoli

John McGarry
Department of History and Political Science
King's College (Canada)

Brendan O'Leary
Department of Government
London School of Economics and Political Science

Ugo Pagano
Dipartimento di Economia Politica
Università di Siena

Pierre Salmon
Faculté de Science Économique
Université de Bourgogne

Paul Seabright
Faculty of Economics and Politics
University of Cambridge

Ronald Wintrobe
Department of Economics
University of Western Ontario

Introduction

The literature on nationalism is enormous. Economists, historians, philosophers, political scientists, psychologists, sociologists, and other scholars as well as lay observers and commentators have all brought their particular skills and methods to bear on the phenomenon which, it would be easy to argue, has dominated human affairs for a good part of the nineteenth century and throughout the twentieth. The contribution of what we may call the rational choice paradigm to that literature has, however, not been large. The questions posed by the contemporary reemergence of nationalism, often in populations where it had once been virulent but for a good part of this century seemed to have vanished, as well as the challenge of providing answers to these questions based on the assumption of rational behavior, motivated us to choose nationalism as the topic of the Fifth Villa Colombella Seminar.[1]

The papers prepared for the seminar range widely. This notwithstanding, we believe that the collection of papers which follows makes a novel, interesting and rigorous contribution to the problem of nationalism. In particular, one or more of the papers deal with the following three questions that are surely central: (1) What are some of the factors, rooted in the self-interest of actors, which can account for the emergence of nationalism? (2) Is nationalism efficient from an individual and from a social point of view? and (3) Are there effective ways

---

[1] The Proceedings of the first four seminars have been published: *Villa Colombella Papers on Federalism*, European Journal of Political Economy (Vol. 3, Special Issue, Nos 1 and 2, 1987); *Villa Colombella Papers on Bureaucracy*, European Journal of Political Economy (Vol. 4, Extra Issue, 1988); *The Competitive State. Villa Colombella Papers on Competitive Politics* (Dordrecht: Kluwer, 1991); and *Preferences and Democracy* (Dordrecht: Kluwer, 1993).

of dealing with the inefficient and destructive manifestations of nationalism?

Specifically, a number of papers suggest mechanisms capable of explaining, from a rational choice perspective, the rise of nationalism. To illustrate, Coleman argues that when the allocation of "rights" is in doubt in a given society, different groups will attempt to appropriate these rights to their advantage and use nationalism as a mobilizing force. Hardin proposes an approach to the search for identity and emphasizes that this search and the identity itself act as motivation for nationalism. Congleton models ethnic clubs as suppliers of goods and services and argues that this activity serves as a spur to nationalism. Wintrobe models the central role of families as generators of ethnic capital which can then support nationalism; while Breton and Breton model economic nationalism as a phenomenon which gives rise to asset redistribution between social groups in a jurisdiction and argue that cultural nationalism and xenophobia serve to undergird that redistribution.

Further, a number of papers contain new and provocative analyses of the individual and social efficiency of nationalism, analyses which were only possible because of the systematic application of economic reasoning to the phenomenon of nationalism. Many of the papers that follow stress that nationalism is *individually* rational and efficient. A few also make the point that nationalism can be *collectively* or *socially* inefficient. For example, in Breton and Breton, in Wintrobe and in Coleman individual rationality leads to collective overinvestment of resources in the pursuit of nationalist objectives and is therefore socially inefficient, while in Salmon's paper there is underinvestment in what could be called a "broader" identity – one that is "less ethnic."

The collection contains attempts, especially in the O'Leary and McGarry paper but also in scattered remarks throughout, to examine ways and means of dealing with some manifestations of nationalism.

In addition, some papers are devoted to what we could call the micro foundations of nationalism, while others focus on the big picture from the outset and are, therefore, more macro analytical in orientation. Some are concerned with the forces and mechanisms that root nationalism in ethnicity; others propose an analysis which is consistent with the view that nationalism is not always ethnically based. Some papers or parts thereof are more concerned with what we could call – using the language of "applied welfare economics" – the benefits of nationalism, whereas others focus more exclusively on its costs; in some approaches, it is indeed fair to say, there are virtually no benefits to nationalism, while in others it is the costs that are dimmed.

Introduction xi

We provide the barest outline of the papers simply to whet the reader's interest.

James Coleman argues that the allocation of "rights" is central to an understanding of the rise and fall of nationalism and of nationalist struggles within states. He develops a model based on the idea that the struggles arise at points in time when particular allocations of rights have come to be in doubt, so that the struggles are attempts to register a claim for the rights, that is, to have an allocation enforced to the advantage of a particular group. He shows that such struggles can be rational given the benefits that holding those rights confer on group members. Coleman also suggests that one of the reasons why nationalisms and nationalist struggles are often grounded in ethnicity is that members of ethnic groups act together toward a common goal and are acted upon together as members of a common group.

Russell Hardin's paper focuses directly on the issue of the formation of groups such as ethnic groups. He insists that this formation is not "primordial" but rational. Individuals, in other words, identify with such groups because it is in their interest to do so. Individuals may find identification with their group beneficial because those who identify strongly with the group may gain access to positions under its control. Hardin argues that individuals create their own identification with the group through the information and capacities they gain from life in the group. A group gains power to take action against other groups. Therefore, the group may be genuinely instrumentally good for its members who may, in turn, think the group is inherently, not merely contingently, good for them.

Ronald Wintrobe proposes a model of ethnic group competition which rests on the assumption that both entry and exit from ethnic groups are "blocked" – one cannot change one's ethnic background. Ethnic loyalty within the group means that the costs of trading within the group are reduced – ethnic loyalty is, as a consequence, a valuable capital asset – but, because entry and exit are blocked, competition among ethnic groups cannot equalize returns on ethnic capital. It is for this reason that successful ethnic groups tend to engender fear and jealousy, while members of ethnic groups with low returns become stigmatized. Conflict among ethnic groups is, therefore, inevitable and is not reduced by market forces. Conflict between groups is particularly exacerbated when families "overinvest" in the ethnic loyalty of their children.

Roger Congleton argues that the ebb and flow of ethnic nationalism can be explained with a "club" model of the production of ethnic services. He makes the point that from a theory of clubs perspective, the extent of "ethnic nationalism" is a matter of the extent to which clubs are important sources of services and duties. The more important the services provided by ethnic clubs, the greater is the importance of ethnic affiliation and the more extensive is ethnic nationalism. Assimilation occurs as ethnic group members demand and receive fewer services from ethnic clubs and rely more extensively upon state and community services based on citizenship rather than ethnic heritage. The comparative statics of the demand and supply of ethnic club services thus provides the basis of a model of the intensity of ethnic nationalism.

Congleton then argues that state activities affect the market demand for ethnic services by producing complements or substitutes for ethnic services and/or by adopting policies which affect the cost of producing ethnic services. Moreover, politically active ethnic clubs may be able to influence state fiscal and regulatory decisions in a manner which yields net benefits for their own members but net costs for nonmembers. Because the resources used to provide services are inherently scarce, ethnic rent seeking generally pits the welfare of one ethnic group against that of other groups. Independence movements gain popular support when group members expect to gain more from direct control of a smaller state than they sacrifice by giving up various economies of scale in governance associated with continued membership in a larger multicultural state.

Stéphane Dion proposes a framework to explain why and when a linguistic, religious or ethnic group will want to leave a political union. He studies the case of Quebec. The framework suggested is based on the idea that any secessionist movement is rooted in three basic feelings. First, a feeling of *fear* – a feeling of being weakened or even of disappearing as a distinct people if the group stays in the union; second, a feeling of *confidence* among group members that the group can perform well, or even better, on its own and that secession is not too risky; and third, a feeling of *rejection,* that is, a feeling of no longer being welcomed in the union. Dion then argues that when these three feelings are at high levels, secession is likely to occur. He suggests, based on a careful analysis of the available evidence, that although these three feelings are (at the time of writing) high among French-speaking Quebecers, they are not high enough to lead to a secession from the Canadian federation.

In their paper, Albert Breton and Margot Breton recognize the value of ethnic loyalty and acknowledge that individual members of society will want to invest in that form of capital. They argue, however, that the "elites" of ethnic groupings will find it in their interest to "exploit" ethnic loyalty by using the state to alter the distribution of tangible assets in a given jurisdiction away from the "foreigners" in that jurisdiction toward themselves. Because of this added value of ethnic loyalty to the "elites," they will want to invest in that loyalty over and above what individuals would themselves commit to that asset. That is how, they argue, cultural nationalism, overinvestment in ethnic loyalty, is related to political nationalism – the use of the state to change the interethnic or international distribution of tangible property, including territory. They also argue that xenophobia is a device that makes it possible for the elites to overinvest in ethnic loyalty.

Ronald Findlay looks at nationalism from the standpoint of the tensions arising from the lack of congruity between the state, as the sovereign authority over a specified territory, and the nation, considered as an "imagined community" bound together by ethnic, religious, or cultural ties. Specifically, Findlay examines some existing theories of nationalism, particularly that of Ernest Gellner, in the light of this relationship and concentrates on some contemporary manifestations of nationalism in the advanced industrial democracies, the former Soviet Union and Eastern Europe, and the Third World, particularly South and Southeast Asia.

Jean-Dominique Lafay's paper concentrates on what he calls "conservative nationalism" – in contrast to expansionist and separatist nationalisms – which, he argues, is governed by the maintenance of the national *status quo* and the reinforcement of the national identity. Under conservative nationalism, the social games within the nation are played more cooperatively, thus lowering transactions and other like costs. Physical, social, and cultural capital, which also reduces the costs of social interaction, is accumulated and a sense of belonging flourishes. Lafay, then, within a simple median voter model in which principal-agent problems are assumed away and in which competition between political parties is perfect, analyzes the factors that shape the demand for and the supply of conservative nationalism, as well as some of the properties of the static equilibrium. He also considers some factors that can lead to alterations in these equilibrium outcomes.

Ugo Pagano asks whether economics can explain nationalism. To answer the question, he begins by looking at the contribution of nations to the division of labor we observe in well-functioning market economies. He argues that even if "rent-seeking nationalism" can cause inefficient "institutional equilibria," because it supports a division of labor, nationalism may be included among the possible causes

xiv   **Introduction**

of the accumulation of wealth. Pagano then considers the limits of the economic explanations of nationalism and looks at some possible extensions to the economic approach that may help to provide a rationale for nationalistic activities that seem to defy any rational choice explanation. As part of that exercise, he considers whether an evolutionary approach would be more appropriate than a rational choice approach to explain nationalism; whether it is the "meme" of nationalism, instead of nationalists, that is maximizing its objective function.

Mario Ferrero's paper focuses at the outset on the spread and success of national liberation movements in which the "working classes" were actively involved – a fact which appears to contradict a basic prediction of Breton's (1964) model – and asks what happens when "bourgeois" nationalism à la Breton, which promises no further change beyond the transfer of foreign-held assets and managerial jobs to nationals, is faced with competition from "socialist" nationalism, in which nationalist and socialist goals are merged into one program and leadership is taken by a communist party. Ferrero's basic argument is that, when adequate political entrepreneurship is available, socialist nationalism tends to drive out bourgeois nationalism as a solution to the national question in dependent countries, because it can supply "voters" with a package that bourgeois nationalism cannot match: an enlarged pie available for redistribution to supporters, a redistribution of these benefits among a much broader constituency (the "working class" appropriately defined), and an increased likelihood of success. He also suggests that the current resurgence of aggressive nationalism in post-communist countries is not the legacy of a precommunist past, but the logical product of the redistributions that lay at the roots of the socialist solution to the national question. This is argued by examining the pattern of who is fighting who after the collapse of communism.

Brendan O'Leary and John McGarry develop a taxonomy of macro-political methods that are used to eliminate and manage national and ethnic conflict. Genocide, mass-population transfers, secession/partition, and integration/assimilation are shown to be ways of eliminating national and ethnic conflict. Control, arbitration, federalism/cantonization and consociationalism are presented as ways of managing national and ethnic conflict. O'Leary and McGarry discuss the circumstances under which the various methods are likely to be used, and to be effective. The normative merits of the various methods are also explored. The authors display some skepticism about economic reductionism in accounting for national and ethnic conflict, but they are not skeptical about the possible insights which rational choice or game

Introduction

theory may bring to the formal modeling of national and ethnic conflict regulation.

Pierre Salmon's paper examines the obverse of nationalism, namely the "transfer" of attachments from a smaller to a larger community through integration. He starts from the observation that European integration looks like a conspiracy and he tries to explain why it takes this aspect. He argues that the main long-run objective of integration, shared by the voters themselves, is to tie together the member countries and that, for that purpose, the building up of attachments to the European Community is necessary. The problems involved in building up or transferring attachments explain why the process of integration is typically roundabout and its objectives disguised. Salmon suggests a model in which the attachments of citizens to their country and to Europe, as well as the powers available to both jurisdictions, are considered as factors of production. Because the distribution of attachments is assumed to be fixed in the short run, a transfer of powers from one level of jurisdiction to the other causes a decrease in the overall level of production. It is only in the course of time that powers, in parallel with a changing distribution of attachments, can be transferred from the level of national states to that of Europe. This process is not reversible in the short run, which means that an integration process of that kind achieves the objective of tying together the member states.

The reader will notice that we are a long way from a tolerably complete, consistent, and empirically relevant theory of nationalism based on the axioms of the rational choice paradigm. We are not even close to the possibility of a generally agreed upon explanation of why nationalism sometimes reveals itself simply as nationalism whereas at other times it disguises itself along ideological lines as communism or as religious fundamentalism; of why nationalism is sometimes racist while at other times it is more tolerant of racial and ethnic differences; and of why it sometimes degenerates into terrorism and inhumanity. So much has to be acknowledged. But the reader will also notice, as he or she tries to synthesize the material in the various papers, that progress has been made. Indeed we believe that many building blocks for what will one day emerge as a rational choice theory of nationalism are discussed in the following pages.

The Seminar was held at Villa Colombella, near Perugia (Italy), September 2 to 4, 1992. We are grateful to the Lynde and Harry Bradley Foundation and to the Consiglio Nazionale delle Ricerche for their generous financial assistance, which made the Seminar possible. We are also grateful to the Maison des Sciences de l'Homme for providing facilities that allowed us to prepare the publication of this book and to the Università di Perugia for secretarial and technical assistance.

Albert Breton
Gianluigi Galeotti
Pierre Salmon
Ronald Wintrobe

CHAPTER 1

Rights, rationality, and nationality

James S. Coleman

The post communist conflicts among various ethnic and national groups in the former Soviet Union came as a surprise to many social scientists.[1] What I want to do in this paper is to lay out a conceptual framework that, if used as a lens for viewing the postcommunist period, would have made the emergence of conflict less surprising. Further, this conceptual framework should help more generally to account for the rise and fall of nationalist conflicts in various places of the world.

Intrinsic to this conceptual framework is the idea of "rights." The concept of rights, in the form of property rights, underlies much of economic theory, though property rights are often taken for granted and ignored in theoretical work. But it is also true that much of what is exchanged in economic markets consists of rights, with new markets constantly emerging as new rights are defined: common stock, preferred stock, bonds, futures, options, to name a few of the most common. Much of social exchange as well can be conceived as an exchange of rights. In other parts of social theory, concepts such as legitimacy and authority have the concept of "right" as part of their definition. To begin an examination of these matters, an example will help.

An example[2]

In a small village in the Basque region of Spain, there was, on one Saturday evening in July 1990, an elaborate performance by a set of

---

[1] See Kuran (1991) for a discussion of reasons why the downfall of communism was itself such a surprise.
[2] The description here is a minor modification of the example given in Coleman (1993).

professional dramatists in the town square. The performance was putatively for the children of the village, but a large fraction of the adults of the village were there as well. Draped on buildings around the square were banners demanding amnesty for those Basque men held prisoner in Spanish jails.

The drama had the following plot: A structure representing a castle, with a bull's head as the pinnacle, was inhabited by four players, three men and a woman. From the far corner of the square came another structure on wheels, but designed to represent a ship. It was manned by three tough-looking, somewhat unsavory characters, one wearing a beret. The three invading men attacked the castle, and a fierce fight ensued. One managed to climb the tower and bring down the bull's head. He and a second sailor carried the bull's head to the ship and placed it atop the cabin, while the third held off the remaining resistance from the castle. The ship with its three sailors began to pull away from the castle, as the last of the castle's inhabitants was subdued. Then came two huge creatures (actors shouldering hooded structures to make them larger than life) with fireworks spouting from their extended fingertips. They attacked the ship, in an effort to recapture the head of the bull. Spouting fire, as if from guns, they attacked again and again, only to be repulsed by the rifles of the three members of the ship's crew. Finally they sank to the earth, and the ship escaped with its trophy. The children shouted with glee, the adults clapped, and there was noise and tumult as the performance ended. The banners calling for amnesty flapped in the wind.

What did all this mean? The performers did not explain the symbolic significance of the play, but it clearly had the character of a medieval morality play. Like a medieval morality play, this performance had normative content; it was not morally neutral.

A plausible interpretation of the performance is consistent with the banners waving in the background. The castle was Spain, and the head of the bull the prized symbol of Spanish rule. The three toughs on the ship, one with a Basque beret, symbolized the Basques. Their victory in capturing the head of the bull and their successful defense against the military force brought in to subdue them, symbolized the victory of the Basques against Spain.

This performance occurred on Spanish territory. Who or what gave the performers the right to carry out an anti-Spanish morality play? The first simple answer is that in most authority systems there exists a right, embodied in law as a legal right, or in common consensus as a norm, for freedom of expression. The right is especially strong when the expression is veiled in artistic symbolism, and cannot be construed

Rights, rationality, and nationality

as breaking a law. It is a right that has existed to various degrees even in despotic regimes.

But the answer is more complicated than this. The performance was carried out not only on Spanish territory, but also in the Basque region, and in a village in which sentiment for Basque autonomy is strong. In order to carry out the performance at that time and place, the troupe needed not only the right that was (implicitly) granted by the Spanish authorities, but also the right, at the explicit disposal of the local authorities, to perform in the village square that Saturday evening. If the general symbolism of the play was known to the local authorities, then their granting of that right (a right more specific than the right to freedom of expression, because it included occupying village property at an important time, and probably some payment of fees for performance) was very likely contingent on their agreement with the normative content of the play.

Finally, we can ask about an even more intangible right, a right under the control of the audience: the right to be heard. That the audience controls this right is evident from numerous examples, in which performers have been booed off stage, or speakers on college campuses have been prevented from speaking by vocal student groups who oppose their views. Suppose that in this case the troupe had transmitted the opposite moral with their morality play, with the Basque sailors chased off or killed by the Spanish. The audience might well have withdrawn the right they had granted to the troupe to perform, and shouted them off the village square.

This explanation thus derives the right to perform this play jointly from three other rights. But if these three rights necessary for the performance are under the control of Spanish central authorities, local village authorities, and the audience, then where does each of these actors get those rights?

The very term "authority" begins an unraveling that leads to an answer for the two sets of authorities involved, for the definition of authority is the legitimate exercise of power. In turn, the definition of legitimacy of an action is the recognized *right* to carry out the action. Thus the authorities, by virtue of their official position, have the legal right to grant the right in question. (In the case of the Spanish central authorities, the matter can better be described in different terms, since the right to freedom of expression is contained in law: They have the obligation to protect the performers' legal right to freedom of expression.) This implies a hierarchy of rights, as shown in Figure 1.1. The hierarchy can be best seen by examining the right granted by local authorities, to perform on Saturday evening in the village square. That

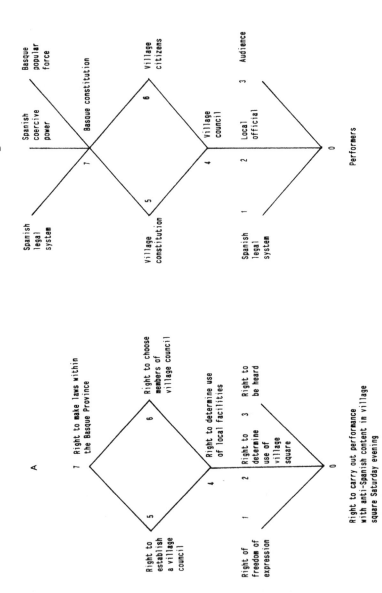

Figure 1.1 Actors Holding Rights

right was probably granted by a local official, occupying a position to which the right was delegated by the village council. The council in turn gained that right through two sources: The village charter gave that right to the village council, and the citizens of the village elected particular persons as members of the council. The charter in turn derives from the Basque constitution.

All appears to be sweetness and light, a hierarchical system of authority within which rights cascade down from one level to another, with the extent of rights cascading down determined by the legal structure or the authorities at the higher level.

But there is an unsettling note, not directly affecting the rights at issue, but relevant to the question of what rights the people of the Basque region have to establish their own constitution, and how those rights originated. The unsettling note is that the Basque region has certain rights that Cantabria, next to it, and existing under the same Spanish legal system, does not have. For example, the Basque region has the right to have all highway signs in its own language as well as in Spanish. It also has the right to collect all taxes, from which it gives a fraction to the central government of Spain. In Cantabria and other regions, Spanish taxes are collected by an agency of the Spanish government, with a fraction returned to the local province.

Why does the Basque region own these rights, while others do not? Alongside this, we may ask why it does not have another right, a right claimed on the posters and banners that surrounded the village square on the night of the performance. This is the right to have those of its citizens now held in Spanish jails for acts of terrorism transferred to a jail within the Basque region.

These two questions point directly to the ongoing conflict between Spain and the Basques. The allocation of legal rights to the Basque region does not merely result from a legally regulated cascade of rights from central government to local government, but reflects the status of that conflict. The conflict is one between two kinds of power, the control of extensive resources including armed forces (held primarily by the Spanish central government) and the power to mobilize large numbers of people willing to act collectively (held primarily by the Basque activists). The activists in the Basque region have wrested extra rights for the region from the Spanish government through demonstrations, protests, terrorist acts, and threats of secession. This popular force has not had the power to gain all the rights demanded by many Basques, but has had the power to gain certain of these rights. One might say that the set of rights held by the Basque government derives from three forces: the legal system of Spain, the coercive force of the Spanish military and police forces, and the power exhibited by political actions (including acts of violence) of Basque activists, supported by Basque citizens. Figure 1.1a shows the partly hierarchical, partly not, structure of rights, and Figure 1.1b shows this same structure, but as a structure of relations between actors holding rights.

This does not, of course, end the regress backward from the right with which we began. It carries this regress back only to the Spanish legal system, to the police force of Spain, and to the popular force of the Basques. Yet by carrying the regress this far, the example indicates something about how legal rights come to be held by one party rather than another.

The right to collect taxes is in the hands of the Basque officials but not in the hands of Cantabria officials, because the balance of power between the central government of Spain and the Basque government and its people is less on the side of the central government than is true for the balance between the central government and Cantabria. The legal right to hold members of its population, convicted in Spanish courts, in jails of its own choosing is not held by the Basque region but by the central government, because the power of the Basques is not sufficiently great to gain this right from the central government. A large number of Basques believe that they have the right, or *ought* to have the right, to have these men held in the Basque region, but this belief is opposed by the Spanish government and indeed by many Spaniards who are not Basques.

The holding of legal rights is in continual flux as the balance of power changes. There are claims of rights by those who do not hold them, such as the claim by Basques to hold convicted Basque terrorists in their own jails. There is a claim by some Spaniards outside the Basque region of the right of the central government to eliminate the teaching of Euskara (the Basque language) from schools in the Basque region, but until this claim is recognized by the legal structure which is backed by police power, the right remains in Basque hands.

The two sources of rights

This example illustrates the two quite different sources of a right. Figure 1.1 shows how the right initially in question derives from the conjunction of three rights. It shows as well the derivation of one of these rights (the right to determine use of the village square) from a more encompassing right, and traces that right all the way up to the right to make laws within the Basque region.

Rights, rationality, and nationality 7

This shows one kind of rights source: A right may follow directly from a broader right, above it in a hierarchical structure of rights. Insofar as the broader right obtains, it implies a set of specific rights which are, in effect, contained within it. Most rights have this kind of source: They are, like rights 2, 5, and 6 in Figure 1.1a, directly derivative from a higher-order ("broader" or "more inclusive") right. Others, like rights 0 and 4 in the figure, gain their existence from the simultaneous existence of two or more higher-order rights.

The second source of rights, however, is quite different. It is illustrated by right 7 in Figure 1.1a, the right to make laws within the Basque region. This right, as shown by Figure 1.1b, does not derive entirely from a higher-order right, but derives in part from the balance of power between a Basque popular force (or Basque "terrorists") and Spanish coercive power. The right to have road signs in Euskara and the right to collect their own taxes do not derive from a higher-order right, nor from the simultaneous existence of two or more higher-order rights. They result from a negotiated settlement of a claim for greater "Basque rights" on the part of some Basques, and an opposition to that claim by the Spanish government.

It is this latter source of rights which is most closely related to nationalist conflicts within a country. One may look at the matter in the following way: The constitution, implicit or explicit, of a state allocates rights to various actors: to the state itself, to be exercised by agencies of government, to individual citizens (as occurs in a "bill of rights"), and to particular subgroups within the state. The last of these may be defined geographically, as are provinces (the Basque region of Spain, the province of Quebec in Canada), or they may be defined by other characteristics, such as gender (for example, the proposed Equal Rights Amendment in the United States) or age (for example, minor children lack certain rights that adults have) by race (for example, the different rights held until recently by different races in South Africa) or national subgroups recognized by the constitution, or still other characteristics. The rights allocation produced by the constitution determines the specific rights of subgroups within the state – so long as the state has the capacity to enforce the existing rights allocation. It may well be that there is great disagreement within the society on this allocation, but so long as the power of the state is sufficient to enforce its authority, the allocation of rights will be as effective as if there were full consensus on the rights allocation.

Just as in the case of a market in which property rights are well defined and enforced, the actors within the system (individuals and corporate actors) will act so as to optimize *given the allocation of rights*. The result will be a system equilibrium resulting from these actions.

The optimizing behavior, however, and the equilibrium to which it leads, is, as in the case of a simple private goods market, specific to the existing rights allocation. If, for whatever reason, this rights allocation can no longer be enforced and the hierarchy of rights it produces crumbles, then the actions that were previously rational are no longer so. Different actions become individually optimal, and a different equilibrium results.

This can be seen most easily at the microlevel, in the case of a natural disaster or other event that results in looting. Looting occurs when property rights can no longer be enforced by the authorities. What was not rational for a person motivated purely by material self-interest before the event, when property rights were enforced, becomes rational when property rights are no longer enforced.

At the level of a state, the same phenomenon can be seen. East Germans, who with rare exceptions did not attempt to escape to West Germany so long as the authority of the East German state, backed by the authority of the Soviet army, was enforced by armed guards. But when Gorbachev was no longer willing to provide this backing, it suddenly became rational for many East Germans to flee to West Germany, through Hungary and Austria. The prospective new equilibrium was one in which East Germany would be denuded of most of its population, and West Germany would be deluged with the bulk of the East German population. It suddenly came to be in the interest of most of the corporate actors in both East and West Germany, including both governments, to immediately bring about reunification, which had seemed a highly unlikely prospect only a few months before.

An example somewhat closer to that of national conflicts when state authority is no longer enforced is the conflict among heirs of an estate after a wealthy man's death. When the will is disputable, rights to the wealth are no longer well defined, as they were before the death, and heirs who were quite compatible before the death suddenly become opponents, each claiming rights over a portion of the wealth that overlaps with others' claims.

National groups as actors

The above examples of the crumbling of a system of authority – and thus a system of rights allocation – illustrate individual actions toward purely individual goods. The case of nationalist conflicts when overall state authority vanishes or weakens involves an additional process. Individuals do not automatically come together along nationalist or ethnic lines when a system of rights collapses. First, there is a free-rider problem. A person defined as a member of a national group can experience the benefits of that group's gaining rights without participating in the conflict which will determine the rights allocation between national groups. Second, "nationality" is only one basis of individuals' self-identification (as Ukrainians, Lithuanians, Azerbaijanis, Russians, Serbs, Czechs, Croats). There are others as well. However, there is one element which may lead groups to claim rights *as* members of the national groups. Just as the claims of heirs to an estate are almost universally claims to portions of the wealth of the estate, the national group claims are almost universally claims to geographic territories. Thus apart from free-rider problems involved in any collective action, there are strong economic reasons for nationality, rather than age, or gender, or race, coming to be the basis of identity around which rights conflicts turn when territory is in dispute.

The main body of individuals in a national group constitutes a resource for those persons whose interests lie in success of the national group's rights claims. The success will ordinarily, in the absence of an authoritative and enforced allocation of rights, depend on the successful use of force.[3] But the successful use of force will in turn strengthen the self-identification of the members of the national group. Jews in Palestine, after the British left in 1947 and after their success in the Jewish-Arab war, gained a stronger identity as Jews, once the territory was conquered and the state of Israel was formed. If success in the use of force to win a rights claim is achieved, then the group rights once won constitute a resource with which to bind those who are included in the group to the group. As an almost trivial example, one which does not involve territory, the success of Indian (that is, Native American) leaders in wresting rights from state or federal governments of the United States has led some persons with an almost-forgotten Indian ancestor to claim membership in the group in order to claim the rights.

There is, then, this reciprocal use of resources by leaders of poten-

---

[3] The earliest work I have seen which pointed to differing interests of different members of national or ethnic groups in the acquisition of group rights is in a paper by Albert and Raymond Breton (1980). They showed that among the leaders of the separatist movement in Quebec in the 1960s were especially to be found employees of the French-language division of the Canadian Broadcasting Company. This was a group whose very livelihood depended on the maintenance of a vigorous French-language culture.

tially viable national groups: The members of the group, whatever their degree of identification with it, constitute resources in the latent struggle against other bases of identity (i.e., race or ethnicity vs geographically defined national identification, as exemplified by the identification as Kurds, whether Iraqi or Turkish, against the identification as Iraqis or Turks, whether Kurdish or not), and the manifest struggle against opposing groups (as exemplified by the struggle of Iraqi Sunnis against Iraqi Kurds). In turn, group rights that have been won become a new resource which can attract to the group identity all those who can claim group membership and for whom the group right is valuable. These rights sometimes include private goods, as, for example, when the resources obtained include land which can be distributed to group members. Such private goods may be made to serve as selective incentives to overcome the free-rider problem, by being made available only to participants in the struggle.

One can easily see how such a mutually reinforcing pair of processes can lead to the strengthening of group identity, whether it be a group defined along national, religious, gender, age, or country lines. What may not come so easily to mind but is equally a consequence of the mutual reinforcement is the extinction of contending group identities that are unsuccessful in the acquisition of group rights. The positive feedback can lead to extinction just as it can lead to intensification.

National groups engaged in common defense

Matters are, however, more complex. Persons who have a potentially common identity may come to have that identity reinforced by being subject to common treatment at the hand of another actor. This is true of a cohort of medical school students who, having had various individual self-identifications, gain a sense of common identity when required to jump over the same academic hurdles at the same time, just as it is of Jews in Germany in the 1930s who, having thought of themselves as Germans, came to gain self-identification as Jews when treated according to this single basis of identity.

This is not always the outcome: Treatment as a member of a particular group can be sufficiently harsh that when combined with the offer of escaping the identity, it can lead to extinguishing the group identity. An example is the case of Jews and Muslims who converted to Christianity in fifteenth-century Spain, when subject to the Inquisition plus the possibility of converting. The general phenomenon seems to be explicable in rational terms, as follows: When persons are treated as a group it may be rational to respond collectively (if the free-rider problem is overcome) because of the spillover benefits of the actions of each for the others. But if offered an opportunity to defect, this may be the rational course of action. The result at the level of the system is that two equilibria are possible, one a dissolution of the national group and the other a strengthening of it. It is important not to forget that under certain circumstances, national groups vanish *as* national groups as their members assimilate into a surrounding group, or as their members take on a broader national identity. The multitude of ethnic groups who settled the United States have lost their members to a larger "American" identity. As Eugen Weber points out in his *Peasants into Frenchmen: The Modernization of Rural France, 1870–1914,* French was a foreign language to about half the Frenchmen who came of age in the last quarter of the nineteenth century.

The ubiquity of nationality

One question not addressed in the above is the question of why nationality is such a common basis for identity. The question might be regarded as meaningless, for nationality can be seen as consisting of whatever components form the basis for the members' identity. That is, "nationality" has different concrete referents for different national groups. It sometimes, but not always, includes a common language, a common religion, a geographic territory, ethnic consanguinity. For Jews it has, until the founding of the state of Israel, included all these except a geographic territory (though the consanguinity of Ethiopian Jews, Moroccan Jews, Indian Jews, and European Jews is more fictive than real, and the Hebrew language was not everywhere taught). For most other national groups (though not for gypsies), occupancy of a contiguous geographic territory is one of the components of their nationality. For Englishmen, consisting of a body of Celts, overlaid by various conquerors and immigrants ranging from Romans to Angles, Saxons, Normans, East Indians, and West Indians, nationality has consisted primarily of a common language and geographic territory called England. Probably the element which is most often a component of nationality is ethnic consanguinity. Walker Connor (1991, 6) defines a nation as "a group of people who believe they are ancestrally related. It is the largest grouping that shares that belief." This definition, however, excludes those groups, such as "Americans" or "Canadians" which have been created as national groups by the existence of a state. Perhaps the only satisfactory definition is one that is almost circular: A nation is a group of people who regard themselves as members of the nation and who regard one another as members of that nation.

Such a definition then modifies the original question to become: What creates national groups, groups which satisfy this definition? The answer should be one which accounts for the fact that national groups which originated in ancient times (whether they have vanished, like the Hittites and the Canaanites, or survived, like the Israelites) almost always have ethnic consanguinity as a central component, and that national groups which originated in the eighteenth and nineteenth centuries almost always have a territorial state as a central component (such as Italy, France, Germany, the United States, Canada, Mexico), and often lack a belief in a common ethnic heritage.

The answer lies, I believe, in two phenomena: acting together, toward a common goal, and being acted upon together, as members of a common group. In antiquity, when primordial institutions deriving from the family were the basis for a society's structure, then most groups which acted together or were acted upon together in wars and disputes had a common ethnicity: family, clan, tribe. Thus the primordial bases, ethnicity and religion, came to be the central elements around which a nation was defined. In the era of the modern state, when migrations have mixed ethnic groups together but states go to war to conquer or defend geographic territories, the groups which act together or are acted upon together are defined by their common citizenship in the state. Thus the constructed entity, the state as a geographically and constitutionally defined entity, comes to be the central element around which new national identities are defined.

The question remains, however: Under what conditions will new state-generated identities – like Czechoslovakia, or Yugoslavia, or the Soviet Union, or Canada, or Belgium – overwhelm the narrower and older primordially based national identities, such as Czech, Slovak, Serb, Croat, Bosnian, Armenian, Ukrainian, Azerbaijanian, French Canadian, Walloon, Flemish. I will not attempt to answer this except to mention the most obvious elements. One of these is the degree to which an industrial economy has undercut the strength of the primordial institutions. Another is the number of elements on which the narrower national groups differ from one another (ethnicity, language, religion, economic status). Still, a third is the geographic concentration of the narrower national groups.

Conclusion

In this paper I have argued that we may think of action taking place under either of two conditions: first the condition in which the allocation of rights is well defined, is enforceable and enforced; and second, the condition in which the structure of rights is no longer enforced, and is not agreed upon. In the first of these conditions, nationality as a basis for collective action is dormant, or nearly so. Persons act, individually or collectively, to maximize their returns given the constraints imposed by the allocation of rights. In the second condition when rights are no longer well-defined and enforced, national identity serves as a basis for collective action, action that is just as rational, given the absence of rights-generated constraints, as is the action taken in the first condition. Indeed, it is more consequential, for upon the outcome of this action depends the new allocation of rights under which actions must subsequently be taken.

References

Breton, A., and R. Breton. 1980. *Why Disunity? An Analysis of Linguistic and Regional Cleavages in Canada*. Montreal: Institute for Research on Public Policy.

Coleman, J. S. 1993. "The Role of Rights in a Theory of Social Action," *Journal of Institutional and Theoretical Economics*.

Connor, Walker. 1991. "From Tribe to Nation," *History of European Ideas* vol. 13, no. 1/2.

Kuran, Timur. 1991. "Now Out of Never: The Element of Surprise in the East European Revolution of 1989." *World Politics* 44:7–48.

Moynihan, Daniel Patrick. 1992. *Pandemonium: Ethnicity in International Politics*.

Weber, Eugen. 1976. *Peasants into Frenchmen: The Modernization of Rural France, 1870–1914*. Stanford, CA: Stanford University Press.

CHAPTER 2

Self-interest, group identity

Russell Hardin

Self-interest

How far can ethnic and nationalist identification in politics be understood to result from essentially self-interested behavior? At first thought, plausibly not very far. Nationalism and ethnic loyalty are commonly viewed as inherently irrational or extrarational in the sense that they supposedly violate or transcend considerations of self-interest. Surely this common view is correct to some extent. Still, it is useful to draw out the self-interest incentives for such commitments and behaviors. There is yet another category of motivations – those that are arational. For example, you want only to sit on the beach and watch seagulls. This is not strictly a matter of your interest but of your pleasure or whatever in consuming your time and energy that way. Similarly, we all have arational drives that make us want things. When we act from those drives, we may lack reasons that could define our actions as rational. These four terms – rational, irrational, extrarational, and arational – are not strictly parallel.

Throughout this paper I use the term "rational" to mean to have narrowly self-interested intentions, and I do not constantly restate this qualification. Rationality is, of course, typically a subjective or intentional notion, not a purely objective notion. You act rationally if you do what you believe serves your interest. Self-interest might better be seen as an objective notion. Its service is the object of rational action, although one may fail to understand what is in one's interest. George Washington presumably acted rationally, but mistakenly, when he allowed himself to be bled, perhaps with fatal consequences. I will refer to primordial, atavistic, inconsistent, and other motivations not intended to serve either the individual or the group interest as "irrational"; and I will refer to individual motivations to serve the group- or national-level interest more or less independently of immediate individual costs and benefits as extra-rational. It is possible, of course, that rational and extrarational motivations will lead to similar actions in some contexts. The rational choice account of ethnic, nationalist, or other group loyalty will be compelling if (1) *it often happens that self-interest and group identification are congruent* and if (2) actions that are costly to the individual but beneficial to the group or nation are increasingly less likely the higher the individual costs.

In some ways, it would be more assertively clear to speak of self interest rather than of rationality. But there is no simple equivalent of the range of terms we want here: rational, irrational, and extrarational. Moreover, we may often accommodate extra-rational concern for the well-being of others by speaking of it as a concern for others' interests, and we can then rationally choose best means to fulfill those interests. You may be an altruist or an ethnic loyalist who has a group interest as well as a self-interest. Finally, and most important, self-interest is not generally treated as a subjective notion – even if I like the taste of some poison, it may not be in my interest to eat it and, if I knew enough about it, I would actively prefer not to eat it. Limits to knowledge lead all of us to mistaken beliefs about our interests even when it would be silly to say we had mistaken intentions. George Washington had mistaken beliefs about the benefits of bleeding to treat a bad cold. This fundamental problem of subjectivity often complicates any account of intentional action, as it will complicate our account of group identification.

Much of the work on nationalism is primarily concerned with will, interests, and identity. It is about the cognitive aspects of actors' being nationalist. Writings on ethnicity may more commonly invoke primordial and other emotional motivations. There are many other identities that might underlie conflict as nationalism and ethnicity seem to do. Many of these, however, do not seem to be of much concern to us in explaining major conflicts up to and including war and internal war. Indeed, many of them seem to be trumped by nationalism in times of war, as identification with class in the Socialist International was, to Lenin's disgust, widely trumped by nationalist identities at the advent of World War I. In a multiethnic state, nationalist and ethnic identities may clash even while the state goes to war.

Often it is claimed that there is something natural about ethnic identification. As there are arguably genetic grounds for physical identification *of* a particular ethnic group, so there might be genetic grounds for psychological identification *with* the group by those who have the relevant physical characteristics.[1] I will take more or less for granted that this presumptive genetic basis of the psychological identification *with one's particular group* is most likely false. Surely it is not merely false but also preposterous for, say, the nationalist identification with the United States, such as was displayed at impressive levels during the Persian Gulf crisis and war against Iraq.

Whatever genetic basis we might find for ethnic and nationalist identification is at most a genetic basis for the propensity to identify with *some* larger group.[2] How we might select a group for identification or how identification may just grow up for some group of which we are part is likely still to be a cognitive problem of making choices. Those choices may be about matters other than direct identification with the particular group or nation. But they will have implications for such identification, which may be an unintended by-product. It is such choices and their grounding in self-interest that are of concern here. One might go further than I wish to go to say that even the basic urge to identify is itself a cognitive result. At the very least, the data on such identification may not readily differentiate biological from cognitive explanations.

Throughout the discussion, there will be two partly separable issues: the role of interest in an individual's coming to identify with a particular group, and the interest an individual has in supporting that group as a beneficiary of the group's successes. The second issue may seem more readily than the first to be about deliberate action. Of course, one could see that membership in a particular group would be beneficial and could therefore develop an apparent or even real identification with it. But for very many identifications, it would be odd to suppose the individuals had deliberately set out to develop or adopt the relevant identity. Hence, the explanatory concern must be with the rationality of various choices they make that eventually lead them to identification with a particular group, identification that, again, may be an unintended consequence of many rational actions.

There are two main moves in the arguments that follow. First, I consider the rationality of an action given one's available knowledge, theory, and so forth at the time of choosing. Second, I consider the rationality of *coming to have* the knowledge and theory one now has. These two moves are independent and one may reject one while

---

[1] E. J. Hobsbawm canvasses difficulties in the definition of nationalities and ethnic groups. Hobsbawm, *Nations and Nationalism Since 1780: Programme, Myth, Reality* (New York: Cambridge University Press, 1990), 1–13.

[2] Among others, see Thorstein Veblen, *An Inquiry into the Nature of Peace and the Terms of Its Perpetuation* (New York: Augustus M. Kelley, 1964 reprint [1917]).

accepting the other. They seem too sensible to be objectionable, but they are also commonly not overtly made by rational choice theorists or their critics. Both moves enormously increase the demand for data in trying to assess the rationality of actions.

Group identification from coordination

How can we plausibly associate nationalist, ethnic, or other strong group identification with self-interest? Surely, it seems, such commitment is beyond the self, it is a commitment to a community of some kind. To get beneath this superficial appearance, first note that many national and ethnic group conflicts are likely to have outcomes that will favor or disfavor members of the relevant group. Contributing to the potential success of the group to which one belongs therefore benefits oneself. Unfortunately, as we well know from the logic of collective action, such considerations are typically outweighed by the costs of contributing.[3] For example, by voting in an election, I may help my candidate win. But to do so, I have to go to the trouble of voting, trouble that can be substantial in many locations. Unless the probability that my vote will make a real difference in the outcome is extremely high, I cannot justify, from my own interest alone, taking the trouble to vote. Then how can I justify contributing to the collective purpose of my nation or ethnic group?

The first answer is that there may be no costs of my joining in the relevant activities of my group. The second answer is that, even if there are costs, I may also expect specific rewards or punishments that will be tailored to whether I contribute. The first answer will apply to many contexts that essentially involve coordination but no expenditure of resources by many of us. The second answer will apply to many contexts in which there are real costs of contributing – so that the problem is not simply one of coordination – but in which rewards of leadership or spontaneous punishments by one's peers are possible.

Of course, a nationalist or ethnic commitment might be purely ideal or normative in that it might involve only ideal-regarding and other-regarding motivations. But it might also be strongly correlated with individual interests. Suppose the commitment is to a nation or ethnic group in conflict with others and with a prospect of success in that conflict. Then it is likely that the nationals or the ethnic group mem-

---

[3] Mancur Olson, Jr., *The Logic of Collective Action* (Cambridge: Harvard University Press, 1965); Russell Hardin, *Collective Action* (Baltimore: Johns Hopkins University Press for Resources for the Future, 1982).

Game 1: Prisoner's dilemma or exchange

		Column	
		Cooperate	Defect
Row	Cooperate	2,2	4,1
	Defect	1,4	3,3

Game 2: Coordination

		Column	
		I	II
Row	I	1,1	2,2
	II	2,2	1,1

bers will jointly benefit from that success. The benefit is often likely to be collectively provided but individually distributed. The group wins or loses together, but winning means that each member or many members of the group benefit individually. Indeed, one need not be committed to the group in any normative or additional psychological sense to see one's interests served by its success.

There are generally two forms that collective, mutually beneficial endeavors may take. These may be represented game theoretically by the prisoner's dilemma and coordination games, as shown in games 1 and 2. The prisoner's dilemma is perhaps the best-known game in all of the massive game theory literature, especially in the discursive applied literature in the social sciences. In this game, I as the Row player face a choice between two strategies, didactically labeled cooperate and defect. You as the Column player face a similar choice. In the end, we will each receive the payoff determined by our simultaneous choice of joint strategies. Our payoffs in the various outcomes are listed ordinally, with 1 as the most preferred and 4 the least preferred outcome; and the first payoff in each cell goes to the Row player, the second to Column. If we both defect, we each receive our third best payoff. If we both cooperate, we each receive our second best payoff. If I cooperate while you defect, I receive my worst payoff while you receive your best; and vice versa. Hence, there is incentive for both of us to try to cheat the other by defecting while the other cooperates.

In the coordination game of game 2, you and I have harmonious interests. We wish either to coordinate on both choosing our strategy I or on both choosing our strategy II. There is no conflict. In the prisoner's dilemma there is both a coordination interest in choosing the (2,2) over the (3,3) outcome and a conflict of interests in which I prefer the outcome (1,4) while you prefer (4,1).

Many of the standard problems of political mobilization are generalizations of the prisoner's dilemma strategic structure. Each of us has an interest in not contributing a personal share to, say, a political campaign, because each of us will benefit from all others' contributions while our own contribution may cost us more than it is worth to us alone. Hence, each of us has incentive to try to be a free-rider. (This is what Mancur Olson calls the logic of collective action.[4])

Many other problems of political mobilization are more nearly generalizations of the structure of the simple two-person coordination game represented here. In such problems, all that is needed to achieve successful mobilization is relevant communication to coordinate on doing what we would all want to do if only we were sure others were also doing it. In what follows, most of my account of group identification, as opposed to action on behalf of a group, will argue or assume that the central strategic problem is merely one of coordination.

There is something objective and something subjective in the idea of an ethnic group or a nationality.[5] This is true in general of coordination points. There are good objective reasons for me to coordinate on X rather than fail to coordinate by choosing Y. But there may be no a priori objective reason for the choice of X rather than of Y apart from knowledge of how you and others are choosing. Hence, group coordination is an achievement that likely turns on highly subjective considerations such as the psychological prominence of particular points in the set of all possible coordination points.[6]

A peculiarity of explanations from coordination is that they often have an important chance element. We might have coordinated on driving on the left, as the English do, or on the right, as North Americans do. There might be no rational ground for the original selection or, rather, for the early pattern of order that turns into a hard coordination. Similarly, we might coordinate on linguistic, religious, or ethnic affinity. If all of these come together to define our group, we may be much more likely to succeed in adopting a strong commitment to the group. If they do not come together, some of us may nevertheless define ourselves as a group on the basis of some attribute that excludes others with whom we might have associated. But the chance element may be more fundamental than this. We might simply fail to coordinate at all in any active sense, even if we have language, religion, and ethnicity in common. Whether we coordinate might turn in part on whether there is someone urging us to recognize our identity and coordinate on it. I may fully identify with my group but take no action on its and my behalf until an Alexander Herzen, Adolph Hitler, Martin

---

[4] Olson, *The Logic of Collective Action*.
[5] Cf. Hobsbawm, *Nations and Nationalism*, 8.
[6] Thomas C. Schelling, *The Strategy of Conflict* (Cambridge: Harvard University Press, 1960).

Luther King, or Ruhollah Khomeini mobilizes those of us with similar identifications.

Moreover, successful mobilization may be a tipping phenomenon in large part. What would not make sense for a self-interested individual when very few are acting might begin to make sense when many others are acting.[7] At that point the relationship changes from a potentially risky prisoner's dilemma to a virtual coordination involving very nearly no risk. Both before and after tipping, the interaction might be successful in providing the group with a collective good whose benefit is distributed among group members. It is such distributed collective goods that give individuals direct interest in identifying with the relevant group.

A prisoner's dilemma can tip into a coordination problem in at least two ways. First, when the number acting on behalf of the group interest becomes large enough, the possibilities of punishment and suppression of individual coordinators may dwindle. When too few are acting, the prospects of punishment may be great enough to make participation costly, as in the logic of collective action. If enough are acting, however, the state's capacity to respond might be swamped and the state might let the crowd go while its police or military concentrate their attentions on channeling the crowd rather than suppressing it outright.

Second, an interaction might tip when those who are cooperating can impose retribution on those not cooperating by inflicting harm on them. It might be supposed that the costs of punishment are somehow closely related to the disvalue of the punishment, as though the act of punishing were potentially a constant-sum game. For example, to impose a ten dollar sanction on you might cost me about ten dollars. This relationship might hold in some cases, but there is no reason to suppose it holds generally. Sanctions can be radically cheaper than the harm they cause. The costs of producing a sanction and the costs of suffering one need not be in any way logically related. The story of Lebanon and Somalia is one of the trivially cheap production of dreadful harms. William Rees-Mogg wrote that, in an Irish Republican Army (IRA) bombing in the City of London, a hundred pounds of Semtex did a billion pounds of damage.[8] One of the threats – seldom actualized – of antiwar groups in the United States during the Vietnam

---

[7] Russell Hardin, "Acting Together, Contributing Together," *Rationality and Society* 3 (July 1991) 365–80.

[8] William Rees-Mogg, "The Sheriff Fiddles While the Town Burns," *Independent*, 4 May 1992, p. 17. Quoted in Daniel Patrick Moynihan, *Pandaemonium: Ethnicity in International Politics* (New York: Oxford University Press, 1993), 24.

Self-interest, group identity

War was to do grievous damage to corporate and university installations. The people who did or threatened the harms in Lebanon and the United States arguably could not have done as much good for their efforts as they did harms. This may be typically true of virtually all of us. Indeed, if there is a very important element of seeming irrationality or extra-rationality in nationalist and ethnic commitments, it is the fact that many people derive great pleasure from inflicting harms on certain others, including those of their own group who seem treacherously not committed to the group's ends.

This insight, that harming can be cheap, is a central underpinning for Hobbes's theory of government and its great value.[9] It also undergirds Robert Axelrod's theory of meta-norms for punishing those who fail to punish defectors in collective actions.[10] Indeed, one might suppose Axelrod's punishment schedule of bearing a cost of two units for nine units of punishment inflicted is not steep enough for many contexts. *When harming is intended to be deterrent, so that it need not be coherently related in kind to the action it is to punish, the form it takes can be specifically selected for its effectiveness and cheapness.* The nuclear deterrent of the Cold War era was ridiculously cheap in comparison to the harms it could have inflicted, and that is a major reason for our resorting to nuclear deterrence: We could afford it. Moreover, in collective action contexts, effective punishment can be decentralized to one-on-one and small-group actions, often more easily than effective rewards can be.

Information through coordination

Joining a coordination with a group of people who share one's interests in some way can also produce information that makes further identification rational. To see this most clearly, we should consider a case in which there can hardly be any argument that the coordination or identification is somehow intrinsically related to the group or the object of its identification. Let us therefore consider loyalty to a sports team, which afflicts remarkably many people but seldom afflicts all those it might.

Why is anyone loyal to any sports team, such as the Chicago Cubs baseball team? Clearly, this is not a biological or in any sense native or primordial identification. Perhaps the urge to identify, to put us

---

[9] Russell Hardin, "Hobbesian Political Order," *Political Theory* 19 (1991): 156–80.
[10] Robert Axelrod, "An Evolutionary Approach to Norms," *American Political Science Review* 80 (1986): 1,095–112.

against them, is biological. Still, however, there remains the difficult question: Why identify with this *particular* group? We could ask this question of any group: the Cubs boosters, Armenians, or whatever. But let us focus on the Cubs boosters.

The local community of sports fans has an easy time coordinating on the local team. News media, neighborhood banter, and on-the-job talk can all focus on the Cubs. Circles of friends and other groups in the local community could not so easily sustain diverse attachments. This is not to say that people sit back and select the local team for these reasons but only that these factors are real constraints that affect the pleasures fans get from their game. They also affect how much a potential fan is likely to know about any team. The local team has privileged access, fans can know more about it, they can see and come to like its star players. Fans who go to games are virtually bound to know the local team better than they could know any other. In the end, many might become critics rather than boosters, but still they may focus their concern on the local team. Again, the reason for such a focus is that the local team is in a privileged position with respect to local loyalties.

Locally there may be claims for why the home team is special and therefore merits support. This result may be a case of the is-ought fallacy: What *is* is taken to be good. Fans in Chicago used to say that, among basketball players, Michael Jordan was the most beautiful to watch. Fans in Los Angeles said Magic Johnson was most beautiful. One suspects that both judgments were at least as much derivative from local loyalties as they were causes of such loyalties. Much of their substantive basis is similar to that of the views of the ethnic loyalist. The loyalist's experience of knowing her own ethnic group gives her special entrée to the pleasures of its practices and customs. From these comes the sense of comfort and well-being that seems to recommend the superiority of that group over others.

For the present discussion, the example of identification with a sports team has the odd advantage that it is purely a consumption good, it is not sensibly seen as an interest one has in the way one has an interest in a higher salary or a windfall profit. Ethnic identification might, in many contexts, actually be in one's interest. I may reasonably be said to have an interest in the resources necessary to get the daily pleasures of fans of the home team, just as I have an interest in the money necessary for satisfaction of other desires, such as those for food and shelter. In a sense, then, it is in my interest that others around me are also followers of the home team so that I may have a context in which to enjoy my own commitment to the team. Here, my interest is directly in the availability of others with similar pleasures and in successful coordination with them.

In a similar way, I might have an interest in the workings of my national or ethnic group, with which I might be especially comfortable for the simple reason that I know it well. But there is also a quite different way in which I have an interest in the workings of my national or ethnic group. From the fact that, say, my ethnic group prevails politically, I may personally benefit because I may get a better job. Hence, I have an interest in the participation of others not because that participation directly gratifies me, as it does in the case of a sports team. I have that interest because I have an interest in what can be accomplished by substantial coordination. I share with others of my ethnic group in the benefits that may flow from our achieving greater political power. In this latter case, the coordination is itself a means to an end. Therefore, as is typically true of means, it may turn out finally not to lead to the benefits that the members of the group hope to get – it may fail. Coordination around the home team, on the contrary, is immediately beneficial to the individual who joins in the coordination. We may therefore expect coordinated action for ethnic or national interests will be harder to motivate than coordination on support for the local sports team.

Indeed, we may even go further to suppose recoordination around a new team will often be easy for one who moves from one city to another. This seems especially likely if the role of the particular team is merely as a coordination point as a means to the pleasure of being a sports fan. The role of a particular ethnic identification is clearly much stronger, it is constitutive of the collective good that will benefit the loyal individual. And it cannot easily be replaced for the individual by coordination on participation in some other group that might provide an alternative route to distributed collective benefits.

Nationalism is intermediate between identification with a sports team and identification with an ethnic group. For example, French, German, and Japanese national identifications might continue to motivate those who migrate from France, Germany, and Japan; they might even be hard to give up after a generation away from home. That may in large part turn on the facts that these identifications involve ethnic as well as nationalist coordinations and that family members may still be in their original home countries. But clearly many people find it relatively easy to become American nationalists, not to say superpatriots, when they migrate to the United States. They can do so because they can plausibly see their personal interests as now associated with the successes of the United States.

One of the most important ways information affects groups is in giving group members an understanding of their common interests. This is one half of Marx's theory of revolution, which requires the development of class consciousness before there can be class-oriented action. Workers in a factory share so much time together that they begin to understand their common fate much better, not least because each can benefit from the insights of all. Peasants scattered across the countryside cannot spend enough time together to gain a comparable sense of class identity. Hence, they are unlikely to become a class for themselves.[11] They are, Marx says, like potatoes in a sack without benefit of manifold relations.[12] Hence, even when given opportunity to act for their interests, French peasants failed to do so and voted for Louis Napoleon out of failure to understand their own interests. The mothers of the Plaza de Mayo movement in Argentina had very nearly the factory experience of Marx's workers. They encountered one another repeatedly in the same revealing contexts as they went to bureaucrat after bureaucrat trying to locate their "disappeared" children. Through this experience of each other's experience, they discovered the real nature of their problem and soon mobilized to help topple the military regime that had murdered their children.[13] Part of the cause of the explosion of ethnic identification and ethnic political agitation in parts of the former Soviet Union now may be the sudden openness of the society that lets groups openly discuss and pool their knowledge and views and openly organize for political action.

Conflict from group coordination

Explanations of ethnic conflict often invoke emotions. Unfortunately, explaining ethnically oriented behavior as emotional may not be explaining it at all or may be explaining only aspects of it given that it happens. The part we most need to explain is why the behavior happens, why such behavior is ethnically oriented. And we need to explain why one group falls into conflict with another. Why these groups? In the preceding discussion, the process of group identification seems to be sanguine. But we know that it often leads to deep

---

[11] Hardin, "Acting Together, Contributing Together," esp. 374–7.
[12] Karl Marx, *The 18th Brumaire of Napoleon Bonaparte* (New York: International Publishers, 1963 [1852]), 123–4.
[13] Marysa Navarro, "The Personal Is Political: Las Madres de Plaza de Mayo," in Susan Eckstein, ed., *Power and Popular Protest* (Berkeley and Los Angeles: University of California Press, 1989), 241–58, esp. 250; John Simpson and Jana Bennett, *The Disappeared and the Mothers of the Plaza* (New York: St. Martin's, 1985), 156–7.

enmity, bloodshed, and even genocide and ethnic cleansing. Benign phenomena apparently produce the conditions for malign phenomena.

The benign phenomena are well understood. Among the benign sources of group coordination are language, religion, local community, mores, customs, and so forth. All of these affect individuals' costs of transactions with one another and stabilize expectations. They may also affect the development and maintenance of group consciousness and, hence, identification. Characterizing these influences as economic is not standard in much of the literature on ethnicity and ethnic and other group politics. For example, it is sometimes contended that Québécois sentiment for secession derives from a noneconomic fear of loss of language.[14] But loss of language is clearly an economic concern in the sense that it affects the interests of most people in the two or three current generations of Québécois. Not everything that greatly affects our interests falls into standard business accounts of monetary income and expenditure.

What is the source of conflict? Suppose two groups have formed different ethnic identifications in a society. Each of their coordinations may be innocuous and fully beneficial to their group's members. But coordination of each group provides the basis on which to build many things, including political action against the other group. To a political conflict over allocations, a coordinated group brings advantages of reduced transaction costs and, often, strong identification and agreement. Hence, *coordination of a group is potentially political.* If two groups seek to achieve collective resolutions of various issues, they may come directly into conflict with each other. My group wants its language adopted as the official language, your group wants its language adopted. My group wants more access to land and jobs for its members, and so does your group, although the supply of each might be relatively fixed. Within each group, the initial problem was one of coordination on common interests; in the larger society the eventual problem is often grim conflict of interest made grimmer by the fact that one of our groups may defeat the other.

To keep the nature of the conflicts clearer, note that there are three classes of issues. There are *positional goods,* such as public office, *distributional goods,* such as income and welfare benefits, and *interac-*

---

[14] Stéphane Dion, "The Importance of the Language Issue in the Constitutional Crisis," in Douglas Brown and Robert Young, eds., *Canada: The State of the Federation 1992* (Kingston: Institute of Intergovernmental Relations, 1992). See further discussion in Russell Hardin, *Contested Community* (Princeton, NJ: Princeton University Press, forthcoming), ch. 6.

tions between these two.[15] Tutsis might wish to hold power in Burundi because a large percentage of available jobs – positional goods – are government jobs that must be filled but that are likely to be filled by the winners in the political conflict. They might also wish to receive certain benefits – distributional goods – from government, such as support for the expenses of maintaining cattle. And, finally, they might wish to hold power and to fill many government positions because the government has control over certain distributional goods.

Consider positional goods of public office. When Rwanda gained independence, it was to begin with a majority Hutu government. Prior to that moment, Tutsis had favored access to native offices under the colonial administration, just as they had dominated control of the nation before colonial domination. Tutsis seemingly spontaneously rose to attempt to block the transfer of power to Hutus, and Rwanda had a bloody civil war that ended with the expulsion of many Tutsis and the dominance of Hutus. The response might not have been spontaneous, however, because among those whose positions were threatened were many in positions to organize and lead a rebellion. When, a generation later, Burundi had its first democratically elected majoritarian government, thereby switching central power from Tutsis to Hutus, Tutsis again rebelled under the leadership of the Tutsi-dominated military. There have been many similar explosions in other states. For example, majority Buddhist Sinhalese governments in Sri Lanka adopted many preferences for Sinhalese. When a later government began to reverse these policies in order to equalize opportunities for Tamils in state-controlled jobs, Sinhalese rioted against the slight reduction in their status.[16] All of these actions were focused on control of positional goods.

Conflict over distributional goods is a commonplace of political life. The standard example in American politics for most of United States national history is conflict over tariffs. Agrarian interests (especially in the south and west) long wanted low tariffs on industrial goods (which they needed to buy and for which they naturally preferred to pay low prices), while industrial interests (especially in the north) wanted high

---

[15] Fred Hirsch distinguishes between positional and material goods and their interaction in a growing economy. Hirsch, *Social Limits to Growth* (Cambridge: Harvard University Press, 1976), esp. ch. 3. The roles of positional and distributional goods in ethnic conflicts were analyzed earlier by Daniel Bell in "Nationalism or Class? – Some Questions on the Potency of Political Symbols," *The Student Zionist*, May 1947 (cited in Moynihan, *Pandaemonium*), 59.

[16] See further cases in Donald Horowitz, *Ethnic Groups in Conflict* (Berkeley and Los Angeles: University of California Press, 1985).

Self-interest, group identity

tariffs to protect their domestic markets. In Nigeria, Yoruba from the northern region benefited from regional control of agricultural (especially cocoa) revenues and state control of mineral (especially oil) revenues, while the Igbo from the eastern region would have benefited from the opposite arrangements.[17] The Igbo attempted to secede as Biafra, but were crushed in the ensuing civil war.

In Yugoslavia, disproportionately many of the positional goods of military and governmental leadership have gone to Serbians, who have also done well in receiving distributional goods allocated by the government. The latter have reputedly been disproportionately funded by the more productive Croatians and Slovenians, who therefore subsidized Serbia. That the distributional result follows in part from the positional advantages of the Serbs is a natural inference. In any case, when the Serbs under Slobodan Milosevic changed the rules and expectations on the sharing of positions, the Yugoslav civil war and breakup were virtually secured. Similarly, when the Croats chose to change the status of Serbs in Croatia, removing them from positions in the police force and reducing their status to "protected minority" rather than full citizens, the Serbo-Croatian war over Krajina was virtually secured.[18]

Note that in good economic times, state-managed distributional goods matter less because private opportunities are very good. Indeed, in very good times, even the positional goods of government may be far less attractive. But in harsh times, when the prospects of individual achievement are dim, the possibility of using government to transfer goods from others to one's own group may offer better hope of improving one's position. Failing to provide an economy that generated private opportunities, one of the great failures of socialist governments in the former Soviet Union and eastern Europe, was almost ordained by definition. But it helped to set the stage for massive ethnic conflict upon the end of the Soviet Union. Giving a former republic autonomy opens opportunity to fill extant positions – hence, to offer positional goods. From the Baltics to the Urals to the Steppes, ethnic groups have wanted to seize government in order to allocate positions.

A similar malaise befell many, perhaps most, newly decolonized states, as in Africa. In an act of gross cynicism or stupidity, the Portuguese government transferred power in Angola to the Angolan people rather than to a government.[19] They thereby invited the three

---

[17] David D. Laitin, *Hegemony and Culture: Politics and Religious Change Among the Yoruba* (Chicago: University of Chicago Press, 1986), 133–4.
[18] See further in, Hardin, *Contested Community*, ch. 6.
[19] Moynihan, *Pandaemonium*, 37.

main groups to fight out the definition of that people. Many formerly colonial states have chosen to follow the statist path to economic and political development and have therefore made their populations too dependent on government for their own opportunities. The statist path might have been almost unavoidable in underdeveloped nations, because it immediately offered positions to enough people to build support for the new native governments. Alas, it may also be a sad accident of history that many of these states gained independence at the apex of belief that the Soviet Union had a better way.

Ethnic conflict often cannot be defused through control over complementary functions. The members of one group might be virtually perfect substitutes for the members of another. Hence, they may benefit best from the group's achieving full control over allocation of positions. In general, when benefits are provided through government, they can have a strongly conflictual quality. Any policy that benefits one group through a general tax or regulatory scheme typically harms some other group relative to its position before or without the policy. Consider two forms of discrimination on the basis of group identity, one that is quite deliberate and one that is largely accidental. Both, however, are conflictual.

First, on Gary Becker's account of its economics, ethnic discrimination in employment and sales can only occur where markets are not fully competitive because discrimination is not efficient and is costly to firms that practice it.[20] Ethnic conflict in parts of the former Soviet Union is in areas from which the market is nearly absent. In some of these there may be active opposition to the market for ethnic reasons. If the opportunities from market reorganization were believed to be great enough, dominant groups and their leaders might relax their grip and let the market allocate positions, thus undercutting discrimination. If the gains from market organization do not seem compelling, then the economy offers a straight conflict between two groups, each of which would be best served by having its members given preference by government. Giving preference to members of my group reduces prospects for members of your group.

Second, when two groups speak different languages, they have in fact each coordinated on a language. If one of the groups gains a dominant position in politics or in the economy, it may discriminate against those who speak any language other than its own. This discrimination need not be economically inefficient, as straight racial discrimination typically may be. Indeed, it could be driven chiefly by

---

[20] Gary S. Becker, *The Economics of Discrimination,* 2nd ed. (Chicago: University of Chicago Press, 1971 [1957]).

concern with productivity, which is likely to be greater if members of the firm can coordinate more easily with each other and if they can communicate better with the principal clientele of the firm. Letting the two languages be used without any government regulation in favor of either may lead to the disadvantage of the speakers of the minority language. Their job opportunities may turn heavily on whether they master the majority language.

To impose rules against racial discrimination can enhance economic productivity. This may not typically be true for rules against language discrimination. To impose such rules might benefit the current generation or two of the minority language speakers. But it is likely to reduce economic efficiency. Language policy is inherently conflictual because different policies differentially affect relevant parties. The current two or three generations of speakers of the minority language will be losers if their language loses its utility. The present generations of speakers of the majority language will be losers if the minority language is kept viable.

From conflict to violence

Suppose we face limited, relatively fixed resources. If some of us can form a group that gains hegemony over our society, we can extract a disproportionate share of total resources for members of our group. The remainder of the society has incentive to counter-organize against us to protect its welfare. If it does so, we are now two groups in manifest conflict. Any would-be political leader may find that asserting the predominance of a particular group is key to gaining substantial support. All that is required to make the conflict between the two groups manifest are plausible definitions of group and counter-group memberships. Slight differences might suffice. More dramatic differences, such as race or ethnicity, language, or religion, might allow for easy mobilization. No one in group A need be personally hostile to anyone in group B for the two groups to be politically hostile simply because they have a conflict of interest. Their conflict is one over which there may be perfect agreement: both groups want the same thing, namely, the available resources.

Shortly after Tito's death, Milovan Djilas said that the Yugoslav system could only be run by Tito:

> Now that Tito is gone and our economic situation becomes critical, there will be a natural tendency for greater centralization of power. But this centralization will not succeed because it will run up against ethnic-political power bases in the republics. This is not classical nationalism but a more dangerous, bureaucratic nationalism built on

economic self-interest. This is how the Yugoslav system will begin to collapse.[21]

Norms of difference and exclusion can establish in and out groups and thereby ground a conflict of interest between the groups. Having a conflict of interest is not, however, sufficient for producing violence. You and I may have a conflict of interest over a job that only one of us can get. One of us might attempt to prevail in that conflict by hiring a hit man to kill the other, but we might also simply compete to the best of our abilities and then let the loser make the best of other options. Ethnic conflicts commonly lead to mere competition, as they may have done to a large extent in the period of economic progress in Tito's Yugoslavia, when Slovenians and Croatians did relatively well, Bosnians did less well, and Serbs and Macedonians did relatively poorly, but no one turned to massive violence to change the results.

Why violence? Many reasons are proposed in varied literatures on ethnic conflict. The reason most commonly asserted for the travails in Yugoslavia since 1991 is ethnic hatred, which will be discussed more fully below. Another that was once high in the list of causes, especially among writers under the sway of Thomas Hobbes, is anarchy that leaves no institutional barrier to conflict so that we all tend to match the lowest common denominator established by the most violent among us. Of these two, that of Hobbes has the greater claim on our attention. On a Hobbesian view of political life, without institutions to help us stay orderly we take a preemptive view of all conflicts. If conflict can lead to violence, I can improve my prospects of surviving the conflict if I preemptively suppress those with whom I am in conflict. I sneak up on you before you sneak up on me.

Self-defense against possible (not even actual) attack suffices to motivate murderous conflict. Risk aversion is enough. And the risk, unfortunately, of not preemptively attacking may be heightened by the fact that the other side – such as an ethnic group – cannot commit to not attacking, and therefore cannot be trusted beyond what can be inferred from their interests. An ethnic group that depends on relatively spontaneous organization, as the Bosnian Serbs did at least in large part, cannot make credible guarantees about what it might do. Indeed, in the cases of the IRA and the Bosnian Serbs, internal competition for leadership might make any commitment automatically the target of some faction among those supposedly making the commitment. Proclaimed commitments are virtually meaningless.

[21] Robert D. Kaplan, *Balkan Ghosts: A Journey Through History* (New York: St. Martin's, 1993), 75.

Self-interest, group identity

In 1991, virtually all political leaders in Yugoslavia must have seen the potential for the breakup of the Yugoslav regime in the morass of post-Tito and post-Communist politics. The two most prosperous republics, Slovenia and Croatia, wanted independence. Unfortunately, Croatia included within its borders a large Serbian community. If Croatia seceded from Yugoslavia, the resident Serbs could wonder about their minority status in the new nation. Because Serbs dominated the national government and the army, there was some prospect of Serbian intervention in a rebellious Croatia. But there could not soon have been a more propitious moment for Croatia to hope to secede successfully, because the central Yugoslav government and economy were weak. The Croatian government opted for secession and then it preemptively turned on the Serbs within Croatia. Croatians have paid dearly for attacking the Croatian Serbs, but they have also been made partner in the subsequent destruction and dismantling of Bosnia. The bloody collapse of Yugoslavia has been a product of this series of opportunistic grabs and pre-emptive violence.

The Hobbesian view seems to fit ethnic conflicts that have turned violent in Lebanon, Azerbaijan and Armenia, Rwanda and Burundi, Iraq, and many other societies, as it fits Yugoslavia. Destabilized governments, brought to weakness by war, economic failure, or fights over succession, cannot maintain adequate barriers to violence. Conflicts that are already well defined then escalate to violence. Once the violence is underway, as in Yugoslavia, preemption becomes an unavoidable urge. One need not hate members of another group, but one might still fear their potential hatred or even merely their threat. Hobbes's vision of the need of all to preempt lest they be the victims of the few who are murderous still fits even in the relatively organized state of ethnic conflict, except that it applies at the group level.

Incidentally, this modified Hobbesian view also fits the apparent results of the various rebellions: Almost all are worse off in the short run. Hobbes supposed that revolution against a going government is inherently harmful even to those who rebel, as seems to be true for the mass of people in, for example, Yugoslavia.[22] Only certain leaders

---

[22] Belgrade, the capital of Serbia, is far from the war zones of Yugoslavia, but many of its people have been brought to poverty by the wars and the collapse of the economy. In December 1993, there was a bread line that stretched three miles through the city (*New York Times*, 19 December 1993, p. 1.20). Part of the problem is the imposition of economic sanctions against Serbia by other nations. But Serbia's economy likely could not support free market importation of necessities of life even without sanctions – rather, it would have to rely on charity from abroad. And its economic hardships had begun well before the war with a slow slide into severe crisis.

(and perhaps occasional others) may have improved their lot and their prospects. Oddly, these leaders have improved their lot not by raising the level of welfare for their groups but through individually specific rewards of leadership. They are unlike the Jimmy Hoffas of the labor movement. Hoffa extracted wealth from his teamsters but he more than made up for his extractions by raising the level of welfare for the bulk of the members of his union (while lowering the welfare of some teamsters and of vast numbers of people not in his union). For the short run, at least, Franjo Tudjman, Slobodan Milosevic, and Radovan Karadzic lack Hoffa's saving grace. They are merely parasitic on their societies. They use ethnic differences to justify murder, mass rape, the destruction of cities, and even genocide while reducing the lives of their own ethnic compatriots. As Faoud Ajami and many others remark, they call on "brotherhood and faith and kin when it is in their interests to do so."[23]

For Hobbes's reason, it would be wrong to say, in the sloppy way some people talk about Yugoslav and other conflicts, that real-world conflicts are zero-sum. They might be fixed-sum in one limited sense or another. For example, when Croatians and Serbs have a conflict over some bit of land, there is a fixed supply of land available. But if they fight over control of the land, they destroy resources and people on both sides and the resulting outcome is one in which total gains are swamped by total losses. It is not fixed-sum, it is negative-sum. Latent conflicts may be zero-sum, but manifest conflicts must typically be negative sum, at least in the short run. In game theoretic language, all that we need say is that, in a pure conflict, any change that makes one party to a conflict better off must make the other party worse off. It is possible for both to become worse off in a pure conflict, but not possible for both to become better off or for one to become better off without harm to the other.

One could imagine a manifest, even violent, conflict that could lead to net gains in the somewhat longer run. For example, one state might seize part of another because the inhabitants are all of the nation of the first state. This is a pristine variant of the conflict between Romania and Hungary over the Hungarian nationals in Romania. If these Romanian Hungarians became part of Hungary, they might immediately become more productive and prosperous and the welfare of all three of the groups – Romanians, Romanian Hungarians, and the original Hungarians – might rise. The welfare of Romanians might rise only to the extent Romanian resources no longer were spent to keep

---

[23] Faoud Ajami, "The Summoning," *Foreign Affairs* 72 (September October 1993): 9.

Self-interest, group identity

the Romanian Hungarians under control. But for most of the violent conflicts of our time, it seems likely that the outcomes are severely negative-sum. And, if it would be mutually beneficial to all three groups to transfer part of formerly Hungarian Transylvania to Hungary, then the situation between Hungary and Romania is not conflictual but is misunderstood.

It is common in the literature on nationalism to assert that the underlying issues are not economic and that the events are not matters of rational choice.[24] As in the discussion of ethnic hatred below, the real motivators are metaphors and likely false beliefs that define the world. Many strong nationalists suffer the solipsistic and egotistical belief that they are *the* chosen people. This belief can coexist with reasoned understandings of its irrationality.[25] Although it might be a benign belief, it has a natural tendency to include the further belief that other peoples are inferior, even bad. It is very hard to disprove a metaphorical thesis, which in the end is at best a form of description of the matter we would like to understand. But even for one who accepts the metaphorical thesis, it merely pushes back the matter to be explained: How and why do people come to have such systematically odd beliefs?

Walker Connor seems to hold that it is nationalist beliefs which cause the behaviors associated with nationalist movements and that various economic explanations can be shown not to be "essential prerequisites for ethnonational conflict."[26] Unfortunately for showing their irrelevance, the way economic issues matter is not merely through a linear causal effect. Economic issues (in the broad sense that includes politicians' career incentives and citizens' comforts) merely construct the range of possibility of conflict. Violence is then a sepa-

---

[24] See, for example, the essays of Walker Connor, *Ethnonationalism: The Quest for Understanding* (Princeton, NJ: Princeton University Press, 1994).

[25] Connor (*Ethnonationalism*, 203) quotes a Ukrainian nationalist who believes his people are chosen by God:

> I know that all people are equal.
> My reason tells me that.
> But at the same time I know that my nation is unique . . .
> My heart tells me so.

Living with contradictions may be especially common for rabid nationalists. Greek nationalists think it only natural that the Greek part of Albania should be made autonomous or part of Greece, but also natural that minorities inside Greece should have no recognition (Hugh Poulton, *The Balkans: Minorities and States in Conflict*, (new ed. London: Minority Rights Publications, 1993 [1991]), 225.

[26] Connor, *Ethnonationalism*, 146.

rate matter that very likely depends on tipping phenomena. Among the tipping events might be the death of Tito, the struggle a few years later of Milosevic and his fellow failed Communists to hang onto power despite their demonstrated incapacity to run the Yugoslav economy, and the desire of leaders in Slovenia and Croatia to be free of the economic losses of greater Yugoslavia. The worst excrescences of nationalism in Yugoslavia followed these events – they did not precede or cause these events. Indeed, the worst excrescences followed only after a period of harsh warfare, as discussed below under "Ethnic hatred."

The order of beliefs and events is important because the content of the falsehoods of nationalism may be determined or manipulated by their fit with political agendas. Connor asks, "What is a nation?" He answers that it is "the largest group that can command a person's loyalty because of felt kinship ties." Emphasis is on *felt*, because I might be led to feel a tie that I cannot objectively claim to have. Connor speaks of intuitive, in contrast to objective, conviction.[27] The distortion of history, the distortion of reports from the battle zones, distortions of claimed ethnic and linguistic differences, and distortions of leaders' intentions can all be used, especially in a nation with centrally controlled television, to instill an intensity of nationalist commitment that did not cause the events that brought about such intensity but that may then be put to use in other events. It is because these odd beliefs must be manipulated into being that mass nationalism is a strictly modern phenomenon – it requires extensive communication, the very communication that also spreads the cosmopolitan vision of humanity. Perversely, we may see grotesquely violent assertions of ethnic superiority just because extensive communication has been laid onto the ignorance of village culture.

Ethnic hatred

Robert Kaplan quotes a 1920 story by the Bosnian Croat, Ivo Andric, the 1961 Nobel Prize winner in Literature: "Yes, Bosnia is a country of hatred. That is Bosnia. . . . [In] secret depths . . . hide burning hatreds, entire hurricanes of tethered and compressed hatreds. . . . Thus you are condemned to live on deep layers of explosive, which are lit from time to time by the very sparks of your loves and your fiery and violent emotion."[28] This sounds like Dostoevsky, Kafka, or

---

[27] Ibid., 202, 212.
[28] Quoted in Robert D. Kaplan, "A Reader's Guide to the Balkans," *New York Times Book Review*, 18 April 1993, p. 31. Kaplan quotes Andric in order to refute the

Poe on a particular fictional person, a person worthy of fictional treatment just because the character is so dramatically unlike the normal. It does not sound like the characterization of a whole people. But Kaplan and Andric evidently take it as characterizing Bosnians in general, and Kaplan takes it as definitive of Yugoslav culture. Further, the view that "visceral hatred of the neighbors" is "the main ingredient" in violent ethnic conflict is a commonplace in journalistic accounts.[29]

The view that the peculiarities of Balkan hatred drives the Yugoslav horrors infuriates humane Yugoslavs who write on the sufferings of their fellows.[30] The thesis of ethnic hatred cannot be established by anecdote, not even by the fictional musings of a Nobel laureate. If it systematically underlies history, it must be systematically evident. The overwhelming problem of the thesis that ethnic hatred motivates the ethnic conflict we see is that, for most of the groups in conflict, relations have generally been good through most of history. In the scale of history, the moments of catastrophic breakdown into violence are just that: moments. Between these moments, there is often substantial mixing. For example, in Yugoslavia, Croatians and Bosnians have typically been next-door neighbors of Serbs; they have been cooperative with them in institutional and economic arrangements; and they have even heavily intermarried with them.

Moreover, many of the participants in the grisly Bosnian wars deny that they hate. One of the young killers in a brutal and merciless paramilitary force of several hundred Croatians at Mostar said, "I really don't hate Muslims – but because of the situation I want to kill them all."[31] He had intended to sit the war out, but the "situation in Mostar caught up with him, labeled him, made him choose: stand with your own or leave your city like a dog and a traitor."[32] Perversely, *he had either to leave his community altogether or he had to identify with it altogether.* He had grown up with Muslims and Serbs among his friends, but when he saw them after the conflict hardened, he had nothing to say to them. Rather than leave his community, he chose to identify altogether with it and he soon became a systematic murderer

---

common claim that Bosnians could not hate so much if they were as thoroughly intermarried and as neighborly as in Sarajevo.

[29] The quoted phrases come from the ordinarily sane *Economist* in a survey of current ethnic conflicts. *The Economist*, 21 December, 1991, p. 45.

[30] See, for example, Bogdan Denitch, *Ethnic Nationalism: The Tragic Death of Yugoslavia* (Minneapolis, MN: University of Minnesota Press, 1994).

[31] Robert Block, "Killers," *New York Review of Books*, 18 November 1993, p. 10.

[32] Ibid., 9.

of trapped civilians. He murdered men, women, and children, armed or not, because, after all, in this preemptive world, someone who is not dead might shoot you in the back as you leave. His method was to watch Muslims to determine their patterns of activity in order to know where to lie in ambush to murder them.

The Croatian killer's alternatives were grim and therefore his choice was grim. But he was not so different from the *gentilhomme* of centuries past in France who chose to risk committing murder in a duel rather than be banished from his community. The saving grace for the *gentilhomme* is that we know him primarily from literature, where he is often presented with style and even humanity. The killers have so far not been romanticized in the world at large.

The killer is striking in the extent to which he seems not to have needed to justify his actions morally by anything more than the grim situation. He does not seem to need to make his victims be deserving for wrongs they have done – he evidently knows they deserve none of it, they are merely unfortunately there. For many of the participants in such carnage, their own gruesome actions seem to lead to putative beliefs in the wrongs of the other group. Serbs, say, begin to believe Croats or Muslims or Albanians are guilty of atrocities as a rationalization for their own atrocities. If the claim cannot be grounded in fact, it is simply grounded in myth. But the Croatian killer of Mostar does not need Milosevic's or Tudjman's lies and mythologies to give him license. He openly confesses to having nothing other than interests at stake.

Ethnic hatred might prevail in some contexts, such as those that involve a long history of overt subjugation of one race or ethnic group to another, as in South Africa, the United States, Guatemala, and many other places, such as Rwanda and Burundi after thirty years of ethnic slaughter. But a genuine hatred that is not reinforced by something from the hated, such as regularly occurring hostile actions, can hardly last over generations. The term "primordial" is often attached to such a seeming impossibility. By labeling it primordial, we seem to have explained something, when we have in fact only labeled it. Thereafter, we can proceed with a know-nothing stance that labels what we do not understand and cannot really believe when it is more fully spelled out.

Durkheim quotes a primordialist statement that is sufficiently lunatic as to be almost charming, especially since it is not invidious: "Woe to the scholar," writes the nineteenth-century historian of religions, J. Darmesteter, "who approaches divine matters without having in the depths of his consciousness, in the innermost indestructible regions of his being, where the souls of his ancestors sleep, an unknown sanctuary from which rises now and then the aroma of incense."[33]

Perhaps the fundamental supposition of the primordialists is an unstated Lamarckianism that attributes current human nature to what was *learned* in earlier generations. On such a theory, the Texan and the Serb, the Australian Aborigine and the Parisian dilettante, the Igbo and the Armenian, the Japanese and the Sri Lankan Sinhalese all have their independent human natures derived from the accidents of their history. Of course, on this theory, some of us are grotesque messes, with such diverse elements tossed together as to create a terribly overdone and botched salad. At least such messes are not likely to abound in adequate numbers of identical types to be capable of ethnic dominance over anyone else.

The quasi-Lamarckian vision of ethnic identification is patently silly, and its silliness pervades much of the commentary on ethnic conflict, both in the press and in more substantial works. Such identification is not primeval, original, primitive, or fundamental – in particular, it is not presocial. Some things about us may reasonably be called primordial. For example, certain instincts, many of which we share with numerous other species, are surely primordial. But nothing that must first be socially learned can be primordial. Ethnic identification is a theoretical, not an instinctive notion. If you have it, you learned it in your own lifetime, you did not somehow learn it at the Battle of Kosova in 1389. History that predates us may play a role in our concern with ethnic conflict because it may show a range of possibilities that might not have been intuitively obvious. History might well suggest that we have a potential interest in preemptively protecting ourselves.

Assuming they do not learn through Lamarckian mechanisms of genetic inheritance, how do young adult Bosnians come to hate Bosnians of other ethnicities? It is plausible that, say, Muslims could do so in the grim conditions of their civil war, with Serbian soldiers raping Muslim women in evidently well-organized and deliberate attacks condoned by Serbian leaders and with Muslim mosques and homes being systematically destroyed by Serbian and Croatian mortar and rocket fire and even by prosaic and methodical dynamite squads. But how do they do so after more than four decades of peace, cooperation, neighborliness, and intermarriage? Of course, it was this last that

---

[33] Emile Durkheim, *The Rules of Sociological Method* (New York: Free Press, 1964 [1895]), 33. Darmesteter goes on to include childhood memories of religious ceremonies in the list of things a competent scholar of religion needs.

preceded the war of the 1990s and, in turn, it was the war that preceded whatever ethnic hatred there now is. It therefore seems likely a canard on humanity to assert that ethnic hatred played the leading causal role in the Yugoslav violence.

Group identification and war

In relatively casual language, nationalism is associated with two very different phenomena involving war. First, it is often associated with national states that go to war against each other. Second, it is often associated with internal "nations" such as Irish Catholics in the United Kingdom, Armenians and Lithuanians in the former Soviet Union, Hutus and Tutsis in Burundi and Rwanda, and Kurds in various countries. In the case of national states, war may often be causally prior to nationalism. In the case of internal nations, civil war is typically caused at least in part by the domestic nationalism.

For the first phenomenon, to say that war is causally prior to nationalism is not, of course, to say that nationalism develops only after a particular war starts. Rather, nationalism is often used *as a means to mobilize* a population for war, both during war and, often, in preparation for war. For example, the Nazi leadership first used nationalist appeals to mobilize the German people and then went to war. During that war, of course, they continued to use nationalist appeals. The Nazi leaders were presumably themselves acting from nationalist concerns, in which case the war was therefore partly caused by nationalism. But one may still suppose that the popular nationalist intensity was heightened by national leaders as a means to mobilize for war.[34] Such mobilization makes sense because coordination of a large population is a form of power. The ideal level of coordination for a government interested in fighting a war is likely to be at or near the whole-nation level.

In the case of subnationalisms, members of a subnational group may believe they can benefit individually if the group gains at the expense of some other group. Then they may respond to nationalist, ethnic, or religious appeals that come up spontaneously or through the deliberate efforts of potential leaders. *The possibility of coordination of an ethnic group entails the possibility of intergroup conflict.* If coordination were not possible, so that a particular group could not gain ascendancy in government, there would be no ground for conflict.

---

[34] This is the general form of nationalism of concern in some of the best recent literature. For example, see Hobsbawm, *Nations and Nationalism*, and John Breuilly, *Nationalism and the State* (Chicago: University of Chicago Press, 1985 [1982]).

Self-interest, group identity

Or, if there were nothing to gain from another group or from ascendancy over it, there would be little incentive for coordination of one's own group. But often there are ready advantages from coordinated action to gain political power.

At least in part, the role of nationalism in war is opportunistic. It can be the great coordinator not for collective action by the population so much as for charismatic power for mobilization of a kind that is especially needed for war. It is simply available as a focus for such coordination and therefore it is used. Other possible motivations, especially universalistic motivations, may not be as effectively available as such foci. Woodrow Wilson's appeal to universalistic ideals after World War I foundered both at home and abroad on nationalist opposition. Stalin mobilized the Soviet people with nationalist and not merely communist rhetoric. The power and immediate success of Sergei Eisenstein's movie, *Alexander Nevsky* (1938), lay in its ethnic and nationalist portrayal of Germans versus Russians as the rising power of Hitler's Germany seemed to threaten the Soviet Union.[35] Class, religion, and even humanitarianism could all work to mobilize people under relevant circumstances, and the first two of these might be used to coordinate peoples for war, as religion has been used during the Crusades and in other times and places. But nationalist and ethnocentric identities seem especially suitable for warlike manipulation.

There need be nothing inherently warlike in nationalism itself. There may be instances of "pure" nationalism in the sense that individuals merely identify with a particular nation or subgroup without having an out-group against which to direct hostility and without having a goal that could be better achieved through massive coordination, as ethnic goals may be. Melville Herskovits supposes that much of the ethnocentrism of anthropological peoples is benign in this way.[36] The eighteenth-century German poet, Johann Gottfried Herder, defended a nonaggressive nationalism on the claim that, as Isaiah Berlin argues, to be human means something like having the epistemological comforts of home, of being among your own kind.[37] There might even be a

---

[35] It was also, no doubt, that nationalist portrayal that forced the withdrawal of the film after the German-Soviet Pact óf 1939. See Ephraim Katz, *The Film Encyclopedia* (New York: Putnam, 1982 [1979]), 383.

[36] Herskovits, *Cultural Relativism*, 102–3.

[37] Isaiah Berlin, *Vico and Herder* (New York: 1976). Also see Berlin's more recent views in the light of the new nationalisms of Eastern Europe and the former Soviet Union in Nathan Gardels, "Two Concepts of Nationalism: An Interview with Isaiah Berlin," *New York Review of Books* (21 November 1991), pp. 19–23.

psychology of nationalist commitment that is not motivated by interest in any central way. But, again, a leadership bent on war can take advantage of Herskovits's simple reasoning from the is–ought fallacy to amass popular support and to turn the nationalist sentiment militant.

Finally, note that if there are interests in group fates, as outlined above, then it may be virtually impossible to resolve many ethnic and nationalist conflicts directly. If a particular ethnic group or nation is to benefit from some policy, the benefit may be purchased at the cost of another group or nation. The conflict between two groups may not be resolvable through compromise that implies mutual gain over the status quo. Such conflicts might be finally trumped by dramatic economic benefits of cooperation, as in the West European community since sometime in the 1950s when the benefits of trade and open economies may finally have swamped the benefits of nationalist separatism. Québécois business leaders in the 1970s seem to have concluded that cooperative gains from staying in the Canadian federation outweighed potential gains from separation. The woeful irony of the current upsurge of ethnic conflict in the former Soviet Union is that the Soviet economy failed to lead people past the possibility of gaining at each other's expense. It failed to make the prospect of mutual gain better than that of conflictual gain. If we run up against severe limits to growth around the world, we may expect ethnic conflicts over limited opportunities to become harsher. In part this is for merely opportunistic reasons: Because a supposed ethnic group can proclaim its identity and take action against others, it may do so for the benefit of its members.

Unfortunately, if a group can benefit from gaining ascendancy over another, then the other has incentive to deter the first group. David Hume argued that there were two ways in which the ancient Anglo-Saxons under King Edgar deterred the Danes. They deterred the foreign Danes, who sometimes attacked from the sea, by maintaining navies to destroy them wherever they attacked. And they deterred the domestic Danes by suppressing them where they lived. "The foreign Danes dared not to approach a country which appeared in such a posture of defense: The domestic Danes saw inevitable destruction to be the consequence of their tumults and insurrections."[38] In the jargon of modern deterrence theory, they practiced deterrence by denial

---

[38] David Hume, *The History of England*, vol. 1 (Indianapolis, IN: Liberty Press, 1983 [1778]), 97.

against the foreign Danes and deterrence by punishment against the domestic Danes.

The chief form of deterrence that conflicting ethnic groups in the same state have against each other is yet a third variety: They deter through preemptive attack. They strive to suppress members of an opposing group where they are in order to prevent their eventual rise. Against the foreign Danes the Anglo-Saxons needed only to be strong to ward off violent conflict. Against the domestic Danes they had to engage in violence in order to retaliate for violence against themselves. Ethnic groups in almost all quarters of the globe seem deliberately to engage in violence in order to pre-empt violence against themselves. In this, they are like Mafia leaders, who strive to murder rivals for the leadership in order to preempt suffering further themselves.

Conclusion

In sum, individual identification with such groups as ethnic groups is not primordial or somehow extrarational in its ascendancy of group over individual interests but is rational. Individuals identify with such groups because it is in their interest to do so. Individuals may find identification with their group beneficial because those who identify strongly may gain access to positions under the control of the group and because the group provides a relatively secure and comfortable environment. Individuals create their own identification with the group through the information and capacities they gain from life in the group. A group gains power from coordination of its members, power that may enable the group to take action against other groups. Hence, the group may genuinely be instrumentally good for its members, who may tend, without foundation, to think it is inherently, not merely contingently, good.

Much of the detail of human nature is a social construction in each case. But this means primarily that opportunities and their costs and benefits are largely a function of what others have done or are doing. A North American can become a wealthy lawyer or entrepreneur because the relevant opportunities are there. Such options are far less readily available to a typical Kenyan or Bangladeshi, or in the early 1990s to a typical Bosnian. But there are constraints that seem even more perversely the product of social interaction. For example, people in different societies are seemingly constrained by different norms. Such constraints seem to play a large role in defining the groups to which individuals become committed. In the rise and maintenance of group identification in many and diverse groups, the role of socially constructed norms is central. The argument for many of these norms, and especially for those that help to motivate loyalty to groups, is that they work as well as they do because they serve relevant interests, even if often in complicated ways that may be opaque to the participants.

CHAPTER 3

Some economics of ethnic capital formation and conflict

Ronald Wintrobe

I **Introduction**

In this paper, I attempt to use simple tools of economic theory to understand ethnicity, ethnic conflict, and nationalism. The starting point of the analysis is a set of circumstances in which there are gains from trade, as in standard neoclassical theory, but that property rights are not costlessly enforceable. Once the latter fiction is discarded, the situation is that people still wish to exchange, but they always have to worry about being cheated. There are reputation mechanisms for solving this problem (Klein and Leffler 1981, Shapiro 1983), but they tend to be expensive. Similar problems arise in politics, interpreted as political exchange in the absence of legal enforcement (one cannot sue a politician in court for breaking a campaign promise), and within families (parents cannot sue their children for not supporting them in their old age).

Indeed, I have argued elsewhere (Wintrobe 1992) that the central barrier in modern economic theory to our understanding of social and economic relationships is arguably the (often implicit) assumption of costlessly enforceable property rights. Once this fiction is discarded, it is possible to interpret much of human behavior – specifically, attempts to form *relationships,* such as trust, love, authority or power relationships, as rational attempts to provide a foundation for exchange. Behavioral models of this sort are central to much of the recent work which attempts to link economics and sociology [e.g.,

---

* I am grateful to Joel Fried, Hilton Root, Theo Offerman, Robert Young, and the participants in the Villa Colombella Seminar on Nationalism for helpful comments and suggestions. Previous versions of this paper were also given at the 1993 Public Choice Society and European Public Choice Society Meetings. I wish to thank the Lynde and Harry Bradley Foundation for financial assistance.

Coleman (1990), Akerlof (1991), or Frank (1988)]. In all these works, one can discern a new character, *homo (femina) socio-economicus (a),* who differs from *homo economicus* in that her behavior is determined not just by her utility function and an income or wealth constraint as in standard economic theory with costless property rights, but by the nature of the relationships he or she is involved in as well.

One particularly effective way to provide a foundation for exchange under many circumstances is to invest in ethnic networks or "ethnic capital." The central feature of ethnic capital is the peculiarity of blood as a basis for network "membership." To the extent that this criterion is used, entry and exit from the network (within a generation) are blocked. I suggest (in the next section) that this gives ethnic networks some advantages as a support for exchange, and partly explains the persistence of ethnicity in modern societies. But if ethnic capital cannot move from one group to another, it also follows that competition among ethnic groups does not equalize returns among them. Consequently, differences in returns and therefore in incomes will persist. The result is that successful ethnic groups tend to engender fear and jealousy on the part of outsiders, while members of ethnic groups with low returns tend to become stigmatized. These disparities combined with the zero-sum nature of economic rents implies that there is an inevitable potential for conflict among ethnic groups ("if you can't join them, beat them"), which is not regulated or reduced by market forces. Instead, ethnic power is *contagious:* The strengthening of one ethnic network breeds fear on the part of outsiders in the same way that one nation's decision to increase its stock of weaponry breeds fear on the part of other nations. And the response tends to be similar: as Barbara Ward suggests, "Nothing so concentrates one's national feeling as being aware of someone else's" (Ward 1959, 19).

The outline of the paper is as follows: Section II shows how the pervasive existence of transactions costs in the modern economy gives rise to economic rents and the demand for trust or networks to seek those rents efficiently. Section III examines the peculiar strengths and weaknesses of ethnic networks. Section IV then looks inside the ethnic group, and in particular at the process of formation of ethnic capital, investments which are largely made by parents for their children. I assume for the purpose of analysis that parents are selfish, and invest in their children in the hope of being repaid in later life. I show that a second peculiar feature of ethnic investments, compared to other kinds of investments in children such as general human capital, is that they are *self-enforcing,* in that the children cannot get the benefits of the capital without exposing themselves to "ethnic pressure" to repay their parents for their sacrifices. This self-enforcing feature makes ethnic investments very attractive to the parents, but not necessarily to the children. Consequently, parents will tend to over-invest in their children's ethnic capital from the children's point of view. I show the circumstances under which this intergenerational conflict can lead to "authoritarian" attitudes in the children, as described in the classic work *The Authoritarian Personality* by Adorno, et. al. (1950). Section V applies the model to the problem of nationalism, and in particular its recent reemergence in the former Soviet bloc.

II The demand for trust or networks

The starting point for our analysis consists of two assumptions, which will be maintained throughout this paper, except in section IV, where, as noted there, assumption 1 is relaxed. They are: (1) All individuals are rational, in the standard sense of that term in neoclassical economic theory, i.e., faced with any two alternatives the individual is capable of making a choice between them, and his or her choices are consistent, and (2) property rights or contracts are not costlessly enforceable, and sometimes may not even exist.

The second assumption implies that in any exchange, there is the possibility that one of the parties will cheat or renege on his or her commitments. In markets, this problem was considered by Klein and Leffler (1981) and Shapiro (1983), in the context of markets for high-quality goods. They assumed that, prior to purchase, consumers cannot distinguish high quality from low. What prevents the firm from producing low-quality goods and selling them as if they were high quality? Shapiro showed that there are three conditions required for it to be in the firm's interest not to cheat its customers: (1) the prospect of future sales, (2) the firm's past reputation as a seller of high-quality goods, and (3) the firm's receipt of a price premium on high-quality goods, both to compensate it for its past investments in reputation and to serve as a deterrent to cheating. If the present value of the premiums received from future sales is large enough to overcome the onetime gains from cheating ("milking" its reputation), it will not be in the firm's interest to cheat. In essence, the existence of the price premium provides the consumer with a reason to *trust* the firm. As Klein and Leffler put it, the consumer pays the firm "protection money" in the form of a price premium to ensure contractual fulfilment. In this way, markets can solve the trust or contractual enforcement problem even in the absence of legally enforceable property rights.

One problem with this solution from the consumer's point of view is that it is expensive. Consumers are forced to pay a premium, the present discounted value of which is at least as large as the gains to the firm from cheating in order to deter the firm from acting that way. Consumers willing to pay this premium are not cheated, but they do not get good value for their money: They stay in Holiday Inns, buy Bayer Aspirin, IBM computers, Samsonite luggage, and so on. An alternative solution for the consumer is to establish a trust relationship with a local seller – the local drugstore, computer hack, and so on. The costs of "signaling" or building trust on a one-on-one basis may be reduced considerably when there is genuine interaction between the parties, as opposed to impersonal market signals. In these cases trust can describe a relationship which is, at the limit, completely private; it exists between a seller and only one buyer – a "network." Trust relationships like these are analyzed by Breton and Wintrobe (1982), and Coleman (1990). Breton and Wintrobe pointed out that trust relationships like these are capital. They yield a stream of future returns which are the profits on the exchanges that trust makes possible and that could not otherwise take place. We also suggested a process by which this capital is formed. To illustrate, suppose that one party, A, presents a second party, B (whom A desires to trust) with an opportunity to cheat him, i.e., to make himself better off at A's expense. The cost to A depends on the size of the opportunity offered since this will be the amount lost if B does decide to cheat him. To the extent that B does not take advantage of this opportunity, he shows that he may be trusted. The cost to B is again equal to the opportunity forgone. The net result of this process whereby A signals and B responds is that some positive amount of the asset "A trusts B" is formed. Trust may be accumulated further if A and B trade with each other, since trade provides opportunities to cheat, and therefore to forego cheating. However, the process is complex, in that the "signals" being given can easily be misinterpreted. Consequently, the process is simplified, and the costs of trust formation are lower, when the two parties share common traits, such as a common language, ethnicity, and so on (cf Landa 1981).

Trust relationships are also important – indeed, probably much more important – in labor markets. Again, the key is to drop the assumption of costlessly enforceable property rights. One way in which enforceability problems can arise is that employees may try to shirk if monitoring their effort level is not costless to the employer. Bulow and Summers (1986) developed a model in which the economy can be divided into "good" jobs and "bad" jobs. Good jobs are jobs in which monitoring performance is difficult – hence the firm will offer high wages, job security, promotion possibilities, and so forth, in order to deter shirking. Bad jobs are jobs in which monitoring performance is easy. Workers with "good" jobs will be tempted to shirk unless the firm can punish them for doing so. However, if markets clear, a worker who is fired for shirking can always get another job at the same wage as he is currently earning, and punishment is impossible. Consequently, wages in the good sector will have to be increased above productivity in order to provide a punishment mechanism. Workers in good jobs who are tempted to shirk then face the possibility that they will be caught, fired, and end up in the secondary sector. In equilibrium, the utility of shirking to the worker must be less than the probability of being caught shirking multiplied by the cost of job loss (the difference between the anticipated present value of income earned in the good vs. the bad sector). Put simply, jobs in the good sector are rationed, and those who have them earn rents which are precisely analogous to the premiums earned by producers of high-quality goods in the Shapiro model.

For our purposes, perhaps the most important lesson of these models is that once the assumption of costlessly enforceable property rights is dropped, the existence of economic rents becomes a pervasive feature of industrial economies. The absence of enforceability generates a demand for trust, and *markets do not supply trust except via rents:* The market mechanism deters cheating only if rents are paid which are at least equal to the gains from cheating.

Of course the same problem of enforceability arises in political markets, in which politicians make promises, especially at election time, and hope to obtain support in exchange for them. What prevents politicians from reneging on the exchange? And what motivates citizens and interest groups to deliver the support that they have promised? Again, the answer suggested here is that both sides of the market will try and look for devices which engender trust (political loyalty) and that these devices imply the distribution of rents. To illustrate, two institutional mechanisms that engender loyalty in politics are pork-barrel projects and political patronage – the exact analogue in political markets to price and wage premia in economic markets. Thus, only to the extent that a pork-barrel project is genuinely wasteful, or that a patronage job has gone to someone who is genuinely less qualified for it than someone else, do these devices distribute rents, and therefore engender loyalty.

To summarize, rents exist to "cement" trust relationships in product and labor markets, within firms, and in political processes. They are a pervasive feature of modern industrial society. A typical individual within that society who wants to buy goods and services at reasonable prices and not be cheated, who wants or wishes to keep a "good" job, who wishes to get his share of the largesse being distributed by politicians, or even to have his views reflected in public policy, therefore has a very complex pattern of network investments to make. For each good or service or political service that he wishes to purchase, where there is some prospect of being cheated, he will have to invest in a specific trust relationship. Some goods and services will be bought so infrequently that such investments will not be worth their cost. The individual will also calculate that investments in these relationships would be lost if the person moves to another jurisdiction. It follows that, in general, the optimal investment strategy (distribution of investments in trust among all the different possible relationships involved) is truly complex. What this individual really wants is a mutual fund. These funds exist, in the form of ethnic networks. They are discussed in the next section.

III Ethnic capital investments

Advantages

1. General purpose: Ethnic networks are often untied to a society's economic structure. Thus, unlike other kinds of networks, such as professional, occupational, social, religious, or other networks, ethnic networks are multipurpose. To illustrate, an Italian moving to Toronto, Canada (where there is a very large Italian community) could use his Italian connections for finding an apartment, a good plumber, buying a car, getting a job, finding a mate, and so on. Like other ethnic networks, those in the Toronto Italian community have two different sources of yield: *private* – as in the examples discussed in the previous section; and *public* – to the extent that the Italian community in Toronto forms a voting bloc and uses this political power to obtain political rents for members of the network. Consequently, upon his or her arrival in Toronto, an Italian has a choice: He can begin the process of looking for a mate, a job, an apartment, a plumber, etc. (not necessarily in that order) in the marketplace, in which case he runs the difficulty of either being cheated a few times or paying market premia in every case (choosing an apartment in a luxury building owned by the financially rock-solid Reichmann brothers, getting a job at IBM, choosing his or her plumber according to the size of the firm's advertisement in the yellow pages, etc.). The third alternative is to join the Italian community: Go to church and social events, vote as instructed (i.e., for the Liberal Party), get a job in a construction firm, and so on. This investment process is easy, and the individual will be guided every step of the way.

2. Blocked entry and exit: Ethnic networks are unique in that "membership" is determined by blood, and it is very difficult for outsiders to enter, or for insiders to truly exit. This solves one of the problems characteristic of networks – namely that if the returns turn out to be substantial, others will want to enter, hence lowering the yield on the initial investments of "insiders." Moreover, because membership is to some extent at least not subject to choice, part of the difficulties normally encountered in establishing a trust relationship are resolved. Thus, a German who meets another German and contemplates a transaction with him that requires trust does not have to worry that the other party is German only *temporarily* because the yield on German capital is temporarily high. Of course, the *level* of German-ness exhibited – the extent to which the other person uses German phrases, pretends to like *rouladen,* goes to German social events, and so on may be precisely subject to such calculations, but, fundamentally, either he or she is German (or Francophone, or Jewish), or not. In part, this is because one's ethnicity is not completely subject to choice, but is also determined by the attitudes of others (as Jews in particular found out from the Germans under the Nazi regime).

Just as it is difficult if not impossible for an outsider to enter an ethnic group, it may also be difficult if not impossible for insiders to exit. A black man can marry a white woman, live in a white suburb, work for an all-white firm, and so on, but he can still find himself greeted by shouts of "Hey, brother!" when he finds himself in the "wrong" neighborhood. And he may also find, to his surprise, that while other connections come and go, the permanence of the ethnic connection can sometimes come in handy. This is particularly likely to happen if he discovers that just as insiders would never completely let him go, so outsiders never really let him in, and he is passed over for promotion or turned down in romance because he "is" black. To be sure, any individual is free to foreswear association with other members of his ethnic group; he can tell his friends and family to get lost, move to another city and refuse to give out his address, never phone his mother again (even on her birthday), change his name to Smith, and so on. Even if he did all these things, however, he will still not be in the same position vis-à-vis his ethnic group as an outsider. To be sure, his ethnic networks will depreciate through lack of use, *but they will not depreciate to zero*. This takes a generation or more. And, should he have a change of heart later on in life and decide to recontact the old network, he will be able to rebuild his capital at less cost than an outsider would incur. It is in this sense that exit from ethnic networks is blocked-an individual is free to reduce his gross investment in this form of capital to zero, but he cannot sell, transfer or dispose of the "sunk" capital which has been accumulated through upbringing, socialization, and ascription by others.

3. Ethnic networks have an infinite life: Another unique feature of ethnic networks is that they go on forever, indeed, backward as well as forward in time. This means that ethnic networks solve the "hangman's paradox" often discussed in game theoretic analyses of the cheating problem. Thus, if the game is finite, cheating is guaranteed on the last play (because there is no possible sanction after the end of the game); if the second party (who has the last move) is going to cheat the first party on the last move, the first party should obviously cheat the second on the next-to-last move; hence the game unravels and cheating takes place on the first move. Whatever importance this analysis has in real life, and there are many who believe it to have some, the problem raised is solved by ethnic networks, since blood ties may thin out but never disappear. Because of this longevity, there is always the prospect of punishment if one ethnic member cheats another in the same group, and there is always the prospect that members of one ethnic group will punish the descendants of another for some transgression or other. In these and other ways, ethnic networks often have a superior capacity to sanction transgressors, both by "insiders" and "outsiders." Thus, the Serb leader Slobodan Milosevic was able to raise genuine fears of conquest and occupation by reminding the Serbs of what the Ottomans did to them at the Battle of Kosovo in 1389. The tactic was apparently effective in building his power base (Ramet 1992, p. 228).

4. (Relative) homogeneity of tastes: Jews like Chinese food, tend to be in favor of human rights, and feel comfortable in big cities. Germans and Japanese people are more willing to work hard compared to Americans. The Irish like to drink. Of course, these ethnic stereotypes are often invalid, but to the extent that tastes do tend to be relatively more homogeneous within ethnic groups than between randomly chosen individuals, collective decision making within the group is made easier. The capacity of the group for collective action is further enhanced in that the willingness of a political system to act on important issues tends to be greater when preferences are homogeneous, as demonstrated elsewhere (Howitt and Wintrobe 1992). Finally, the costs of forming trust will be lower if signaling and communication is easier, as it often is between members of the same ethnic group (Breton and Wintrobe 1982).

5. Ethnic capital investments are subsidized through inheritance and upbringing: An individual whose parents are members of an ethnic group will, by the time he becomes an adult, have already accumulated a substantial amount of ethnic capital. Some of it is "in the genes," some will have been accumulated through education and forced socialization with other members of his or her ethnic group. Of course, at some point the individual is free to choose a different ethnic identity but in that case he will have to accumulate all of the costs at his own expense. A Frenchman who decides that he really wants to be a Pakistani can of course try to do so, but his parents are probably unlikely to help him, and he will be throwing away all of his French connections.

Problems

1. Difficulty in forming other networks: A person who is "too" ethnic tends to cut herself off from the rest of society, and the possibility of forming other connections. Francophones who refuse to speak English have difficulty getting a job in an English firm. Rastafarians with dreadlocks, Yiddish speaking Jews with skull caps on kosher diets, and Sikhs carrying ceremonial daggers are not normally invited to WASP social functions (sometimes one is invited, but not more). Iannaccone (1992) suggests that cults often adopt what to outsiders appear to be weird customs so that their members will have difficulty enjoying themselves outside the cult, hence raising the marginal rate of substitution of cult sanctioned consumption goods and services against other types.

The costs which may arise from the difficulties of having experiences with or forming relationships with outsiders are purely private, in the sense that they are borne entirely by the individual, who, if he or she feels them to be excessive, can reduce his or her investments in ethnic capital accordingly. The rest of the costs to be considered in this section are all to some extent external to the individual or ethnic group involved, and hence full account of them may not be taken in decision making.

2. The "cult" element: Because of the mysteries of blood relationships, and because ethnic groups have a history and a culture which can be "rediscovered" or passed on from generation to generation, ethnic leaders ("managers" of ethnic capital) can see themselves as accountable to history as well as to the current membership and their interests. Partly for this reason, in many instances, the legitimation of ethnic leadership or actions is "top down" rather than bottom up. This lack of responsibility or accountability to their membership gives such leaders an extra degree of freedom of action in deciding how to allocate ethnic capital investments, e.g., which political party to support, what sorts of issues will be emphasized, what types of private facilities (churches, social centres, clubs, sports facilities) will be built. This extra freedom of choice (compared to say a democratically elected politician) means that ethnic leaders might try to enlarge their scope of action or to increase their power in ways that might not be sanctioned by the group. Alternatively, they might form an elite within the group which attempts to monopolize rents. However, at the same time as their freedom is enhanced, their power is diminished by this fact because it is never clear that they have the support of their membership on any particular issue. Thus, it is never clear how much Jesse Jackson speaks for the American black population, Arafat for the Palestinians, etc. As a consequence (unlike managers of, say, financial capital) ethnic managers may have to demonstrate that they have control over their membership or the commitment of their membership in order to reallocate their political capital resources.[1]

3. Blocked entry and exit: In the standard economic theory of markets, two broadly conceived assumptions are necessary to ensure the efficiency or (Pareto) optimality of competition: (i) The absence of externalities, "publicness," or other factors which would lead to the systematic under- or overpricing of economic costs or benefits. (ii) Free entry and exit of capital. As is well known, the second assumption implies that capital will flow out of those industries where its yields are relatively low and into those industries where yields are relatively high. So rents will not persist in long-run equilibrium but will be eliminated as capital flows to those industries where it is most valuable, and the supply of goods and services from those industries expands, driving down their prices and reducing economic rents. This

---

[1] The same implications would follow if, instead of stressing the "cult" element, one focussed on the competition among different aspirants to ethnic leadership. I am grateful to Brendan O'Leary for this point.

mechanism assures the efficiency of competition in economic markets. As discussed above, entry to or exit from ethnic networks is blocked. Consequently, if one ethnic group experiences abnormally high returns (e.g., U.S. Jews) and another group abnormally low returns (e.g., U.S. blacks), there is no mechanism whereby the returns to ethnic capital can be equalized across ethnic groups.

To illustrate this point with a simple model, suppose that there are only two ethnic groups, the Golds and the Silvers. Assume that all individuals of either type are identical. However, although the individuals are identical, the yield to forming network capital need not be. Suppose that the returns to network capital formation are higher among the Golds than the Silvers. The Golds might have a superior capacity to sanction deviant or non-participating members, or they may be able to communicate better with each other, or they may be more isolated from the rest of society and therefore interact with each other more, and so on. Finally, assume that, for either group, there are diminishing returns to aggregate ethnic capital. Let d = the depreciation rate of ethnic capital, and C' = the marginal cost of its formation. The benefits are the increased likelihood of obtaining a rent (p) multiplied by its value (R). For example, the rent from a good job is

$$R = \frac{W_g - W_b}{r + q + q\frac{E_g}{E_b}} \quad (1)$$

where $w_g - w_b$ is the wage differential between "good" and "bad" jobs, r is the interest rate, E_g and E_b are the number of good and bad jobs, q the exogenous rate of turnover, and $q\, E_g/E_b$ is the probability that one could get another good job if one lost the first one (the exogenous rate of turnover multiplied by the proportion of good jobs in the economy).[2] Other rents can be described similarly, e.g., those from obtaining a "good" apartment are

$$R = \frac{A_g - A_b}{r + q + q\frac{A_g}{A_b}} \quad (2)$$

is the utility from obtaining a good apartment, A_g and A_b the number of good and bad apartments, q the rate at which occupants of good apartments lose them for reasons that have nothing to do with their own behavior, etc.

---

[2] This formula for labor market rents is analogous to that presented in Bulow and Summers (1986).

The return to ethnic capital is the sum of these rents $\sum_i p_i R_i \ \forall_i$ where i denotes all the "uses" of ethnic capital (jobs, apartments, plumbers, mates, investments counsellors, political patronage, etc.). Each member of the Golds will invest in ethnic capital to the point where the marginal return just equals its cost, i.e.,

$$(\sum_i p_i R_i)'_G = C_G'(r + d_G) \tag{3}$$

where p is the probability that the ith individual will obtain the rent, d is the rate at which ethnic capital is expected to depreciate, primes denote partial derivatives, and G indexes variables for the Golds. The same equation holds for the Silvers. Individuals in either group will invest until the *marginal* yields are equal to their costs (and therefore to each other's costs). However, if infra-marginal yields were high for the Golds and low for the Silvers, the total amount invested would be high for the Golds and low for the Silvers.

In equilibrium, then, the average yield is high for the Golds and low for the Silvers. Golds will get more of the good jobs, good apartments and so on than Silvers do. If mobility were possible between groups, Silvers would enter the Gold network and average yields would fall there and rise among the Silvers. However, blocked entry and exit prevents this mechanism from operating. Returns could be equalized by differential rates of population growth, if the high yield to Gold ethnic capital resulted in high population growth rates there, and the low yield to Silver ethnic capital resulted in low rates of population growth for that group. However, if anything, this mechanism appears to work in reverse: High-income groups appear to have low rates of population growth and low income groups high rates of growth. Consequently, high yields among some ethnic groups will persist, giving rise to fear, envy and possibly hatred among other groups who will never share those yields. Low returns among other groups will result in stigmatization, or statistical discrimination (Arrow 1972) as individuals within an ethnic group are judged on the basis of the performance of the average for that group. Borjas (1992) presents highly suggestive evidence of the persistence of differential earnings capacity among ethnic groups across generations. Clearly, the phenomenon of blocked entry and exit, more than any other property of ethnic capital, explains why market mechanisms do not eliminate ethnic conflict and why competition among ethnic groups tends to breed ethnic conflict and violence.

Finally, I would also like to suggest that blocked entry and exit is the primary or fundamental characteristic of ethnic networks, not only in the sense of the importance of its effects, as just discussed, but in the sense that all of the other characteristics can be derived from it. Thus, if entry to and exit from a network are blocked, that network is automatically general purpose, has an infinite life, membership with relatively homogeneous tastes, subsidized investments, difficulty in forming other networks, and cult element. So, this would appear to be the defining characteristic of ethnic relations from an economic point of view.

In short, the phenomenon of blocked entry and exit explains why market mechanisms do not eliminate ethnic conflict and why competition among ethnic groups has the potential to breed conflict. To some extent, individualism is devalued as the characteristics of the group become more important as determinants of individual welfare. There is also a natural tendency for ethnicity to be linked to territory, as in the "principle of nationality" that the boundaries of the state should be linked to those of the "nation" or ethnic group (Hobsbawm 1990). The absence of the market regulating mechanism implies its replacement by evolutionary or conflict mechanisms, as groups either prosper or decline as a whole. And there is a natural demand for leadership in the management of ethnic capital. In *extreme* form, all of these characteristics – the importance of the group over the individual, the leader and evolutionary principles, and the stress on struggle and the inevitability of conflict are precisely the characteristics of fascism, as we discuss further below. However, the extremity or the viciousness of *some* ethnic conflicts, such as that under the Nazi regime, or perhaps the contemporary conflict between the Serbians and Croatians, is still, I believe, difficult to account for with a model like this one. To do this, it is necessary to look more deeply inside the ethnic group and to investigate in more detail how ethnic capital is formed.

IV Intra- and inter-group ethnic conflict

So far, I have suggested that ethnic investments can yield a positive return, and have assumed in the last section that individuals accumulate the optimal level of this form of capital. Intergenerational harmony was thus assured, despite the fact that much of the investment in ethnic capital is performed by parents for their children. I also assumed that entry and exit from the network are blocked. In this section, I want to elaborate a more complicated model, in which parents make investments in their children in exchange for control over the behavior of their children in later life, and in which this exchange is "enforced" by the pressure which can be brought upon the children by other members of the ethnic group.

Thus, suppose that parents invest in the ethnic capital of their children by sending them to ethnic schools, inculcating ethnic customs and rituals, language, and other communication techniques, restricting their socialization while young to other members of the ethnic group, etc. Parents expect to be repaid for these sacrifices through the obedience of the children in later life to norms of the ethnic group, which presumably include support and attention to their parents in their old age, but may also encompass other aspects of their children's behavior, e.g., that they will marry within the group and raise children who will continue to participate within it, that they participate in ethnic cultural activities, rites and rituals, respect and/or worship ancestral heroes, take credit as members of the group for the accomplishments of their forefathers, assume the debts of previous generations, and so on. In short, children may repay their parents not only directly with support, but also indirectly by making decisions based on their parents' wishes or utility function, and by participating in the activities or adhering to the norms of the ethnic group.

But what mechanism can parents count on to enforce the implicit contract between them and their children? The children can't be sued in court if they don't repay. There are obvious reasons for this. One reason is surely that the contract may not be voluntarily entered into by the children, or even if it is, the children may be too young to be deemed capable of "credible" or enforceable commitments. Another is that the preferred form of repayment can take subtle forms, e.g., that the children's career or marriage choices are those that their parents would have liked them to make. With these forms of repayment, it may be difficult for an outsider to ascertain whether repayment has in fact occurred, and to adjudicate disputes between parents and their children over this matter. Yet both parents and children might prefer these forms of repayment to, say, cash repayments.

So how can parents be confident that their children will in fact repay them for the sacrifices they have made on their behalf? Clearly, the problem is a general one, i.e., it applies to all forms of parental investment, e.g., to investments in general human capital such as their childrens' education or occupational training, and to "gifts" of land, houses, cash, and so on.

I can think of at least five mechanisms which can act as substitutes for legal enforcement: (1) altruism, (2) bequests, (3) trust, (4) guilt, and (5) shame. Becker (1974, 1976), Frank (1988), Hirshleifer (1977) and others have argued that altruism is a powerful force in family life, as indeed, it no doubt is. In the famous "rotten kid" theorem, Becker argued that, under certain conditions one-sided altruism, i.e., the parent loves the child but not *vice versa,* is sufficient to motivate the child's cooperation. However, this argument only holds under certain conditions.[3] In any case, it relies on the mechanism of the expectation of further transfers from parent to child, which we rule out here, except for bequests, which are discussed separately below. Altruism *on the part of the child* will no doubt motivate the child to repay his parents. The problem is that altruism within the family is sometimes insufficient. Becker and Murphy (1988) explicitly acknowledge this and suggest that state intervention (compulsory schooling, pension plans, etc.) often mimics the kinds of contracts that the family would have entered into if legally enforceable contracting were possible. But they do not inquire into the private behavior that ensues where love is insufficient, i.e., there is no analysis of alternative bases for exchange within the family. Yet, even where love is plentiful, so long as it is not complete, i.e., the child cares for the parent as much as he does for himself (Becker calls this "full caring"), interaction will sometimes occur between parent and child on the basis of self-interest. For all these reasons, it is necessary to look beyond altruism in discussing family interaction.

Bernheim, Shleifer and Summers (1985) suggested that, in addition to caring for their children, parents want attention from them, especially when they get older. Children may not mind visiting their parents at first, but after a while they get tired of it, and further visits bring disutility. Parents never tire of seeing their children (at least, never before their children tire of visiting them), and so, at the margin, parents are willing to trade larger bequests for more visits. Amazingly, data exist on the level of attention children give to their parents, in the form of indices of the number of weekly visits paid by children to their parents. Their analysis of the data showed that the larger the potential bequest, the more frequent the visits. Most sadly, perhaps, visits to parents who were poor and became ill dropped off, while those to parents who were rich and became ill increased. Here, the strategic threat of the withdrawal of the bequest is used by parents to enforce their wishes on their children. Note that the mechanism does not precisely mimic legal enforcement, because with legal enforcement, it would not always be necessary to give all the bargaining power to the parent. Perhaps it is this problem which explains why in some coun-

---

[3] See Hirshleifer (1977), Wintrobe (1981, 1983).

tries (Germany, France) parents are legally proscribed from depriving a child of his parent's estate beyond a certain point (for example, in a two-child German family, each child is entitled to a minimum of one-fourth of the estate).

Both the analysis and the evidence on bequests show that family relations can be illuminated using the model of exchange. However, it still appears that poor parents with no planned bequest have nothing to protect them in their old age. One other possibility is that the parents might simply trust their children to look after them. However, if we rule out the altruistic and economic motives already discussed, and we also assume that the children are rational, then there must be some explanation of why the children would behave in this way. The most obvious motives are shame and guilt. The two are commonly distinguished (e.g., Freud 1929, Kandel and Lazear 1992) on the basis that shame ("external pressure") requires external observability whereas guilt ("internal pressure") does not. Freud interprets much of the advance of civilization to this economy of guilt as a mechanism in enforcing behavioral codes and norms. I will not attempt a comprehensive analysis of the operation of these two motives here, but I will suggest that ethnic capital is an investment vehicle for which they are particularly suited, and discuss their operation in this context.

In brief, the argument is that parents can partly "bind" their children to the ethnic group by ethnic capital investments in them while young. The children are bound not just because the yield on this form of capital is specific to the ethnic group in question, and cannot be sold or otherwise transferred. The reason is that, in order to obtain the yield on this form of capital, the (grown) children will have to associate with other members of the ethnic group, and other members of the ethnic group can be counted on to pressure or shame them into repaying their debts to the parents and to adhere to the other norms of the group. So the "contract" is "self-enforcing" from the parents' point of view – the children can only obtain the benefits from this form of capital to the extent that they repay their parents for the investments made.

To illustrate, imagine a mythical ethnic group, the Harriets. Two Harriets, HI and HR are discussing a business deal over lunch. Because they are both Harriets, it is easy for them to communicate,[4] and they feel free to ask personal questions. Here are some standard ones

---

[4] I would argue that two members of an ethnic group do not necessarily like or trust one another, but do find it easier to communicate with one another, thus making it easier to establish whether or not they can trust or like each other.

(HI is the Interlocutor, HR is the Respondent): "So, HR, your wife is also a Harriet?" "How many little Harriet children do you have?" "Your mother lives with you, or did you put her in a home?" If the answer to questions like these are all negative, the respondent may find the deal coming unstuck, as the interlocutor discovers that he is not maintaining his ethnic capital.

Why does the interlocutor (HI) want to enforce the norms? Even if they are beneficial to the group, why doesn't HI free ride, and leave it to other members of the group to police behavior? Although I will not give a comprehensive analysis of this problem here,[5] I will suggest three reasons why other members of the ethnic group can often be counted on to apply the required pressure: (1) *Ordinary self-interest:* If the respondent didn't honor his implicit contract to repay his parents, there is, ipso facto, some reason to believe that he is more likely to renege on his current obligations; hence it is worthwhile to get this information. (2) *Guilt:* By pressuring other members of the group to honor their obligations, a group member in part fulfills his own, and lessens his sense of guilt. (3) *Sanctions for not enforcing the group norm:* Ethnic groups may have a particularly powerful capacity to use sanctions effectively. The reasons are implicit in their value as exchange networks discussed earlier: subsidized early socialization with other members (hence facilitating mutual monitoring), infinite life (therefore implying common ancestry and descent, and therefore a long period over which transgressions can be punished), multipurposeness, and so on.

To the extent that members of the ethnic group, for these reasons, can be counted on to encourage, pressure, or police each other's obedience to group norms, parents who invest in the ethnic capital of their children can count on them to repay. Hence ethnic investments are self-enforcing.[6] In this respect, ethnic networks differ from other forms of parental investment (e.g., general human capital), for which parents may have to rely entirely on the affection of their children, or on internal pressure (guilt), to be repaid.

It follows immediately that there will be "overinvestment" by parents in the ethnic capital of their children, compared to other types of

---

[5] A more general analysis would derive the level of enforcement from the characteristics of the ethnic group, and from its environment; I hope to do this in another paper. Here, I will just assume general obedience to the norm, and suggest why this could be the case. On some conditions for the persistence of codes, see Wintrobe (1983).

[6] Indeed, the self-enforcing nature of ethnic capital provides a further reason for the persistence of ethnicity.

capital. Because no other form of capital has this self-enforcing aspect,[7] parents are guaranteed a return on ethnic capital investments, while for other forms of investment in their children, they are forced to rely on their children's affection for them, guilt or trustworthiness to be repaid for their sacrifices. Consequently, this biases their investments in the direction of ethnic capital investments: Given two investments of equal yield to their children, parents will strictly prefer the ethnic over the non-ethnic investment. Indeed, they will prefer an ethnic investment of lower yield, and the potential differential will be larger, the more militant and committed are members of the ethnic group (the more that members are willing to act to enforce the repayments of debt).[8]

Of course, to the extent that the parents love their children, they will take their children's welfare into account in deciding on their investments. Here, we have assumed that the parents are entirely selfish, and decide on the level of investment which is optimal from their point of view alone. It is worth noting, however, that the over-investment theorem will still hold in the case of altruistic parents, though the level of over-investment will presumably be smaller as the degree of altruism (and hence concern for the welfare of the child)[9] gets larger.

In any case, at some point the child will reach maturity, and at that

---

[7] The statement in the text is obviously too strong; other parental gifts, interpreted here as loans, may be partially self-enforcing, e.g, the gift of a house next door to one's parents keeps the children next door, and therefore encourages attention, so long as the house is illiquid.

[8] To demonstrate this point, let p = the level of ethnic pressure which the parents can anticipate can be brought to bear on the next generation, i.e., p = the estimated probability that the children will be forced to repay their debts by pressure from their fellow ethnics, t = the extent to which parents trust their children to repay out of a sense of moral obligation (guilt) in the absence of pressure, and A_k = the probability that the children will want to repay out of a sense of affection or altruism towards their parents. Suppose the parents invest $\$X$ in their children, which yields $\$X(1+\pi_e)$ in the case of ethnic capital, and $\$X(1+\pi_g)$ in the case of general human capital. Suppose for simplicity that the fraction k of it must be repaid in either case. Then the parents will be indifferent between two investments, one ethnic and one general, where $kX(1+\pi_e)(t+A_k+p) = kX(1+\pi_g)(t+A_k)$. The required ratio between the yield on general vs. that on ethnic capital is $(1+\pi_e)/(t+A_k) = (1+\pi_g)/(t+A_{k+p})$ i.e., investments in general human capital will be "artificially" discounted by the factor $1/1+p$.

[9] Note that for altruism to reduce overinvestment, the altruism must take the form of concern for the child's own welfare or utility, and not for the child's consumption pattern, i.e., the parent's utility function must have the form $U_p = U_p(c_p, U_k)$, where p = parent, k = kid, c = a vector of consumption goods, and not $U_p = U_p(cp, c_k)$. Increased altruism of the latter variety can lead to *more* ethnic investment if the parent believes that ethnic capital is particularly good for the kid.

point will find that he has involuntarily been made a partner to these contracts with his parents (and perhaps with other relatives). Unless the child's preferences are identical to those of his parents, the mature child will find that he is "out of equilibrium" – his desired level of ethnic capital is different from the stock which has been accumulated for him. From the overinvestment theorem, it follows that typically the individual will want to allow some of his or her ethnic capital to depreciate, although those children whose tastes or opportunities lie heavily in the direction of the ethnic group may want to invest more (the overinvestment theorem only holds on the average.) Perhaps it is for this reason that many ethnic groups have institutionalized "rites of passage" signaling the onset of maturity: At this point the individual, by participating in the ritual, indicates his acceptance of the responsibility for the debts that have been incurred on his behalf. It is peculiar, and deserves further exploration, that while these rites are common to many ethnic groups, the age at which they take place appears to vary enormously among different groups. Thus, for some Chinese groups, it only takes place just before marriage (hence never at all for those who don't marry), while for Jews, it happens at the age of thirteen. The strategic aspects are obvious enough: in the Chinese case, the pressure to marry (and perpetuate the group) is increased as the individual who never marries is in effect considered never to have grown up; in the Jewish one, "maturity" (and the onset of responsibility for debt) is deemed to have taken place at an age when the individual is too young to resist.

Note that the overinvestment theorem obviously neglects possible external effects due to ethnic capital. Thus, if, as de Tocqueville suggested, and as Hechter (1992) reemphasized, ethnic groups impart useful social values to their members, and these contribute to the creation and maintenance of social order, overinvestment from the viewpoint of the children invested in might easily be an underinvestment from the social point of view. On the other hand, to the extent that ethnic investments create prejudice and hostility among groups, raising tensions, hostility and leading to wasteful expenses on rent seeking, the level of overinvestment discussed here could easily be an underestimate of the socially optimal level.

To model the effects of parental investment in ethnic capital, let π = the gross yield to ethnic capital to individual i at his or her maturity (subscripts are suppressed for notational simplicity), r = the rate of interest on the debt which must be repaid to the parents, and $K = i$'s stock of ethnic capital. Let p = the level of ethnic peer pressure on i to repay his parents for their investments in ethnic capital, so $r = r(p)$.

To derive a very simple picture, assume that marginal = average yields and rates of interest, so that π and r are constant (given p). Then the marginal net yield to i's ethnic capital is π-r, and total net profits are $(\pi$-$r)K$.[10]

Because ethnic capital is a sunk investment whose value is specific to ethnic networks, and which cannot be sold or transferred, the gross yield on this capital is a quasirent (in the sense of Klein, Crawford and Alchian (1978). Its main value is to permit trade with other members of the ethnic group. Consequently, the yield on this capital (π) will be high when other mechanisms which can enforce trade (such as legal enforcement) are weak, and vice versa. Space prohibits consideration of all of the possibilities, but one interesting case is that where: (1) K is relatively high, (2) π is low, and (3) p is high, so that π-$r<0$, and with K high (relative to other forms of capital) the individual is incurring substantial losses. However, exit is difficult because p is high. What can the individual do? I suggest that individuals in this position are particularly likely to develop prejudices against members of other ethnic groups, and have the potential to engage in conflict with them and to encourage antidemocratic forces in order to raise the yield on ethnic capital. To buttress this assertion, I will try to show that the constellation of returns just described is consistent with the peculiar syndrome described in the classic work by Adorno and others, *The Authoritarian Personality* (1950).

The authoritarian personality was a personality structure or constellation of attitudes which was believed to show, as one of the concept's inventors later described it, a *potential* for fascism, a *susceptibility* to anti-Semitic propaganda, and a *readiness* to participate in antidemocratic social movements.[11] The essential technique used in the original work was to discover, on the basis of interviews, attitudes that linked, in a nonobvious way, with general prejudice, anti-Semitism, or fascism, giving rise to the *"E"* (ethnocentrism), *"A-S"* (anti-Semitism) and *"F"* (fascism) scales. As might be expected the scales are highly correlated with one another.

Thus, one item, to which respondents were asked to express agreement or disagreement, was: "He is indeed contemptible who does not feel an undying love, gratitude, and respect for his parents." Agreement with this statement was held, because of the way it is expressed, to mask an underlying or unconscious hostility toward the

---

[10] A more complete model would also specify the action f for nonrepayment, so that, at maturity, an individual would have the choice between repayment, and earning π-r, and non-repayment, yielding expected profits of $(1-p)\pi$-$p(\pi$-$f)$.

[11] Sanford (1950), p. 142.

Economics of ethnic capital formation and conflict

parents. The overt glorification and unconscious hostility towards one's parents, (other evidence of which became apparent during the interviews), was held to be a distinguishing feature of the highly ethnocentric person.

A second characteristic was an exaggerated, emotional need to submit to authority, again springing, according to theory, from an underlying hostility to ingroup authorities, originally the parents.[12] Other characteristics were superstition (a tendency to shift responsibility from within the individual to forces outside his control), stereotypy (a tendency to think in rigid, oversimplified categories), and a narrow range of consciousness.

Adorno, et. al. found no specific relationship between the scales and socioeconomic factors. But they did find that people who scored high on the E-scale tended to express similar political and religious preferences to those of their parents. Subsequent work on the correlates of the F-scale found a correlation with an emphasis in upbringing on obedience and strict control, and with low education.

The foregoing is a very brief summary of some of the main themes of *The Authoritarian Personality* and subsequent work in that vein. Its purpose is to illuminate my conjecture above that hostility toward other ethnic groups can be predicted on the basis of a particular constellation of returns to ethnic capital: relatively high K and p combined with low net yield or π-r. Thus, consider the likely attitudes of a person in such a position who is rational in every respect save one: he must follow the norm of honoring one's parents. So, the person is unlike *homo economicus* in that he is capable of repressing unpleasant emotions. I assume that the more the parents have invested, the more unpleasant it would be to think negative thoughts about them. Now, suppose that the investments are low-yielding, and that K and p are high. The individual in this position is awash in debt to his parents and other ethnic group members, but the yield on the capital investments they have sacrificed so hard to give to him is low, too low to cover his debts to them. Because he has substantial ethnic capital he venerates his parents and his forefathers, and they cannot be overtly blamed for the pickle he is in. (But unconsciously, he knows they have plied him with excess ethnic capital.) He has very little space to exercise his own choices in life because in order to repay debts his behavior is largely dictated by his parents' wishes and the norms of the ethnic group. So, his political and religious choices are their choices, and his range of consciousness and capacity for conscious choice is narrow.

[12] Sanford (1973), p. 144.

In a sense he is quite rightly superstitious (his behavior is largely outside his control, given his adherence to the norm). Thus the "authoritarian personality" can be made sense of as a response to this constellation of returns to ethnic capital.

Why is he prejudiced? To the individual in question, his problem is not that his parents invested too much in his well-being, but that, through no fault of theirs, the yield on this capital is low. Whose fault is that? "The Jews," of course, with their tight, high-yielding international network, and their connections with the state and to international markets[13] (the development of which lowers the yield on other ethnic capital). What to do about it?: (A) Get rid of them, and (B) engage in other collective actions to raise the yield on ethnic capital. The Nazi ideology of blood and ethnic purity as a means of organizing society was certainly an extreme response, but it is one which is precisely along this line. It certainly raised (for a time) the yield on the right kind of ethnic capital. In general, the extremity of some ethnic conflicts, such as the behavior of the Nazis, and perhaps the contemporary conflict between Serbs and Croatians can be explained with the approach suggested here, (and is difficult to explain with a strictly rational approach): Because the ethnic group which is the object of conscious hatred is not the real enemy, acts of hatred and destruction toward members of it are inherently unsatisfying and result only in frustration, breeding further hatred and violence.[14]

Finally, I cannot resist pointing out at least one other novel and testable implication: The argument suggests that, *ceteris paribus,* ethnocentrism, ethnic conflict and authoritarianism will be lower in societies with generous pension or social security systems. In those societies, parents will feel it less necessary to invest heavily in their children's ethnicity in order to gain support in their old age; as a result, the children will be less likely to develop and repress hostile emotions toward their parents and to project these onto other ethnic groups if the yield on these investments falls.

---

[13] Arendt (1951), Part I: Anti-Semitism, discusses these factors in the context of anti-Semitism in the nineteenth century.

[14] In other respects, the implications of the present approach accord with those which might be predicted from completely rational models: Ethnic conflict would appear more likely, *ceteris paribus* the greater the difference in wages or other factor returns between groups, the smaller the complementarity between their factors (hence the less they "need" each other) and the more similar they are in terms of tastes or resource utilization (hence the more they are in direct competition with each other for scarce resources).

V   Contemporary nationalism in the former Soviet bloc

Nationalism may be defined as the striving of members of a culturally defined group for territorial autonomy (e.g., Rogowski 1985). In our terms, this would presumably occur when the returns to ethnic capital are perceived to be higher if the ethnic group in question were to form a sovereign state. The returns to ethnic capital are determined by the supply of rents available, and the probability that these rents can be obtained by members of the ethnic group in question (the *power* of the ethnic group). The supply of rents available depends on economic growth while the power of the ethnic group presumably depends on its position within the wider society. Does the ethnic group control its own territory? Do members of the elite have access to public and private rents, or are these controlled by a *nomenklatura* which is blocked to members of the ethnic group? Do members of the ethnic group have a sufficient supply of elite skills to run their own country? Structural factors such as these, analyzed in a number of recent writings on nationalism (e.g. Rogowski 1985, Laitin 1991, or Hechter 1987), combined with economic variables such as the rate of economic growth in the group's territory (and hence the supply of rents there) vs. the rate of economic growth at the "center" determine the relative yield of ethnic capital under (ethno-) federalism vs. that under sovereignty. Space prohibits a general analysis of these issues, but a possibly general line of analysis can be indicated by considering one important case of the reemergence of nationalism – namely that in the former Soviet bloc.

Nowhere are standard views of totalitarian dictatorship more misleading than they are in the case of the "nationalities question" in the former Soviet Union. There are two standard views: (1) Communist regimes ruled by repression alone (Kirkpatrick 1982); (2) Communist dictatorships, like other totalitarian dictatorships "atomize" the interest groups within them (Arendt 1951). Elsewhere (Wintrobe 1990), I have suggested a different approach to understanding the behavior of totalitarian dictatorships. I tried to show that they typically accumulate power, using loyalty or support as well as repression as instruments. This point is well illustrated by Soviet policy with respect to the nationalities. Thus, although the role of the state in destroying both real and imaginary ethnic oppositions is well known, the Soviets also sought to tie the various minorities to the Soviet regime through the Stalinist linkage of ethnicity, territory, and political administration. Zaslavsky (1992) documents how the Soviets created a federation of ethnoterritorial units, "governed by indigenous political elites and organized in an elaborate administrative hierarchy. Ethnicity was also institutionalized on the individual level through the introduction of a comprehensive internal passport system which fixed the ethnic affiliation of every Soviet citizen."[15]

Ethnic identification in turn provided an objective basis for affirmative action policies oriented towards territorially based nationalities (well described in Roeder 1991). While the activities of dissident nationality groups were repressed, in part this was done by giving the indigenous cadre an institutionalized monopoly on the public expression of ethnic identity. Moreover, as Roeder goes on to point out, "within each Republic this cadre was assigned the role of gatekeeper, to determine when the ethnic group would be mobilized politically . . . the means of communications, particularly the indigenous language press and broadcast media, were monopolized by the Republican institutions controlled by this cadre. Access to meeting places such as auditoriums and public squares within the Republic was at the discretion of this cadre."[16] Roeder also documents the numerous "affirmative action" policies which permitted these cadres to build more secure political bases within their ethnic communities.[17] However, although Soviet federalism fostered preferential treatment of the representatives of local nationalities within their own territories, top-level positions in the all-union service were largely reserved for Russians (the *nomenklatura*) (Laitin 1991).

In sum, far from "atomizing" ethnic networks, the Soviet strategy was to encourage them by making rents available to their leaders for distribution to their membership, *provided* that in return the leadership would channel their ethnic resources into loyal party service. Distrust among ethnic groups was sown, and formal links among them existed only via the Party. In this way, the various ethnic groups were co-opted into the Party structure and the system built on the loyalty of these groups to the center.

A second distinctive feature of the Soviet system is that it mimics ethnic networks in having a cultlike aspect, namely its ideology, which competes with the cultures of ethnic groups. Giuseppe di Palma summarizes a number of features which mark Communist legitimation from the top:

> (1) "tasks" and "campaigns" (to conquer new heights or stamp out evils) replace legal frames as the language of the state . . . (2) Soviet bureaucracies (the Party in particular) lay claim to command because

---

[15] Zaslavsky (1992), p. 99.   [16] Roeder (1991) p. 205.
[17] Loc. cit.

Economics of ethnic capital formation and conflict

their tasks are guided by a superior truth. They claim a monopoly on political discourse. Thus their truth cannot be falsified by reality, their commands are always correct, and their task can never fail by their own shortcomings. . . . (3) Authentication of the truth does not need the people. On the contrary, the truth enjoins the people to learn and disseminate it, to bear witness to it.[18]

As Brecht put it "the Communist party might just as well dissolve the people and elect a new one."[19]

The third distinctive aspect of Soviet policy was that, like other industrial societies its legitimation rested to a considerable extent on the promise of continuous economic growth. The causes of the steady decline in growth rates since the 1960s are too complex to discuss here. However, its implications are worth summarizing:

(1) So long as economic growth continued at a satisfactory rate (at least until the 1960s) the various ethnic groups obtained a satisfactory "return" on the loan of their ethnic resources to the Soviet state. However, when economic growth declined, the supply of rents began to dry up, and these became increasingly reserved for the Russian *nomenklatura* at the center. Consequently, the ethnic groups began to withdraw their loyalty.

(2) Less obviously, the capacity of the center to maintain its power by repressing the population collapsed as well, because repression and loyalty are positively correlated for totalitarian societies (as shown in Wintrobe 1990).

(3) With the collapse of economic growth came the collapse of the belief that the system could ever fulfill its ideology. As Poggi nicely puts it, "the promises had been made for too long to be believed, and for too long to be surrendered" (Poggi 1990 168–9).

(4) The removal of the Party at the center left a power vacuum, and also removed the only network links between ethnic groups, leaving them only with Communist-encouraged antagonism and distrust for one another.

(5) The collapse of the economic system and the switch to a market system in which property rights are still extremely underdeveloped means that the returns on both the major alternatives to ethnic capital investment – the old, collapsed Party system and the marketplace – are low.

---

[18] di Palma (1991), p. 57.   [19] Cited in di Palma (1991), p. 57.

It is hardly surprising, then, that ethnic leaders wanted to reallocate their capital away from the central institutions of the USSR (The Party, etc.), whose decline appeared inevitable. Demonstrations and uprisings were therefore orchestrated by ethnic leaders (using the tools of control which the Party had previously allocated to them), sometimes with the support of many of the members, in order to make the collective transfer of the capital away from the center (where its yield has fallen) and toward the region (where its yield has increased) possible. Indeed, Roeder (1991 197) has shown that it is the nationalities with the highest level of educational, occupational, and often political attainment rather than the disadvantaged or marginal ones, that have advanced the most ambitious agendas for change and engaged in the most extensive protest. The upsurge of nationalism among ethnic groups in this region is therefore not necessarily irrational, and can, I believe at least partly be explained with a model along the lines suggested here.

VI   Conclusion

In this paper, I have presented a simple model of ethnic group relations. In it, ethnic networks are a form of capital which allow "members" of ethnic groups to make exchanges at low transactions costs, and to seek rents from the public sector. The basic point of the chapter is that, compared to other groups, the fundamental characteristic of ethnic groups is that entry and exit from the group are blocked. This accounts for the strength of ethnic groups in that it solves a number of exchange problems, including the problem of opportunistic entry or exit. But it also implies that competition among ethnic groups does not equalize returns among them. Consequently, differences among these returns persist, and the result is that successful ethnic groups tend to engender fear and jealousy while members of ethnic groups with low returns tend to become stigmatized. As a result, there is a potential for conflict among ethnic groups ("If you can't join them, beat them."), which is not reduced by market forces. The reason is that the essential quality of competition which accounts for its efficiency in industrial life – free entry and exit – is missing in this sphere.

Of course, in reality, entry and exit are usually not completely blocked, and, in fact, it is easier to enter in or exit from some types of ethnic groups than others. A more general analysis would allow the level of barriers to entry and exit to vary and develop an "industrial organization" of ethnic groups. In this paper, I have simply assumed blocked entry and exit in order to bring out the implications of this assumption. I have, however, in the last two sections, tried to use the model to explain the "authoritarian personality" construct, and applied the model to the recent upsurge of nationalism in the former Soviet bloc, and shown that the approach is capable of throwing some light on that construct and those events.

References

Adorno, Theodor W., Else Fenkel-Brunswik, Daniel Levinson, and R. Nevitt Sanford. 1950. *The Authoritarian Personality*. New York: Harper.
Akerlof, George A. 1991. "Procrastination and Obedience." *American Economic Review Papers and Proceedings* 81 (May): 1–19.
Arendt, Hannah. 1973. *The Origins of Totalitarianism*. 2nd ed. Orlando, FL: Harcourt, Brace, Jovanovich.
Arrow, K. J. 1972. "Models of Job Discrimination." In Pascal, A. H., ed. *Racial Discrimination in Economic Life*. Lexington, MA: Heath.
Becker, Gary. 1974. "A Theory of Social Interactions." *Journal of Political Economy*. 82:1,063–1109.
  1976. "Altruism, Egoism, and Genetic Fitness." *Journal of Economic Literature*. 14:817–26.
Becker, Gary, and Murphy, Kevin. 1988. "The Family and the State." *Journal of Law and Economics* 31:1–19.
Bernheim, B. Douglas, Shleifer, A., and Summers, L. H. 1985. "The Strategic Bequest Motive." *Journal of Political Economy,* 93:1,045–76.
Borjas, George J. 1992. "Ethnic Capital and Intergenerational Mobility." *Quarterly Journal of Economics* 107:123–50.
Breton, Albert. 1964. "Economics of Nationalism." *Journal of Political Economy* 72:376–86.
Breton, Albert, and Wintrobe, Ronald. 1982. *The Logic of Bureaucratic Conduct*. New York: Cambridge University Press.
Bulow, Jeremy, and Summers, Lawrence. 1986. "A Theory of Dual Labor Markets with Applications to Industrial Policy, Discrimination, and Keynesian Unemployment." *Journal of Labor Economics* 4:376–414.
Coleman, James S. 1990. *Foundations of Social Theory*. Cambridge: Harvard University Press.
di Palma, Giuseppe. 1991. "Legitimation from the Top to Civil Society: Political Cultural Change in Eastern Europe." *World Politics* 44:49–80.
Frank, Robert H. 1988. *Passions Within Reason*. New York: Norton.
Freud, Sigmund. 1991 [1929]. *Civilization and Its Discontents*. Reprinted in the Penguin Freud Library vol. 12, *Civilization, Society and Religion*.
Gellner, Ernest. 1983. *Nations and Nationalism*. Ithaca, NY: Cornell University Press.
Hechter, Michael. 1987. *Principles of Group Solidarity*. Berkeley and Los Angeles: University of California Press.
Howitt, Peter, and Wintrobe, Ronald. 1992. "Equilibrium Political Inaction in a Democracy." In Breton, A., et al., eds. *Preferences and Democracy*. Dordrecht: Kluwer Academic Press.
  1994. "The Political Economy of Inaction," *Journal of Public Economics*. (1994).

Iannaccone, Laurence R. 1992. "Sacrifice and Stigma: Reducing Free-Riding in Cults, Communes and Other Collectives." *Journal of Political Economy* 100:271–91.
Kandel, Eugene, and Lazear, Edward. 1992. "Peer Pressure and Partnerships." *Journal of Political Economy* 100:801–8.
Kirkpatrick, Jeane. 1982. *Dictatorships and Double Standards: Rationalism and Realism in Politics*. New York: Simon & Schuster.
Klein, Benjamin, and Leffler, Keith B. 1981. "The Role of Market Forces in Assuring Contractual Performance." *Journal of Political Economy* 89:615–41.
Laitin, David D. 1991. "The National Uprisings in the Soviet Union." *World Politics* 44:139–77.
Landa, Janet. 1981. "A Theory of the Ethnically Homogeneous Middleman Group: An Institutional Alternative to Contract Law." *Journal of Legal Studies* 10:349–62.
Poggi, Gianfranco. 1990. *The State: Its Nature, Development and Prospects*. Stanford, CA: Stanford University Press.
Ramet, Sabrina P. 1992. *Nationalism and Federalism in Yugoslavia, 1962–1991*. 2nd ed. Livingston: Indiana University Press.
Roeder, Phillip G. 1991. "Soviet Federalism and Ethnic Mobilization." *World Politics* 43:196–232.
Rogowski, Ronald. 1985. "Causes and Varieties of Nationalism: A Rationalist Account." In Tiryakin, Edward A., and Rogowski, Ronald, eds. 1985. *New Nationalisms of the Developed West: Toward Explanation*. Boston: Allen & Unwin.
Sanford, Nevitt. 1973. "The Authoritarian Personality in Contemporary Perspective." In *Handbook of Political Psychology*. San Francisco: Jossey-Bass Publishers.
Shapiro, Carl. 1983. "Premiums for High Quality Products as Returns to Reputations." *Quarterly Journal of Economics* 98:659–79.
Ward, Barbara. 1959. "Nationalism." In Ward, Barbara, ed. *Five Ideas That Changed the World*. New York: Norton.
Wintrobe, Ronald. 1981. "It Pays to Do Good, But Not to Do More Good Than It Pays." *Journal of Economic Behavior and Organization* 2:201–13.
1983. "Taxing Altruism." *Economic Inquiry* 21:255–70.
1988. "The Efficiency of the Soviet System of Industrial Production." In Villa Colombella Papers on Bureaucracy. *European Journal of Political Economy* 4:159–84.
1990. "The Tinpot and the Totalitarian: An Economic Theory of Dictatorship." *American Political Science Review* 84:849–72.
"Homo (Femina) Socio-Economicus (a): Reflections on Models of Trust, Power, Love and Authority." *Economic Inquiry*. Forthcoming.
Zaslavsky, Victor. 1992. "Nationalism and Democratic Transition in Post-Communist Societies." *Daedalus* (Spring): 97–122.

CHAPTER 4

Ethnic clubs, ethnic conflict, and the rise of ethnic nationalism

Roger D. Congleton

I Introduction

The "reemergence" of nationalism with the collapse of the Soviet empire has surprised many Western scholars, although it should not have. Such occurrences have happened many times before and for the most part along similar lines. A brief consideration of the reemergence of tribalism in Africa at the time of the cessation of European colonialism, or in Central Europe with the end of the Austrian-Hungarian monarchy, or in the Middle East after the collapse of the Ottoman Empire reveals patterns which are fundamentally similar. All appear to be responses to a decline in the productivity of formal state institutional arrangements with a subsequent substitution of production by the less formal institutions of tribe and family.

Consistent with this theory, the opposite phenomena tends to occur in states with a well functioning government. During the mid-nineteenth century, the Hapsburg reign of the Austro-Hungarian monarchy generated a period of relative ethnic tranquillity (Sipos 1991, 102). Moreover, the lessening importance of *ethnic* forms of nationalism in much of Western Europe and in the United States during the mid-twentieth century appears to be a result of increased effectiveness of formal state arrangements. However, even within well-functioning democratic states, ethnic politics (often termed regionalism in Europe) remains an important electoral and cultural force.[1]

---

[1] For the purposes of this paper, as may already be evident, the words "nation," "ethnic group," and "tribe" are used as synonyms. These are groups of people who share common antecedents and consider themselves for a variety of historical reasons to be members of a group. A common culture, religion, and language facilitate transactions between individuals by facilitating communication and allowing more accurate predictions about the behavior of fellow group members.

This paper analyzes the individual demand for ethnic services as a basis for characterizing larger group responses to changes in political and economic circumstances. The extent of ethnic nationalism varies with the level of ethnic-based production and distribution of services in a particular society. If a wide range of services are produced and paid for via fulfillment of ethnic duties, then ethnic nationalism is important. If such services are a relatively minor portion of a typical individual's life, then ethnic nationalism is relatively important. Which kind of production system an individual makes use of varies with the costs and benefits of his alternatives. The more personally valuable are services provided by "ethnic clubs," the greater is the demand for ethnic affiliation, and the more extensive is ethnic nationalism. Assimilation occurs as ethnic group members demand and receive fewer services from ethnic clubs, and rely instead on services produced by other groups they are affiliated with, often groups based on citizenship or achievement rather than ethnic heritage.[2] The comparative statics of the demand and supply of ethnic "club" services, thus, provides the basis of a model of the intensity of ethnic nationalism and ethnic conflict.

It bears noting that the general structure of informal groups resembles that of federal governments. Just as residents of a small village may obtain various services directly from their local community and others from regional, national or supranational organizations; members of a family may obtain services based on their extended families, clan, tribe, ethnic group, race, or culture. Similarly, the extent to which individuals identify themselves with one group rather than another, or are identified as members of one group rather than another, parallels the pattern of citizenship in various levels of government. Both sorts of affiliation are affected by economic concerns (transaction costs, individual gains to trade, and ease of collective action), political expediency, natural boundaries, and historical accident.

However, the procedures by which an individual can become a full member of another clan or ethnic group are generally far more stringent than those required to change government service districts. The

---

[2] State and ethnic forms of nationalism differ largely because of the prerequisites for membership. A state generally has formal proceedures by which currently unaffiliated individuals may become full citizens eligible for all state services. In contrast, membership in an ethnic group is largely based upon blood ties to individuals in an ethnic homeland. Although it is possible for currently unaffiliated individuals to gain some ethnic membership rights through marriage or outstanding service to an ethnic club, generally it is substantially more difficult to join an ethnic group than to become a citizen in a state. The former tend to be exclusive, the latter inclusive.

Ethnic clubs, ethnic conflict, and ethnic nationalism 73

latter is an important distinction between familial based organizations and modern states. For the purposes of this paper, membership in a particular ethnic group is taken as given, and implications of incentives to participate more or less in ethnic-based activities are analyzed.[3]

The analysis and discussion is organized as follows. Section II develops a model of an individual's decision to participate in ethnic club activities. The model is based on the observation that individuals contribute to ethnic activities partly to obtain services available to active members, and partly to avoid sanctions imposed on inactive members. In this context, state activities affect the demand and supply of ethnic services to the extent that the state produces complements or substitutes for ethnic services, and/or adopts policies which affect the cost of producing ethnic services. A substantial part of the ebb and flow of ethnic nationalism can be explained by the variation in state services and policies.

Section III of the paper develops some properties of ethnic conflict in a multinational state based on an Olson-Becker model of special interest group activities. In a reasonably well-functioning state, ethnic groups may use their resources to influence policy making on matters of interest to their membership. Because the resources used to provide state services are inherently scarce, ethnic rent-seeking pits the welfare of one ethnic group against that of other groups, which tends to increase the importance of ethnic identification and intensify ethnic conflict. A state's institutional arrangements, therefore, may encourage or discourage ethnic political conflict to the extent that they promote ethnic-based rent-seeking activities by allowing them to be profitable for well-organized ethnic groups. In states with overly permissive institutional arrangements in this regard, the dynamics of the sequential ethnic rent-seeking game may undermine the state's own stability insofar as losing groups expect to be made increasingly worse off by their continuing affiliation with the existing multiethnic state.

The final section summarizes the results and applies them to analyze the independence movements of Eastern Europe. To the extent that active affiliation with ethnic groups is based on expected services and sanctions, it is clear that the attractiveness of ethnic club services increased in the former Soviet empire as the Soviet government became less effective at producing state services and as sanctions on the

---

[3] A careful examination of the manner in which individuals become classified as members of a particular ethnic group is beyond the scope of this paper. (Some progress on this issue is made in the pieces by Russell Hardin and Ugo Pagano elsewhere in this book.)

provision of ethnic services declined. Ethnically based independence movements gain popular support when individuals expect to gain more from direct control of smaller ethnically based state than they sacrifice from the loss of various economies of scale in governance associated with continued membership in a multicultural state. Consequently, independence movements tend to arise when it is expected that future government services will be inefficiently managed or, that other ethnic groups will be able to gain control of state institutions and obtain large transfers from the groups desiring to secede. All of these factors were present during the reemergence of ethnic nationalism in Eastern Europe and in the former states of the Soviet Union.

II   Ethnic clubs: Enforcement and group services

A cohesive ethnic group is a service producing club with a more or less fixed membership composed of *all* individuals within an ethnic group. In this respect, ethnic clubs differ from those most closely examined by the economic literature on clubs which generally focuses on club size and individual mobility between clubs. (See Buchanan 1965, Cornes and Sandler 1986). Membership in such ethnic clubs, or "nationalities," is not entirely voluntary in the sense that belonging to a political party or most private clubs is voluntary. Rather affiliation with an ethnic or tribal nation is a consequence of hereditary links to particular groups of families or clans. Ethnic affiliation is less a birth right than a birth consequence.[4]

Nonetheless, it is clear that members of an ethnic group may provide more or less resources to the groups they are affiliated with, according to their own circumstances. In this respect membership in an ethnic group is analogous to membership in a college alumni associ-

---

[4] Productive states (or governments) are also a form of club, but one generally based on geographical areas rather than ethnicity per se. States generally have more formal institutional arrangements than ethnic groups which make political choices and administer "the law" within a particular geographical part of the world. Governments may be larger than nations, as is clearly case for geographically large countries like those of India, the United States, and Russia. Or, governments may be smaller than nations as was clearly the case for Germany until the recent reunification (and may still be true) or in Italy before the success of the risorgimento. The relationship between membership in a "nation" and citizenship in a state is largely indeterminate.

This footnote is meant largely for American, Canadian, and French readers for whom nationalism is allegiance to particular institutions and geographical land masses rather than identification with a particular ethnic group. For the purposes of this paper and to avoid confusion, such feelings might better be called patriotism.

ation after graduation. However much one might regret or appreciate one's association with a particular university after graduation, the historical fact remains, and individuals remain alumni, but *not* necessarily active alumni.[5] As is the case for other alumni associations, their continuation and importance is largely a matter of the net value of services provided to active members of the relevant group. Although ethnicity is for the most part exogenously determined at the level of the individual, individuals may participate more or less in the production of output via groups based on ethnic heritage.

A   *Sanctions, services and active participation in ethnic clubs*

The success of any club is partly a matter of the value of the services provided, partly a matter of the "dues" which must be paid for continued membership, and partly a matter of sanctions imposed on members who fail to contribute to club activities. A proper combination of services, fees, and sanctions allows a private club to produce local public goods for its membership. Ethnic groups address these same problems and are able to provide a wide array of club services – for example, a common language, education, social insurance, collegiality, entertainment, and enforcement of codes of conduct and obligation.[6] Sanctioning mechanisms determine the bounds of club membership, and mitigate public goods problems associated with club production. No club can function without effective sanctions.[7]

In small clubs, the principal sanction available is exclusion from club services. Consequently, some private and excludable benefit must exist for those who sponsor club activities. In clubs providing a

---

[5] The psychological theory of cognitive dissonance suggests that individuals will tend to be proud of these historical facts.
[6] The term "ethnic services" is used here in a very general and abstract sense. It includes the familiar services already mentioned as well as other services such as collegiality and to some extent pride and immortality: Members gain partial responsibility for the actions of all fellow ethnic members at all times. Modern nationalism clearly offers a substitute for these services as well insofar as patriotism allows one to "take pride" in the accomplishments of one's fellow citizens (as in science, war, or more recently the Olympics).
[7] Groups that produce only nonexcludable services have a difficult time because of the well-known free-rider problem. Beneficiaries of nonexcludable group activities need not pay their "dues" to realize all the advantages of membership in such clubs. A club that produces only excludable services can force members to pay their dues if they desire club services. See Olson 1965 and Sandler 1986 for more on the economic theory of clubs.

variety of services, exclusion may be finely adjusted. Failure to abide fully by club rules can be sanctioned by excluding members from a subset of club services rather than expulsion from the group.

Excludability of at least some club services is less important in large multifaceted clubs where other sanctions are available. In more violent (or less legally inhibited) settings force and threats of force may be used. (It bears noting that a club's exclusionary practices often are directly or indirectly enforced with threats to life and property.) In such cases, active membership is not entirely voluntary, although some discretion generally remains at the margin. In less extreme settings, milder nonexclusionary sanctions are available. Individuals who perform their club duties poorly or unenthusiastically, and yet because of club size must continue to interact with other club members, can be sanctioned with "disapproval" and low status assignments.[8]

Ethnic groups have made use of all of these sanctioning devices. Informal suasion and approbation of fellow ethnic group members to be "true to their culture" (participate in ethnic group activities) are commonplace. Formal and informal access to ethnic-based services such as job referral and social insurance are linked to past performance of familial and ethnic duties and obligations. Historically, banishment and other all-or-nothing methods of exclusion have also been used as sanctions. Many ethnic groups appear to have originally been based on the administration and provision of local public goods within stable communities of affiliated individuals. It seems likely that production of such location specific services accounts for the historical origins *and bounds* of many ethnic groups. (Banishment forces individuals to live outside the region of local public services.) Club sanctions directly affect individual decisions to participate in ethnic club activities.

Essential features of private decisions to contribute to the production of club services can be illustrated with the following model. Consider the choice of an individual who must allocate his time between producing private (nonclub) consumption and club activities. To simplify the exposition at this point, suppose there is a single

---

[8] Congleton (1989) analyzes how the rules of status games can be varied to provide informal solutions to public goods problems and reduce unproductive conflict. "Rules" for assigning status to ethnic group members are generally an important part of any ethnic group's culture. Timur Kuran (1987) has argued that even mild sanctions like disapproval and discrimination may be sufficient to cause many individuals to publicly conform to prevailing rules of conduct, even those which they privately disagree with. Doubtless, a good deal of ethnicity is simply displayed for pragmatic private purposes rather than as personal affirmation of local codes of conduct.

Ethnic clubs, ethnic conflict, and ethnic nationalism

nonclub good (C_i) purchased in the market, a single nonexcludable club service (S) available to active members and a local government service (G_i). In order to mobilize the resources necessary to produce desired services, clubs direct sanctions at prospective club members with the greatest sanctions imposed on those who provide fewest resources to the club.

The individual values private consumption, C, government services, G, and club service, S, but is made worse off by the level of club sanction, F_i, directed at him by other club members. Initially, government services, G, are assumed to be beyond an individual's direct control and are treated as exogenous for the purposes of individual decisions. The individual allocates his time, T_i, between nonethnic production, W_i, and ethnic group production, D_i, which together with the efforts of all other members generates ethnic service level S. Ethnic production is undertaken only with other members. These assumptions imply that the typical ethnic club member faces an optimization problem of the following sort.[9] Individuals maximize

$$U_i = u_i(C_i, S, F_i, G_i) \tag{1.0}$$

subject to:

$$T_i = W_i + D_i \tag{2.1}$$

with

$$F_i = f(D_i) \tag{2.2}$$
$$C_i = c_i(W_i, G_i) \tag{2.3}$$
$$S = s(\Sigma D_j) \tag{2.4}$$

Substituting, then differentiating with respect to D_i yields the first order condition which describes a typical individual's inclination to provide resources to the ethnic club.

$$U_S S_D + U_F F_D = U_C C_W \tag{3}$$

Equation 3 indicates that an individual will participate in ethnic group activities (provide personal resources to the club) up to the point where the marginal reduction in nonethnic private consumption generated from further ethnic club activities equals the marginal utility of club services and marginal reductions in penalties imposed by club sanctions. Equation 3 clearly indicates that both individual tastes and constraints and club services and sanctions affect decisions to provide

---
[9] The utility function is assumed to be strictly quasiconcave with $U_{Ci} > 0$ $U_S > 0$ and $U_{Fi} < 0$
Subscripted variables denote partial derivatives of the variables subscripted.

resources to ethnic group activities. Each of the three terms combines an objective factor with a subjective taste (marginal utility) factor.

The left-hand side of the equation is the marginal benefit of active participation. Other things being equal, an individual will spend more time on club activities as the subjective value of club services increases at the margin, and as the disutility of club sanctions becomes more negative at the margin.[10] Members will also participate more as their contribution generates a larger increment in overall club services and/or a larger reduction in club sanctions. The right-hand side is the marginal cost of participation, and indicates that as either the marginal value of private consumption increases or the marginal productivity of time used to produce private consumption (after tax wages) increases the individual will devote less time to ethnic activities.

The club itself directly controls two of the nonsubjective elements of the individual's choice problem: the production of services and the sanction schedule.[11] The more productive the club is at the margin (the larger S_D is) and the greater the penalty for inactivity (the more negative F_D is) the more inclined individuals will be to donate time and effort to club activities. The latter makes it clear that a club that is unable to penalize those who fail to participate will also be less able to provide desired club services. Given a distribution of individual tastes and circumstances, an increase in these club productivities increases the likelihood that a given individual will make contributions and thereby the production of ethnic services.

The model also indicates that exogenous changes in conditions which affect the opportunity cost of participating in ethnic clubs or the value of club services cause changes in each prospective members willingness to participate in club activities. Here, a change in either the individual's real wage rate, C_D, or government service level, G_i, affects the extent to which an individual contributes to ethnic activities. As wages fall the opportunity (time) cost of nonclub consumption tends to increase. Consequently, one expects *greater* ethnic contributions and service demands from relatively *low income* members of ethnic groups – in the usual case where the substitution effect dominates the income effect of this relative cost change. Similarly, a deep

---

[10] Some club sanctions depend almost entirely on individual tastes for their effect. For example, to the extent that individuals seek "approval" from fellow club members, disapproval can be used as a sanction. Naturally the stronger the need for approval the more potent this sanction is.

[11] It might be argued that the common transmitted culture of an ethnic group affects individual tastes in fundamental ways. But current club leadership has relatively little control over such effects.

recession tends to *increase* time contributions to ethnic activities insofar as after tax wage rates tend to decline.

Changes in the price or availability of government substitutes for club services affect the extent of ethnic nationalism in two ways. First, insofar as government services are substitutes or complements to club services and/or private consumption it affects the marginal utility of club and private consumption. Second, insofar as service increases are financed with income taxes the marginal cost of private consumption tends to increase relative to club services. The latter tends to encourage untaxed production via informal organizations. The former may increase or decrease the demand for ethnic services depending upon the relative size of the effects on the marginal utility of private and club goods, U_{SG}, U_{FG} and U_{CG}.

B   *A digression on state and ethnic group provision of substitute public services: The case of law enforcement*

A well-organized club responds to changes in demand by varying the level of services provided club members and adjusting membership fees to maximize the net advantage of club membership. The above analysis indicates that the individual willingness to supply resources to ethnic clubs varies with the changing economic and government services. Consequently, the production of ethnic services tends to vary, more or less spontaneously, if the resources provided are productively employed, as government services and/or economic circumstances vary. The manner in which such changes take place is less clear and depends on the manner in which group activities is organized. More centralized ethnic group organizations would also tend to vary service levels as individual member demands vary as a method of maximizing leadership power and wealth. In either case, variations in the willingness to pay for ethnic services tends to induce similar variations in the supply of ethnic services.

One of the most important service areas in which ethnic groups compete directly with the state is a fundamental one for civilized societies: namely the enforcement of codes of conduct. Effective codes of conduct facilitate intragroup economic activities, and to some extent promote the decentralized production of public goods. Enforcement of codes of conduct reduces uncertainty about transaction outcomes and increases the likelihood that mutually desired outcomes can be achieved by reducing the return to predatory behaviors. Awareness that trading partners are members of "the group" implies that "misbehavior" is subject to group sanctions. The latter makes mal-

Prisoner's Dilemma Game

	B Cooperate	B Cheat
A Cooperate	B,B	D-F,A
A Cheat	A-F,D	C-F,C-F

$A > B > C > D$

Table 4.1

feasance less attractive than would have been the case for transactions between unaffiliated strangers. Naturally ethnic sanctions are most valuable when individual interaction is most problematic, as tends to be the case when state enforcement activities are relatively ineffective.

Essential features of the demand for sanctions can be illustrated using pairwise games in which interaction is problematic. Club sanctions change the relative payoffs in "games" between club members. Two problematic structures of payoffs are represented in Tables 4.1 and 4.2 for prisoner's dilemma and coordination games, respectively. The payoffs for nonmembers have the usual ordered structures. Active club membership affects behavior insofar as club sanction, F, has

Coordination Game

	B Use Rule 1	B Use Rule 2
A Use Rule 1	B-F, B-F	C-F, C
A Use Rule 2	C, C - F	B, B

$A > B > C$

Table 4.2

Ethnic clubs, ethnic conflict, and ethnic nationalism 81

positive values. When F has the value 0, interaction of club members in these games suffers from the usual problems. A prisoner's dilemma outcome results in the first case, were both individuals "cheat." In this case, there is no general enforcement value associated with club membership. The prisoner's dilemma game generates the (C, C) payoffs which is Pareto dominated by the (B, B) payoffs generated when both players cooperate. The ambiguity of the coordination game means that any outcome is possible. The role of club sanctions is apparent. As club sanction F increases, there is a point at which new dominant strategies emerge which are mutually beneficial. In this manner, club members may benefit from collective steps to sanction relationships between individual members.[12]

To analyze the relationship between ethnic and state enforcement services, consider a typical ethnic group member's demand for sanctions in various problematic social settings.[13] In any social setting, a wide range of gamelike settings may be confronted. Let there be a finite number of prisoner's dilemma and coordination problem settings, N, and suppose that the probability of the ith game setting, with payoffs, Ai, Bi, Ci, Di, is Pi. The potential advantage of sanctions in a particular game is the movement from outcome (Ci, Ci) to (Bi, Bi). Sanctions are a combination of expected state, F_i^s, and ethnic, F_i^e penalties or "fines" which yields a total penalty of $F = F_i^s + F_i^e$ for noncooperative behavior. The cost of producing expected sanctions (a combination of monitoring and punishment) is assumed to be an increasing function of the sanctions level to be imposed. This would be the case if the probability of detection and the penalty imposed is produced via an ordinary production function. The typical member's

---

[12] As indicated above for the general demand for club services, individual efforts to provide or support club sanctions depend in part on the level of sanctioning behavior of other club members, and in part on an individual's own circumstances. In cases where the necessary sanctions can be imposed at little cost, providing enforcement activity can be a dominant strategy for all club members and little formal organization is required to secure club benefits. Every individual who benefits of his fellows always cooperates regardless of his own intended strategy. Thus every individual has an incentive to encourage his fellows to cooperate. In an ongoing community, as Axelrod's (1984) tit-for-tat strategy results indicate, active support of group sanctions are privately worthwhile as long as the expected improvement in member interactions exceeds the cost of participating in the sanctioning process.

[13] Sociologists often emphasize the role of social norms within an ethnic group. The cooperative strategy of a prisoner's dilemma game represents a class of norms: Don't cheat, don't steal, be civil, cooperate. Any solution to a coordination game can also be thought of in terms of a norm. Here there is not efficiency case for a particular kind of behavior, so the norms can be arbitrary, although there is an efficiency case for enforcing whatever norm is selected.

cost shares is denoted $C^s = c^s(F_i^s)$ and $C^e = c^e(F_i^e)$ for state and ethnic sanctions, respectively.

The expected net benefit, N_i, from sanction level F_i for a typical participant in game i is:

$$E(N_i) = P_i(B_i - C_i) - c(F_i) \text{ for } F_i > A_i - D_i \qquad (4.1)$$
$$\text{and } E(N_i) = c(F_i) \text{ for } F_i \leq A_i - D_i \qquad (4.2)$$
$$\text{where } c(F_i) = c^n(F_i^n) + c_s(F_i^s). \qquad (4.3)$$

In the usual case, individuals prefer the division of sanctioning responsibilities between their ethnic group and government that minimizes the total cost of implementing desired sanctions. This requires that sanctions for each game type to be produced at least cost, and that each game's sanction be the minimum required to eliminate the dilemma or coordination problem.[14] (Imposing sanctions on malfeasors is a costly activity, and penalties greater than $A_i - D_i$ yield no additional benefit. Consequently, when a sanction is desired, the sanction adopted should impose an expected cost that only slightly exceeds $F^* = A_i - D_i$.)

The ideal allocation of sanctions minimizes $c(F^*) = c^n(F_i^n) + c_s(F_i^s)$ subject to the constraint that $F_i^n + F_i^s = F_i^s = F^*$. Differentiating with respect to F_i^s and F_i^n yields the first order condition for the cost minimizing combination of state and national sanctions.

$$dc/dF_i^e = dc/dF_i^s = \lambda \qquad (5)$$

In cases where the expected gain from a sanction satisfying equation 5 is below this least costly combination of effective sanctions, because the situations are rare or the cooperative solution is only slightly better than the Nash solution, the optimal sanction is 0.

In cases where a nonzero sanction is applied, individuals generally prefer a combination of formal state and informal ethnic sanctions that reflect the diminishing returns to the production of sanctions over the range of interest. The usual solution implies that, *ethnic and state sanctions are substitutes for each other at the margin.* For example, in the case in which the costs of producing sanctions are the same for ethnic groups and states, the state and ethnic groups would each

---

[14] The possibility of such a joint optimization provides a basis of an argument for ethnically homogeneous states, that is a one-to-one mapping from ethnic groups (tribes) into governments. However, it should be noted that although ethnically homogeneous states potentially allow interaction problems to be solved at least at cost, they may because of other aspects of nationalism lose potential gains from trade with other ethnic groups.

Ethnic clubs, ethnic conflict, and ethnic nationalism 83

ideally provide half of the penalties associated with "antisocial" behavior. The above analysis clearly indicates that the individual's preferred distribution of enforcement services between formal state and ethnic organizations varies as his share of the production costs varies.[15]

The cost of state and tribe production of sanctions tends to vary for several reasons. For example, in most cases the probability of detecting misbehavior is higher within an ethnic group than within the state. Fellow members of an ethnic group can generally recognize each other by common names, patterns of speech, dress, or countenance. Historical commonalities manifest themselves via transmitted culture and genes as common behaviors and appearance. Within an ethnic group, detection is done by essentially all members of the group who, besides being more numerous, often have more direct knowledge of the behavior of fellow members than is available to state law enforcers. The greater probability of detection and conviction within an ethnic group or tribe, implies that any desired expected sanction can be achieved with a smaller punishment than required under a state system.[16] On the other hand, ethnic groups may not be inclined to penalize transgressions against nonmembers (because of high costs) or able to penalize transgressions by their leadership, and thus some classes of misconduct may be enforced by state sanctions alone.

As was the case for the abstract government service level examined above, exogenous changes in the level of enforcement activity by the state also tends to affect the actual as well as the ideal level of enforcement by the ethnic groups. A diminution of state enforcement effort increases the productivity of ethnic enforcement efforts at the margin, and thereby induces increased efforts by ethnic group members to sanction ethnic group-based codes of conduct. That is to say, any exogenous decline in a government's ability to provide enforcement

---

[15] If the cost of one agency is uniformly below that of the other, it is possible that all the enforcement will be produced by the state or by ethnic groups for particular games. Such corner solutions do appear to exist for somewhat obscure crimes and minor cultural transgressions, but generally we observe many cases where there are both informal and formal sanctions for crimes. Thieves may go to jail but are also to be disapproved of (assigned lower status) when they are released. Moreover, having proved themselves untrustworthy, they may be excluded and denied any preferential treatment that (trustworthy) "members" are normally eligible for in market and other transactions.

[16] The standard finding in the literature on the effectiveness of criminal sanctions suggests that potential transgressors are more sensitive to the probability of capture and conviction than to the severity of the punishment. See Ehrlich (1975) or Witte (1980).

services, or increase in the tax price for those services, *is sufficient to cause the reemergence* of ethnic nationalism in groups with a functioning cultural affiliation.

III   Ethnic conflict in a multinational state

The economic foundations of a multiethnic state are in many respects similar to those of ethnic groups. Various economies of scale in the production of services implies that large organizations are more efficient at producing *some* services over *some* ranges of output than smaller organizations. As in the theory of fiscal federalism (see Oates 1972), the ideal assignment of responsibility for a given service should reflect tradeoffs between the realization of various economies of scale and losses from greater uniformity and other organizational diseconomies. Just as the services provided by ethnic clubs should be those which are too costly to be produced by individual families or clans, the services provided by multinational states should be those which are not efficiently provided by smaller and more homogeneous governments.

A multiethnic state is, for example, better able to resist outside conquest. Multiethnic states have larger markets in which specialization, innovation, and competition can operate to advance individual welfare. A uniform legal system and system of standards can reduce transactions costs. Moreover, regional externalities can be more easily addressed by a country whose jurisdiction spans the entire region of interest. Ideally these advantages are balanced against the costs of more diffuse political control and greater conflict, but this is not always the case.[17]

For example, it bears noting that in multinational states, state enforcement efforts are unlikely to be those which minimize the cost of providing every ethnic group's desired pattern of enforcement. A uniform level of enforcement activity across all ethnic groups may be cost minimizing for one group but is unlikely to be so for all groups. Here informal group mechanisms will be more or less heavily used than in the ideal case according to whether state enforcement is deficient

---

[17] From an ethnic group perspective, an ideal federal state would be a federation of ethnic groups formed to mutually profit from the realization of various economies of scale. A multinational state founded by conquest rather than cooperation would also be able to realize economies of scale in the provision of many services, although the principal economic explanation of such states would be the realization of economies of scale in coercion.

or excessive from the point of view of a particular ethnic group's membership.[18]

However, the policies adopted by a multinational state are always at least partly determined by the interests of ethnic groups. This contrasts with decisions within an ethnically homogeneous state in that disagreements over policy, naturally, can not be based on ethnicity. The decisions of dictators and elected representatives in multinational states are responsive to the welfare of such groups because in both cases those in power wish to remain so. Dictators have an interest in the continued acquiescence of their population, and elected representatives have an interest in the future votes of ethnic group members. Consequently, state-sponsored ethnic-based programs would tend to exist even if ethnic groups, themselves, are entirely passive. However, in most cases ethnic groups can advance the interest of their membership by actively attempting to influence policy.

A   *Ethnic rent seeking*

In a multinational state, the political effort of every ethnic group to obtain preferential treatment for itself tends to threaten the interest of other groups who will be ineligible for preferential treatment. Consequently, both the groups who expect to gain and lose from programs are inclined to invest in the production of political influence. The former attempt to maximize their gains, the latter to minimize their losses. The ethnic conflict thereby engendered may be peaceful, as in well functioning democracies where tribal groups lobby legislatures for particular favors, or may be violent in countries in which government functions poorly or have been captured by one ethnic group and used to exploit others.[19]

---

[18] In this case, the ethnic group would ideally adopt the sanction level which minimizes their total cost, given the state enforcement level.

The ideal joint optimization case is, of course, ideal only with respect to enforcement. But it does suggest that in the case in which a state's citizenry is ethnically homogeneous, the distribution of enforcement efforts might be closer to the ideal than in a multinational state. An implication of this is that crime rates (for both formal crimes and informal trespasses) generally would be higher in multinational states than in ethnically homogeneous states other things being equal.

[19] Yugoslavia and South Africa are examples of the latter. It also bears noting that attempts by one ethnic group to exact transfers from other groups may also proceed directly without using a formal government apparatus. Well-organized groups may attempt to extort or take from other groups by pooling resources for use in threats of force or force itself. These efforts may also be resisted by the pooled efforts of the groups at risk of being exploited. Tribal-ethnic wars and extortion may be modeled in a similar fashion to that modeled above.

86   Roger D. Congleton

The level of resources invested to acquire rents or transfers from other groups varies with the effectiveness of group organizations and the extent to which such efforts affect policy outcomes. The production of political influence is a public good for a group's membership. Voluntary contributions to such activities would tend to be small, but for the provision of other excludable ethnic services and the existence of club sanctions, as discussed above.

To gain some insight into the structure of political conflict, consider the following Olson/Becker special interest-group model of ethnic political activities. In a highly politicized state, government service levels and rents obtained from various occupations reflect the relative political power of politically active groups. Suppose that every ethnic group has its own influence-generating function, $I_j = i_j(D_j, N_j)$, which maps membership, N_j, and pooled resources, D_j, into effective political power,

$$P_j = i_j(D_j, N_j) / \sum_k i_k(D_k, N_k). \tag{6.0}$$

To simplify for purposes of illustration, suppose that each ethnic group's share of the national government services and payment for those services is determined by the effective political power of the ethnic group. As an ethnic group's power increases, its share of government services increases and/or its share of the cost of government services diminishes. Suppose further, that the advantages of power for the ethnic group as a whole similarly affect the situation of the typical member of the ethnic group. This allows the model of individual contributions developed above to be extended to account for the effects of ethnic-based political activities on government service levels.

In this case the typical ethnic group member receives, in effect, a combination of direct ethnic services, Si, and indirect services insofar as Gi and after tax income are affected by the ethnic group's relative political power. The member again allocates his time between ethnic group activities, D_i, and earning after tax income, W_i, to maximize a utility function defined over private consumption, C_i, club services and sanctions, S_i and F_i, and government services. The ethnic club member maximizes:

$$U_i = u_i(C_i, S, F_i, G_i) \tag{7.0}$$

subject to

$$T_i = W_i + D_i \tag{7.1}$$
$$F_i = f(D_i) \tag{7.2}$$

and

$$S = s(\Sigma D_j) \tag{7.3}$$

but now:

$$C_i = c_i(W_i, G_i, P_j) \tag{7.4}$$
$$G_i = g(P_j) \tag{7.5}$$

Personal consumption and governmental service levels are now partly determined by the ethnic group's political power which in turn is determined by influence relative to other groups.

Substituting, then differentiating with respect to D_i, yields the first order condition which describes a typical individual's inclination to provide resources to a politically active ethnic group.

$$U_S S_D + U_F F_D + P_D(U_G G_P + U_C C_P) = U_C C_W \tag{8}$$

Equation 8 indicates two general features of politically active ethnic groups. First, they tend to increase the demand for ethnic services. The marginal benefits of a donation (here time) to ethnic activities is increased to the extent that it now generates indirect effects on state fiscal policies. As long as $P_D (U_F G_P + U_C C_P) > 0$ the marginal benefits of contributing to ethnic group activities is larger for politically active groups than for pure service groups. Second, relative to other potential political pressure groups, the presence of direct ethnic services implies that contributions will be greater for ethnic groups than for groups which either do not provide direct benefits to members or who lack an effective sanctioning system. Consequently, political interest groups based on ethnicity tend to be more effective than those based on purely economic or public service agendas alone.

The first two terms capture what might be interpreted as the nonpolitical demand for group solidarity, $U_S S_D + U_F F_D$, which, as indicated above may be largely determined by sanctions and/or excludable ethnic group services available to those who contribute generally to ethnic activities.[20] Note that if these partial derivatives sum to zero over the range of interest, individual group members behave as simple net transfer maximizers who happen to be affiliated with the ethnic group of interest. If, on the other hand, other aspects of club membership, "solidarity," are important, then the partial derivative of utility with

---

[20] New services may also be produced as part of the process of generating an effective political organization. For example, individuals may enjoy meetings with fellow members of their ethnic clubs accompanied with food, drink, songs, and speeches.

88	Roger D. Congleton

respect to D is greater than zero, and political contributions produce "solidarity" as well as political influence.

In the context of this political game, individual members of ethnic groups contribute resources to their respective ethnic groups as utility maximizing participants in a Nash game. Applying the implicit function rule to equation 8 allows the ith member of the kth ethnic group's player's best reply function to be characterized as function of variables beyond his direct control.

$$D_{ik}^* = d_{ik}(T_i, N_k, \sum_{j \neq k}^{N} D_j) \qquad (9)$$

Equation 9 can be interpreted as the demand for ethnic services by a given member of an ethnic group. The portion of ethnic contributions accounted for by the political consequences of ethnic activities can be considered to be the demand for ethnic conflict by a typical member of the ethnic group. The overall level of resources devoted to ethnic conflict is the sum of such efforts by all ethnic group members.

The ethnic group donation functions characterize the resources at the disposal of each nationalist ethnic group; which, at the game equilibrium, characterize the political apportionment of the state fiscal policies, service levels and personal consumption, at the equilibrium of the political game.

$$D_k^* = \sum_{i=1}^{M_k} D_{ik}^* \qquad (10.1)$$

$$P_k^* = \frac{D_k^*}{\sum_j^N D_j^*} \qquad (10.2)$$

$$G_{ik}^* = g(P_k^*) \qquad (10.3)$$

$$C_{ik}^* = c_i(T - D_{ik}^*, G_{ik}^*, P_k^*) \qquad (10.4)$$

To the extent that ethnic politics determine the apportionment of economic resources by determining the pattern of government services, tax obligations, and rents, the relative positions of ethnic groups in a multinational country depend upon the numbers and motivation of group members, and the technology of the production of political power. The right-hand term of equation 10.4 represents the equilibrium apportionment of private services at the individual level at the Nash equilibrium.

A substantial portion of the increase in ethnic resources brought about via political activities may be a source of social deadweight loss to the extent that these resources are devoted to ethnic political conflict. A proportional reduction in efforts by all politically active groups would reduce the overhead cost of the political process, freeing resources for other uses, without affecting the overall disposition of government policies. This rent-seeking cost of politicization of ethnic groups is partly a matter of the interests that ethnic group members have in increased government services and reduced tax burdens, U_G and U_C, partly a matter of the technology by which influence is produced, P_D, and partly a matter of state institutions which determine the extent to which political influence generates policy changes, G_P and C_P. It is clear that the larger the effects of political influence on government services regulations and tax burdens the greater is the marginal advantage of the ethnic group's political activities. In this manner, government institutional arrangements that facilitate the adoption of transfer policies or ethnically targeted policies, tend to call forth greater political efforts by ethnic groups and result in greater ethnic political conflict. Ethnicity, per se, will be relatively important in such states. The conventions of the rent-seeking literature imply that *such societies will be relatively poorer as a whole* insofar as societal resources are consumed in unproductive political influence games.[21]

It bears noting that an ethnic group that does poorly in the political process of resource allocation may find that the advantages of contin-

---

[21] Disputes over the disposition of existing resources are inherently nonproductive, although they nonetheless consume the valuable time and effort of all active participants. This suggests that institutional and other factors which increase the importance of ethnic political conflict or reduce its cost thereby diminishing the total wealth of society by diverting more and more social resources to be devoted to socially unproductive conflict. See Buchanan, Tullock and Tollison (1980) for an overview of the methodology of the rent-seeking approach.

Sociologists and historians who study ethnic conflict report that multinational states which mandate ethnic neutrality are most stable and successful. Here the experience of New Zealand and the early period of the Austro-Hungarian monarchies are held out as exemplary cases. See Armstrong (1987) and Sipos (1991). Such observations are very much consistent with the club theory advanced here. For true ethno-neutrality reduces incentives for ethnic groups to control the power of the state which in turn limits a potent source of exploitation and also wasteful investment in ethnic conflict.

ued association within the existing multinational state are below the costs of continued exploitation. Consequently, ethnics who feel exploited or threatened by an existing political equilibrium will naturally seek greater independence and autonomy. Moreover, the intensity of conflict in exit games of this sort tend toward escalation, as in all-or-nothing games, because groups which gain from state transfers will attempt to block the exit of those from whom the transfers are being taken. In this manner, ethnic conflict may destabilize a multinational state.[22]

B *A digression on the dynamics of ethnic groups' power and wealth*

The solution to the ethnic power game developed above may be interpreted as a long-term political equilibrium which characterizes equilibrium levels of ethnicity and distributions of national income and wealth. Given the political equilibrium apportionment of wealth implicit in government policies, the services provided ethnic groups are also characterized insofar as individuals contribute directly productive ethnic activities according to equation 9. Full ethnic equilibrium requires the political and nonpolitical activities of all interest groups to be simultaneously in equilibrium. The analysis, thus may be used to characterize a long term equilibrium between state and ethnic services within a given polity. (One of the services provided by ethnic groups is to encourage individuals to think in terms of centuries or millennia.) However, generations do pass and individual preferences and service demands change as innovation in lifestyles takes place.

[22] There are advantages of small homogeneous nation-states which partly offset the loss of economies of scale. As noted above, a government that governs a single national group is able to less expensively solve the variety of social interaction problems faced by its citizens by adopting an efficient balance of formal and informal enforcement mechanisms that may be adopted. A greater level of consensus about fundamental values may reduce internal political conflict as well.

On the other hand, ethnic favoritism tends to encourage intolerance and reduce prospects for free trade which in turn tend to impede innovation and material progress. Consequently, it is generally the case that citizens of a small homogeneous nation-state have a somewhat lower income and somewhat greater risk of conquest than is the case for well-functioning multinational states, although crime rates might be a bit lower. Other things being equal, this suggests that individuals will prefer a federation of ethnic nations, to an ethnically homogeneous state – unless other ethnic groups are expected to use the powers of the state to make large transfers to themselves, or the multicultural state itself is expected to be fundamentally inefficient and exploitative.

If one imagines the struggle for societal resources being an ongoing game in which players consider only finite time horizons or, equivalently, in which capital markets are imperfect, the above game can be used as the basis of a dynamic analysis of interest ethnic group power. In a sequential game, the resources available to individuals in successive rounds of the game are determined by outcomes in previous rounds of play. Because group resources affect the extent to which they will be successful in any particular round of political intrigue, it is clear that a series of play generates a time path of wealth shares. Figures 4.1 and 4.2 depict two scenarios of interest for a two ethnic group state. In each case, the initial power of the two groups is assumed to be essentially equal, until a small shock upsets the balance of power.

Figure 4.1 depicts movement to a new stable equilibrium where) a balance of power is eventually found, at the margin, as assumed in the Becker (1983) type models of special interest groups interaction. In this case, group 1 gains political power as a consequence of the shock, and is able to acquire a larger share of national resources through its greater political effort. The effect of this increase in wealth gradually diminishes the intensity of group 1 efforts because of the diminishing marginal utility of wealth, while for the same reason calling forth sufficiently more intense resistance on the part of members of the exploited group to offset the successful group's greater economic resources.

Figure 4.2 depicts a degenerate case in which the shock leads to complete dominance of one of the ethnic groups. Initially, group 1 and group 2 have essentially equal political power. A small perturbation increases group 1's power relative to that of group 2 and again allows it to secure relatively a larger share of national wealth which implies relatively greater political power in the next round. As long as members of ethnic group 2 do not respond to their losses with substantially increased contributions to their defense, they will enter the successive rounds of the game with ever diminishing resources and political influence. In the case depicted, the only other equilibria are at the two corners in which one of the interest groups is completely dominant.

Insofar as wealth and numbers jointly generate power, any change in the initial balance of power will tend to enhance one group's power and thereby its ability to secure transfers for itself and further power. In this manner exploitation may emerge without ethnic hatred or intense nationalism, simply as a wealth maximizing attempt to use gov-

92 Roger D. Congleton

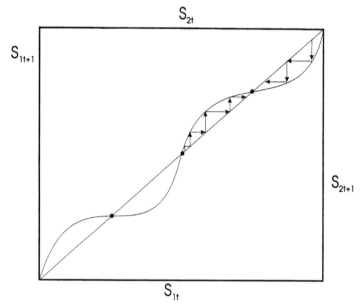

Figure 4.1

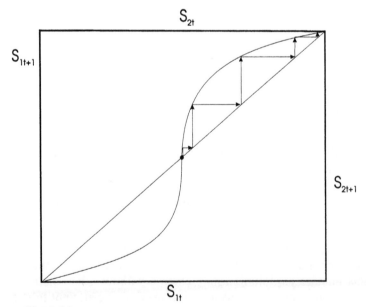

Figure 4.2

ernment to secure advantage for the members of a tribal-ethnic group.[23]

IV Ethnic clubs and the rise of independence movements in Eastern Europe

This paper has argued that the demand and supply of ethnic services are affected by the production of state services. This interdependence occurs at two levels of analysis. At the level of independent ethnic groups, "ethnic clubs" produce services which are substitutes for government services and consequently as state production declines, the demand for ethnic services tends to increase. State governments also adopt policies which affect the cost of supplying ethnic services. For example, repressive regimes often attempt to increase the cost of providing ethnic services as a method of reducing organized resistance to state activities. A decline in the effectiveness of state sanctions against ethnic activities increases the supply of ethnic services by reducing the overall cost of producing ethnic club services. A good deal of the ebb and flow of nationalism can thus be explained by fluctuations in the productivity of state institutional arrangements.

However, a complete analysis of the rise and fall of ethnic nationalism must take account of interactions between ethnic group demands and state activities. State institutional arrangements tend to encourage or discourage ethnic conflict to the extent that they encourage or discourage transfers from one ethnic group to another. In extreme cases, ethnic conflict within a multinational state can lead to ethnic-based independence movements as the losses from ethnic conflict exceed the perceived benefits of continued membership in a multinational state. The results of both dynamic and static versions of the national ethnic group power games indicate that relatively small or poorly organized ethnic groups may significantly benefit by leaving an exploitative state.

The resources devoted to ethnic conflict may be substantial. An

[23] The current taking of the wealth of non-Serbians from Bosnia in the former Yugoslavian republic appears to be an example of the degenerate case. Necak (1991, p. 131) reports that the "creation of the Yugoslavian state represented a success for the Serbian people, since . . . it created the preconditions required for it to assume the leading role in the state and to replace the Germans or the Hungarians as far as the Slovenes and the Croates were concerned." Peter Maass (1992) reports that "Across the devastated swath of northern Bosnia-Hercegovina that Serb militia forces control, there is little activity aside from the ransacking of deserted and often shattered houses. Serb militiamen usually get first pick – the stereos and television sets. Local [Serbian] farmers take the bulky leftovers."

exploited ethnic group would be willing to devote as much as the discounted value of future net losses it bears to establish an independent national state organized around ethnic lines. The beneficiaries of exploitative policies adopted are willing to pay as much as the value of all future net benefits, including net transfer receipts and various economies of scale in public services, to prevent the secession of exploited groups. Similar amounts would be sacrificed to add new ethnic subjects to an existing group's dominion. As in any rent-seeking game, conflict over secession tends to diminish the resources of both states without contributing any value. Moreover, the all-or-nothing nature of independence games tends to imply escalation in a sequential game with very substantial costs to all sides.[24]

In the former Soviet Empire, the reemergence of ethnic nationalism in the form of independence movements, reflects all of these problems. With the rapid decline in state services from former communist regimes, and the decline in effective sanctions against ethnic group activities, both the demand and the supply of ethnic club substitutes naturally increase.[25] This increase in services necessarily increases ethnic nationalism as defined here, but it does not necessarily generate independence movements. For broadly supported independence movements to arise general dissatisfaction with expected future government services must be such that independence is preferred to continued association.

The decline of imperial powers naturally tends to encourage the formation of ethnic-based independence movements as services decline and penalties mandated for nationalistic activities become less credible. Moreover, imperial states are not voluntary federations of ethnic groups, but rather the results of conquest. Thus individual members of ethnic groups have little reason to believe that continued affiliation in a multiethnic state will yield benefits from economies of

---

[24] Note that the avoided rent-seeking expenditures create a slight asymmetry favoring independence movements. The independence movement would invest resources to avoid their current expenditures on political conflict, while the group favoring continued association would invest *less* because of anticipated savings from reduced internal dissention. Occasional remarks made by Czech officials suggest that such savings are a sufficient reason to let Slovakia quit the "federation."

[25] The services provided by the former Soviet empire were, of course, a mixed blessing. The widespread use of and greater threat of coercion clearly made many citizens worse off than they are today in terms of various indices of freedom, including the freedom to engage in ethnic activities. The decline of the productivity of Soviet government services is reflected in the decline in measured per capita income in *all* the countries and regions within the empire as the empire disintegrated.

scale in state operations that outweigh the risk of exploitation by previously dominant groups.

The former Communist governments either intentionally or unintentionally engaged in ethnic favoritism. For example, the effective control of the Czechoslovakian and Yugoslavian governments by the Czech and Serbian ethnic groups resulted in net transfers from Slovakian and Croatian regions to government centers in the Czech and Serbian regions of the two countries. Combined with the failure of the previous national governments, there was, consequently, no experience-based reason for those who were exploited in the past to expect to do significantly better in the future. Similar histories and policies occurred in the former Soviet Union vis-à-vis Russians and other ethnic groups, which have lead to similar demands for independence. It is not surprising that independence movements arose in these countries.[26]

However, this is not to say that the long-run future of Eastern Europe is a series of unaffiliated ethnically homogeneous states. The existence of economies of scale in government services – for example, national defense, trade policy, environmental matters – and in private production implies that in the long run a process of reagglomeration is likely to occur. Western European nations realize economies of scale are realized via membership in supranational organizations (European defense through NATO and market economies via membership in the European Community) and federal governments. To the extent that services provided by such organizations substitute for those accorded ethnic group members, the future will entail less rather than more ethnic nationalism. But this is the long run, and until functioning democratic institutions and markets emerge in Eastern Europe, the immediate future seems likely to entail increased ethnic nationalism and reliance on informal arrangements between peoples of common blood and history.[27]

---

[26] The Québécois movement of Canada is more difficult to explain. Canada is a multinational federal government formed more or less voluntarily by the included groups as a means of realizing economies of scale (trade and defense) for their mutual advantage. However, as noted above, even reasonably well-functioning federal systems can manifest ethnic rent-seeking and nationalist movements.

[27] If ethnic rent seeking is inevitable in multiethnic states (or other organizations) then it seems likely that the long run will exhibit cycles of confederation, exploitation, and secession. This is partly a matter of institutional design, but also of the extent to which assimilation takes place. With assimilation, rent seeking will not be conducted along ethnic lines.

References

Akerlof, G. A. (1985) "Discriminatory, Status-Based Wages among Tradition-Oriented Stochastically Trading Coconut Producers," *Journal of Political Economy* 93:265–276.

Armstrong, M. J. (1987) "Interethnic Conflict in New Zealand," in Boucher, J., Landis, D. and Clark, K. A. Eds. *Ethnic Conflict: International Perspectives*. London: Sage Publications.

Axelrod, R. (1984) *The Evolution of Cooperation*. New York: Basic Books.

Becker, G. S. (1983) "A Theory of Competition among Pressure Groups for Political Influence," *Quarterly Journal of Economics* 98:371–399.

Boucher, J. Landis, D. and Clark, K. A. Eds. (1987) *Ethnic Conflict: International Perspectives*. London: Sage Publications.

Breton, A. and Wintrobe, R. 1986 "Bureaucracies of Murder Revisited," *Journal of Political Economy* 94:905–926.

Buchanan, J. M. (1965) "An Economic Theory of Clubs," *Economica* 32:371–384.

Buchanan, J. M., Tullock, G. and Tollison, R. D. Eds. (1980) *Toward a Theory of the Rent-Seeking Society*. College Station: Texas A&M Press.

Buchanan, J. M. and Brennan, G. (1985) *The Reason of Rules*. Cambridge: Cambridge University Press.

Congleton, R. D. (1980) "Competitive Process, Competitive Waste, and Institutions," in Buchanan, J. M., Tullock, G. and Tollison, R. D. Eds. *Toward a Theory of the Rent-Seeking Society*. College Station: Texas A&M Press.

Congleton, R. D. (1989) "Efficient Status Seeking: Externalities and the Evolution of Status Games," *Journal of Economic Behavior and Organization* 11:175–190.

Cornes, R. and Sandler, T. (1986) *The Theory of Externalities, Public Goods and Club Goods*. Cambridge: Cambridge University Press.

Frank, R. H. (1987) "If Homo Economicus Could Choose His Own Utility Function, Would He Want One with a Conscience?" *American Economics Review* 77:593–604.

Friedman, D. (1977) "A Theory of the Size and Shapes of Nations," *Journal of Political Economy* 85:59–77.

Ehrlich, I. (1975) "The Deterrent Effect of Capital Punishment: A Question of Life and Death," *American Economic Review* 65:397–417.

Hunt, C. L. and Walker, L. (1974) *Ethnic Dynamics*. London: Dorsey Press.

Kuran, T. (1987) "Preference Falsification, Policy Continuity and Collective Conservatism," *Economic Journal* 97:642–665.

Landa, J. (1981) "A Theory of the Ethnically Homogeneous Middleman Group: An Institutional Alternative to Contract Law," *Journal of Legal Studies* 10:349–362.

Maass, P. (1992) "Serb Looters Pick Bones of 'Cleansed' Bosnia," *Washington Post*. (August 17):A1, A20.

Mcguire, M. (1974) "Group Segregation and Optimal Jurisdictions," *Journal of Political Economy* 82:112–132.

Necak, D. (1991) "The Yugoslav Question: Past and Future," in Ra'anan et. al.: 125–134.

North, D. C. (1991) *Institutions, Institutional Change, and Economic Performance*. Cambridge: Cambridge University Press.
Olson, M. (1965) *The Logic of Collective Action*. Cambridge: Harvard University Press.
Olson, M. (1982) *The Rise and Decline of Nations*. New Haven: Yale University Press.
Ra'anan, U., Mesner, M., Armes, K. and Martin, K. Eds. (1991) *State and Nation in Multi-Ethnic Societies: The Breakup of Multinational States*. New York: Manchester University Press.
Roback, J. R. (1989) "Racism as Rent-Seeking," *Economic Inquiry* 27:661–682.
Sipos, Peter (1991) "National Conflicts and the Democratic Alternative in the Austro-Hungarian Monarchy and its Successors." in Ra'anan et al.: 98–109.
Tullock, G. (1974) *The Social Dilemma: The Economics of War and Revolution*. Blacksburg VA: University Publications.
Witte, A. D. (1980) "Estimating the Economics of Crime with Individual Data," *Quarterly Review of Economics* 94:57–84.

CHAPTER 5

Nationalism revisited

Albert Breton and Margot Breton

In spite of the fact that it has retained the attention of countless scholars and commentators nationalism is a poorly understood phenomenon. One of the reasons for this state of affairs is that, like other big realities, nationalism is multidimensional, and it is difficult to ascertain which of these dimensions are fundamental and permanent and which are accidental and transitory. This problem of multidimensionality is made worse by the fact that virtually all participants in debates and discussions on the subject have consciously or unconsciously held prior beliefs about the phenomenon: Those whose prior beliefs are supportive of nationalism emphasize the dimensions which, in their eyes, confer virtue to the phenomenon and label these basic and essential; the dimensions which in their view denote evil, they call contingent and ephemeral. Those whose prior beliefs go in a different direction invest the same dimensions with the opposite qualities.

These difficulties are not the only ones which scholars must confront in their effort to model nationalism. There is also what could be called the problem of selecting the "proper" level of abstraction for formulating a hypothesis; in other words, there is the problem of deciding which, among the multiplicity of real world factors that appear related to the phenomenon, must be retained to capture its fundamental and permanent dimensions – whatever these may be – and which factors can be left aside as secondary. To illustrate we mention some of the criticisms that were made of the model of nationalism suggested by Breton (1964) almost thirty years ago and to which we return in more detail below. That model was based on the idea that nationalism revealed itself in the allocation of resources to alter the

---

The financial assistance of the Lynde and Harry Bradley Foundation is gratefully acknowledged.

distribution of tangible (measured) assets or wealth between the "foreigners" and the "nationals" of a jurisdiction[1]. The model assumed that owners of assets were wealth maximizers. Nationalism, therefore, could not do anything else but redistribute wealth, proximately at least, between "foreigners" and "nationals." Moreover, it was argued that not all the "nationals" of a jurisdiction would gain equally from the redistribution; the model suggested a rationale to explain why, ultimately, the "middle classes" would gain more than the "working-classes." The model was, *avant la lettre*, at once one of rent seeking (Tullock, 1967) and one of income redistribution à la Aaron Director (Stigler 1970), though nationalism was the driving force.

As was to be expected, the model was criticized. For example, Gilles Paquet (1972, p. 17, n. 45) argued "that nationalism is an ingredient that makes the sedentary [*less mobile*] inputs [the *nationals?*] more productive by galvanizing their energies" and, therefore, that the use of scarce resources to alter the interethnic (say) distribution of asset ownership could (would?) be productive. Paquet, in effect, argued that even though all asset owners are wealth maximizers, because nationalism kindles what Keynes called the "animal spirits" of "nationals," the redistribution of assets makes wealth-maximizing "foreigners" look indolent in comparison to the newly energized wealth-maximizing "nationals." Paquet may or may not be right, but the fundamental question is whether what is emphasized in the original 1964 model is more basic to an understanding of nationalism than what Paquet chooses to underline. Whether, in other words, the alleged capacity of nationalism to galvanize energies for productive purposes – and not only, we assume, for ostracism, scorched earth policies and genocide – is more important than the suggested redistributive aspect of the phenomenon.[2]

Mel Watkins (1978) criticized the model for, among other things, assuming that the political, cultural, social, and everyday economic life of a country would not be adversely affected by the "foreign" ownership of its assets; in other words, for assuming that it was a

---

[1] In some circumstances, it is easy to identify who the "foreigners" and the "nationals" are, but in others that task is not easily performed. Indeed, one important barrier to a tolerably complete and consistent theory of nationalism and, therefore, to a better understanding of the phenomenon, is the lack of simple criteria that would permit an easy identification of the relevant groups.

[2] Among the most ascerbic criticisms of Breton (1964) are those of Stephen Clarkson (1978) and Mel Watkins (1978). Both reject all the empirical evidence, such as it is, which lend some credence to Breton's model. Paquet's remark is, at most, a conjecture; he evokes a possibility and certainly provides no evidence. Yet both Clarkson and Watkins – the latter at length – use Paquet as evidence against Breton.

matter of indifference, in terms of quality of life, what fraction of a country's assets were owned by "foreigners" and what fraction by "nationals." Watkins has a point. However, we must correctly appreciate its significance. Suppose that we knew the "optimal" fraction of a country's assets which, taking everything into account – that is, all the benefits and all the costs of foreign ownership – should be owned by the "nationals" of that country. Let that fraction be v^*. Now assume that the actual fraction is $v < v^*$ and, therefore that it is productive to invest resources in buying "foreign" assets to raise v by dv to where $v + dv = v^*$. Consequently, unless the real world is generally characterized by $v < v^*$ – a fact which we ignore and one on which the literature (including Watkins' paper) is not enlightening – Watkins' criticism can legitimately be taken as pertaining to "distortions" in a model which, at a licit and customary level of abstraction and as a first approximation, neglects distortions.[3]

Though we recognize that nationalism is multidimensional, we submit that one permanent and essential dimension of the phenomenon is national, ethnic and/or racial ownership of property – for example, of territory (land), factories, refineries, infrastructures, government machinery, bureaucracies, and movie studios – and of the flows which derive from these assets. That proposition is not different from the one underlying Breton's (1964) model. However, that model also rested on assumptions which, in our view, are overly restrictive and which, unless jettisoned, do not permit the exploration of behaviors, such as xenophobia, which appear to be closely related to nationalism. In addition, the 1964 model tacitly assumed that nationalism would exist always and everywhere. The assumption mirrors the real world closely enough to be innocuous. Indeed, in the literature that followed the original paper, no one, to our knowledge, remarked on it – though virtually everything else in the model was singled out for comment! However, it is enlightening to see what happens when the assumption is abandoned.

Consequently, after a reformulation of the 1964 model under less restrictive assumptions in the next section and a brief digression in Section II, we provide, in Section III, a rationale for xenophobia which is not only consistent with the model of Section I, but which is capable of explaining why some nationalisms are, while others are not,

---

[3] The argument in the text is framed in terms of an optimal fraction of a nation's assets owned by the "nationals" of the country (v^*); there must, however, be a v^* for every province, state, or canton and for every municipality and parish in a nation. "Foreigners" are foreigners surely, whatever the jurisdiction.

xenophobic. In Section IV, we examine briefly the factors that help determine the reemergence of some nationalisms. Section V concludes the paper.

I   A reformulation of the 1964 model

Almost everyone who writes on nationalism, recognizing the multidimensionality of the phenomenon, distinguishes between types of nationalisms. In Breton's original 1964 model, two kinds of nationalisms were identified – namely cultural and political nationalisms – and it was assumed that the first is inconsequential. Specifically, it was asserted (p. 376) that cultural nationalism "has no direct effect on economic behavior other than increasing the consumption of flags, of materials on which national anthems are printed and other kindred products." The paper focused only on political nationalism as the driving force leading to alterations in the international or interethnic distribution of asset ownership.

However useful the assumption may have been for the early formulation by allowing an undistracted concentration on the ownership-of-property dimension of nationalism, we believe that it is an impediment to a more complete understanding of the phenomenon.[4] Consequently, though we continue to distinguish between cultural and political nationalisms, we do not take the volume[5] of cultural nationalism as

[4] It was the need to remove this assumption that led Harry Johnson (1965) to transform Gary Becker's (1957) notion of a "taste for discrimination" into a "taste for nationalism" as a characteristic of individual persons which then allowed them, in the presence of things national or ethnic, to enjoy psychic or utility income. We do not find this way of dealing with the problem attractive in part because, if not carefully construed, it makes cultural nationalism more innate or "primordial" than we believe it to be. Johnson's "taste for nationalism," however unsatisfactory it may be, did nonetheless allow him to meaningfully distinguish between "output" and "income" – or, we would say, between tangible or money wealth and the subjective valuation of the flow of services it generates – and to explain why the "working classes" would willingly pay the price of redistributing tangible wealth from "foreigners" to "middle class" nationals. Lafay's (this book) failure to appreciate Johnson's contribution mars his criticism of Breton's (1964) model in that it prevents him from seeing that what nationalism does is give "pride" to the "working classes" and tangible monetary wealth to the "middle classes."

[5] Cultural nationalism has an intensive as well as an extensive margin. The first relates to the *strength* of belief in, and commitment to, "things" national or ethnic – some of which we describe below; the second pertains to the *number* of persons who believe and are committed to the same "things." Wealth maximization implies that, in equilibrium, the yield at the two margins are equalized. We assume, to simplify the presentation, that the equality holds at all times. We do not address the question of what it is that wealth maximizers do to maintain the equality.

given. We instead assume that resources can be invested in that productive opportunity just as they can be invested in political nationalism. The capital formed by investing in cultural nationalism is in the nature of national or ethnic loyalty (it is more or less like the "ethnic capital" analyzed by James Coleman, Russell Hardin, and Ronald Wintrobe elsewhere in this book).

It is beyond anyone's capacity and certainly beyond ours to completely describe the variety of resources that can be invested in national or ethnic loyalty. We can do no more than illustrate. Robert Dernberger (1967) in his perceptive analysis of "The Role of Nationalism in the Rise and Development of Communist China" notes that what we here call investment in cultural nationalism had two main components. There was first the development of an "official doctrine that Western religion, institutions, social science theories, literature, and in fact almost every aspect of Western civilization, were not applicable to China" (p. 54); and second, the demonstration "that most of China's ills were the responsibility of the West" (p. 55).

In his monumental study of Nazism, Karl Bracher (1970) traces the evolution of an idea he identifies as a "*volkisch* sense of special destiny" in Germany from Johann Fichte's widely read *Addresses to the German Nation* (1807–8) to the writings, speeches, and declarations of Adolf Hitler and of his colleagues, notably Joseph Goebbels. Bracher points to "the emergence of a special German sense of destiny with anti-Western overtones" and to the elaboration of "the idea of the superiority of German culture, extremely profound and imbued with the idea of a universal mission, set against the superficial, imitative civilization of others" (p. 23). He then shows how these ideas were nurtured by and, in turn, nourished the distinction between community and society – between *gemeinschaft* and *gesellschaft,* later given more form by Ferdinand Tönnies – and how it led to the idea of strengthening the "communal spirit of the people" by "the separation of one nation from the other, and even by war" (p. 25). Bracher finally shows how the notion of "*racial purity* as the basis of historical national grandeur" (p. 26, italics in original) grew from these doctrines and how, in universities, it came to be believed that "the education of the future was to be based on a popularized national history, on a language cleaned of all foreign words, on physical labour and military sports, on the glorification of national symbols and heroes" (p. 26).

The articulation and dissemination of doctrines promoting distinctiveness, exculpation and/or a sense of special fate and their modification as circumstances change are obviously not unique to China and Germany. Such doctrines, in more or less explicit garbs, can be found in many other countries. We can point to the doctrines of "exceptionalism" and of "manifest destiny" in the United States and to innumerable other doctrines based on the idea of the spiritual superiority of a particular group of people which appear to have remained alive among Slav peoples, that is, among Russians, Serbs, Croats, Slovenes, etc. The presumption of spiritual superiority also found echoes in the notions, now defunct, of the "mission civilisatrice de la France"[6] and of Quebec as the "plaque-tournante" of North America – the turntable or rotating platform that would reorient all of North America's misguided civilization.

The marshaling of resources for investment in national and ethnic loyalty, in addition to the cultivation of a sense of distinctness and of special destiny, also takes the form of pledging allegiance to flags (in some societies every school day of the year), of singing national anthems (during certain events, such as Olympic games, many times a day), of organizing and participating in parades or other manifestations designed to reinforce national or ethnic pride, and of promoting and diffusing national or ethnic literature, folklore, music, theater, cinema, and other kinds of cultural expressions.

What is the yield on resources invested in cultural nationalism or in national or ethnic loyalty? We suggest that it has two components. One is to create in individuals a sense of belonging and of identity. It is that component which allows some trades in interethnic groupings or networks to be sometimes consummated at lower transactions, or contractual enforcement, costs. (See Roger Congleton and Wintrobe, this book.) The savings on transactions costs period after period correctly measure that first component of investment in ethnic capital.

The second and, in our view, the much more important component of the yield on cultural nationalism takes the form of a reduction in the resource cost of a dollar's net yield on political nationalism.[7] What we are proposing and was missing from Breton's (1964) original model is the idea that those who seek to change the international or interethnic distribution of asset ownership – who invest in political nationalism –

---

[6] "In the preface he wrote for a handbook published in 1955, E. Louveau, who had recently completed a six-year term as governor [of French Sudan, later Mali], explained that the country was so poor that from a utilitarian point of view its development might well appear doomed to failure." 'Hence, it is not from this point of view that France considered the problem. Faithful to her generous tradition, she sought to win hearts rather than earn dividends'." From Aristide Zolberg (1967 p. 102).

[7] That second component of the yield on ethnic capital is, we believe, so much more important than the first in understanding the multifaceted phenomenon of nationalism that, in the remainder of this paper, we concentrate on it to the exclusion of the first.

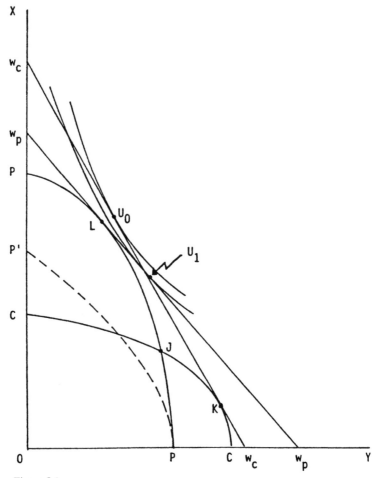

Figure 5.1

can increase the yield to themselves on every dollar invested in that type of opportunity by "initially" allocating resources to capital formation in cultural nationalism or ethnic loyalty.

The argument can be formalized and expanded by adapting the standard analysis of interdependent investment opportunities as interpreted by scholars such as Jack Hirshleifer (1970). Figure 5.1 depicts, for a two-period model, three investment opportunities loci. All three are characterized by continuous smoothly flattening slopes as we move in the northwest direction, indicating diminishing marginal returns as the scale of investment increases. CC tells us what happens to the yield on cultural nationalism, while PP and PP' do the same for capital formation in political nationalism. The difference between the PP and PP' curves is that the second depicts the yield on political nationalism in the absence of investment in cultural nationalism, whereas the first reflects the behavior of marginal returns after prior investment in cultural nationalism up to point J. For that case, the relevant investment opportunity locus is, therefore, CJP. (Note that the CJP curve could be continuous; all that is needed for the analysis is a region of increasing absolute (algebraic) slope in PP after the initial investment in cultural nationalism.)

As the diagram indicates, if the rate of interest is "high," thus generating a steep wealth constraint like $w_c w_c$, resources will be invested in cultural nationalism alone up to point K, because $w_c w_c$ is the constraint which, given the long-term ruling rate of interest, permits the most desirable consumption vector of X and Y, namely U_o – the point at which wealth, on Fisher's definition, is maximized. With a lower rate of interest, the wealth constraint is less steep (less negative); wealth is maximized by investing along CC to point J and then along PP up to L and choosing the consumption bundle U_1 on $w_p w_p$.

The relationship of cultural to political nationalism, therefore, depends on the "technical" properties of the investment opportunity loci and on the height of the rate of interest. For example, if a dollar's worth of cultural nationalism produces a "strong" sense of belonging and identity in those in which it is invested, the marginal return to a dollar's worth of resources allocated that way is high: Investment will occur even if the rate of interest is also high – even if, in other words, the demand originating elsewhere in the economy for the available flow of savings is strong. A similar argument can be made for political nationalism. An understanding of nationalism will, therefore, require a comprehension of the factors that help determine what in diagrammatic terms is the degree of concavity of the CC and PP investment opportunity curves as well as a comprehension of the forces that determine how they relate to each other. We propose a hypothesis in Section III.

Before doing so we must, however, ask two complementary questions, even though the answers we provide to these questions will only be complete after the discussion of Section III. The questions are: (1) who invests in nationalism; and (2), who benefits from the yield on the accumulated capital? We consider these questions in sequence. In the original model (Breton 1964), political nationalism was assumed to be a pure Samuelsonian public capital good. We hold to this assumption for the present reformulation and, indeed, we extend it to cultural nationalism.

From Paul Samuelson's (1954) work on public goods, we know that these goods, by their very nature, induce individuals to misrepresent their true preferences, that is to free ride. In his *Logic of Collective Action*, Mancur Olson (1965) made the point that the free-rider problem is sometimes solved by the offer of private goods which one can only access by paying one's proportionate share of the cost of the public good. The supply of public goods becomes, in effect, a by-product of the purchase of one or more private goods. Two years later, James Buchanan (1967) showed that if the (marginal) tax prices of public goods are given, the incentive to free ride vanishes completely. Still later, Ronald Coase (1974) and Alan Peacock (1979) showed that in the case of lighthouses in Britain, Ireland, and Scotland — the services of lighthouses presumably being quintessential pure public goods — the free-rider problem had been resolved by two government decisions: one granting monopoly privileges to the private owners of lighthouses and the other requiring customs and excise officials to deny clearance for any goods unless light dues — a sum per ton of cargo per voyage — had been paid. Finally, Burton Weisbrod (1988) argued and demonstrated empirically that the free-rider problem is solved, in some contexts, by making use of moral suasion and social pressures.

These writings and others we have not mentioned make two things abundantly clear: (1) organizations of all sorts and of all sizes are able to resolve the free-rider problem that derives from the technical properties of Samuelsonian public goods and are, therefore, capable of supplying these goods; and (2) all the solutions — and there are more than the preceding paragraph discloses — entail the use of coercion by the organization that undertakes to provide the public goods[8]. (There is, indeed, only one case when the provision of public goods is free of coercion and that obtains when one individual provides for himself or herself alone an amount which is greater than or equal to that which the group would provide for itself.)

Most if not all the literature on free riding assumes that the demand functions for public goods are either ascertained or are easily ascer-

---

[8] Because coercion, in one form or another, is needed to deal with free riding, the claim by Coase and by Peacock that the institutional solution to the lighthouse problem adopted in Britain, Ireland, and Scotland was a "market solution" is, to say the least, misleading.

tainable by suppliers in such a way that, when the free-rider problem is resolved, the desired quantities of the public goods can be provided. For example, in the Coase-Peacock lighthouse case, the light dues collected (which, we may recall, are a function of tonnage) and the quantity of light signals provided are on the shipowners' demand-for-protection-against-navigational-hazards curve – not above or below that curve – a position that is not easily obtained.

In addition to a free-rider problem, there is, therefore, an information problem that must be resolved: Suppliers must ascertain the height as well as the slope of demand curves – the relationship between quantities, tax prices, incomes and so on. Suppliers of public goods are in effect organizations which, making use of the best available production technologies, are most efficient at solving these two problems. A casual look around us reveals that very many organizations are capable of dealing with the free-rider problem and with the problem of obtaining information about the position of the demand curve for a sense-of-belonging-and-identity, and are, as a consequence, capable of supplying the collective capital good which we have called national or ethnic loyalty or simply cultural nationalism. Indeed, countless organizations – trade groupings, newspapers and magazines, reading societies, fraternities and associations of all sorts – exist to extol the courage and valor of national or ethnic heroes, to erect monuments to their glory, to celebrate the spirit and virtues of ancestors, to eulogize the grandeur and beauty of the land, to praise the virtues and superiority of nationally or ethnically produced goods and services, to cultivate a feeling of distinctiveness and destiny, to organize sports and other national and ethnic competitions, and to keep alive grievances against other national and ethnic groups. The list could be extended almost without end.

The number of organizations that can invest in political nationalism, in that capital good which we identified as the fraction of a jurisdiction's assets owned by its "nationals," appears to be smaller than for cultural nationalism. There are, to be sure, small coteries that engage in "buy local" campaigns, in boycotts or in discouraging the ownership of foreign assets by refusing to refuel Soviet made cars, for example, or by smashing the hoods or the windshields of Japanese-made vehicles. However, the main investors in political nationalism are most certainly governments through purchases (nationalizations), confiscations, harassments, prohibitions, and conventional commercial policies.

It is time to turn our attention to the question of who benefits from investment in nationalism. To simplify the answer to this question, suppose that everyone in a given society has the same preferences in respect of things national or ethnic, in such a way that everyone derives equal (marginal) utility from the yield on both cultural and political nationalisms: that is from the sense of belonging and identity that flows from a feeling of distinctiveness and of special destiny as well as from the benefits that result from a larger fraction of national or ethnic ownership of assets. As the proportion of assets owned by the "nationals" of a jurisdiction increases, the utility attached to belonging and identity also rises. In the original model (Breton 1964), that dimension of nationalism was implicit. It was made explicit by Johnson (1965).

The original model focused on the tangible and monetary amenities that flow from the national and ethnic ownership of assets, from political nationalism, and argued that these amenities were in the nature of "good jobs" – jobs characterized by high monetary rewards, security of employment, genuine responsibilities and the possibility of promotion – and that these would be available primarily to the "middle classes" or "elites." It was further argued that if the increase in the fraction of "nationally" owned assets was effected primarily by the government of the jurisdiction through direct purchase and state ownership, through financial participation in private ownership, loan guarantees, tax holidays, public procurement of a part of the asset's product, the free or subsidized provision of land (industrial parks), free or subsidized labor training, or through any of the other instruments that can promote the private ownership of assets, the "good jobs" accruing to the "middle classes" or elites would be "paid for" by all tax-paying citizens of the jurisdiction and, as a consequence, from an income distribution point of view, political nationalism would be regressive.

The empirical work inspired, at least in part, by the model is mostly concerned with the Canadian tariff. (See Richard Caves 1976 and Donald Daly and Steven Globerman 1976). It is a literature which is difficult to interpret but provides no ground for rejecting the hypothesis about the incidence – in the sense given that word in Public Economics – of political nationalism.[9] Much more, however, can be understood about the benefits of cultural and political nationalisms

---

[9] There is another reason why the Caves-Daly-Globerman studies should be interpreted with some circumspection in respect of the model of nationalism we are proposing. As mentioned in the text, these studies focus on the Canadian tariff. Theoretical discussions of that tariff, if they point in any direction in the matter of ownership, indicate that it was as much an incentive to "foreign" ownership as it was to an increase in "national" ownership. Political nationalism may not have been a strong motivation behind the Canadian tariff.

and their incidences by turning our attention to a phenomenon that is closely correlated with them. We do this after a brief discussion of homesteading in the next section.

II A brief digression

By 1850, after fifty years of purchases, annexations and negotiations for land with a succession of foreign powers, the government of the United States owned over 1.2 billion acres of public lands – an amount approximately equal to half of present-day America. Ownership, following acquisition and arrogation, must be enforced, otherwise it risks being usurped or supplanted altogether. Enforcement can be achieved by force through the deployment of constabulary and/or military power. Such enforcement will be costly and would be inordinately so when the landmass whose ownership must be secured is as large as that which was owned by the American government in 1850. Furthermore, the U.S. government was surely contemplating additional acquisitions – as witness the 1867 purchase of Alaska from Russia – and/or further annexations which would demand more enforcement personnel. The presumption must be that such aggressive political nationalism, nurtured in a cultural nationalism based on the doctrine of "manifest destiny," would lead to the search for a substitute to force in securing ownership which, though not altogether eliminating the use of such an enforcement instrument, would at least reduce it.

Douglas Allen (1991) convincingly argues that the conventional economic analysis of homesteading – the restricted tenancy and cultivation of surveyed public lands generally obtained at a zero money price on a first-come, first-served basis – which is habitually cast in a framework of rent dissipation and waste, is seriously misconstrued. Instead, Allen argues, homesteading should be conceived as an instrument used to insure property rights in land and to economize on the use of force. Allen's model allows him to coherently interpret a large body of evidence and to explain, among other things, the similarities and differences between the practice of homesteading in the United States and in Canada, where it was used to establish ownership against a presumed American takeover of some Canadian territory.

We accept Allen's analysis. What we wish to underline, which retains little, if any, of his attention, pertains to the incidence of homesteading. It is well to recall that only a relatively small fraction of public lands was available for homesteads. Millions of acres were granted to railroads or allocated to wagon roads and canals as well as to state governments either for sale to generate revenues or as endowments for state institutions. On the basis of secondary evidence, Allen (p. 9) reports that "of the 1,031 million acres of public land disposed of, 285 million acres went to homesteads, the rest went to states, railroads, and private claims."[10]

There is widespread agreement among historians of the American frontier that the misery and suffering endured by the settlers was enormous (see Richard Stroup 1988 and the references he cites). One of the reasons for this misery is no doubt that "of the land that was set aside for homesteading, there seems ample historical evidence to suggest that it was the least valued of the frontier land" (Allen, p. 9), in addition to the requirement that the land be improved, cultivated, and inhabited for at least five years.

We also accept this evidence and suggest that it supports our hypothesis that political nationalism benefits the middle classes and the elites – the railroad owners, the canal users and the state university faculty and students, among others – and much less, if at all, the "working classes" who, in this case, were the homesteaders. The institutional forms which govern the regressive incidence of political nationalism vary from place to place, from period to period, and from circumstance to circumstance, but when correctly analyzed, they are seen to generate the postulated regressive outcome.

III   Xenophobia

Our four dictionaries – two English and two French – define xenophobia as fear or hatred of foreigners and hostility toward them. The definition is at once evocative and misleading. It is misleading first because it gives the impression that people are or are not xenophobic, while, in reality, xenophobia is a continuous variable which, properly measured, could be normalized to vary between zero and one. It is also misleading or should we say uninstructive because it gives no indication of the kind of behaviors that xenophobes adopt. The common habit of rewriting history by exalting national or ethnic protagonists and depreciating others and the practices associated with "ethnic cleansing" are both manifestations of xenophobia, but even if they are on the same continuum, they are poles apart.

Xenophobia, we suggest, is best understood as consisting of the whole set of actions, whether or not motivated by fear or hatred, aimed at excluding, physically or symbolically, "relevant" foreigners from the lives, activities, and institutions of nationals or ethnics, at

---

[10] The number in Allen is "1,031 billion acres," which is surely a typo.

downgrading, often humorously (ethnic jokes), their way of life, their speech, their eating habits, their leisure activities, and so on, at ostracizing them, and at eliminating them by willfully creating uncertainty, by deporting them, and at the extreme, by killing them.

Why are nationalists, whether wittingly or unwittingly, often xenophobes? For the simple reason, we suggest, that the ability of foreigners to fit into the host society, to make a life for themselves, to prosper, in other words to act as people who belong and are identified with the rest of the people around them, provide, by these deportments and activities, information that denies the claim of cultural nationalists that ethnic loyalty, as an especially favored basis for a sense of belonging and identity, reduces the transaction costs as much as or more than other more cosmopolitan and liberal forms of loyalty (such as loyalty to neighborhood organizations and other local institutions, to business and professional partners, to political parties, etc.). Xenophobia, as we have defined it in the previous paragraph, is therefore best conceived as a barrier that protects the national or ethnic masses from information originating in "foreign" groups that would allow them – the masses – to discover that what we have called belonging and identity can have very little or nothing at all to do with national or ethnic background, folklore, distinctiveness, and feeling of special collective destiny.

Xenophobia, then, increases the rate of return on investments in cultural nationalism and, because of the relationship which we have described in Section I between political and cultural nationalisms, on investments in political nationalism as well. Referring to Figure 5.1, we would say that xenophobia increases the concavity of the CC-curve as well as the length of the segment JL of the PP curve which has high absolute (algebraic) slope.

The mechanism which underlies the hypothesis we have just proposed rests on the idea that the authority of elites and of all those who impart direction to any group or collectivity, whether national or ethnic or whether of some other variety, is to a considerable extent determined by the competition which governs their relationship with other groups or collectivities, as the theory of reference groups indicates (see, for example, Merton 1957). Indeed, the stronger the competition, the more will the elites have to cater to the preferences of the group's members and the weaker, as a consequence, their authority and power. Pierre Salmon (1987), borrowing from the economic theory of tournament or rank-order competition, has formalized the mechanism for the case of intergovernmental competition. His analysis is, however, easily adapted to the present context and when this is done it shows that members of one group or collectivity can evaluate the performance of their own elites by reference to the conduct and undertakings of elites in other groups or collectivities. Xenophobia destroys this type of rank-order competition and leaves all members of the collectivities, except their elites, worse off.

If the foregoing is accepted, it can help us understand why all nationalisms are not xenophobic. Indeed, it tells us that xenophobia, like other protectionist measures, will be fostered by national or ethnic groups that are not able to sustain what Schumpeter called "the gail of competition." Competitive national or ethnic elites will be able to invest in the formation of ethnic loyalty and in increasing the fraction of domestically owned assets without making use of xenophobic measures.

These propositions may help us understand why Quebec nationalism, rooted in a context in which the Anglophone and Jewish communities of the province were more cosmopolitan, has historically been intensely xenophobic and why, in recent decades, as the Francophone community itself has become more cosmopolitan and competitive – in part, but not exclusively because of the departure of a significant fraction of the Anglophone and Jewish populations – xenophobia is less virulent, though by no means extinguished. It can also help us understand why American nationalism which, from the days of Alexander Hamilton has been the preserve of a urbane white Anglo-Saxon Protestant elite, has historically been so vigorous and aggressive without being xenophobic, and why, in recent times, with an increasing fraction of "national" assets owned by Japanese interests, that nationalism shows unmistakable signs of xenophobia. We suspect but cannot demonstrate, because of a lack of even casual evidence, that the above analysis could be applied with benefit to what is happening in the former Soviet Union, in the former Yugoslavia, in much of the Balkans and Eastern Europe where, in many instances, xenophobia has reached new historical heights.

IV Sundry notes on the reemergence of nationalism

Political nationalism, proximately, and cultural nationalism, ultimately, are about the ownership of assets. Under communism, all assets are owned by the state and, as a consequence, political nationalism has no ground to take root. The fires of national or ethnic loyalty can obviously be stoked and they will be if nationalists become the fulcrum toward whom opposition to the regime gravitates. However, the conflation of cultural nationalism with political opposition will make it difficult, in most cases, to disentangle the two phenomena and to correctly diagnose the depth and strength of national or ethnic loyalty.

When communism vanishes, assets find themselves without owners. If capital formation in cultural nationalism has been significant during the period of communist governance, the national or ethnic elites – many of whom will be per force, former communists – will organize themselves and seek to lodge the ownership of assets in their own hands. If the working-class population is poor, the instrument of acquisition that will be used will be confiscation, as was argued in Breton's (1964) original paper. If the confiscator has authority and legitimacy, confiscation can be effected peacefully; if not it will lead to turmoil, unrest, and even to war. This will be especially likely if the asset over which ownership is claimed happens to be land inhabited by populations invested with different cultural nationalisms.

If the model we are suggesting does capture essential and permanent dimensions of nationalism, we would have to conclude that it was not the totalitarian component of communism in the former Soviet Union, in the former Yugoslavia, and in East European countries that was inimical to nationalism, but the state ownership of almost all assets and most surely of land. The rush for national or ethnic ownership of assets is consequent on the demise of public ownership and would have occurred even if the governmental structures had continued to be totalitarian.

If confiscation is ruled out, nationalism will ebb and flow with permanent changes in long-term real interest rates, increasing when these rates are lower. It will also ebb and flow with variations in Friedman's permanent or expected long-term real incomes, falling as incomes fall, essentially because the ability of governments to raise the needed revenues to finance the investments will be adversely affected. However, because of the nature of the resources involved and because of the nature of the investing organizations, political nationalism could be more severely affected than cultural nationalism by falling income, so that cultural nationalism would be relatively more salient in "hard times." All in all, however, the behavior of investment in nationalism should parallel the behavior of capital formation in the rest of the economy.

We have offered a model of cultural and political nationalisms which integrates these two kinds of nationalisms in a way that makes it possible to explain the level of investment in political nationalism and, therefore, to gain an appreciation of the extent to which this kind of nationalism is regressive. As such the model captures what we believe are fundamental and permanent dimensions of nationalism. The model, in addition, can be used to derive a number of testable propositions. It has also allowed us to integrate a phenomenon which often appears to be a strong correlate of nationalism, namely xenophobia, and through this integration to make it possible for us to shed light on old as well as on reemergent nationalisms.

References

Allen, Douglas W. 1990. "Homesteading and Property Rights; or, 'How the West Was Really Won.' " *Journal of Law and Economics* 34, no. 1 (April): 1–23.
Becker, Gary S. 1971 [1957]. *The Economics of Discrimination.* Chicago: University of Chicago Press.
Bracher, Karl D. 1970. *The German Dictatorship.* Translated from the German by Jean Steinberg. New York: Praeger.
Breton, Albert. 1964. "The Economics of Nationalism." *Journal of Political Economy* 72, no. 4 (August): 376–86.
Buchanan, James M. 1967. *Public Finance in Democratic Process. Fiscal Institutions and Individual Choice.* Chapel Hill: University of North Carolina Press.
Caves, Richard E. "Economic Models of Political Choice: Canada's Tariff Structure." *Canadian Journal of Economics,* (Vol 9, No 2, May 1976), 278–300.
Clarkson, Stephen. 1978. "Anti-Nationalism in Canada: The Ideology of Mainstream Economics." *Canadian Review of Studies in Nationalism* 5, no. 1 (Spring): 45–65.
Coase, Ronald H. 1974. "The Lighthouse in Economics." *Journal of Law and Economics* 17, no. 2 (October): 357–76.
Daly, Donald J., and Globerman, Steven. 1976. *Tariff and Science Policies: Application of a Model of Nationalism.* Toronto: University of Toronto Press for the Ontario Economic Council.
Dernberger, Robert F. 1967. "The Role Of Nationalism in the Rise and Development of Communist China." In Johnson, Harry G., ed. *Economic Nationalism in Old and New States,* 48–70.
Hirshleifer, Jack. 1970. *Investment, Interest, and Capital,* New York: Prentice-Hall.
Johnson, Harry G. 1965. "A Theoretical Model of Economic Nationalism in New and Developing States." *Political Science Quarterly* 80, no. 2 (June): 165–85. Reprinted in Johnson, ed. *Economic Nationalism in Old and New States,* 1–16.
— 1967. *Economic Nationalism in Old and New States.* Chicago: University of Chicago Press.
Merton, Robert K. 1957. *Social Theory and Social Structure.* New York: Free Press.
Olson, Jr., Mancur. 1965. *The Logic of Collective Action. Public Goods and the Theory of Groups.* Cambridge: Harvard University Press.

Paquet, Gilles. 1972. "The Multinational Firm and the Nation State as Institutional Forms." In Paquet, Gilles, ed. *The Multinational Firm and the Nation State*, 2–19. Don Mills: Collier-Macmillan.
Peacock, Alan T. 1979. "The Limitations of Public Goods Theory: The Lighthouse Revisited." In Peacock, Alan T., *The Economic Analysis of Government and Related Themes*, 127–36. Oxford: Martin Robertson.
Salmon, Pierre. 1987. "Decentralization As an Incentive Scheme." *Oxford Review of Economic Policy* 3, no. 2 (Summer): 24–43.
Samuelson, Paul A. 1954. "The Pure Theory of Public Expenditure." *Review of Economics and Statistics* 36, no. 4 (November): 387–9. Reprinted in Stiglitz, Joseph E., ed. *The Collected Scientific Papers of Paul A. Samuelson*. Vol. 2, 1,223–5. Cambridge: MIT Press, 1966.
Stigler, George J. 1970. "Director's Law of Public Income Redistribution." *Journal of Law and Economics* 13, no. 1 (April): 1–10.
Stroup, Ricard L. 1988. "Buying Misery with Federal Land." *Public Choice* 57, no. 1 (April): 69–77.
Tullock, Gordon. 1967. "The Welfare Costs and Tariffs, Monopolies, and Theft." *Western Economic Journal* 5, no. 2 (June): 224–32.
Watkins, Mel. 1978. "The Economics of Nationalism and the Nationality of Economics: A Critique of Neoclassical Theorizing." *Canadian Journal of Economics* 11, no. 4 (Supplement, November): S86–S120.
Weisbrod, Burton A. 1988. *The Nonprofit Economy*. Cambridge: Harvard University Press.
Zolberg, Aristide R. "The Political Use of Economic Planning in Mali." In Johnson, ed. *Economic Nationalism in Old and New States*, 98–123.

CHAPTER 6

The reemergence of secessionism: Lessons from Quebec

Stéphane Dion

Why does nationalism take a secessionist tone in some circumstances, and not in others? Authors have identified a huge number of determinants of ethnic mobilization: various historically rooted inequalities, cultural threats or clashes, ethnic diversity and segmentation, unbalanced political institutions, liberal belief in self-determination, the size of the stratum of intellectuals, and so on (Gellner 1983; Pinard 1992, pp. 472–8; Smith 1991). The list of such determinants is so long that it may discourage one from assembling it in a simple framework.

In order to explain secessionism, I propose to study the level on which three basic feelings are shared by any linguistic, religious, or ethnic group looking to leave a union. First, a feeling of *fear*, of being weakened or even of disappearing as a distinct people if the group stays in the union. Second, a feeling of *confidence* among the group that it can perform as well, or even better, on its own and that the secession is not too risky. And third, a feeling of *rejection*, the sensation of no longer being welcomed in the union. When these feelings are all at high levels, secession is likely to occur.

By using the word "feeling," I do not want to suggest that nationalism is only, or even mainly, a matter of emotions, an irrational manifestation of some kind of primordial sentiments (Geertz 1963). I just want to imply two things. First, the gains and losses perceived to be linked to nationalist options are affected by emotions, which have a distorting power: "Emotions matter because they move and disturb us" and because "they also interfere with our thought processes, making them less rational than they would otherwise be" (Elster 1989, pp. 69–70).

Second, the use of the word "feeling" does not lead one to overestimate the degree of information on which citizens build their political expectations. This level of knowledge is usually very low. Such a phenomenon is understandable on a rational basis: Since each citizen is aware that his or her individual vote or political contribution is unlikely to affect the collective future, he or she has little incentive to spend a large amount of time and energy to improve his or her comprehension of political life. Because the level of information is usually low, organizational theory considers that feelings are somewhat rational (Waring 1991). When one does not have a high level of knowledge of a field, it is more rational to have a "sense," a feeling, than a firm expectation.

For a study of nationalist and secessionist feelings, the Quebec–Canada question constitutes a very specific case among a huge amount of various situations. The world is experiencing the strongest fever of nationalism since the postwar decolonization movement. Many countries are facing ethnic tensions, and some (the Soviet Union, Yugoslavia, Czechoslovakia, Ethiopia) will not survive the challenge of secession. The Quebec–Canada question bears little similarity to these cases. The Canadian federation is not a decaying, totalitarian regime, a new democracy, or an unstable third world country. Quebecers have freely elected pro-Canada politicians since the beginning of the federation, in 1867. It seems harder to explain the challenge of secession when it occurs in such a wealthy modern welfare state, envied by the world. Never has a liberal democracy split except Norway and Sweden in 1905, and Ireland and Britain in 1922. Still, the basic question remains the same, whatever the kind of state and the level of economic development: What are the factors that affect the feelings of fear, confidence, and eventually, rejection, among the linguistic, religious or ethnic groups seduced by the secessionist idea?

The Quebec–Canada question bears more similarity with the reemergence of autonomist movements in some Western European countries. But neither Scotland, Catalonia, nor any other region in Western Europe is as likely as Quebec to become an independent country during the near future. Quebec is a striking case which may have important leading effects on what will happen in Europe. In that sense, it must be regarded as a very instructive case.

Although the secession of the province of Quebec from Canada is a true possibility, I already committed myself in September 1991 to predict that, in the end, Quebecers will stay in the Canadian federation (Dion 1991b, p. 14). I repeat this prediction in November 1992. Indeed, it seems to me that both the feeling of fear to be weakened as a distinct people in the union, and the feeling of confidence in a costless secession, although they have been exceptionally high for the past two years, are not strong enough to lead to secession. However, the feeling of rejection is currently very intense among Quebecers and may spoil my prediction. It is a fluctuating and sporadic phenomenon, a catalyst which may generate unpredictable developments in the short term.

The importance of considering fluctuations over time is the most important lesson to draw from the Quebec case. Secessionist movements are not stable and monolithic forces; at least in Quebec support for an independent country has many shadings and has fluctuated considerably over time.

In Quebec the feeling of fear is a long-term factor that was strengthened by some recent events. This feeling is connected with a sense of linguistic insecurity and fear of being anglicized. The feeling of self-confidence that Quebec has the economic and governmental institutions necessary to survive on its own grew up in the last three decades, but became stronger in the last years with the higher visibility of a Francophone business class. The sense of rejection by the rest of Canada is, as I said, a short-term, catalytic feeling in the wake of the 1990 Constitutional crisis. I will review the roots of these three feelings after describing how much they have taken a separatist tone in recent years.

The course of the secessionist idea in contemporary Quebec

Although nationalism has always existed in Quebec, the secessionist idea ceased being politically marginal only in the 1960s. By 1968 an important separatist party was created, the Parti Québécois. Its raison d'être has been labeled *souveraineté-association* – political sovereignty combined with economic association with Canada. This association would imply a common market with mobility of goods, services, capital, and people in a monetary union. The Parti Québécois won majority control of the provincial legislature in November 1976, after a campaign focused on issues other than sovereignty: integrity, good government, good leadership, linguistic security for French-speakers (Pinard and Hamilton 1978, pp. 745–56). The party had promised not to implement sovereignty unless it received majority support in a referendum to be held later. The Parti Québécois won the 1976 election with 41 percent of support, the remaining votes being split among three "federalist" parties – that is, those that support the Canadian federation.

After waiting four years, the Parti Québécois held its referendum in May 1980. Even then the sovereignty question was formulated in such a way as to postpone a final decision. Quebecers were asked simply to give the government of Quebec a mandate to negotiate sovereignty-association, a new arrangement with Canada that would then be submitted for approval in a second referendum. This second referendum was never held because 60 percent of voters in the 1980 referendum denied the government authority to initiate negotiation over sovereignty-association.

The 1980 referendum defeat disheartened the nationalist troops to the point that the idea of secession appeared dead (Clift 1982). The Parti Québécois cautiously avoided discussing the sovereignty issue during the 1985 campaign, won by its old rival Robert Bourassa and the Liberal party. A moderate leader, Pierre-Marc Johnson, initiated a drift of the Parti Québécois platform toward a position favoring autonomous status in the Canadian federation. The mid-eighties were a very tough time for the Parti Québécois, which suffered an important drop in membership and funding. The support for independence was very low in the polls (Pinard 1992, p. 480, table 1). A January 1985 CROP poll showed that 52 percent of Quebecers chose the status quo as their first constitutional option, 23 percent a particular status for Quebec in the federation, 15 percent sovereignty-association, and only 4 percent independence (Cloutier, Guay, and Latouche 1992, p. 62).

The Parti Québécois lost the September 1989 elections and made no substantial gain with 40 percent of the votes. However, by this time the party had as its head a clear prosovereignty leader, Jacques Parizeau. In this way the 1989 campaign indicated a renewal of the nationalist mood. This renewal was connected to the fact that a constitutional deal, called "The Meech Lake Accord," aimed to accommodate Quebec, was in discussion. After the rejection of this deal in June 1990, support for sovereignty spectacularly increased in the polls. It rose from 27 percent to 42 percent between October 1985 and August 1989 and peaked at about 65 percent of support in some polls during the second half of 1990 (Cloutier, Guay, and Latouche 1992, pp. 62–3). Support was even higher among Francophones since the rest of the Quebecers (about 17 percent of the provincial population) tended to be strong supporters of the Canadian federation.

Facing this renewal of the nationalist mood, the provincial ruling party, the Liberals, switched to a far more nationalist platform. On March 10, 1991, the Liberal party endorsed the Allaire report (1991), which claimed for the Quebec government virtually every power possible, leaving to the exclusive care of the federal government only defense, customs, currency, post, the debt, and equalization payments to provincial governments. This massive transfer of powers was described in the Allaire report as a necessary condition if Quebec was to stay in the federation. On March 27, 1991 Liberal members of the

National Assembly endorsed the report of the provincial Commission on the Political and Constitutional Future of Quebec (Bélanger-Campeau Commission, 1991). It recommended that a referendum be held in spring or fall 1992 on the constitutional future of Quebec. This nationalist drift of the Liberal party did not stop the Parti Québécois from increasing its popularity. It has taken the lead in the polls.

The new strength of the secessionist movement has had important repercussions in the federal legislature too, with the creation of the Bloc Québécois. This parliamentary group was created by a former minister of the Mulroney government, Lucien Bouchard, who left the Conservative party during the Meech Lake crisis in the spring of 1990. Since that time the Bloc Québécois has become the most popular federal party in Quebec.

However, the fervor of the secessionist movement cooled since the spring of 1991. A June 1992 CROP poll showed 46 percent of Quebecers in support of sovereignty, 40 percent against, and 14 percent undecided. This figure stayed broadly the same since April 1991 (Lessard, 1992, A-1). Considering that the undecided are less likely to vote for the most risky option, the secessionist idea might not gain the support of a majority of voters. Moreover, "sovereignty" became a catch-all notion that generates a large amount of confusion: a March 1992 CROP poll showed that 20 percent of those in support of this option thought that a "sovereign Quebec" would still elect MPs to the Canadian federal Parliament.

It is clear that Premier Bourassa himself has not been seduced by the secessionist idea. He rapidly put some distance between himself and the very nationalist Allaire report, endorsed by his own party, by stating that Quebec's real purpose was to work with all Canadians to make the federation more manageable.

A referendum was held on October 26, 1992 on a new constitutional deal reached by all the first ministers on August 28. Among many provisions, the deal included a devolution of powers to the provinces considerably limited compared to what the Allaire report requested. Canadians at a rate of 55 percent, and 56.6 percent of Quebecers voted against the deal. This referendum leads to the conclusion that it will be impossible to renew the Constitution for the forthcoming future. This may convince many soft nationalists in Quebec to join the secessionist camp. But, during the referendum campaign, support for sovereignty decreased in Quebec. An October 24 CROP poll showed that for the first time in three years, opposition to sovereignty was higher than the support for it (44%–40%). Moreover, support for the Liberal party tied support for the Parti Québécois, even though the latter was clearly ahead before the referendum campaign (Falardeau 1992). This drop in secessionist fervor can be explained by the fact that the economic costs of sovereignty were an issue during the referendum campaign.

To sum up, the secessionist idea was unpopular during the years following the May 1980 referendum on sovereignty-association, to the point that the whole question seemed to be out of date. But it enjoyed an unprecedented popularity at the end of 1990 before declining in 1991, and remaining stable around the majority level until the 1992 fall referendum campaign. It dropped under the majority level at the end of the campaign.

To explain this impressive variation in the support for the secessionist idea, we will review the roots of our three nationalist feelings: fear, confidence, and rejection. They explain the rise of support for secession; they suggest also the reversibility of such support.

Feeling of fear: A permanent sense of linguistic insecurity

Language is not always the basis for political identity, which may lie elsewhere, in religion or ethnicity for instance (Edwards 1984). But in Quebec, since the rapid drop of the Catholic church's influence during the sixties, language certainly has been the primary source of identity.

Obviously such an intricate and complex phenomenon as the strength of the secessionist movement in Quebec is not explicable by a single factor. Factors other than language – history, culture, territory – are also important parts of the nationalist credo in Quebec. But if I had to choose the main reason to explain why nationalist feeling has fueled a powerful secessionist movement, I would select, without any hesitation, the fragility of the French language in North America.

Francophone Quebecers account for only 2.4 percent in an overwhelmingly English-speaking North America. Canada is rightly known as a bilingual country, but most of its French-speaking population lives in Quebec (86.3 percent in 1986). Francophones account for less than 5 percent of the population in every Canadian province except Quebec and New Brunswick. Overall, the proportion of French speakers in the Canadian population dropped from 29.1 percent in 1941 to 24.2 percent in 1986 (Statistics Canada 1988–89).

Within Quebec itself, however, Francophone dominance grew. French speakers represented 82.9 percent of the total population in 1986, up 2.2 percentage points from 1971 (Conseil de la langue française du Québec, 1992, 2–3). The decline of English speakers in Quebec is primarily the result of an exodus following the 1976 Parti Québécois election. This emigration of Quebec's Anglophone population, together with a lower capacity of the French province to attract and keep new immigrants and the spectacular drop of the French speakers' birthrate, decreased Quebec's demographic weight in the whole Canadian population from 29 percent in 1941 to 24.8 percent in 1986. As a result, the share of MPs from Quebec in the federal Parliament dropped from 28 percent of the total in 1974 to 25.4 percent in 1990. The same decline in Quebec's population political weight will presumably occur in all federal institutions.

The crucial issue is obviously the Montreal area, which accounts for 44.7 percent of the total population of the province. Quebec's Anglophone and immigrant populations are concentrated in this area (at rates of 75 and 90 percent, respectively). Historically, the Anglophone population was powerful. The attraction of the continental language is very strong on the immigrant population. Francophones fear losing control of their metropolis. If Montreal became English, the rest of Quebec would no longer be in a position to shape a strong French community.

The immigrant population, once primarily from European countries such as Italy and Greece, now comes primarily from third world countries (Forbes 1992). This pattern is familiar in most Western countries. In many places the insertion of these growing heterogeneous ethnic groups among an aging white population created social tensions and reinvigorated ethnicity as an important political variable. But in Quebec these problems are complicated by the language question because the attraction of English is so strong on immigrants (Lambert and Curtis 1982). The days when the French Canadians had the highest birthrate in Western countries ended with the secularization and modernization of the province. The fecundity rate was 1.43 among French-speaking women in 1986, when the rate needed to replace a population is 2.1, according to demographers (Conseil de la langue française du Québec, 1992, pp. 10–11). Thus, each event suggesting that the integration of new immigrants into the French community is incomplete, fragile, or easily reversible, nourishes the secessionist feeling. It is easy to convince oneself that the security of the French language would be strengthened if Quebec was an independent French-speaking republic. Then the signal given to all inhabitants and new immigrants would be clearer.

In short, the rest of Canada is increasingly English, the demographic weight of Quebec is decreasing within the federation, and everything suggests that these two trends will continue in the foreseeable future. Quebec is increasingly Francophone, but the aging population of French descent is facing growing young immigrant populations attracted by the continental language. Thus it is hardly surprising that the Francophone population of Quebec has a strong feeling of linguistic isolation in Canada and North America.

Obviously Quebecers do not have an exact knowledge of all those statistics. There is a low level of public awareness of the proportion speaking each language, French or English. Only 30 percent of college-aged French Quebecers have a realistic idea of the percentage of Francophones in the total Quebec population (Nadeau and Niemi 1992). But the sense of linguistic fragility is fully a part of French Quebecers' beliefs, and from it stems their fear of disappearing.

Nationalism finds its central roots in this structural situation. The history of Quebec is haunted by fear of Anglicization, obsessed by the examples of Louisiana and parts of Canada where the French presence survives only as folklore. The manner in which other Canadian provinces historically denied their Francophone minorities any bilingual facilities, particularly regarding the language of instruction, did nothing to cool Quebec's linguistic insecurity.

The linguistic context described above may easily become an explosive political problem. In reviewing the course of the Quebec nationalist movement since the 1960s, one finds a linguistic crisis at the beginning of each new outburst of nationalism. At issue was the nationalists' claim to have a compulsory law to protect the French language over the Quebec territory. Only nine months after its 1976 election, the Parti Québécois government passed such a compulsory law, Bill 101, stipulating that in Quebec French must be the usual language of work, instruction, communication, trade, and business. The English-speaking minority could retain its own language in publicly funded health care and social institutions, public schools, and universities, but access to English elementary and secondary schools was denied to French speakers and "Allophones" – those whose native language is neither French nor English.

Bill 101 automatically received full support from nationalist groups. English-speaking groups and the business community opposed it, and it was criticized as "retrograde" by the Canadian prime minister of the time, Pierre Elliott Trudeau (quoted in Fraser 1984, p. 105). Despite the protests, Bill 101 was implemented. It rapidly appeared to be a success for the defense of the French language in Quebec. The impact can be shown in a single statistic: The percentage among the Allophones who went to French schools increased from 38.7 percent to 75.5 percent between 1980 and 1989 (Conseil de la langue française 1992, pp. 28–9).

Bill 101 generated a new perception of linguistic protection among Francophones. But this simple fact had an effect not expected by the Parti Québécois: it dissuaded many moderate nationalists from joining the sovereignty camp. If linguistic insecurity is what has triggered all of the outbreaks of nationalist fever since the 1960s, the reverse is also true: Times of linguistic security are not favorable to the secessionist movement. The cooling of linguistic insecurity following the implementation of Bill 101 decreased secessionist sentiment and, by doing so, was an important factor in the defeat of the prosovereignty position during the 1980 referendum (McRoberts 1988, pp. 389–90). This feeling of linguistic security remained strong during the years following the referendum, and it helped to maintain secessionist support at a very low level.

The linguistic question was not an issue at all during the 1985 provincial campaign, and it was possible to assume at the time that a durable consensus had been reached on the matter. But this linguistic peace was frail for two reasons. First, the fact that the Parti Québécois was in power was an important factor for this sense of linguistic security. The defeat of the Parti Québécois and the election of the Liberals in December 1985 changed the situation. Pushed by its Anglophone lobby, the Liberal party had been a vehement critic of Bill 101 at the outset and still in 1985 was less firm on linguistic matters than the Parti Québécois. Quickly linguistic tensions rose in Montreal in 1986. The warning "Ne touchez pas à la loi 101 ("Don't touch Bill 101") was visible everywhere in Montreal as secessionist feelings were still very low and as the Parti Québécois was trying to put off its sovereignist option.

The second threat to the linguistic peace was the 1982 Constitutional law endorsed by all the provinces but Quebec. This Constitutional law contains a Charter of Rights which enshrined the federal government's conception of linguistic rights. The federal government defines its role as the protector of linguistic minorities throughout the country. It considers its role in a strictly symmetrical manner – that is, that both minorities (the French outside Quebec and the English inside Quebec) must receive protection. This symmetrical linguistic concept was enshrined in the Charter of Rights of 1982 without the consent of the government of Quebec. With its unilingual prescriptions, the compatibility of Bill 101 with the Charter was uncertain. Never has a law enacted in Canada been so contested in the courts. When came a Supreme Court's judgment on a particular emotional and visible issue – language in commercial signs – the storm began.

On Dec. 15, 1988, the Supreme Court ruled that the Bill 101 unilingual requirements for commercial signs were inconsistent with the Quebec and Canadian Charters of Rights because they violated freedom of expression. The Bill 101 "French only" policy has always enjoyed the full support of nationalist groups. For them a policy of unilingual French signs is very important, especially in Montreal, because a "French face" in the street is one way to signify to everybody – in particular to new immigrants – that in Quebec things happen in French. Among the whole Francophone population, the prescriptions to banish other languages in many areas of public life, especially commercial signs, were never popular, but the fear was to see a step-by-step dislocation of the linguistic protection. That is why the Supreme Court decision increased secessionist support. A panel survey, done with Montreal students, in December 1988–January 1989, showed that the Supreme Court decision created a strong radicalization among those students (Cloutier, Gay, and Latouche 1992, pp. 62–3).

Premier Bourassa was pressed by nationalist groups to ignore the Supreme Court judgment. They urged him to use the "notwithstanding" clause" – a provision of the 1982 Constitution that allows governments to avoid conforming with Supreme Court decisions. Bourassa tried to find a middle way between the conflicting points of view. He used the "notwithstanding clause" but passed a new law, Bill 178, which legalized the use of languages other than French for commercial signs inside but not outside commercial buildings. Bill 178 failed to cool the new nationalist fever in Quebec. In the context of the Supreme Court decision about the language of advertising in Quebec, and the so-called inside-outside Bill 178, the pressure group *Mouvement Quebec Français* was able to hold the biggest political meetings and demonstrations since the 1980 referendum, and the prosovereignty idea gained significantly in popularity in public opinion polls.

The language issue had a tremendous impact in the rest of Canada as well. The federal language policy aimed to promote French outside Quebec, in provinces where the French fact is hard to perceive, created a lot of hostility against the French-speaking province, even though Quebec's government had nothing to do with this federal policy. The government of Quebec's own linguistic policy, aimed at resisting the encroachments of the English language, did not foster popular support for promoting French in the rest of Canada (Young 1991). Quebec's Bill 178 angered English speakers in Quebec and elsewhere in Canada, and it contributed to the widening disenchantment with the constitutional negotiation with Quebec and to its failure in June 1990. The law provided a convenient reason for sixty-two Ontario municipalities to declare themselves English-unilingual in the first three months of 1990, and helped new parties openly hostile to the French fact to gain popularity. These events were seen in Quebec as instances of rejection, and they had a tremendous effect on nationalist feelings in Quebec.

But some factors are working to cool off the fear of Anglicization. Objectively speaking, the French-speaking population is growing relatively to the English one in Quebec. Bill 101 is effective, especially in bringing immigrants to French schools. Linguistic insecurity is not strong enough to keep the secessionist support to the majority level. But other factors are active too, especially a new confidence of French speakers in their own abilities.

The fragile new feeling of confidence

During the 1980 referendum, the feeling of confidence in a costless secession was low. A pervasive argument against sovereignty was that it would cause big business and foreign capital to flee Quebec. A widely held opinion was that the Quebec government, institutions, and citizens were broadly funded by the rest of the country, mainly through equalization payments and the transfer policies of the federal government.

Ten years later, several economists and experts argued for the possibility of a quiet and costless shift to sovereignty (Fortin 1990; Proulx 1990; Tremblay 1990; Chambre de Commerce du Québec 1990). No one claims that there would be a significant short-term increase in wealth following sovereignty. Many claim, however, that there would be no significant economic deterioration during the transition period and probably an overall improvement in the long term. Even some important business people have expressed this view. Almost half of 200 chief executives (48.5 percent) of the 500 biggest Quebec enterprises surveyed in a 1990 poll said that independence would have a positive effect in the long term, and only 13.3 percent believed that there would be a negative effect (reported in the business weekly *Les Affaires* 62, May 12–18, 1990). This optimism is in stark contrast to the pessimism during the 1980 referendum, when the business class was almost unanimously hostile to the secessionist idea.

What happened? How to explain that, in 1991, no less than 84 percent of the French Quebecers agreed (and 55 percent agreed strongly) with the statement that "Quebec is more capable of becoming an independent country today than it was ten or twenty years ago" (Pinard 1992, p. 494)?

The feeling of confidence grew since the 1960s, and especially during the last decade, with the economic advancement of Francophones, the consolidation of a Francophone business class, the improvement of provincial institutions to the point where they reached the level of a quasistate, and external factors like free trade and the various difficulties of the federal government. All this led to optimistic perceptions about sovereignty.

Until the 1960s English was undeniably the language of prestige in Quebec. French speakers had little control of the ownership of the private enterprises operating in the province, and they were strongly underrepresented at managerial levels. Today, Quebec is still in many ways a fragile economy with an unemployment rate and a poverty rate higher than the Canadian average (Noël 1993). But there has been an improvement of the Francophones' economic situation relative to the Anglophone population in Quebec. An English speaker earned 44.7 percent more than a French speaker in 1970, but 16.3 percent more in 1980. The proportion of workers employed by Francophone-owned enterprises increased from 47.1 percent in 1961 to 61.6 percent in 1987 (Vaillancourt 1989). French speakers accounted for only 30.5 percent of the managerial category of enterprises operating in Quebec in 1959, but 58 percent in 1988 (Conseil de la langue française 1992, pp. 50–1). Moreover, French-speaking large enterprises grew, and some of their presidents became well-known figures.

This economic advancement gave tremendous confidence to the Francophones, in particular among the elites. A striking point was the rising of the Francophone business class and its visibility and prestige during a decade of neoconservative mood. It generated the opinion that the new capitalist spirit in Quebec would inspire confidence and credibility in international investors and that the local business class was solid enough to support the transition costs of sovereignty.

The fact that prominent members of this business elite became well-known supporters of sovereignty is also an important factor. This is a new phenomenon. Before the 1960s, traditional nationalism in Quebec was mainly communitarian, centered on the Catholic church, and antistatist (Bélanger 1974). From 1960 until the 1980 referendum, nationalism was somewhat connected with the growth of the provincial government, and widely identified with the public sector and the new middle class of artists and intellectuals (Beaud 1982; Blais and Nadeau 1984a, pp. 293–4 and 1984b, p. 329; Pinard and Hamilton 1989, p. 294). But in 1990, with some support from the business class, sovereignty became a nonideological or catchall idea and thus better placed to seduce all groups and social classes. The impact of socioeconomic variables on support for sovereignty substantially decreased between 1980 and 1990 (Cloutier, Gay, and Latouche 1992, p 146; Pinard 1992, p. 490; Meadwell 1993, p. 211, table 1). The age variable alone remains – slightly – significant after multivariate control (Blais and Nadeau 1992, pp. 93–5).

Moreover, the policy networks which link this business class and Quebec government officials are strong. But the same may be said about various elites: professionals, scholars, artists. The Quebec government and institutions expanded in so many directions that it came to have a firm grip on almost all the sectors of the society. It came to form a quasistate. This also strengthens the feeling of confidence in an easy and profitable sovereignty.

In fact, Canada is the most decentralized OECD country, along with Switzerland (Gray 1991, p. 19). And even Canada's provinces are much more powerful than Switzerland's cantons. If we take the usual indicator for measuring the extent of a country's decentralization, namely, the distribution of autonomous revenues among the levels of government, we see that Canada is the only country in which the central government controls less than one half of the mandatory levies of governments (48.1 percent in 1988 according to the IMF). It is followed closely by the provinces, which, even before they received the manna of federal transfer payments, in 1988 received 41.3 percent of government revenues, compared to 24.6 percent for the Swiss cantons, 24.4 percent for the American states, and 22.1 percent for the German lander. The municipal level is less well-off in Canada, with 11.5 percent of government revenues, compared to 22.1 percent in Switzerland, 16.5 percent in the United States, and 13.8 percent in Germany. Canada, moreover, is the only one of these federations in which the trend is toward increasing the relative share of the provinces in relation to the central government (Dion 1992, p. 84, table 2). Since we know that Quebec is itself a particularly centralized provincial government that intervenes in more sectors of activity than the other nine provinces, with its pension fund, its international role, its accepted autonomy in matters of taxation and immigration, we can conclude that Quebec is the most powerful second level of government of all OECD countries.

Very few Quebecers are aware of this fact. But it generates the sense that the step would not be so big to change this quasistate in a true sovereign country. It induces a taste of independence among Quebec bureaucrats and politicians to the point that any intervention from the federal government is received as an intolerable intrusion by many of them. Since so many federal and provincial jurisdictions overlap, new initiatives of the federal government inevitably lead to protests. For example, in 1992 jurisdictional conflicts arose over communication and environmental policies. The Parti Québécois, with the support of many experts, is confident that under a sovereign Quebec, a lot of economies would be easily made by eliminating federal and provincial duplications (but see Treasury Board of Canada 1991).

Since the beginning of 1990, with secessionist sentiment higher than ever before, federal institutions have been under attack in French Quebec. More and more politicians and experts are confident that the help of the federal government is not essential. The perception that a sovereign Quebec would be able to maintain the level of public services without necessarily increasing the fiscal burden was well served by the budgetary policy of the current Conservative government. In order to decrease its huge annual deficits, the federal government began to restrict the growth in the amount of money that is sent to the provinces for such services as health, welfare, and higher education and for equalization payments to the poorer provinces. It further reduced its economic role by privatizing important crown corporations.

The opinion that "Canada is useless now" has gained extensive credibility because of another factor: the challenge of the international economy. The perception is that the federation no longer offers useful economic protection in a time of trade globalization and liberalization. The 1989 Free Trade Agreement with the United States helped to generate this opinion among many economists, business people, politicians, and citizens (Courchene 1986; Landry 1987; Martin 1994). The impression is that the future of the Quebec economy will be increasingly north-south. Regarding the east-west market, many believe that access to this market is already secured by the free-trade agreement, GATT rules, a mutual interest in commerce, and globalization of the economy, irrespective of whether Quebec remains a province of Canada or secedes. During the 1980 referendum campaign, this optimistic view was not really shared outside the circles of the Parti Québécois. In 1990-2 it probably would have rallied the majority of French-speaking economists in Quebec.

One very popular concept is "Quebec Inc," – the idea that a compact elite and a homogeneous society are better able to foster cooperation and to cope with international competition than is a heavy and heterogeneous federation paralyzed by regional jealousy and incessant intergovernmental conflict.

The confidence of the French-speaking political and economic elites in their ability to independently manage a modern state without a decline in the standard of living has never been so high. Still, this optimism has its limits.

It has been strongly challenged by the deep economic recession that hit the eastern part of North America since 1990. Unemployment in Quebec reached 12 percent. Month after month enterprises went bankrupt. Many new stars of the Quebec business establishment struggled financially. Beginning in February 1991, prominent business leaders in Quebec began to warn that independence would be a very risky business (Guay 1992). Both the federalist and the sovereignist camps created associations of business leaders supporters – the *Regroupement Economie et Constitution* and the *Regroupement Souveraineté-Québec Inc.* – but the former is much more important.

The most important set of uncertainties is related to the maintenance of a close economic association between an independent Quebec and Canada, after a likely acrimonious breakup (Banting 1992, pp. 166–7). Even though the weight of the U.S. market is increasing in Quebec imports and exports (Meadwell 1993, pp. 227, table 4), Quebec remains the most dependent of all provinces on the internal Canadian market. Thus the assumption that the rest of Canada will not engage in protective policies damaging to the Quebec economy is all the more risky. The most important Quebec business association, the *Conseil du patronat*, stressed its concern on this matter (Raynaud, 1991, pp. 13–14, 55).

The debate about currency reinforces the impression that secessionist arguments are fragile. One would expect that a confident Quebec would be eager to create and control its own currency. In fact, even Parti Québécois leader Jacques Parizeau said that he would keep the Canadian dollar, even without the agreement of the Canadian Parliament and without holding any control over the central bank of Canada. The idea of an autonomous monetary policy is not popular.

Another concern is Quebec's share of Canadian debts. With an accumulated debt of $450 billion, more than 60 percent of the GNP, the Canadian federal government has one of the worst financial records in the OECD. Moreover, Quebec is itself the Canadian provincial government with the worst financial record, after Newfoundland. This enormous debt contracted in Canadian dollars would be even harder to reimburse with a devalued Quebec currency (McCallum 1992).

An issue that is gaining visibility is the integration into the Quebec public sector of more than one hundred thousand Quebecers currently employed by the federal government. This would be an enormous task that may easily become an inextricable mess (Corbeil 1991; Dion and

Gow 1992, pp. 80–1). The Parti Québécois committed itself to hiring all those Quebecers, with the same status and working conditions that they enjoyed, but the Liberal party said that that would be too costly. In addition would come the cost of economic support to the Quebec part of the national capital region, which is currently heavily dependent on the Canadian federal government.

Many other doubts have been raised about the profitability of sovereignty (among them: the emigration of thousands of Quebec's wealthiest and most educated citizens). But the matter is no longer only an issue of profitability, since recently it has been complicated by territorial issues. First, native peoples warned with more insistence than ever that they would not allow their ancestral territories to be annexed to an independent Quebec. They started an intensive Canadian and international lobby to win support for their cause. Second, a few English-Canadian intellectuals have argued that if Quebec secedes it should leave with no more than the territories it had in 1867, when the confederation began. All lands ceded to Quebec by federal laws in 1898 and 1912 should be given back, they claim (Bercuson and Cooper 1991). Such a point of view has been echoed by at least one prominent Canadian politician: Clyde Wells, premier of Newfoundland. These territorial claims mean that Quebec might lose three-quarters of its territory – all the northern land – with the natural resources and the hydroelectric dams and potential. In practice, it would be reduced to the Saint Lawrence valley.

In short, the new self-confidence extended optimism about the profitability of sovereignty, but not to the point of building a firm consensus blotting out numerous sources of doubt.

Feeling of rejection: The constitutional crisis

English Canada's refusal in June 1990 to include in the Constitution proposals that were almost unanimously viewed in French Quebec as minimum conditions had a very strong effect on public opinion in the province. It generated an intense feeling of rejection. A common interpretation was that *"les Anglais* do not want us anymore." According to a 1991 poll, "as many as 67 percent of Quebec respondents (and 75 percent of the Francophones) agreed, most of them strongly, with the statement that 'Québécois were right to feel humiliated by Meech Lake's rejection' " (Pinard 1992, p. 488).

To understand this current French Quebecers' feeling of rejection, one must go back to the 1980 referendum campaign. At that time, Canadian Prime Minister Trudeau pledged to renew federalism if the referendum of the Parti Québécois was rejected (Clarkson and McCall 1990, pp. 238-9). In Quebec the expression "renewed federalism" was broadly understood as synonymous with "new powers for Quebec in the federation," that is, the traditional claim of the Quebec government. But no gain of that sort for the Quebec government was included in the Constitution Act of 1982. The idea that Trudeau made a voluntarily ambiguous statement in 1980 to attract the votes of soft nationalists is a major claim of the nationalist camp.

The second important event was the way the Quebec government was isolated during the 1981-2 Constitutional negotiations. The final negotiation occurred during the night of November 4, 1981. René Lévesque, then premier of Quebec and leader of the Parti Québécois, was absent. Such an isolation of Lévesque has been clearly perceived as unfair to the point that many nationalists deny any legitimacy to the Constitutional Act, 1982 (Laforest 1991).

So the Constitutional Act was implemented in 1982, without the consent of the province of Quebec. The next significant event is the federal electoral campaign of 1984. Brian Mulroney and Progressive Conservative party candidates endorsed the point of view that Trudeau's ambiguous statement in 1980 was an intellectual fraud, that the way Quebec was isolated in 1981-2 was a shame. Brian Mulroney solemnly committed himself to reintegrate Quebec in the Constitution with "honor and enthusiasm" (Fournier 1991, p. 32). In other words, the new prime minister of Canada legitimized the view that the rest of Canada owed reparation to Quebec.

By 1987 it was not the secessionist René Lévesque who sat at the negotiating table but the federalist Robert Bourassa, reelected in December 1985. Robert Bourassa brought the shortest list of constitutional demands ever requested by a government of Quebec: recognition of Quebec as a distinct society; a greater role in immigration; a role in appointments to the Supreme Court; limitation on federal spending power; and a veto on Constitutional amendments. His conditions roughly reflected the terms of the agreement reached at Meech Lake on June 3, 1987, between the prime minister of Canada and the ten provincial premiers. The government of Quebec, as well as the Quebec federal MPs of the Conservative party, and Prime Minister Mulroney claimed that they had indeed succeeded in reintegrating Quebec in the Constitution with "honor and enthusiasm."

Yet the story did not proceed as they hoped. The federal Parliament and ten provincial legislatures had three years to ratify the accord. Newly elected premiers declared themselves not committed by the signature of their predecessors. The Meech Lake agreement failure resulted, ultimately, in June 1990, from the refusal of two small provinces, Newfoundland and Manitoba, to give their assent to the accord.

Then, Premier Bourassa decided to boycott any negotiations with the other first ministers as long as the Meech Lake conditions were not accepted. The federal government engaged in a huge number of consultations, commissions, and reports (Rocher 1992). All this resulted in July 7, 1992, in a frail accord involving all parts of Canada outside Quebec: the federal, provincial and territorial governments and representatives of aboriginal peoples (Government of Canada 1992). That the Meech Lake conditions were met in this accord was still an open question, but the innovation was elsewhere. Two new provisions were very badly received in Quebec.

First, there would be a senate in which all the ten provinces would share equal representation, as in the U.S. Senate. This is mainly a demand from the Western provinces, claiming that what they call "Central Canada" – that is Ontario and Quebec, the two most populous provinces – is overrepresented in the Executive as a result of the electoral system of single-member constituencies (for evidence of this, see Weaver, 1992, pp.36–7, table 1). Such a senate reform means that Quebec would have 10 percent of the senators, like tiny Prince Edward Island – and even less because the native peoples and the northern territories would have some senators as well. This Senate, however, would have only a veto power, and this under specific conditions. Yet, this equal senate quickly has been rejected by all political circles in Quebec. But at least three premiers of Anglophone provinces said that the new senate is a sine qua non condition for any agreement.

The other provision would give native peoples a Constitutional inherent right to self-government. The concrete meaning of this "inherent right" would be defined through negotiations and, in case of impasse, by the courts. That means that Quebec's territorial integrity would be an issue in the courts. Premier Bourassa committed himself to never accept it. The fact that English Canada conceded to native peoples such a huge power of negotiation, when it is so reluctant to even acknowledge Quebec as a "distinct society," is broadly perceived in Quebec as an unfair rule of double standard.

Robert Bourassa came back to the negotiation table, and after five days of long and tough discussions, on August 22, 1992, a unanimous deal was reached. The new senate was weaker than in the July 7 proposal, and Quebec was permanently guaranteed 25 percent of the seats in the first Chamber, the House of Commons. An inherent right to aboriginal self-government was recognized, but this would give no new territorial rights, and laws enacted by these governments would have to be compatible with provincial and federal laws. A devolution of powers to provincial governments was included in the accord, but this devolution was considerably less important that the one requested in the Allaire report.

Robert Bourassa geared up to fight for this accord. But, as we know, he lost. On Oct. 27, 1992, 56.6 percent of Quebecers and 55 percent of all Canadians rejected the deal. The *No* got the majority in six provinces out of ten. Many factors may explain this result: the unpopularity of the Conservative federal government, the complexity of the deal, some dissensions and bad strategic moves on the *Yes* side, and the fact that the deal was somewhat unachieved, leaving many clauses to be negotiated after the referendum. The divergence of views between the provinces are certainly a fundamental part of the explanation. Western provinces wanted a stronger senate, whereas Quebec thought that the one proposed was already too much. The proposed devolution of powers was described as a disappointment by *No* supporters in Quebec, whereas some poor provinces were concerned by a possible weakening of the federal government capacity to help them. The linguistic rights provisions seemed unclear and failed to secure French Quebecers.

The Meech Lake failure was overwhelmingly perceived as an affront in Quebec, and the subsequent negotiations failed. For the near future, there is no possibility to renew the Constitution. Quebecers will probably have to make a dramatic choice between the Canadian federation, as it is, and sovereignty. This choice is likely to be made in a referendum called after the next provincial election.

How to explain this impossibility to reach a Constitutional agreement? To answer, one must take a look at other provinces and not only at Quebec. English Canadians did not intend to reject Quebecers in rejecting Meech Lake, polls said *(La Presse* February 27, 1992, p. A–2). The answer is elsewhere.

First, there is the unanimous rule to be reached for any modifications of the Constitution concerning federal institutions. The federal Parliament and the legislatures of the ten provinces must agree on these issues. And even this was not regarded as sufficient in 1992: The majority support of the population in each province, expressed in a referendum, was now requested. It is doubtful that any democracy would be able to proceed to an important Constitutional change under such an iron collar. A Constitutional deal would have been adopted with a less rigid rule.

Second, there is the linguistic issue. I have already explained how much the language crisis over the Supreme Court decision interfered with this Constitutional debate. The "inside-outside" Bill 178 was opposed everywhere in English Canada and damaged the reputation of the Meech Lake Accord. It nourished anti-French and anti-Québécois attitudes.

Third, the constitutional negotiations created the rise of Constitutional lobbies, each one focusing on a specific issue. At the outset, Quebec's claims alone were on the table. Meech Lake allowed some gains only for Quebecers, although it gave them a veto power over further changes on federal institutions. For French-speaking Quebecers, this long-lasting Constitutional negotiation was supposed to be their round, the "Quebec round," the reparation that English Canada owed to them. But across Canada, various feminist, aboriginal, ethnic, and regional groups complained that the accord gave them nothing. This was a powerful strike against Meech Lake in the English-speaking provinces. In particular, the equal senate issue was on the back burner from the outset: The smallest provinces knew that they would never have the senate they dream about once a veto was given to Quebec. In fact, the Quebec government's claim for a massive devolution of power because of its cultural distinctiveness opened a Pandora's box. Some other provinces claimed to be distinct communities as well, and native leaders were in a position to claim the championship of distinctiveness. The Constitutional debate encouraged an escalation of confrontations and became a forum for battling interests. The mood was certainly not one of compromise during the 1992 referendum campaign.

But the main reason why these negotiations were so difficult is that they reached the level of symbolic politics. Abstractions like "distinct society," "equality among provinces," and "inherent rights" can easily set one population against another by presenting simplistic symbols leaving little room for compromise.

The strong impact of such symbols explains the puzzling results of attitudinal polls. On one hand, "support for sovereignty does *not* result from the belief that Quebec has been unfairly treated in the present federal system" (Blais and Nadeau 1992, p. 100). Indeed, Quebecers' retrospective judgments about the equity of the existing federal system are not particularly negative and sovereignty supporters are not significantly harsher than other respondents. Yet, a majority of Quebecers wish to exit from this federation. On the other hand, "Quebecers interpreted the failure [of the Meech Lake Accord] as the rejection of

Quebec's distinct society" (ibid). This underlies the highly symbolic character that the debate took when it was focussed on a notion as emotional as that of "distinct society."

A parallel analysis may be done about the Western provinces' commitment to senate reform. Polls indicate that even in Alberta, public support for a "Triple E" senate – that is, elected, equal, and effective – is surprisingly soft (Urquhart 1992). But acceptance of the Triple E became the symbolic evidence that central Canada cares about Western concerns, and not only about Quebec ones. It is clearly symbolic politics.

Such an abstract idea as the concept of "strict equality between provinces" seemed impossible to accommodate with a distinct-society clause that applied only to the province of Quebec. But the truth is that Quebec has long had a special status. Since the beginning of the federation, it has had its own legal system based on the French civil code, and it has expanded its role in important fields since the 1960s, such as a pension plan, immigration policy, fiscal arrangements, and international relations. Such arrangements were negotiated with the federal government in recent decades in a piecemeal fashion. The focus was on means at least as much as ends and on absolute principles. But when the time comes to speak about the Constitution or Supreme Court interpretations, absolute principles, symbolic slogans take precedence in the negotiation. One hardly hears about concrete means and current realities.

The current Constitutional debate puts Canadians in the obligation to all agree on the symbolic representation of their country or, at least, to enshrine a pan-Canadian ideology (Ajzenstat 1992). One may easily list older states than the Canadian federation that would not survive such an exercise. Many Quebecers believe that Canada is a bicultural country, a pact between "two founding nations," that is, the descendants of the British and the French. Many Canadians see Canada as a multicultural country and a pact between equal provinces. In absolute terms, these visions are irreconcilable (Taylor 1991; Stark 1992). But in normal times, outside the Constitutional debate, Ottawa and the provinces have been able to maintain an acceptable level of intergovernmental cooperation (Young, Faucher, and Blais 1984). Comparative studies show that relationships between linguistic groups are less conflictual in Canada than in Belgium, and that mutual appreciation of the French and English in Canada did not deteriorate between 1968 and 1988 (Blais 1991).

In many ways, it is the last round of a nonstop constitutional debate, five years old now, that put Quebec and the rest of Canada in the situation of feeling rejected by each other.

Conclusion

I began this paper by pointing out that the Quebec–Canada question must be regarded as a very instructive case study. Some lessons may be found for the purpose of comparative studies.

With respect to the feeling of fear, a country exposes itself to the challenge of secession if its Constitutional rules do not grant a solid protection to its minority. This is particularly true concerning language policy. Students of multilingual countries reached the conclusion that a fully bilingual region is impossible to achieve because when two languages freely compete in a territory, the dominant one displaces the other. This is why countries like Switzerland and Belgium built their unity in using territorial linguistic rules to provide to each linguistic group a full security of its own territory (Laponce 1987; Mc Rae 1983; Mc Rae 1986). This is exactly the aim of the Quebec government language policy except that it has not been endorsed by the Constitutional rules of the Canadian federation. Yet, Bill 101 is a soft policy in comparison with those existing in Switzerland or in Belgium. Anglophone institutions are extensively funded by the Quebec government, whereas there is no way to find public funding for a French school in Flanders, or for a Netherlandish school in Wallonia.

Regarding the feeling of confidence, the striking point is the conviction that the globalization of the economy gives to some regions the impression that their current central state is useless and that they can go on their own. Especially among the elite, there is the feeling in Quebec that the Canadian federation is less useful given international competition and the Free Trade Agreement with the United States. The same phenomenon is seen elsewhere: Edinburgh feels that it may escape from London, Barcelona from Madrid, because of the existence of the European Union. The coincidence of trade globalization and regional fragmentation, macro-economy and micro-polity, is a striking paradox of our time.

I said at the outset that the importance of considering fluctuations over time is the most important lesson to draw from the Quebec case. The short-term outlook may be changed by a variety of phenomena: recessions, wars, the rising or disappearance of a charismatic leader, and so on. In Quebec, such a catalyst came from a feeling of rejection that appeared strongly and suddenly. To this effect, the lesson to draw from the Quebec case concerns the importance of symbols. It is doubtful that French-speaking and English-speaking Canadians understood, or even cared, about the judicial quibbles of the never-ending Constitutional debate. But they understood very simple ideas. Francophones believed that English Canada did not recognize Quebec's distinctiveness because it did not agree to enshrine in the Constitution the obvious fact that Quebec is a "distinct society." This interpretation became a very strong symbol which darkened the perception that many Quebecers had of the rest of Canada.

A last lesson remains to conclude. According to the Quebec case at least, it seems a nationalist ideology performs badly in explaining itself. For Quebec nationalists, cultural distinctiveness is the key point. They claim that Quebec's systematic distinctiveness in comparison with Canada imposes sovereignty, or at least a massive devolution of powers to the government of Quebec. Both the Allaire and the Bélanger-Campeau reports are based on this reasoning.

In fact the distribution of powers between the federal and the provincial governments, as such, has never been a widespread concern among the Quebec population, before the 1990 Meech Lake failure. It simply did not move people to action, to the great disappointment of Quebec government officials who tried to get popular support for their struggles with the federal government (Morin 1991, pp. 598–602). And about cultural differences, some exist in addition to language between Francophones and Anglophones, regarding tastes, behaviors, and attitudes (L'Actualité 1992), but many of these differences are declining, and in the end the cultural convergence of French speakers and English speakers is striking. The two linguistic communities now share the same democratic and liberal values, the same concept of rights and freedoms, and the same range of opinions on the role of the state (Hunter 1977; Simeon and Blake 1980; Johnston 1986; Johnston and Blais 1988; Sniderman and others 1988; Sniderman and others 1989; Bashevkin 1990; Taylor 1991). Never have Anglophones and Francophones been so alike.

Nationalist elites claim that Quebec society is in many ways incompatible with English-Canadian society. This occurs precisely when the cultural dispositions of both societies are more similar than ever before. How to explain this paradox? It is Alexis de Tocqueville who foresaw that modernity would cause cultural convergence of populations and that it would encourage placing extreme value on cultural differences (Dion 1991a). As human groups lose their differences, they view them with nostalgia and put high value on the remaining ones. And because different groups increasingly share the same values, they compete more for the same goods and they also envy each other more. Cultural differences are fading as a strong sociological fact, at the same time that cultural identities are rising as an important political cleavage. That is exactly what happened in Canada. And I suspect that it is occurring in most places where there is the reemergence of nationalism.

References

Ajzenstat, Janet. 1992. "Constitution-Making: The Slipperly Slope to Secession." Mimeo.
Allaire, Report. 1991. Quebec Liberal Party Constitutional Committee. *A Quebec Free to Choose*. January.
Banting, Keith G. 1992. "If Quebec Separates: Restructuring Northern North America." In Weaver, R. Kent, ed. *The Collapse of Canada?*, 159–78. Washington D.C.: Brookings Books.
Bashevkin, Sylvia. 1990. "Solitudes in Collision? Pan-Canadian and Quebec Nationalist Attitudes in the late 1970s." *Comparative Political Studies* 23(1):3–24.
Beaud, Jean-Pierre. 1982. "Hiérarchie partisane et sélection sociale: l'exemple du Parti québécois." In Lemieux, Vincent, ed. *Personnel et partis politiques au Québec*, 229–52. Montreal: Boréal Express.
Bélanger, André J. 1974. *L'apolitisme des idéologies québécoises*. Quebec: Les Presses de l'Université Laval.
Bélanger-Campeau Commission. 1991. *Report of the Commission on the Political and Constitutional Future of Québec*. Quebec: Bibliothèque nationale du Québec.
Bercuson, David Jay, and Cooper, Barry. 1991. *Deconfederation: Canada Without Quebec*. Toronto: Key Porter.
Blais, André. 1991. "Le clivage linguistique au Canada." *Recherches sociographiques* 32 (1):43–54.
Blais, André, and Nadeau, Richard. 1984a. "La clientèle du Parti québécois: évolution de la clientèle de 1970 à 1981." In Crête, Jean, ed. *Comportement électoral au Québec*, 279–318. Chicoutimi: Gaëtan Morin.
　1984b. "La clientèle du OUI." In Crête, Jean, ed. *Comportement électoral au Québec*, 321–34. Chicoutimi: Gaëtan Morin.
　1992. "To Be or Not to Be Sovereignist: Quebeckers' Perennial Dilemma." *Canadian Public Policy* 28 (1):89–103.
Chambre de Commerce du Québec. 1990. *L'avenir politique et constitutionnel du Québec: sa dimension économique*. Report presented to the Commission on the Political and Constitutional Future of Quebec, November.
Clarkson, Stephen, and McCall, Christina. 1990. *Trudeau of Our Times*. Vol. 1: *The Magnificent Obsession*. Toronto: McLelland & Stewart.
Clift, Dominique. 1982. *Quebec Nationalism in Crisis*. Montreal: McGill-Queen's University Press.
Cloutier, Edouard, Guay, Jean H., and Latouche, Daniel. 1992. *Le virage. L'évolution de l'opinion publique au Québec depuis 1960 ou comment le Québec est devenu souverainiste*. Montréal: Québec/Amérique.

Conseil de la langue française du Québec. 1992. *Indicateurs de la situation linguistique au Québec.*
Corbeil, Michel. 1991. "Le grand désordre?" *Expression* (June): 38–41.
Courchene, Thomas J. 1986. "Market Nationalism." *Policy Options* (October): 7–12.
Dion, Stéphane. 1991a. "Le nationalisme dans la convergence culturelle: le Québec contemporain et le paradoxe de Tocqueville." in Hudon, Raymond, and Pelletier, Réjean, eds. *L'engagement intellectuel: Mélanges en l'honneur de Léon Dion*, 291–311. Quebec: les Presses de l'Université Laval.
⎯⎯⎯. 1991b. "Will Quebec Secede? Why Quebec Nationalism Is So Strong?" *The Brookings Review* 9 (4):14–21.
⎯⎯⎯. 1992. "Explaining Quebeec Nationalism." In Weaver, R. Kent, ed. *The Collapse of Canada?* 77–121. Washington, DC: Brookings Books.
Dion, Stéphane, and Gow, James Iain. 1992. "L'administration publique." In Monière, Denis, ed. *L'année politique au Québec*, 67–84. Montreal: Le Devoir-Québec/Amérique.
Edwards, John. 1984. *Linguistic Minorities, Policies and Pluralism.* San Diego, CA: Academic.
Elster, Jon. 1989. *Nuts and Bolts for the Social Sciences.* New York: Cambridge University Press.
Falardeau, Louis. 1992. "Majorité absolue pour le NON." *La Presse*, 24 October, p. A-1.
Forbes, H. D. 1992. *Multiculturalism: Some Elements of an Analysis.* Mimeo. Toronto: Department of Political Science, University of Toronto.
Fortin, Pierre. 1990. *Le choix forcé du Québec: aspects économiques et stratégiques.* Report presented to the Commission on the Political and Constitutional Future of Quebec. November.
Fournier, Pierre. 1991. *A Meech Lake Post-Mortem: Is Quebec Sovereignty Inevitable?* Montreal: McGill-Queen's University Press.
Fraser, Graham. 1984. *P.Q.: René Lévesque and the Parti Québécois in Power.* Toronto: Macmillan.
Gellner, Ernest. 1983. *Nations and Nationalism.* Ithaca, NY: Cornell University Press.
Geertz, Clifford. 1963. "The Integrative Revolution: Primordial Sentiments and Civil Politics in the New States." In Geertz, Clifford, ed. *Old Societies and New States*, 105–57. New York: Free Press.
Government of Canada, Federal-Provincial Relations Office. 1992. *Status Report: The Multilateral Meetings on the Constitution.* July 16.
Gray, Gwendolyn. 1991. *Federalism and Health Policy. The Development of Health Systems in Canada and Australia.* Toronto: University of Toronto Press.
Guay, Jean-H. 1992. "Le patronat: une année de crainte." In Monière, Denis, ed. *L'année politique au Québec*, 181–92. Montreal: Le Devoir-Québec/Amérique.
Hunter, A. A. 1977. "A Comparative Analysis of Anglophone-Francophone Occupational Prestige Structures in Canada." *Canadian Journal of Sociology* 2 (1):179–93.
Johnston, Richard. 1986. *Public Opinion and Public Policy in Canada: Questions of Confidence.* Toronto: University Press.

Johnston, Richard, and Blais, André. 1988. "Meech Lake and Mass Politics: The 'Distinct Society Clause.'" *Canadian Public Policy* 14 (4):25–42.
L'*Actualité*. 1992. "Qui sommes-nous: anatomie d'une société distincte." January.
Laforest, Guy. 1991. "L'esprit de 1982." In Balthazar, Louis, Laforest, Guy, and Lemieux, Vincent, eds. *Le Québec et la restructuration du Canada, 1980–1992*. Quebec: Septentrion.
Lambert, Ronald D., and Curtis, James E. 1982. "The French and English Language Communities and Multicultural Attitudes." *Canadian Ethnic Studies* 15 (2):43–58.
Landry, Bernard. 1987. *Commerce sans frontières: le sens du libre-échange*, Montreal: Québec/Amérique.
Laponce, Jean. 1987. *Languages and Their Territories*, Toronto: University of Toronto Press.
Lessard, Denis. 1992a. "Un Québec souverain ferait toujours partie du Canada", *La Presse*, March 30, A-12.
——— 1992b. "L'appui à la souveraineté se maintient à 46 p. cent", *La Presse*, June 22, A-1.
Martin, Pierre. 1994. "Free Trade and Party Politics in Quebec." In Doran, Charles F., and Marchildon, Gregory P., eds. *The NAFTA Puzzle: Political Parties and Trade in North America*, 143–71. Boulder, CO: Westview Press.
McRae, Kenneth. 1983. *Conflict and Compromise in Multilingual Societies: Switzerland*. Waterloo: Wilfrid Laurier University Press.
——— 1986. *Conflict and Compromise in Multilingual Societies: Belgium*. Waterloo: Wilfrid Laurier University Press.
McCallum, John. 1992. *Canada's Choice: Crisis of Capital or Renewed Federalism*. Toronto: C. D. Howe.
McRoberts, Kenneth. 1988. *Quebec: Social Change and Political Crisis*. 3d ed. Toronto: McClelland & Stewart.
Meadwell, Hudson. Forthcoming. "The Politics of Nationalism in Quebec." *World Politics*.
Nadeau, Richard, and Niemi, Richard G. 1992. "Gaining Knowledge About the Sources of Political Knowledge: A Multivariate Perspective." Rochester, NY: University of Rochester. Mimeo.
Noël, Alain. 1993. "Politics in a High Unemployment Society." In Gagnon, Alain G., ed. *Quebec: State and Society*. 2nd ed., 422–49. Toronto: Nelson Canada.
Pinard, Maurice. 1992. "The Dramatic Reemergence of the Quebec Independence Movement." *Journal of International Affairs* 45 (2):471–97.
Pinard, Maurice, and Hamilton, Richard. 1978. "The Parti Québécois Comes to Power: An Analysis of the 1976 Quebec Election." *Canadian Journal of Political Science* 11 (4):739–75.
——— 1989. "The Leadership of Intellectuals in Traditional Parties: Canadian and Comparative Perspectives." In Gagnon, Alain G., and Tanguay, A. Brian, eds. *Canadian Parties in Transition*. Scarborough, Ont: Nelson Canada.
Proulx, Pierre-Paul. 1990. *L'évolution de l'espace économique du Québec, la politique économique dans un monde de nationalismes et d'interdépendance, et les relations Québec-Ottawa*. Report presented to the Commission on the Political and Constitutional Future of Quebec. October.

Raynaud, André. 1990. *Les enjeux économiques de la souveraineté: Mémoire soumis au C.P.O.* Montreal: Conseil du Patronat. October.
Rocher, François. 1992. "Le dossier constitutionnel." In Monière, Denis, ed. *L'année politique au Québec,* 85–116. Montreal: Le Devoir-Québec/Amérique.
Simeon, Richard, and Blake, Donald E. 1980. "Regional Preferences: Citizen's Views of Public Policy." In Elkins, David J., and Simeon, Richard, eds. *Small Worlds: Provinces and Parties in Canadian Political Life,* 77–105. Toronto: Methuen.
Smith, Anthony D. 1991. *National Identity.* Harmondsworth: Penguin Books.
Sniderman, Paul M., et al. "Liberty, Authority and Community: Civil Liberties and the Canadian Political Culture." Paper prepared for presentation at the 1988 annual meeting of the Canadian Political Science Association.
Stark, Andrew. 1992. "English-Canadian Opposition to Quebec Nationalism." In Weaver, R. Kent, ed. *The Collapse of Canada?* 123–58. Washington D.C.: Brookings Books.
Statistics Canada. 1988–9. *Dimensions Series.* Ottawa: Minister of Supply and Services. Publications 93-151-57.
Taylor, Charles. 1991. "Shared and Divergent Values." In Watts, Ronald, and Brown, Douglas, eds. *Options for a New Canada,* 53–76. Toronto: University of Toronto Press.
Treasury Board of Canada, Secretariat. 1991. *Federal-Provincial Overlap and Duplication: A Federal Program Perspective.* 12 December.
Tremblay, Rodrigue. 1990. *Le statut politique et constitutionnel du Québec.* Report presented to the Commission on the Political and Constitutional Future of Quebec. November.
Urquhart, Ian. 1992. "On Senate Reform." *Constitutional Forum* 3 (3):67–9.
Vaillancourt, François. 1989. "Demolinguistic Trends and Canadian Institutions: An Economic Perspective." In *Demolinguistic Trends and the Evolution of Canadian Institutions.* Ottawa: Commissioner of Official Languages.
Waring, Stephen P. 1991. "The Rationality of Feelings." In *Taylorism Transformed. Scientific Management Theory Since 1945,* 104–31. Chapel Hill, NC: The University of North Carolina Press.
Weaver, R. Kent. 1992. "Political Institutions and Canada's Constitutional Crisis." In Weaver, R. Kent, ed. *The Collapse of Canada?* 7–75. Washington, D.C.: Brookings Books.
Young, Robert. 1991. "How to Head Off the Crisis." *Globe and Mail.* 10, January, p. A-17.
Young, Robert A., Faucher, Philippe, and Blais, André. 1984. "The Concept of Province-Building: A Critique." *Canadian Journal of Political Science* 17 (4):783–818.

CHAPTER 7

Notes on the political economy of nationalism

Ronald Findlay

The resurgence of nationalism all over the world in the last few years can be said to arise, in every case, from a lack of congruence between "state" and "nation." While each of these terms is highly complex and controversial, we all know the main difference between them. The state is a political and administrative unit, claiming the "monopoly of the legitimate use of force" over all the inhabitants of a given territory. The nation, on the other hand, is an "imagined community," including the dead and the unborn, who are bound together by the ties of kinship, language, custom, and shared myths that separate it from other similar collectivities.[1] Thus we can have a nation without a state, as in the case of the Kurds, or states that comprise many nations, such as the former USSR and Yugoslavia, and a nation divided between several states, as in the case of the Italians and Germans before unification in the nineteenth century, or the two Germanys and two Koreas of more recent history.

It is tempting to specify the one-to-one correspondence between state and nation as a sort of long-run equilibrium condition, which generates persistent turbulence whenever it is not fulfilled. There are many ways in which the movement toward equilibrium can take place. A single nation could establish a powerful state that expands to incorporate other nations within it. The "subject" nations might then assimilate gradually to the dominant one, by adopting its language, culture, and religion so that eventually all the citizens of the state come to feel themselves as essentially one nation. Something like this is what happened in the case of the "old continuous nations" of Western Europe,

---
[1] On the concept of a nation as an "imagined community," see the influential work of Benedict Anderson (1983).

such as Britain and France.[2] In the case of movements for national unification, one of the states of the common nation, Prussia under Bismarck or Piedmont under Cavour, prevailed upon the others by force and diplomacy to create what roughly corresponded to genuine nation–states.

The problems of nationalism that are exercising us most today, however, are all the legacy of the collapse of the great empires of the last few hundred years, that of the Hapsburgs, the Russians (first under the czars and then the communists), and the Ottoman, in Central and Eastern Europe and the Middle East, and the European colonial empires in Asia and Africa. In almost *no* case is there a congruence between state and nation in any one of the successor states of those former empires. One exception is Austria, the core of the Hapsburg Empire, where we have a mainly German-speaking Roman Catholic nation. Hungary is itself more or less ethnically homogeneous but about one third of the Hungarians in the world live as minorities in Romania, the Voivodina province of Serbia in Yugoslavia, and the Slovak part of Czechoslovakia, which has split into the Czech lands and Slovakia, so that only the former will be ethnically homogeneous. Yugoslavia is of course the most intractable case of all with the still unresolved secession of Slovenia, Croatia, and Bosnia-Herzegovina, as well as the difficult problem of Kosovo and the Albanians and the many complexities of Macedonia.

In the case of the former Soviet Union, the ethnic problems are also painfully apparent. Substantial Russian ethnic minorities are located in Ukraine, the Baltic states, Kazakhstan and Moldova while ethnic feuds have already broken out in the Caucasus and some of the Central Asian republics. Russia itself has substantial minorities such as the Tartars within it.

In the Middle East, the dissolution of the Ottoman Empire left Iraq a rich and fertile territory very sharply divided on ethnic and religious lines, while leaving a large Kurdish minority in Turkey itself. Sudan has a major ethnic and religious problem between the Arabized Islamic north and the African non-Islamic south. Syria and Lebanon, in particular, have sharp sectarian differences within their populations.

Dozens, if not scores, of new states were created by the successive "decolonizations" after the World War II of the former imperial possessions of the British, French, Dutch, Belgians, and Portuguese. In

---

[2] See, however, the important new study by Linda Colley (1992) who argues that a "British" nation was "invented," *à la* Anderson, between 1707 and 1837, as a result of Protestantism, war, and empire, in a manner that transcended, without blending or fusing, the constituent English, Welsh, and Scottish national identities.

most cases, this process resulted in the formation of states whose borders contained highly disparate populations, that had not constituted integrated communities prior to the European dominion. In many cases, as with the Indians in East Africa, significant components of the populations were immigrants from other, quite distant, colonies. Many of these colonial territories had strong nationalist movements that agitated and fought for independence, under unifying ideologies that stressed the common links of the subject populations as against the colonial rulers. After independence, however, severe conflicts emerged on the basis of what Clifford Geertz (1973) calls the "primordial" diversities of ethnicity, language, and religion.

In many cases the European colonial states were much larger and more integrated than their predecessors, such as the Mughal Empire in India or the sultanates in the East Indies. The newly independent postcolonial states therefore all faced critical secession struggles during or soon after their emergence. In some cases they have been successful, for example Bangladesh, but for the most part they have failed, as with the attempt of Biafra to break away from Nigeria.

Another completely different type of state was also created by the European expansion over the rest of the world during the last few centuries. This is the type of state established in the New World and in Australia and New Zealand with settlers of mainly European origin. Although there are exceptions such as Mexico and Peru, where significant numbers of the indigenous populations survived, for the most part these new European overseas states eliminated the original inhabitants as a result of disease and warfare. In these states there has either been a dominant European group such as the Spanish in Latin America, or a "melting pot" of largely European origin, as in the United States. In neither case has there been a significant "nationality" as distinct from simply ethnic problem within the boundaries of the state. An important exception, of course, is the French-Canadians of Quebec.

The outcome has been very different when Europeans settled in Africa. In Algeria the *pied noir* left after a very bitter war of independence, as did most of the British from Kenya and to a lesser extent Zimbabwe. Thus the potential nationality problem in these cases has been solved by the emigration of the European settlers. In South Africa, however, the peculiarly intractable and potentially still explosive problem remains of how to accommodate three or four million people of European descent with five or six times that number of natives and Asian immigrants.

Nationalism is the ideology that animates a people who feel the sense of cultural identity that we associate with the concept of nation. It stresses what sets them apart from others and thus serves as a support in struggles with other nations within the same state, or in other states. It is generally regarded as having arisen in France during the time of the French Revolution and to have spread to the rest of Europe in the course of the Revolutionary and Napoleonic wars, in imitation of or opposition to the nation that founded it. As Huizinga (1940) has stressed the emotion of patriotism and the sense of national consciousness and identity can be traced back to antiquity and the Middle Ages. These however were subordinated to the influence of the "universal" religion of the Roman Catholic church, the feudal magnates and dynastic states. It was only after national unification had already taken place in France and Great Britain that nationalism in the modern sense emerged. This is the "received doctrine," ably expounded in surveys by Minogue (1970), Alter (1989), Smith (1979), and especially Seton-Watson (1977).

Despite the vast extent of the literature, analytical "theories" or "models" of nationalism that attempt to account for the phenomenon in terms of some unifying *Gestalt* are unfortunately rather scarce.

The most ambitious and stimulating theory of nationalism I have encountered is that of Ernest Gellner (1983). His theory is cast in terms of an evolutionary view of the historical process, in the nineteenth-century manner of Comte, Morgan, and Marx, in which the economic system is first based on hunting and gathering, then agriculture and finally industry. Specialization and the division of labor can be highly developed in agrarian societies, particularly the agrarian empires of the Orient, but "culture" in the sense of an integrated symbolic system based on a written language is confined to a narrow class of priests and bureaucrats. The "cultures" of the peasantry, who form the productive base of the system, are confined to purely local dialects and cults. Conflict in this type of society is confined to peasant rebellions or power struggles over control of the state by different aristocratic or bureaucratic factions, but the higher culture itself remains invariant and common to all contending parties, or is acquired by successful outsiders, as in the case of the "barbarian" invaders of China such as the Mongols and the Manchus.

Specialization and the division of labor take a completely different dynamic form in "industrial" society. Rather than each worker learning a traditional craft and practicing it for life in a closed guild or caste, as in agrarian society, all workers must be highly mobile and versatile between specializations on the basis of a high common level of general education. Integration of the economy through market forces takes the place of rent and tax payments in kind, requiring the transmission and reception of complex "messages" over a wide area in some common medium. Thus we have the development of uniform literary languages for efficient dissemination to a wide public in print. Everyone's horizons are broadened by these contacts and a common "national" culture develops for the whole society instead of the previous diversity of "local" cultures. The incessant technical change of industrial society requires education to be extended to all, with an increasingly high minimal level.

If all these changes take place within a culturally homogeneous society, where "culture" essentially means language and its usual associations of a shared history, all is well and the society can progress in a peaceful manner. Contrary to Marx, class differences based on property and income do not lead to revolution and are eventually ironed out by competition in the market place based on merit and achievement. Rewards are unequally distributed but all have access and the opportunity to compete.

Suppose, however, that there are two "cultures" in the society instead of one, in the Gellner rather than the C. P. Snow sense. Furthermore, suppose that one of them, the "Hapsburg" or the "Ottoman" one, enjoys an effective monopoly of public offices and access to higher education, both of which are conducted in a language distinct from that of the subordinate "Czech" or "Serbian" culture. Economic development is at such a level that Czechs and Serbs are active participants in the economy, but are deprived of the opportunities for higher public office and education.

This situation creates, in Gellner's view, the classic "Hapsburg (and points east and south)" nationalism that has been so potent a force, for good and evil, in Central and Eastern Europe and the Balkans for the last hundred and fifty years and is now raging again after the communist interlude, with the "return of history" as Misha Glenny (1990) calls it. In terms of the simple "two-culture" model that Gellner adopts to derive his typology of nationalisms, the solution is obtained by the subject nation casting off the yoke of the dominant one and expelling it from the territory that both occupied, as a result of war, revolution, or voluntary surrender by the ruling power.

The other main type of nationalism that Gellner identifies is the "Western liberal" or "Risorgimento" type of nationalism exemplified by the efforts of Mazzini, Cavour, and Victor Emmanuel to bring about the unification of Italy. In terms of Gellner's parsimonious theoretical categories, the difference with the "Hapsburg" case is that the subordinate group is deprived *only* of political power, and *not* of access to education and general culture. One way of putting it is that in the "Hapsburg" case the subject people can develop their national culture more fully only *after* political emancipation, whereas they have already achieved their full cultural identity in the "Risorgimento" case. This distinction therefore roughly corresponds to the well-known dichotomy proposed by John Plamenatz (1976) between "Western" and "Eastern" varieties of nationalism.

Although the leaders of nationalist movements may be perfectly sincere in the altruism of their motives, which in fact many of them demonstrate by risking execution and torture in the course of their struggles for independence, once in power they become dispensers of patronage on a lavish scale. Positions once reserved for the alien ruling elite are now occupied by fellow nationals, and additional opportunities are opened up by new "nation-building" activities. Typically it is the intelligentsia among the subject nations that are the beneficiaries of the new dispensation. Middle-class jobs in the public sector for French-Canadians, in replacement of English-Canadians, is the major outcome of nationalism in Quebec, in the refreshingly cynical interpretation of the "economics of nationalism" put forward by Albert Breton (1964). Gellner also is sardonically aware of this point, in his parable of how Ruritania obtained independence from the Empire of Megalomania (p. 61). Examples of massive and economically ruinous expansions of public sector employment are all too plentiful from recent experience in the Third World.

One implication of Gellner's model, which to my surprise does not seem to have been noted, is that it fails to predict any "nationalist" outcome for the "old continuous nations" of England and France and, for that matter, Japan. This is because over the long period of this internal development these states and nations were able to forge a relatively homogenous cultural identity, in Gellner's sense, and so in his view there could not be such a thing as "old industrial country" nationalism. Nationalism therefore becomes exclusively an "ideology of delayed industrialization," in the sense of Alexander Gerschenkron (1962), associated with a movement against an alien ruling elite.

But is there really no such thing as English, French, or Japanese nationalism? The French, after all, are generally regarded as having "invented" nationalism during the course of the French Revolution and to have exported it at the points of the bayonets of their armies to the rest of Europe. The existence of Japanese nationalism would certainly not be doubted by anyone who experienced World War II in the Far East, and was it really in a "fit of absence of mind" that Britain acquired her empire as Gellner (p. 42) implies, even generalizing the idea from Britain to all of Europe?[3]

It seems to me to be a severe defect of Gellner's approach that he adopts, in common with much of nineteenth-century evolutionary type of thinking, a view of history in which the collective units being studied (societies, states, nations) are all lined up on parallel tracks with the trains leaving at successive dates. What is missing (except for the implicit spread of "industrial" technology) is any interaction between the units in either conflict or cooperation. While I have little else in common with the view of Immanuel Wallerstein (1974), I share completely his insistence that it is necessary to study nations interacting within a global *system* to make proper sense of the modern world. I see nationalism emerging from the process of internal integration and unification, which combined political, social and cultural factors such as language and religion, in the "old continuous *states*" of France, Spain, and England, together with their national *rivalry* over commerce and overseas possessions inaugurated by the voyages of discovery. In other words, I would date the emergence of nationalism to the age of mercantilism rather than to the spread of the Industrial Revolution to Central and Southern Europe, a difference of more than two centuries.[4]

As Schumpeter (1951, p. 211) says, "Nationalism is affirmative awareness of national character, together with an aggressive spirit of superiority. It arose from the autocratic state." The competing states in early modern Western Europe, engaged simultaneously in the "internal colonialism" of absorbing border areas and fighting each other overseas for access to the riches of the New World, each developed both spontaneously and by design complex interlocking myths of national identity to support them in the execution of these activities. While much of this activity was focused on the glorification of the monarchs, particularly Elizabeth I and Louis XIV, the extolling of the nation was inseparable from that of the rulers. As many have argued it was this element of incessant competition between the industrial units of the European state system in the early modern period that might account for the "rise of the West" as compared with the agrarian empires of the East.[5] In Northern and Eastern Europe also it is possi-

---

[3] Linda Colley's book, cited earlier, is a convincing refutation of this view in the case of Britain.
[4] See once again the work of Colley, and for the Elizabethan roots of English nationalism the interesting new study by Helgerson (1992).
[5] See Findlay (1992) for a brief survey of these issues, with references.

ble to link the emergence of national consciousness in Poland, Denmark, Sweden, and Russia to their struggles over control of the Baltic trade. Again, strong monarchs such as Gustavus Adolphus and Peter the Great were much involved in the shaping of these images of national identity.[6]

The element of what George Orwell (1945, p. 412) calls "competitive prestige," inseparably associated with the idea of nationalism, also appears to have played a major role in the drive for German unification in the nineteenth century. In terms of Gellner's model it is not clear why there should have been any German nationalism at all. It is true that they were divided into thirty-nine states in the German Confederation devised by the Congress of Vienna in 1815, but the rulers were in every case German. The movement was therefore essentially for unity rather than "independence" from alien domination. What exercised German nationalists was that the division of the nation into so many states put it at a disadvantage with respect to its European rivals, the French in the West and the Russians in the East. This "competitive" factor was significant in the Italian case as well, even though there was foreign domination present in some parts of Italy.

The problems of nationalism in the world today fall into three categories: (1) Movements for autonomy and even secession by ethnically or culturally distinct regions in advanced industrial countries, such as Quebec in Canada, the Basques and the Catalans in Spain, and Northern Ireland, Scotland and Wales in Great Britain; (2) the break-up of the former Soviet Union, Yugoslavia, and Czechoslovakia into component republics on the basis of distinct ethnic and cultural identity; and (3) ethnic tensions and clashes in developing countries such as the conflict between the Buddhist Sinhalese and the Hindu Tamils in Sri Lanka.

The rest of this paper is devoted to examining each of these problems in the light of the approaches considered earlier.

The first set of issues raises the question of why they arise in the first place. In advanced industrial countries which all of them are (with the possible exception of Spain) economic development and "modernization" should by now have welded the different communities together into a homogeneous national consciousness. Regional concerns always arise, of course, but why can they not be settled within a single state, with a federal structure if necessary?

Gellner's answer is that it is not only the level and extent of devel-

---

[6] See Kirby (1990).

opment that matters but whether or not it is "uneven." Systematically underachieving groups in Canada, say, could not have a focal point for their discontent to rally around if they share the language, religion, and other cultural accoutrements of the majority of their fellow citizens. If, however, a substantial proportion of some culturally identifiable group, French-speaking Roman Catholics, who moreover are concentrated in a particular region, Quebec, feel themselves to be denied full equality with their fellow citizens, then we have an instance for an outbreak of a nationalist movement within Gellner's model. Of course, the intellectuals who lead the movement can "do well by doing good" for their community, as in Breton's model which, as we have seen, is fully compatible with Gellner's more general formulation.

The claim by Gellner (1979, p. 275) that the model can account for Northern Ireland is more doubtful. It is true that the Catholics can be considered an underprivileged group, but it does not seem plausible to regard this factor as being responsible for the extraordinary violence and bitterness associated with the nationalist movement. Better jobs and prospects for the Catholics would not assuage the long and tragic history of Irish relations with the English state that is the underlying cause, which only complete British withdrawal could assuage.

Gellner (1979, p. 276) quite frankly admits, however, that his model does not fit the case of Scotland. Here one cannot argue that the inhabitants of the region are systematically disadvantaged relative to the rest of Britain. How then to account for the phenomenon of Scottish nationalism? While there are certainly enough examples of violent repression such as the massacre of Glencoe in the past, it does not appear that Scottish nationalism has the same roots as the Irish, since relations were peaceful after the Jacobite rising of 1745. Scots were active and successful participants in British developments for a long time before the modern revival of nationalist impulses.[7]

What seems to be involved in the Scottish case, and perhaps that of the Basques and Catalans as well, is nationalism as a collective consumer good, that a group demands as a means of overcoming the sterile homogeneity of contemporary culture. All are fluent in the dominant community's language, so that the desire for a revival of Gaelic is not related to economic performance but is rather in the nature of a luxury public good that the group desires to consume. The emphasis here is not on nationalism as a rationalization for a policy of middle-class jobs for members of the group as in the case of Breton's model. Rather it is on manifestations of the group's cultural identity

---

[7] Particularly in the army and the empire, as Colley stresses.

through architecture, monuments, literature, dress, music, and so on, which they fear will not be catered for sufficiently under existing political arrangements.[8]

Such feelings by themselves may be insufficient to generate sufficient separatist sentiment unless reinforced by memories of historical oppression as in the Irish and French-Canadian cases. What may reinforce it is whether or not the region is a net contributor or recipient in relation to the national budget. In the case of Quebec, which is a net recipient, the center can use transfers as a bargaining chip to preserve unity. In the case of Scotland, the North Sea oil was a factor in the opposite direction. The unwillingness to continue sustained transfers to other regions, as in the case of the Lombard League in Northern Italy, is a good indicator of the erosion of the sense of national identity. There is also of course a strong "free-rider" element in many of the secession movements, since they are well aware that defense and other public goods in most cases cannot be effectively withheld from them by the rest of the country in the event of separation.

When the Bolsheviks inherited the Russian empire they were faced with the difficult problem of preserving the revolution in a vast multiethnic territory that had only been held together by force. They were ready to do the same but their rule had at least nominally to be reconciled with their adherence to the principle of national autonomy for all peoples. They adopted a federal structure in which territorial divisions corresponded to ethnic divisions. The structure thus appeared to be one in which the different nationalities were joined together in a genuinely participatory way. As it turned out, however, this was merely a front for a sophisticated system of "imperial" rule from the center, with the hegemonic entity not being the Russian monarchy or even the Russian republic itself but the Party. The ruling elite in each republic was appointed and controlled by the centrally organized Party, with a bias in favor of the titular nationality of each republic, an interesting contrast to the usual imperial practice of appointing outsiders to administer provinces. Since these officials were creatures of the center, however, without any local power base, the essential principle was preserved. With access to higher education carefully controlled, this also ensured that the local intelligentsias

---

[8] Colley argues that the formerly unifying "British" identity no longer serves a functional purpose, with the cessation of war and the loss of empire, thus allowing the old Scottish and Welsh identities to assert themselves once again.

were co-opted into the system since the Party offered the only "career open to talent." Any attempt at independent ethnic organization was suppressed ruthlessly.

This Soviet nationality policy thus served both as the means of implementing the centrally determined plan in each region as well as a method of controlling the potentially troublesome ethnic elites. Movements of population from one republic to another were strictly regulated by an internal passport system. The policy worked remarkably well during the expansionary phase of Soviet development when massive investments under forced draft brought significant returns despite the waste and inefficiency. As development faltered, however, the system could only be propped up by resource transfers from more productive to poorer regions.

Thus, although Marxism, in common with liberalism and other Enlightenment doctrines, anticipated a "withering away" of ethnicity in the process of development, the Soviet system actually preserved and intensified nationality as an organizational principle. As the discipline of the center began to break down in attempts at reform, each republic had to look out for itself. Since the ruling elites reflected the dominant nationalities in each republic, it is not surprising that one solution to the problem of increasing scarcity was harsh discrimination against local minorities, such as that of the Uzbeks against the Meshketian Turks or the Georgians against the Ossetians. Conflicts between neighboring republics also broke out over disputed territory, such as that between Armenia and Azerbaijan over the Nagorno-Karabakh enclave, and over access to water and grazing lands in the Central Asian republics.

The breakdown of the center, in the absence of any intermediate associations of a "civil society," had the effect of "turning nationalities into political parties," as Victor Zaslavsky (1992) points out. This "ethnic mobilization" did *not* lead to demands for separation and independence in the Caucasus and Central Asia since these republics were net recipients of transfers from the center. The Baltic republics and Ukraine, however, on whose "surplus" the center was drawing, moved in the direction of breaking away. As Zaslavsky (p. 114) puts it, the former Soviet Union was "a state which unites a Norway and a Pakistan" (which is probably unfair both to Norway and to Pakistan), and was therefore not viable in the absence of centralized dictatorship.

The bloodshed and intolerance associated with the eruption of ethnic tensions in the southern and eastern republics fed the strongly negative image of nationalism as a destructive atavistic force by Western observers and governments. Two incongruous heirs of the Enlightenment disdain for the politics of ethnicity, Eric Hobsbawm (1990) and George Bush, both denounced what the latter referred to in his speech at Kiev as "suicidal nationalism."

Zaslavsky and many other writers say that this negative attitude towards nationalism in Europe and the United States, while justified for the Caucasus and Central Asia, is unfair and misguided in relation to the more "Western" or "European" nationalities, such as the Baltic peoples and Ukraine and Slovenia and Croatia in the former Yugoslavia with their higher stage of economic development in comparison to the other republics, and their Roman Catholic, Lutheran, or Uniate religious traditions. The Slovenian philosopher Tomaz Mastnak (1992) eloquently defends the idea of the nation–state in relation to these cases, on the same grounds as those enthusiastically supported by Western liberals in the nineteenth century with respect to the Greek, Italian, and other independence movements. He argues that the West, by delaying recognition of Slovenia and Croatia, encouraged Slobodan Milosevic and the Serbs to go on the rampage, thus making "Balkan tribalism" a self-fulfilling prophecy.

These are difficult and controversial issues. On the question of recognition it is very likely that it was *too early* recognition of Croatia and Slovenia that precipitated the horrifying "ethnic cleansing" in Bosnia.[9] There are also very legitimate questions about the commitment to democracy of the mostly communist leadership in these "Western" breakaway states and their treatment of minorities within their borders. The substantial Russian minorities in the Baltic states and Ukraine pose a particularly acute problem. The fact that Milosevic has apparently gotten away with his annexations in Bosnia cannot fail to tempt Yeltsin's successors, whoever they may be, to intervene in the Baltic states and Ukraine.

The discussion of nationalism in the Third World must unfortunately be particularly brief and confined to South and Southeast Asia. Here once again nationalism can be seen as the response of the diverse local cultures and peoples to modernization within a colonial framework, much along the lines of the Gellner model. The existence of high religions and the memory of powerful indigenous kingdoms, only recently overthrown, facilitated the growth of nationalist ideology by Western-educated elites. Unity was made possible between ethnically and linguistically diverse subject peoples by their common opposition

[9] See Glenny (1992, p. 179) for this view.

Notes on the political economy of nationalism   155

to colonial rule, with the language and ideas of the imperial powers providing the means for concerted resistance. In a process greatly accelerated by World War II, and the Japanese occupation of Southeast Asia, several newly independent states emerged.

Even before the colonial powers left, however, the ethnic and religious tensions between the local populations erupted violently, most notably in the separation of British India between India and Pakistan in 1947. India, with its huge population and extreme linguistic and religious diversity, is and will long continue to be a fascinating laboratory experiment in the saga of nationalism and the nation–state. Hugh Seton-Watson (1977, p. 196) asks a good question: "Is India a multilingual nation or a multinational state?" Despite powerful centrifugal forces such as the Sikhs in the Punjab and the Tamils in the south, it would seem that the countervailing forces of economic development and the cultural unity of the huge and rapidly growing middle-class spread all over the country are more likely to prevail in the end. Films and television are other influences that have integrating power at lower educated levels of the population. The commitment of Nehru and the first generation of Congress leaders to the "secular" character of their new polity was unswerving and their legacy might be strong enough to resist the temptation of Hindu hegemony, or so at least one hopes, despite the destruction of the mosque at Ayodhya.

A prominent feature of economic development in Southeast Asia during the colonial period was the role of Indians and Chinese who migrated into the area in response to the opportunities opened up by the expansion of primary exports. These communities mainly were involved in wholesale and retail trade, along with the provision of credit in rural areas. After independence the Chinese communities in Thailand, Indonesia, and particularly Malaysia entered vigorously into the wider range of activities that became open to them in manufacturing, commerce, and finance. Integration with the dominant ethnic group was easy in Buddhist Thailand but tensions were much more severe in the Muslim societies of Malaysia and Indonesia, particularly the former where the two populations are not too far apart in size. In both societies, however, the ruling elites have successfully contained ethnic hostility without discouraging the vivifying enterprise of the Chinese community which, in combination with development strategies that emphasize foreign investment and exports, has brought a sustained rise not only in per capita income but also the share of it accruing to the non-Chinese majority. Control of the state by the Malay-dominated UMNO in Malaysia and the Javanese-dominated army in Indonesia assures sufficient redistribution from local Chinese and foreign businesses to satisfy the Muslim majority people in each case.

There are many reasons to doubt, however, whether the situation will remain stable in the long run. For one thing, the present arrangement has resulted in extensive corruption and highly unequal shares within the Muslim majority in each of these societies. Dissent is contained by tight political control in what are essentially one-party systems. Any opening to a more participatory system carries with it the possibility that the discontent of the masses will be tapped by fundamentalist Islamic groups, as has already happened in the case of Algeria. The combination of a social revolution against a corrupt ruling elite, together with a xenophobic reaction against the wealthy local Chinese would be a powerfully disruptive force. Thus there is a painful dilemma in these cases, between the possibility of democracy on the one hand and ethnic strife on the other.

The example of Sri Lanka is a chilling reminder of what can happen. This abundantly endowed island had a highly literate population and advanced social services, together with a genuine parliamentary democracy. There were many close historical links between the Buddhist Sinhalese and the Hindu Tamils, who lived together peacefully in the colonial era and in the first years of independence. But once the Pandora's box of Buddhist Sinhalese xenophobia was opened by S. W. R. D. Bandaranaike, in the course of competing for political power, the island became doomed to the all-consuming fury of ethnic strife in which it is still engulfed, as perceptively analyzed and documented by Tambiah (1986).

In concluding these notes on the congruence, or lack of it, between state and nation, I would like to cite the opinions of two eminent Victorians of widely divergent views. John Stuart Mill (1861, p. 309) declared "Where the sentiment of nationality exists in any force, there is a *prima facie* case for uniting all the members of the nationality under the same government, and a government to *themselves apart*" (my italics). He goes on to add, however, that "free institutions are next to impossible in a country made up of different nationalities." Thus, he rejects the nostalgia often expressed in many quarters for the good old days of the old empires when different peoples went about their business peacefully under the shelter of an alien ruling class. Mill was a severe critic of the empires of his day, advocating independence for nations that met his high standards of capacity for representative institutions. The dilemma comes when peoples are so intertwined that the "one nation – one state" principle becomes impossible to apply while at the same time the legitimacy of the center has broken down.

Unlike Mill, Lord Acton (1862, p. 150) believed that "The combination of different nations in one state is as necessary a condition of civilized life as the combination of men in society." He had a highly idealized view of the Hapsburg empire, lauding its apparent success in uniting a wide diversity of nations at different stages of development by a system of mutual checks and balances that maintained the effective liberty of each component. In a state based on a single dominant nationality he says (p. 156) that

> The greatest adversary of the rights of nationality is the modern theory of nationality. By making the state and the nation commensurate with each other in theory, it reduces practically to a subject condition all other nationalities that may be within the boundary. It cannot admit them to an equality with the ruling nation which constitutes the state, because the state would then cease to be national, which would be a contradiction of the principle of its existence.

On this subject it is unfortunately Acton, rather than the optimistic Mill, who ought to have the last word.

References

Acton, Lord - "Nationality" chapter 5 of *Essays in the Liberal Interpretation of History*, University of Chicago Press, 1967, pages 131–159 (original published in 1862).
Alter, Peter - *Nationalism*, Edward Arnold, London and New York, 1989.
Anderson, Benedict - *Imagined Communities*, Verso, London, 1983.
Breton, Albert - "The Economics of Nationalism," *Journal of Political Economy*, August 1964.
Colley, Linda - *Britons: the Forging of the Nation - 1707–1837*, Yale University Press, 1992.
Findlay, Ronald - "The Roots of Divergence": Western Economic History in Comparative Perspective", *American Economic Review*, May, 1992.
Geertz, Clifford - *The Interpretation of Cultures*, Basic Books, New York, 1973.
Gellner, Ernest - *Spectacles and Predicaments*, Cambridge University Press, 1979.
  Nations and Nationalism, Cornell University Press, Ithaca, New York, 1983.
Gerschenkron, Alexander - *Economic Backwardness in Historical Perspective*, Harvard University Press, 1962.
Glenny, Misha - *The Return of History*, Penguin, 1990.
  The Fall of Yugoslavia, Penguin Books, 1992.

Helgerson, Richard - *Forms of Nationhood*, University of Chicago Press, 1992.
Hobsbawm, Eric - *Nations and Nationalism Since 1780*, Cambridge University Press, 1990.
Huizinga, Johan - "Patriotism and Nationalism in European History" in *Men and Ideas*, Princeton University Press, 1984, pages 97–158 (originally published in 1940).
Kirby, David - *Northern Europe in the Early Modern Period: the Baltic World 1492–1772*, Longmans, 1990.
Mastnak, Tomaz - "Is the Nation-State Really Obsolete?" *Times Literary Supplement*, 7 August, 1992, page 11.
Mill, John Stuart - *Considerations on Representative Government*, Gateway Editions, 1962 (originally published in 1862).
Minogue, Kenneth - *Nationalism*, Pelican, 1970.
Orwell, George - "Notes on Nationalism," in *Collected Essays, Journalism and Letters*, volume III, Penguin Books, 1970, pages 410–430 (originally published in 1945).
Plamenatz, John - "Two Types of Nationalism" in E. Kamenka (ed.) *Nationalism*, Arnold, London, 1973.
Schumpeter, Joseph - "The Sociology of Imperialisms" in *The Economics and Sociology of Capitalism*, Princeton University Press, 1991, pages 141–219 (originally published in English in 1951).
Seton-Watson, Hugh - *Nations and States*, Westview Press, 1977.
Smith, Anthony - *Nationalism in the Twentieth Century*, New York University Press, 1979.
Tambiah, Stanley - *Sri Lanka: Ethnic Fratricide and the Dismantling of Democracy*, University of Chicago Press, 1986.
Zaslavsky, Victor - "Nationalism and Democratic Transition in Postcommunist Societies" *Daedalus*, Spring 1992, pages 97–122.

CHAPTER 8

Conservative nationalism and democratic institutions

Jean-Dominique Lafay
History and Nature [and Economic Theory] do not tell much, except caution.

Nationalism has at least two very different meanings. It may first refer to an ideology calling for the building of a new nation, because the size and/or composition of the present one is thought to be highly suboptimal. In its expansionist form, this nationalism calls for a nation of a larger size, through conquest or through peacefully negotiated agreements with neighboring countries. In its separatist form, which is the most common, it aims at splitting the existing national club into smaller and more homogeneous ones.

But nationalism may also refer to the desire to maintain the existing nation, with its territory and population, giving the government the right to submit any other objective to it, including the welfare and basic civil rights of individual citizens. In this chapter, we shall concentrate on this second, conservative form of nationalism.

As a political ideology, conservative nationalism has a very bad reputation among its numerous adversaries. It is considered as historically responsible for several major wars, civil as well as international (among which the two World Wars). Ethically, it is charged with being a selfish philosophy, which leads to unjust discriminatory behavior. Economically, it is presented as a source of inefficiencies, because it restricts international competition and specialization, by promoting barriers, regulations, and discriminations against labor, capital, firms, and products of the foreign sector.

Despite this extensive negative rhetoric, measures of a nationalist tone are currently advocated or implemented by political parties, revo-

---

Revised version of a paper presented at the Fifth Villa Colombella Seminar on "Nationalism and Its Re-Emergence," Perugia, Italy, Sept. 2–4, 1992. I thank the participants, particularly Manfred Holler, for their comments and suggestions.
[1] Dahl and Tufte (1973:111). Personal addition in bracket.

lutionary movements, socioeconomic, or ethnic groups. Moreover, in politically unstable regions, such as Lebanon or Yugoslavia, many ordinary citizens support nationalist policies, at the price of high risks for their own lives, by voluntarily joining local armies or, more simply, by staying in their homeland despite intensive fights. The unexpected upsurges of nationalism in the public opinion during the debate on the European Economic Community (EEC) Maastricht treaty are also a clear sign of its persistent weight in Western European countries.

Section I presents the main arguments advanced to justify conservative nationalism. Section II analyzes how nationalist demands emerge and are taken into account in democratic institutions. Section III concludes.

I   The logic of conservative nationalism

A nation is a specific club, with given social decision rules and a given amount of social and cultural capital, accumulated through history. Conservative nationalism corresponds to a set of proposals concerning the existence, membership and functioning of this club.

Maintaining the national club

A nation can be seen as a more or less balanced organizational system that has emerged from an initially chaotic world "à la Hobbes." It gathers citizens on a given territory – voluntarily or not – produces public goods for its members, and takes "sovereign" collective decisions (sovereign meaning that its implicit or explicit social welfare function is independent of the preferences of individuals who do not belong to the club).

The observed equilibrium is only one among many potential ones. It may correspond to a well-shaped territory, with "natural" borders, or to a more or less accidental result of historical events or international decisions. For example, the shape of most of the sub-Saharan countries is simply the result of colonial border cutting. Similarly, the population may be ethnically and/or culturally homogeneous but it may also gather people from very different origins and cultures, as in Switzerland or in the United States. There are several possible explanations for this: People may have historically been forced to group; or they may have had an interest to do so; or, more simply, strong immigration flows may have mechanically created heterogeneity. Finally, the nation may be run by a relatively strong and unified state, as is generally the case now, but history tells us that these kinds of "nation-states" are of recent origin (they were a means for the European kings to establish their power and to put an end to feudalism). National entities have their own existence, independent of the national state (Barry 1991).

Even if the initial political equilibrium is not intrinsically stable, it tends to become more and more so for a number of reasons. First, common social life and habits of cooperation accumulate trust. Individuals feel that they live in a more secure environment. They are less reluctant to engage in intertemporal redistributions in favor of fellow nationals, because they expect that commitments taken for the future are more likely to be met. This increased willingness to wait greatly facilitates collective decisions. In general, the social games are repeated more often and can be played more cooperatively. Second, social capital is continuously accumulated, and national individuals can consume an increasing amount of its services. Third, the psychological benefits resulting from a sense of belonging and from a sense of sharing a common destiny usually increase as the nation becomes older.

For all these reasons, it is interesting to preserve the status quo. Even if a country has no historical, ethnical, or cultural justifications, the mere fact that it has existed for a while will give arguments for conservative nationalism: Keep the nation as it is and further reinforce its identity. The constitutions of many countries in the world are, for a large part, a plea for conservative nationalism, justifying an extended use of force to preserve their "indivisibility," against external as well as internal threats.

This may create severe conflicts between conservative nationalism and the other forms of nationalism, those that demand a different size and/or composition of the national club.

For some groups, the expected benefits from a different level of sovereignty sometimes largely outweigh the costs of changing the status quo. These expected benefits can be: allocative benefits (the new desired size and composition are thought to be socially more efficient); redistributive benefits (the changes in constituencies and/or in decision-making processes are expected to give redistributive advantages or to suppress supposedly undue redistribution to other members of the society); benefits from higher political stability (because it lowers the probability of cycling in decision making when the problem is to split a heterogeneous country or because better coordination is assumed to reduce the risk of disputes when the problem is to aggregate nations).

This form of nationalism may be of an expansionist type: In that sense, the EEC project corresponds to an expansionist nationalism simply because all the arguments saying that the EEC will lower the risks of intra-European conflicts or create a more efficient entity in the world balance of power are justifications for a nation of bigger size.

However, the most successful form of this type of nationalism in the contemporaneous period is separatism, that is, the claim for a smaller national size. The doctrine of the "right of peoples to self-determination," which was forged against the European monarchies during the nineteenth century and in the first half of the twentieth century, has played a great part here. A priori, this "right" may correspond to a bigger as well as to a smaller national size (by splitting and regrouping). However, after World War II, under the pressures of decolonization and other independentist movements, separatist nationalism has been dominant. As a result, the number of sovereign nations has more than doubled since the fifties, a fact that clearly contradicts the common post-World War opinion that the number of nations was bound to decrease rapidly and the prediction that the international system would contain only a small number of big multinational units (Hassner 1965).

Separatist nationalism was also very important in the communist empire, both as a form of opposition to the régime and as a way for some ruling groups to protect themselves in a climate of general suspicion.[2] Its later explicit upsurge has been, in a sense, a "mechanical" phenomenon.

Central governments try to deal with separatism by decentralization and by granting enlarged autonomy to some regions, but these measures do not respond to the main demand: the wish to change the "peak-coordinating policy unit" (Cauley, Sandler, and Cornes 1986). This demand, which is clearly inconsistent with conservative nationalism, is often the starting point of severe conflicts or even of civil wars. Some groups try to leave the national community through secession, because they think the present social heterogeneity has become too costly for them or because they want to escape some unexpected redistributive consequences of previously accepted constraints. Conservative nationalists object to these secessionist pressures on the grounds that a change in the territorial unity creates significant negative externalities for the remaining population (because, for example, some national primary resources will go exclusively to the secessionists or because the new reduced territory will create increased problems for national defense). Because as the constitution generally de-

---

[2] Lafay (1980) on this point.

clares that the nation is indivisible, they feel entitled to use force. This increases the distrust of the separatists and results in a well-known escalation in violence.

Conservative nationalism and social objectives

From a positive point of view, it is now largely accepted that political decision-makers maximize their own utility function. This however, does not imply that the normative social objectives that all political ideologies assign to governments have no positive effect. Referring to specific ideological norms or obtaining the approval of a given ideological leader may be an efficient means to gain the support of some groups. Indeed, some gap may exist between words and actions, but this means that a rhetoric of persuasion is necessary, and one may assume that its cost is an increasing function of the size of the initial gap. Consequently, the social objectives assigned to rulers by ideologies matter, even from a strictly positive point of view.

For nationalist ideologies, the main if not exclusive social objective of governments must be "national interest." But, here again, the concept may have several very different meanings.

In the holistic view, a nation is seen as a superbeing, with its own aims and rights. This superbeing is the sovereign judge of the "national interest," and it has a "natural" right to promote this interest, whatever the consequences for the sovereignty and welfare of other nations or for the sovereignty and welfare of domestic individuals.

Holistic nationalism can be nondemocratic (national interest is considered to exist independently of individual preferences) as well as democratic. In the first case, electoral procedures can be done away, if it is in the national interest to do so. This situation is excluded by definition in the second case, because national interest is supposed to correspond to the Rousseauist "general will" of the nation, as it is revealed by universal suffrage. In this "populist" conception of democracy (Riker 1982), national individuals are, however, only allowed to *participate* in the definition of the "general will." So, as in nondemocratic visions, they do not own inviolable personal rights or individual property rights on national capital: All personal interests are submitted to the "general-national-will."

The holistic versions of nationalism are at variance with what Riker (1982) calls the "liberal" vision of democracy. According to this vision, general will is considered a myth, which cannot be revealed in a consistent and stable way by any form of aggregating procedure, voting included. Direct democracy is consequently inefficient and may give results that are ethically unjust and/or seriously offend individual rights. Then, the central aim of political institutions is to protect a minimum set of individual and minority rights, whatever the general will, and to control the power abuses of the ruling class (which is considered to present permanently a high risk of corruption). The voting procedure becomes only a means, by the threat of non-reelection, to control the government, along with constitutional rules, separation of powers, checks and balances, or reinforced majorities. In such an institutional framework, nationalism can only correspond to national egoism. If national interest is now limited to the interest of national citizens, the fact remains that it has to be promoted whatever the consequences for foreign countries and nonnational citizens. This position raises some consistency problems, because it denies to nonnational individuals and populations the basic individual rights that are claimed to be sacred for national citizens. A way out of this is to say that national egoism is a second-best policy in a world that is known not to play cooperatively. Despite this argument, moderate nationalists of this type usually accept to limit national sovereignty to the respect of a minimum set of basic ethical imperatives and to exclude, whatever the expected gains, attempts to redistribute international wealth to their national benefit by war or threat of war (but not necessarily by nationalization of assets or debt repudiation). A certain amount of voluntary redistribution to poorer countries is also admitted.

Conservative nationalism and the criticism of representative democracy

Historically, conservative nationalism has often been critical of representative democracy. A large majority of politicians was considered self-interested, corrupted, and too isolated from the citizens by the complexity of institutions; for these reasons, they were unable to defend the "true" interests of either the "nation" or the "people" (the two concepts being generally closely associated and their interests presented as highly complementary).

Representative democracy was also accused of placing too much constraint on politicians, who thus were unable to make efficient use of the "strength of masses" and, consequently, unable to exploit the full potentialities of the nation (or to accomplish its "destiny"). This last type of argument was important at the end of the nineteenth century and in the first decades of the twentieth century, when nationalist ideology was actively developing its intellectual basis.[3] From this point of view, the huge popular success of Gustave Le Bon's "Psychology of Crowds" is highly revealing.

If the concepts of "nation" and "people" were generally associated in the different schools of nationalist thought, opinions concerning the way to better satisfy their complementary interests or to realize their "common destiny" were clearly different. Some people were maintaining the populist democratic idea that universal suffrage was generating a correct "general will" and were supporting variants of plebiscitarian régimes; others – and perhaps intellectually the most influential ones – were refusing all forms of democratic institutions, because they supposedly operated an inadequate trade-off between individual and national interests and because they were accused of choosing incompetent and self-interested elites. Alternative mechanisms of social organization were elaborated, grounded on more or less explicit "positivistic" laws (along the lines of Auguste Comte's doctrine), such as natural selection or historical legitimacy. The stress was put on the early social selection of elites and on their education geared to a centrally determined national interest.

Conservative nationalism and nationality

As any club, the national club defines criteria for membership (nationality). Members (nationals) are entitled to participate in collective decisions (but also have to obey all these decisions). They also share the property rights to the social capital accumulated through history.

By social capital, we mean the sum of physical public capital, which is the publicly owned territories and natural resources and the assets accumulated through previous public investment or appropriation; and cultural capital. Community in language, culture, social norms, historical experience, etc., produces psychological benefits and reduces costs, in information, transaction, and coordination. Cultural capital corresponds to the present value of all these elements.[4]

---

[3] The two main and exceptionally active intellectual centers were Berlin for Marxism and Paris for nationalism (France was preparing the "revenge" against Germany to recover the eastern territories lost after the war of 1870). For an exceptional historical synthesis of ideas during that period, see Sternhell (1978). The most significant original texts by nationalist authors are published in Girardet's (1966) anthology of French nationalism.

[4] The cultural capital produces public services that can be of the traditional additive type (identity of language), of the "best-shot" type (individual sense of pride from

In the absolute monarchies of Europe, which historically gave rise to the concept of nation, there were no problems of nationality. The king alone was deciding the geographical and demographic content of the "nation," and he was the only owner of the social capital accumulated in it (hence the well-known statement by Louis XIV: *"L'Etat, c'est moi"*). If citizens felt they were compatriots, it was only to the extent that they were "loyal to the same person" (de Jouvenel 1945, p. 184).

Conversely, the problem of nationality (i.e., entry and membership conditions for the club and property rights to its social capital) becomes central in any country where the ruling class is not considered the legitimate owner of the public assets. It is still more important in democracies where each citizen is entitled to participate in collective decisions; in "old" countries, which have accumulated an important level of social capital; and in countries where the state has a high level of redistributive activity and social security.

Except in countries that are severely underpopulated, conservative nationalism usually argues in favor of a restrictive definition of nationality. The three main arguments follow.

First a citizen must be considered as an heir; he inherits the investment effort of the previous generations, that is, the present social capital, and this provides him with many public goods at much lower costs.[5] Then, the same efficiency and equity arguments used for private inheritance apply, and nationality must obey the same laws (*jus sanguinis*). Opening up nationality on a different basis would present

---

national successes and celebrities), or of the "weakest-link" type (sense of solidarity between compatriots); on these questions, see Hirshleifer (1983).

[5] Economic theory does not detail the production technology of public goods. The specificity of these goods is only linked to their provision method, which must be public, but there is no objection to their *production* by private firms (Musgrave 1959). Thus, any direct production by the public sector results not from a technical choice but from a political choice of the government. In reality, some public goods must not only be publicly provided but also publicly produced. The production of (internal and external) order, particularly, enters this category. It can be produced only through the monopoly of force, and if the government does not own this monopoly, it will not last for a long time as a government (Auster and Silver 1979). Another argument is that some public goods are produced at much lower cost when the citizens participate in their production through civic behavior. Maintainance of the environment, enforcement of property rights, military training, and protection against the enemy's spies are examples of such a productive contribution. Civic behavior is a form of Kantian altruism, of voluntary in-kind transfer to the collectivity. Nationalism insists much on the necessity to preserve and expand a sense of civic duty, through education or propaganda (by demanding that the citizens, after J. F. Kennedy, not ask themselves what their country can do for them but what they can do for their country).

Conservative nationalism and democratic institutions

the risk of reducing the value of cultural capital (as defined previously), assuming that this value effectively depends on the homogeneity of preferences, norms, and experiences in the total population.[6]

Second, individuals born in the country or at least residing in it for a long period have greater incentives to play the social game as a repeated one and to not adopt a hit-and-run strategy when they participate in collective decisions. Consequently, nationality based on jus soli is often accepted in addition to *jus sanguinis*.

Third, in large welfare states, redistribution and social security have distorting effects on the demand for immigration. The higher the expected benefits, the lower the qualifications of potential immigrants (highly qualified immigrants have to pay for national social transfers, while lesser-qualified ones are more likely to be entitled to benefit from them). More generally, problems of "adverse selection" may exist for immigrants, because their adhesion to the national "club" is voluntary. Problems of moral hazard are also more likely to appear: If immigrants integrate fewer social norms, they are more prone to opportunistic behavior.

II Nationalism and the economic theory of democracy

This section examines two questions: What are the main determinants of the demand for nationalism and how does the political market respond to this demand in a democratic setting? and Why does this demand fluctuate so strongly and so suddenly?

Nationalism and the median voter model

The observed level of nationalism in a country depends on both demand and supply conditions on the political market. To simplify our analysis, this market is assumed to be perfect: Competition between political parties is such that programs and government policies reflect the preferences of the voters, who are pivotal, given the aggregation rules of individual choices. The principal (the electorate) totally controls the political agent (the political parties and the government). The analysis will also be limited to the simple deterministic theory of

---

[6] Some extreme nationalists may also use this homogeneity argument retroactively (as in the present "ethnic purification" policy of the Serbian government in the former Yugoslavia). On the contrary, some moderate nationalists accept the idea that, in an uncertain universe or an underpopulated territory, a significant level of permeability to immigration can bring sizeable benefits. However, compared to the policy positions of other parties, the optimal level they set is generally much lower.

voting behavior, so that the programs and policies will correspond to the preferences of the median voter.[7]

Several factors let us think that nationalism has a negative income elasticity (i.e., is an inferior good). If personal wealth presents a marginally decreasing utility, citizens whose private wealth is lower will value their property rights to national capital more than the richer citizens value theirs. Furthermore, demands for strict restrictions in the eligibility conditions for the welfare state will generally be more pronounced in the low-income classes, or receivers, than in the higher ones, or givers. If the total level of redistribution depends only on the income of givers and if immigrants are net demanders of welfare benefits (as discussed above), then, as new receivers, the immigrants tend to reduce the amount received by the present receivers.

Owing to the observed, left-skewed shape of the income distribution curve, the median income, which is supposed to represent the income of the median voter, is smaller than the mean income. Thus, the median voter has a higher than average demand for nationalism for two reasons: first, because he has a lower income and, second, because he is a net receiver in the welfare system.

Nationalism also has strong redistributive effects. Winners will support it and losers will oppose it. The way governments respond to one type of demand or the other depends on the expected net political benefits. For example, some industries will support nationalism and the associated protectionism, because it reduces the competitive pressure of imported goods. On the other hand, protectionism may create high costs for export industries if the other countries retaliate, so they tend to oppose nationalism.

Similarly, nationalism may promote immigration controls and quotas that create price distortions in the labor market. These benefit some categories of workers but correspond to general efficiency losses for all. The beneficiaries depend heavily on the exact regulation structure. Therefore, the rent-seeking capacities of the different social groups and the potential for fiscal illusion (i.e., for concentrating benefits and for spreading or hiding costs) may be of crucial importance here.

---

[7] This would no longer be true in a probabilistic voting framework, where politicians have imperfect information on voters' preferences. Parties' programs and public policies of the government would then correspond, in the political equilibrium, to a weighted combination of individual preferences, with weights being inversely proportional to the probability that a given individual will vote for a given program (see Lafay [1992] on this point).

According to Breton (1964), by protecting and promoting specific categories of inputs, nationalism offers more and better-paid jobs to the middle class. Therefore, "we should expect the working class to be less nationalist than the middle class," a fact apparently confirmed by Canadian data (Breton 1964, 381). Thus government investment in nationalistic rhetoric serves first to "stimulate the support of the working class in favor of politics which are not to their economic advantage" (Breton 1964, 379).

The problem with the above theory is that it does not explain why a rational government would wish to promote middle-class interests. However, if it is assumed that middle-class interests are narrowly correlated with the median voter's interests, Breton's analysis can be changed into a positive theory of the redistributive effects of nationalism in a democratic setting.

To simplify matters, we shall assume that the set of nationalist measures is restricted to the labor market, that is, to the regulation of workers' immigration. Rational democratic governments will severely restrict entrance for workers with medium qualification, because they compete on the labor market with the median voter, and will allow free entrance for the two extreme categories (unqualified and highly qualified workers).[8]

Notice, however, that this policy cannot be pushed too far in practice, or else two types of reactions can emerge from the two extreme income classes: xenophobic attitudes and the substitution of "voice" to their ineffective ballot, because foreign workers compete more directly with these classes on the labor market; and claims for a strong nationalist government and antidemocratic attitudes, because these classes feel like victims of the institutional system.

Consequently, and contrary to Breton's (1964) suggestion, the working class is not less nationalist than the middle class, even if nationalism is seen as only income-redistributing. Its nationalism will simply take a different form, more violent and more politically radical. Moreover, its nationalism may have some similarities with the nationalism of the high-income class; thus, a significant probability of coalition between the two exists, and this may directly threaten the democratic system.

---

[8] The same logic states that foreign students with medium-level formation will generally be pressed to go back to their home countries at the end of their studies. On the contrary, students with high-level formation will be submitted to much lower pressures.

Fluctuations in the demand for conservative nationalism

A major feature of nationalism in democratic systems is that its electoral success fluctuates significantly over time. Nationalist parties generally obtain a significantly higher share of popular vote during political or economic crises. There are at least three explanations for this phenomenon. First, national egoism and redistribution against the foreign sector, which characterize most programs of nationalist parties, have greater appeal in a period of declining real incomes. Second, in periods of high crisis, a growing share of the electorate does not limit its criticisms to the existing government but extends them to the institutional system. The success of nationalist parties in such periods is thus linked to their programs of institutional change and to their violent populist attacks against the parliamentary system (to be replaced, according to them, either by a more direct, plebiscite democracy or by a stronger, less democratic system – supposed to better express the "true will of people"). Third, nationalist parties also take advantage of the mere fact that they are perceived as extremist. According to Enelow and Hinich (1981), the polarization of opinion fluctuates cyclically. During noncrisis periods, centrist parties are perceived as less ambiguous in their expected consequences than the extremist parties, because of their lower destabilizing capacity. Risk-averse voters have a greater preference for them. During crisis periods, the situation is reversed in favor of extremist parties: They benefit from their strong precommitment to settled positions, because it is expected to reduce general uncertainty and to stop negative cumulative processes.

The demand for nationalism seldom fluctuates smoothly. It often experiences very sudden outbreaks in crisis periods.[9] These unexpected bursts of nationalism can be explained as "unanticipated revolution" (Kuran 1989). Nationalism implies, at least to some degree, an egoistic and discriminatory behavior against some human groups, and as we have seen, this class of ideas often has a bad ethical reputation. Public support of them may create social reprobation, violent reactions or other forms of social punishment. Many individuals will then

---

[9] Or, in the case of social choices, it would bear on the content of national sovereignty. A good illustration of this is the attitudes of the French electorate toward the ratification referendum for the Maastricht treaty (assuming that opposition to it is mainly a nationalistic reaction). Surveys show that the percentage of intended votes against the treaty suddenly jumped from less than 30 percent in June 1992 to more than 50 percent at the end of August (and the actual percentage of votes against the treaty stabilized at 48 percent in the final vote in September).

falsify their preferences, and a gap will appear between the true "private preferences" of ordinary (nonactivist) persons and their "public preferences," the ones they express in their social activity. This preference falsification represents a cost to the individual, "who suffers for compromising his integrity" (Kuran 1989, 47). When the gap is bigger than a given threshold and/or when the number of persons expressing publicly nationalistic preferences form a sufficiently important "protocoalition," a large number of the rational nonactivist citizens will align their private and public preferences. The corresponding burst of nationalism appears all the more sudden because information about true private preferences was previously hidden.

III   Conclusions

This paper has analyzed two points: how the nationalist rhetoric, at least in its conservative version, can be reformulated using the analytical framework of club theory and to what extent the political programs inspired by this rhetoric are successful among voters in democratic institutions.

In order to limit the analysis on the second point, a perfectly competitive political market was assumed: To win elections, political parties were supposed to respond to the preferences of the pivotal voters, and neither the government nor the opposition parties had any leeway to implement different policies between two elections (there was no principal/agent problem). In reality, such leeway exists, and this supply aspect of nationalism would be worth studying.

At first sight, governments will use their leeway to oversupply nationalism, because it makes public policy easier and allows increases in their own rent. By referring to the glorious national history and to civic duties of citizens, the present states "advertise their virtues" and manipulate the demand curves to their benefit through education. They can also modify the individual perception of alternatives and increase, through nationalistic persuasion, the opportunity cost of exit (Auster and Silver 1979, pp. 62–5). More abruptly, nationalism may be a pretext to increase by force the costs of emigration, to exploit more the national population, or to raise the military strength of the state in order to conquer or submit adjacent nations (and become an international rent-seeker). Finally, appeal to nationalism encourages "rally round the flag" reactions in periods of difficulties and may contribute much to the success of some crucial policies.

But the opposite government behavior, that is, undersupply of nationalism, is not excluded. For example, the governmental negotiators of the Maastricht treaty have clearly been much less nationalist, in the conservative sense, than their national opinion, at least in some European countries. An obvious extension of this discussion would be the search for positive explanations to these different governmental attitudes.

References

Auster, R. D., and Silver, M. 1979. *The State as a Firm.* Boston: Martinus Nijhoff Publishing.

Barry, B. 1991. "Self-Government Revisited." In Barry, B. *Democracy and Power, Essays in Political Theory 1.* Oxford: Clarendon Paperbacks.

Breton, A. 1964. "The Economics of Nationalism." *Journal of Political Economy* 72, no. 4:376–86.

Breton, A., et al., eds. 1992. *Villa Colombella Papers on Preferences and Democracy.* Dordrecht: Kluwer Academic Press.

Cauley, J., Sandler, T., and Cornes, R. 1986. "Nonmarket Institutional Structures: Conjectures, Distribution, and Allocative Efficiency." *Public Finance/Finances publiques* 41, no. 2:153–72.

Dahl, R. A., and Tufte, E. R. 1973. *Size and Democracy.* Stanford, CA: Stanford University Press.

de Jouvenel, B. 1972. *Du pouvoir.* Paris: Hachette (1st Swiss edition in 1945).

Enelow, J. M., and Hinich, M. J. 1981, "A New Approach to Voter Uncertainty in the Downsian Spatial Model." *American Journal of Political Science* 25:483–93.

Girardet, R. 1972. *Le nationalisme français, anthologie 1871–1914.* Paris: Editions du Seuil (1st edition, 1966).

Hassner, P. 1965. "Nationalisme et relations internationales." *Revue française de science politique.* 15, no. 3:499–528.

Hirshleifer, J. 1983. "From Weakest-Link to Best-Shot: The Voluntary Provision of Public Goods." *Public Choice.* 41, no. 3:371–86.

Kuran, T. 1989. "Sparks and Prairie Fires: A Theory of Unanticipated Political Revolution." *Public Choice.* 61, no. 1:41–74.

Lafay, J. D. 1980. "Empirical Analysis of Politico-Economic Interaction in East European Countries." *Soviet Studies* 33:386–400.

———. 1992. "The Silent Revolution of Probabilistic Voting." In Breton, A., et al., eds. *Villa Colombella Papers on Preferences and Democracy.* Dordrecht: Kluwer Academic Press.

Musgrave, R. 1959. *The Theory of Public Finance. A Study in Public Economy,* International Student Edition. New York: McGraw-Hill.

Riker, W. H. 1982. *Liberalism Against Populism. A Confrontation Between the Theory of Democracy and the Theory of Social Choice.* San Francisco: Freeman.

Sternhell, Z. 1978. *La droite révolutionnaire, les origines françaises du fascisme, 1885–1914.* Paris: Editions du Seuil.

CHAPTER 9

Can economics explain nationalism?

Ugo Pagano

Nations are large "imagined political communities" that have shaped the last two hundred years of human history. Each member of a nation knows only an insignificant fraction of the other members; thus any feeling for them involves some "imagination" of fellow countrymen and some imagination of their differences with respect to "foreigners." The term "imagined communities"[1] does not mean unreal or false communities. It simply distinguishes them from communities like the village, the family or the workplace, where people have a real chance of interacting and meeting each other, and where their sense of community stems from their direct interaction.

Nations are not "natural" institutions; they are fairly recent "institutional innovations" that have characterized the last two hundred years of human history. Before the eighteenth century, wars and dynastic policies (in particular, marriage policies!), often determined the composition and the size of political communities; there was no particular feeling of identity with other (temporary) members of a political community that could often speak different languages and share different social customs. In spite of the sense of antiquity or eternity of many nations, the identification of "political communities" with ethnic groups, which is the central idea of nations and nationalism, is very recent.[2]

I thank the participants to the seminar organized in September 1992, at Villa Colombella, Perugia, Italy, for useful comments. I also wish to thank Sam Bowles, Ha Joon Chang, Marcello De Cecco, Ernest Gellner, Frank Hahn, and Robert Rowthorn for useful discussions on this topic. Financial support by C. N. R. and M. U. R. S. T. is gratefully acknowledged. The usual caveats apply.

[1] This term is due to Benedict Anderson (1991) and it is also the title of his book.
[2] This does not mean that, before that date, there was never a coincidence between political communities and ethnic groups but simply that this coincidence was not

Rational choice and self-interest are the basic assumptions and the starting point of many economic explanations. The fact that, from a certain stage of human history, so many people have become so ready to die and kill for their "nations" seems to contradict these assumptions: People appear to be much more generous and idealistic and much more cruel and perverse than the assumptions of economic theory seem to imply.

Why, at a certain point in human history, does the "nation" become the "natural" political community? Are there "economic" interests that explain the emergence of nationalism and its reemergence today? How is it possible that utility-maximizing individuals, who may free ride on so many simple duties of everyday life, may be ready to die for these imagined communities? And how is it possible that the same utility-maximizing individuals who are so peaceful in everyday life can then kill the members of other nations? Can economics explain nationalism, or should we come to the conclusion that nationalism comes from irrational aspects of human behavior about which orthodox economics has little or nothing to say?

In order to answer these questions we will start by reconsidering the analysis of the division of labor and try to show that nations play a very important role in allowing that division of labor that is associated with market economies. Even though the mutual relationship existing between nation building and the development of the division of labor may cause inefficient institutional equilibria, nationalism must be included among one of the possible causes of the accumulation of wealth.

In the second section we will contrast wealth-creation explanations with rent-seeking explanations of nationalism, and we will argue that both explanations can help the understanding of nationalism: Some analysis of the different periods of nationalism is necessary to understand which one of these two economic explanations of nationalism is more appropriate.

In the third section we will consider the limits of the economic explanations of nationalism. We will consider some possible extensions of the economic approach that may help to provide some rationale for nationalistic activities that seem to defy any rational choice explanation.

considered to be a condition necessary for the viability of a political community. On this point, see Anthony Smith (1991), where he also makes an interesting distinction between the experiences of those countries where the coincidence between ethnic and political communities existed before the age of nationalism and those that realized it after that period.

Finally, we will briefly examine whether an evolutionary approach is more appropriate than a rational choice approach in explaining nationalism.

Nations, markets and the division of labor

Adam Smith attributed the "wealth of nations" to the division of labor that was, in turn, determined by the extent of the market economy.

Smith's analysis relied on the fact that the division of labor would favour learning by doing: The workers could improve their job specific skills if they specialized in one single activity. Nations should eliminate all the obstacles to trade if they wanted to enjoy the full advantages of the division of labor.[3]

The division of labor argument was developed on different lines by Charles Babbage (1832). Whereas Smith saw skills differences as a result of the division of labor, Babbage started from the assumption that individuals are endowed with different skills and have different comparative advantages in various activities. According to Babbage, specialization is advantageous because it makes it possible to exploit the comparative advantages of individuals.

This principle is similar to that used by David Ricardo to explain the advantages of the division of labor among nations. Unlike Smith, Babbage (and Ricardo) saw the differences in skills (and other factors affecting productivity) more as a cause than as a result of the division of labor.

This was not the only difference between Babbage and Smith. Whereas Smith argued that the division of labor maximized the learning that is acquired by doing, Babbage maintained that the great advantage of the division of labor is that it minimizes the learning that it is necessary to acquire before doing: The narrower the content of a job, the less it is necessary to learn before production.

[3] List (1909, 121) pointed out how the principle of the *division* of labor also required "*a confederation or union of various energies, intelligences, and powers on behalf of common production*. The cause of productiveness of these operations is not merely that *division*, but essentially this union." According to List, "Adam Smith well perceives this himself when he states, "The necessaries of life of the lowest members of society are a product of *joint* labour and of co-operation of a number of individuals' (*Wealth of Nations*, book I, ch. 1)." List adds, "What a pity that he did not follow this idea (which he so clearly expresses) of *united labour*." By contrast, List followed this idea and anticipated some considerations on the role of the nation in the organization of the division of labor that have been later independently developed by Gellner (1983; 1987). The roles of nations in creating and sustaining market economies were also the focus of Polanyi (1944).

The degree of specialization that is implied by Smith and Babbage is different. Smith's principles imply that specialization should not be extremely narrow; otherwise it could prevent, rather than favor, learning by doing. By contrast, Babbage's principles imply that extreme specialization and job deskilling may be convenient because they always do decrease the learning required before the doing and allow a better exploitation of given comparative advantages.

Whereas the Smithian principles point to the advantages of a horizontal division of labor where everyone enjoys the learning by doing advantage, the Babbage principle has strong hierarchical implications: The greatest savings on training time are obtained when the most skilled tasks are separated from unskilled tasks, and only the people with the greatest comparative advantage are trained for the skilled tasks.[4]

Even if Babbage and Smith principles are different, and their joint application may require some "compromises," their arguments could be somewhat integrated by observing that, within certain limits, the division of labor can decrease the learning that is required before doing, increase the learning that is acquired by doing, and exploit innate skills and comparative advantages. These principles give the reasons for the wealth of nations in the double sense that the division of labor among the individuals of a nation and among nations both increase productivity.[5]

In spite of all these benefits, national or individual specialization has the disadvantage that the individuals or nations put all their eggs in one basket. If, as Smith maintains, the division of labor maximizes the development of job-specific skills, it also implies that one runs the risk of losing much human capital if a particular occupation becomes redundant. The mobility among occupations that is associated with market economies implies that the extent of the market could limit rather than enhance the incentive to specialize in particular occupations.

---

[4] On the analysis of the principles of the division of labor, see Pagano (1985; 1991).

[5] In these theories, there is a perfect similarity between nations and individuals. In international trade theory, nations are simply areas within which factors, and in which particular individual skills, can move among different uses without meeting the obstacles that they would find when they try to move factors from one nation to the other. Individuals are very much the same: They also define areas within which skills can move among different uses without meeting the obstacles that they find when they try to move skills from one individual to the other. It is not surprising that the same principles, such as comparative advantage, apply to individuals and nations even if the nature of the boundaries of individuals and nations are, of course, very different.

This point is rather important for our topic. Gellner (1983; 1987) argues that the mobility of people among occupations, rather than the division of labor as such, is the novelty of modern industrial societies. According to Gellner, the link between the division of labor and the wealth of nations runs also through the development of nations and nationalism.

In traditional agricultural societies, the risks of specialization are negligible. In these societies, there is no great incentive to innovate and to exploit the profit opportunities that arise from the application of innovation. The consequent low level of productivity implies that many commodities satisfy basic needs for local markets, for which demand is unlikely to be volatile. The absence of innovation and the relative stability of demand imply that these societies are stationary and the activities of the individual can safely repeat themselves over time. Individuals rarely change their occupations, which can be (and often must be) passed on from parents to children. In this situation, each occupation can develop its own idiosyncratic culture by which the skills, the "secrets," and the ethical codes are transmitted from one generation to the other.

In traditional agricultural societies, cultural differentiation is useful. Culture can specialize to satisfy the specific needs of a particular trade and to favor the cohesion of its members. Cultural differentiation enhances the stability of the society.

In agricultural societies, the language of the people in power is often different from the language of the workers. The written language may not be spoken or may be spoken only by priests, bureaucrats, and intellectuals. This diversity of languages does not cause particular problems. It can even contribute to the stability of society because it provides a clear sign of the position that is to be occupied by each one of its members.

Linguistic and ethnic differentiation are enhanced by the fact that spatial mobility also is low; again, given that culture is only locally transmitted, this is not a problem but may rather contribute to the spatial stability of society.

Thus the division of labor in traditional societies can be fairly complex. The complexity and the internal differentiation of their cultures can be even more remarkable.

It is useful to contrast the characteristics of traditional agricultural societies with those of modern industrial economies.

These societies are characterized by frequent technological innovations and greater volatility of demand; this implies that workers often have to move from one job to the other; the content of the jobs is frequently changing, and the division of labor must often be redefined. In this situation, specialization can cause greater risks because the skills acquired performing a particular job can easily become redundant.

The risks associated with specialization in modern dynamic economies can be greatly reduced if the individuals happen to share a general common culture.[6]

A common culture allows people to retrain more easily if they must change jobs. For this reason, in an industrial society, the occupational and spatial cultural idiosyncrasies that characterize agricultural societies can no longer be easily accepted. They limit the mobility of people among the different positions of a mutable division of labor. In contrast, a homogeneous culture, by decreasing retraining costs, reduces the risks associated with specialization and favors the exploitation of the advantages of the division of labor in a changing world.

In a modern industrial society, the division of labor is limited not only by the extent of the market but also by the extent of a certain homogenous culture.

Nationalistic policies favoring the homogenization of culture can favour the development of the type of mutable division of labor that is associated with market economies. In this sense, nationalism may favor the accumulation of wealth.

The risks associated with the division of labor may be decreased by turning many job specific investments into investments in general culture. Many of the old idiosyncratic secrets of a particular trade can be expressed in a clear language that becomes accessible to all the individuals belonging to the same culture.

Written language and a general culture cease to be the exclusive domain of a certain cast of individuals. They must become the bread and butter of all the individuals because only the individuals who master these general skills are able to enjoy the learning-by-doing advantages of the division of labor. Only the individuals who have acquired a general culture[7] can carry (at least part of) what they have learned by doing from one occupation to the other.

---

[6] The need for a general common culture is also due to other reasons. The nature of work in modern society is more "semantic" than physical. It presupposes the capacity to communicate with occupants of other positions, and this requires a shared general culture. The whole of education focuses much more on this shared general culture than on special skills that are required later. This does indeed make new training easier, but is already a consequence of the work itself.

[7] General culture can be thought of as something applicable to more contexts; it also enhances our ability to learn in some contexts by making us understand what these

Thus the members of a mobile market society can benefit from the Smithian advantages only if they have had enough general preliminary learning. Otherwise, they must rely, instead, on the benefits of the division of labor outlined by Charles Babbage: that some jobs requiring little preliminary training can be separated from those requiring greater skills.

Assembly-line workers do not need much general culture and often do not even need to speak the language of the country where they work. Their extreme specialization is advantageous not because it allows any learning by doing benefit but because it minimizes the preliminary learning that is necessary before doing. The labor market becomes a dual labor market divided between Smithian-type and Babbage-type workers and sometimes in Smithian-type and Babbage-type nations.

Sharing a rich general culture is important if individuals wish to become a Smithian-type rather than a Babbage-type of worker. However, a nation is much more than an institution that favors, and is favored by, the development of a general national culture. A nation is also an "imagined community" whose members feel a particular solidarity among themselves. Also, however, the "organic solidarity"[8] of the members of a nation can be related to the dynamic nature of the division of labor of a modern economy.

Even if having a large group of people share a common culture can reduce the risks associated with the division of labor, these risks are still very considerable in a modern economy. Some learning will still be job specific and will be impossible to employ elsewhere. Some form of risk sharing (or some form of organic solidarity) becomes necessary to exploit the benefits of a mutable division of labour. The existence of institutions of national solidarity, such as unemployment benefits and subsidized retraining, becomes necessary to induce people to take the risks of specialization. Otherwise, many individuals may choose to forgo the Smithian benefits and to occupy the bottom ranks of a division of labor organized along the lines suggested by Babbage.

The division of labor may also be limited by the extent of national

---

contexts are and which experiences of other contexts may be applicable. It allows a "learning of a higher order" in the sense that it is about contexts and not simply within contexts. Such a "learning of a higher order" is very important in a dynamic society where contexts are often changing. On the concept of "learning of higher order," see Bateson (1972).

[8] On the difference between the "mechanical solidarity" existing in backward societies and "organic solidarity," see Durkheim (1933), where he considers the relationship between these types of solidarity and the division of labor.

solidarity. Thus economic self-interest can provide some explanation for the fact that nations and nationalism emerged together with the diffusion of capitalism in the seventeenth century. In a world characterized by mobility across occupations, a homogeneous national culture and national solidarity have much economic importance and contribute to the wealth of nations. The intolerance for the multiplicity of ethnic groups and cultures (a multiplicity that characterized the former dynastic states) may also have a similar economic rationale.

Investments in "general culture" are general only in the sense that they can be applied in many jobs, but they are specific to that particular culture. If a particular culture fails to develop, or even to survive, one may lose many valuable investments in human capital. General investments that are specific to a particular culture may be inhibited by these risks. Political safeguards,[9] such as the existence of a state that safeguards ethnic investment, can reduce the risks of culture-specific investments. These safeguards not only protect sunk ethnic investments, they also favor new investments in ethnicity, which in turn makes it convenient to invest in new political safeguards. A cumulative causation process between cultural and political nationalism then takes place.

National culture and national solidarity can be greatly enhanced and sometimes be invented by a national state.[10] Thus the emergence of both cultural and political nationalism can be explained by the advent of capitalism.

If certain "political entrepreneurs" can overcome the free-rider problems that characterize collective action, some investment in nationalism will take place and decrease the risks of the mobile division of labor that characterize market economies.

The existence of a mobile division of labor can make it rational to invest in nationalism. However, the converse is also true. The existence of a national community can induce rational agents to undertake the risks related to a mobile division of labor.

Thus nationalism and the mobility of the division of labor are self-reinforcing: The existence of a mobile division of labor induces rational agents to invest in the institutions of a national community that

---

[9] The role of these safeguards for ethnic-specific or culture-specific investments is similar to the role of the safeguards considered for firm-specific investments by Williamson (1985). This similarity becomes even more striking if we accept with Kreps (1990) that the development of the firm's culture is the key for understanding its nature.

[10] On this point, see Hobsbawm (1992) and Hobsbawm and Ranger (1983).

Can economics explain nationalism?

favor a mobile division of labor and vice versa.[11] Durkheim's organic solidarity and Smith's advantages of the division of labor may feed each other in a self-reinforcing circle.[12]

In this respect, *national capitalist* economies may describe *institutional equilibria*. The institutions of nationalism re-create the conditions under which investments in nationalism are necessary through the division of labor of a capitalist economy. The institutions of capitalism re-create the conditions under which this form of organization is convenient through the institutions of nationalism.[13]

It is in the nature of institutional equilibria[14] that a national capitalist economy, enjoying the Smithian benefits, may never take off.

If the institutions of nationalism are missing, acquiring skills is too risky. On the other hand, if people do not have skills, the investments in the institutions of nationalism, which safeguard these skills, are not convenient. Many people who are not able to associate themselves in viable nations may be left at the periphery of the world economy and at the bottom of a Babbage-type division of labor.

Moreover, it is in the nature of institutional equilibria that one may be stuck in a wrong "nation." Even when a nation of a different size could extend the scope for the division of labor and the efficiency of the economy, solidarity, trust, and political safeguards may induce people to make investments that are specific to a certain national culture (and vice versa). This outcome may also arise because the benefits of nationality are unequally distributed. Small groups, enjoying large and possibly unequal benefits, may invest in the formation of nations that are otherwise "inferior institutional equilibria" for the majority of the population.

---

[11] Other self-reinforcing mechanisms do not work through the interaction with economic factors. One of them was considered by Ernest Renan in his pioneering lecture given in Paris in 1882. He claims that "a nation's existence" is "a daily plebiscite, just as an individual's existence is a perpetual affirmation of life." However, the results of this plebiscite are self-reinforcing because a nation is "a large-scale solidarity, constituted by the feeling of sacrifices that one has made in the past and of those that one is prepared to make in the future" (Renan 1882, 19).

[12] Thus Durkheim's and Smith's contributions, concerning the division of labor, should not be seen as the "private properties" of two different disciplines but as foundations of the analysis of a complex problem.

[13] The concept of "institutional equilibrium" is a close relative of the concept of "organisational equilibrium" developed in Pagano (1993).

[14] Similar inefficiencies arise for the case of "organisational equilibria." See Pagano (1993).

Does nationalism maximize the wealth of the nation or the rents of the nationalists?

The possibility that nationalists may fight for inferior institutional equilibria is consistent with Breton (1964), who proposed an *ante litteram* rent-seeking approach to the study of nationalism.[15]

Breton shows how nationalistic investments can be a rational choice for a group seeking particular privileges at the expense of other social groups of the same nation. In particular, the middle class can gain from investments in nationality. Its members can get better jobs when other ethnic groups cannot compete for them. In this way, investments yielding a higher social rate of return are sacrificed for projects that maximize the privileges of the middle class.

Nationalistic investments may have also the result of manipulating the preferences of the working class so that it may even gain some psychological benefits from the nationalistic policies. However, these psychological benefits are only obtained at the cost of losing the fruits of unbiased investment projects yielding a higher rate of return.[16]

In these cases, nationalists have an effect that is opposite to (but not inconsistent with) that considered by Gellner. Instead of creating cultural homogeneity, solidarity, and market mobility, they invent "old" traditions that bring about intolerance and discord. In this way, they can break a nation into smaller nations where they can hold the best jobs. They tend to limit, instead of enhance, market mobility and the positive effects of the division of labor. They do not create or enlarge markets but break them up in order to gain some rents that would be wiped out by competition in larger national markets.

Other economists have described nationalist movements in ways that are opposite to that taken by Breton. They argue that nationalistic policies are necessary to promote the development of third world countries. Protectionism is seen as a way of maximizing the wealth of the nation rather than the rents of the nationalists.

---

[15] Rent seeking does not occur only in the public sector of the nation but also in the private sector and, in particular, within the firm (Breton and Wintrobe [1982] and Milgrom and Roberts [1990]). Again, there is a certain similarity between the problems of a nation and those that arise within a firm. The classic application of the "collective action" failure problem to the explanation of "the rise and fall of Nations" is Olson (1982).

[16] Breton (1964) shows that the nationalistic policies carried out by the Quebecois government were not *income-creating* but *income-redistributing* in favor of the French Quebecois middle class. This redistribution was obtained at the expense of English-speaking, old middle class *and* at the expense of the French-speaking working class. The working class was, at most, getting some "psychological" advantages.

Nationalistic policies based on active protection of the national "infant" industry have characterized the development of those countries that Marxists call now imperialist countries. For instance, the father of protectionism, Friedrich List (1909), advocated protectionist policies for the German states and formed his views by observing and defending the United States' protectionist policies.

According to these approaches, the nationalistic policies followed by less developed countries are a rational reaction to the fact that free trade inhibits their development.

Alternatively, recent dependency theorists (for instance, Palma [1978]) have maintained that the system of free trade does not completely inhibit development. However, according to them this development is functional to the needs of the countries of the "imperialist centre"; it does not satisfy the needs of the nations of the "periphery."

According to this approach, economic dependency causes political dependency in the sense originally suggested by Hirschman (1945). Even if international trade brings about gains from exchange, the importance of these gains relative to the size of the national economies is asymmetrical and can cause political dependency. In turn, political dependency can cause economic dependency in a self-sustaining vicious circle. The imperialist power can blackmail other nations and inhibit some patterns of development that damage its interests. For instance, the imperialist nations may try to concentrate Smithian-types of jobs in their national territories and try to locate the bottom ranks of a Babbage-type division of labor in the third world.

Sometimes nationalists claim that breaking political and economic dependency is strictly related to the end of the relation of "cultural dependency" from the "imperialist" powers. They mean by cultural dependency that the culture they consume is produced somewhere else and is not tailored to needs of their nations.

The protection of local culture may, however, bring about an inward-looking provincial mentality that is only in the interest of some "rent-seeking intellectuals." Moreover, local culture may segment the market and limit the advantages of the division of labor along the lines that we have already considered.

However, if the development of local culture has the effect of increasing cultural homogeneity and ethnic solidarity,[17] then it can have positive effects on market mobility and deliver some "Smithian advantages" of the division of labor.

---

[17] Also on this ground, Kennan (1993) advocates the breakup of the United States.

By contrast, the role of passive consumers of an alien culture may confine the members of a certain ethnic group to the inferior positions of a Babbage-type division of labor. Skill saving requires that the jobs needing a more active cultural participation are separated from the other jobs. The members of the periphery happen to have a comparative advantage in jobs characterized by little cultural participation. This reinforces their position of passive consumers of an alien culture and, in a vicious circle, their perverse comparative advantage.

Although a self-sustaining situation of cultural dependency is possible, cultural protectionism may make things even worse; only sometimes is cultural protectionism helpful in breaking this vicious circle. In general, cultural protectionism is a bad way of protecting a culture: Each culture can only progress and survive if it is able to integrate in some creative way the best aspects of the other cultures. The exposure of a culture to the outside world may be a condition for its long-term survival.

The nationalistic arguments in favor of the protection of jobs from foreign competition are somewhat more convincing than those concerning foreign commodities and foreign culture. In this case, it also is possible to argue that immigration control simply provides rents for the workers who would otherwise be wiped out by the competition of foreign workers. However, if a state intends to guarantee some form of cultural homogeneity and national solidarity that may favor Smithian-type specialization and market mobility, then some immigration control may become necessary. Any attempt to provide everybody with the same basic skills is doomed to fail if it is impossible to limit the access of foreigners to the nation. If the common culture of a national community is to be preserved (also for reasons other than its economic benefits), the speed of immigration must be compatible with the speed of integration. The feasibility of the institutions of national solidarity (such as full-employment policies, unemployment benefits, and health insurance) requires that their access not be open to an unlimited number of foreigners.

There is some evidence that restrictions on immigration have come together with the growth of the institutions of national solidarity. Indeed, according to Carr (1945), the approach to immigration problems is the crucial characteristic that distinguishes twentieth-century from nineteenth-century nationalism.[18]

---

[18] According to Carr, the difference between these two periods of nationalism start emerging during the last three decades of the nineteenth century but reveal their unexpected dangerous consequences in the first half of the twentieth century when nationalism causes two world wars in the space of a single generation.

According to Carr, the "liberal" nationalism of the nineteenth century was based on the view that the state should simply defend property rights and not interfere with mechanisms of national and international trade. The beliefs in the automatic mechanisms of laissez-faire and in the formal divorce between political and economic power contributed to the relatively peaceful relations among nations that characterize the nineteenth century. During this period, nations were more political and cultural than economic units (or at least many of their members believed that this was their nature). For this reason, they were not an obstacle to international trade or to factors of mobility. Moreover, until 1870, nationalism promoted the unification of smaller states (Italian and German unification) and contributed to the expansion of national markets.[19]

Carr maintains that the different characteristics of twentieth-century nationalism, including its more violent nature, are derived from three factors: the socialization of the nation, the nationalization of economic policy, and the geographical extension of nationalism.

The socialization of the nation, that is, the bringing of new social strata to full membership in the nation, emerged during the last three decades of the nineteenth century. "Its landmarks were the development of industry and industrial skills; the rapid expansion in number and importance of urban population; the growth of workers organisations and of the political consciousness of the workers; the introduction of universal compulsory education; and the extension of the franchise" (p. 18). The democratization of the nation in the nineteenth century was centered on the assertion of the political claims of the dominant middle class. By contrast, "the socialisation of the nation for the first time brings economic claims of the masses into the forefront of the pictures" (p. 19). The levels of wages and employment become

---

[19] Even if it is always dubious to formulate these distinctions in terms of a single date, it is convenient to set clear limits to some historical periods with certain common characteristics. However, the choice of the year 1870 can be very misleading without the two following qualifications. First, this date is chosen referring only to European, American, and Japanese history. Second, it does simply distinguish between cases of relatively "easy" nationalism and the cases of difficult or impossible nationalism. Before that date, nationalist activity was carried out by peoples who were already endowed with a compact territory and a reasonably homogeneous culture. After 1870, in Europe, the center of nationalistic activity shifted to Eastern Europe, where this compactness and cultural standardization did not exist or could be only obtained by some suitable "ethnic cleansing." However, in our century, in Asia and Africa some nationalistic movements have faced conditions similar to those obtaining in Europe before 1870.

central issues in national policy, to be asserted, if necessary, against the national policies of other countries.[20]

The nationalization of economic policy was a direct consequence of the extension of national aspirations to the well-being of the entire population. An international economic order could be compatible with national political power only insofar as the economy was not a political issue. When the attention to social issues replaced laissez-faire, the single world economy was necessarily replaced by a multiplicity of national economies, each concerned with the well-being of its own members.

The socialization of the nation and the nationalization of economic policy found their most dramatic expression in the radical changes of immigration policies that occurred after 1919 when all industrial countries closed their frontiers to large-scale immigration.

The nineteenth-century governments could welcome immigration on the ground that a competitive national economy required cheap and abundant labor. By contrast, "cheap and abundant" (p. 22) labor could be a fatal political blow for twentieth-century governments. Cheap and abundant labor disappeared from the political dictionary to be replaced by the unappealing words, "low wages and unemployment."

Immigration restrictions clarified that nationality meant not only political but also economic membership in a community. The nation was not only providing national defense, the definition and enforcement of property rights, and a homogeneous culture, but also providing education, skilled jobs, health, unemployment benefits, and many public goods. Nationality gave an exclusive membership in the enjoyment of these goods.

The effects of immigration restrictions were ambiguous. On the one hand, unrestricted immigration dilutes the incentives to invest in public goods that are necessary for the well-being of the large majority of the population of the nation.[21] In this sense, immigration restrictions can increase the wealth of nations. On the other hand, immigration

---

[20] Carr (1945, 19) observes that "the socialisation of the nation has as its natural corollary the nationalisation of socialism," and in a footnote he points out that "it need hardly to be said that the term 'national socialism' is not a 'Nazi' invention." Seers (1983, 48) shows how (anti-)nationalism and (anti-) egalitarianism can be joined together to draw the ideological map that underlies modern politics.

[21] We are referring to goods that are public in the sense that it is impossible or very costly to exclude the individuals who live in a certain area from their consumption. They are not public goods in the sense that the quantity and quality of the goods consumed by each individual are independent of the amounts consumed by other individuals.

restrictions imply that nations cannot acquire some of the skills they need. Skill shortages tended to produce positions of monopoly and other privileges that cannot easily be eliminated by foreign competition. In this sense, immigration restrictions impoverish the nation and enhance the rents of particular groups of workers.

A similar ambiguity characterizes the various forms of employment protection, job definitions, standardization, and restrictions based on qualifications that characterize much of twentieth-century legislation.

Different forms of regulations may be necessary to induce firm-specific or occupation-specific investments. In the former case, employment protection of a job in a particular firm may be a necessary condition for firm-specific investments. In the latter case, the characteristics of a job, including the pattern of qualifications, are standardized across firms.

Employment protection in a particular firm is associated with the existence of an internal job market, and it is related to the bureaucratic complexity of modern firms. This bureaucratic complexity may be the only way to favor exchanges in situations where property rights in skills cannot be legally defined and must be based on the reciprocal trust of insiders (Breton and Wintrobe 1982).

By contrast, job standardization may be a way of creating property rights and national occupational markets for skilled occupations. In this way, a worker can find the same "slot" defining the same occupation in different firms. Job standardization implies that firm-specific investments are greatly reduced and are replaced by general investments that can be taken by the workers from one firm to the other (Pagano 1991).

The creation of these national markets may be quite complex; employers, possibly in collusion with their own employees, may be tempted to change job specification and make it less general and more specific to the particular needs of their firms. Markets for skilled occupations are a public good, and individuals may free ride in its provisions. National employers and employees' associations may be one way of limiting this free riding. Active state intervention in educational policy and definitions of occupational standards may also be necessary for the institutional viability of occupational markets.

However, state regulations can have the unfortunate effect of segmenting occupational markets into national markets characterized by different systems of regulations. They reinforce the obstacles to free movement due to immigration control and share with immigration restrictions the ambiguity that they can have either wealth-creation or rent-seeking consequences.

The socialization of the nation and the nationalization of economic policy, which started in the last decades of the last century, show how the state can improve the institutions of national solidarity and national culture that are the conditions for an efficient division of labor within the nation. We have seen in the preceding section how the interaction of these elements may imply self-sustaining inferior equilibria by which people may be stuck in the wrong division of labor and in the wrong nation. This limitation of nationalism also becomes more clear after 1870.

The year 1870 marks the end of relatively "easy" nation building: Before that date, new nations could easily be defined either because nation building was attempted where some administrative units preexisted the formation of the nation or because it was attempted where a high degree of cultural homogeneity existed over a compact territory before political unity.

Before 1870, nationalism helped the extension of markets: Nationalists abolished local feudal rights, trade restrictions imposed by the "mother country," or artificial confines that make the size of the state smaller than the nation.

After 1870, smaller ethnic groups, dispersed and mixed with other ethnic groups in the same territory, tried to acquire a status of nations. Nationalism often becomes associated with separatism and intolerance. The inflation of nationalism often tends to break instead of create markets. Rent-seeking explanations become more convincing than wealth-creating explanations of nationalist activities.[22]

The disastrous experiences of the first half of this century have given nationalism a sinister connotation. After the Second World War, for many years, with the exception of the "national liberation movements," nationalism has been replaced by the allegiance to universalistic values such as the free world and communism. Still, national states were the basic organizational form during the postwar period, and nationalism has vigorously reemerged immediately after the definitive end of the conflict between the "free" and the "communist" worlds.

Since 1989, nationalism has reemerged with all the terrible ambiguities that have characterized its history. However, "internationalism" and "cosmopolitanism" also are not free from ambiguities. The forma-

---

[22] This does not mean that there are not many recent cases in which a wealth-creating explanation of nationalism is more appropriate. For instance, the case of South Korea shows how "nationalistic" state intervention can contribute to the development of a country. On this issue, see Chang (1991).

tion of larger communities can mean that many of the functions gradually acquired through the socialization of nations and the nationalization of economic policy are transferred to wider organizations. These organizations can better perform these functions in a world made smaller by multinational firms,[23] communication, media transports, and pollution and where national wars can mean the end of humankind.

However, the decline of the national state may involve the setting aside of those institutions of national solidarity that gradually emerged after 1870 and that have grown considerably since the Second World War. Those who advocate the decline of the powers of the national state have sometimes a vested interest in the dismantling of the institutions of national solidarity. Others try to rebuild the same institutions in wider communities.

Either nationalism or the rejection of nationalism can be due to "general" or to "particular" interests. However, in both cases, the contrast between rent-seeking and wealth-creation approaches should not be overstated. In many cases, both explanations may apply; in some other historical situations, only one explanation is appropriate. Moreover, both approaches explain nationalism as a rational choice of agents who seek to increase their welfare. In this way, they come to share the assumption that factors such as national identity, pride, and power play a negligible, or at least a subsidiary, role in explaining nationalism. For these reasons, we can label both explanations as "economic" explanations of nationalism.

What do nationalists maximize?

Breton points out that "nationality" is a public good. This should imply that each individual should shirk and contribute very little to the production of nationality.

In this respect, it should not be relevant whether the returns of the public good are only the rents gained by the group making the investment in nationality or also the returns generated by the development of the entire nation. If individuals cannot find a solution to the usual free-rider problem they will undersupply investments in nationality.

This free-rider problem should give some hope to those who dislike nationalism. Unfortunately, experience does not seem to support this speculation. Every day we learn from the media that (too) many

---

[23] On the redefinition of national policies in the age of multinational firms, see Reich (1991).

people are ready, and often happy, to sacrifice their wealth and their lives for their nations.[24] These sacrifices are not easy to explain for an economic approach where people seek to maximise their wealth.[25]

We will try to explain the readiness of people to engage in nationalistic activities by addressing ourselves to the following facts. First, many people participating in nationalistic activities claim that living together with people of other nationalities is challenging or preventing them from expressing their way of life and destroying their identity. Second, sometimes national groups seem to accept "cohabitation" with other national groups only if they have the "power" to rule the country. Third, people are sometimes ready to sacrifice their wealth and life for these struggles for national identity and power.

Can economics explain these facts? Can we redefine utility maximization to explain nationalistic behavior? Do nationalists maximize anything or are they crazy and irrational?

In this section, I will try to give a positive answer to these questions. The answer will be based on two possible "extensions" of the textbook description of maximizing behavior: the first considers that individuals also take into account "symbolic utility" whereas the second examines the consequences of the possibility that individuals derive utility from "positional goods."

Utility maximization should not only take into account the utility of what *we have* (and the activities we carry out) but also the utility we get from what (we think) *we are*. In his book, *The Examined Life*, Robert Nozick (1989) has called this type of utility "symbolic utility." The idea of symbolic utility has caused a radical change in his views about state intervention in the distribution of wealth. Many of our actions give us symbolic utility in the sense that they increase our welfare by defining what we are in a way that we find desirable. For instance, we may vote, in spite of the gap existing between the effect of our vote on the outcome of the election and the effort of voting, because we want to define our political identity; similarly, we may decide to redistribute wealth because we want to define ourselves as part of a community that cares for its members.

We can obtain traditional utility maximization as a particular case of the symbolic utility framework. In principle, we may also like to

---

[24] And perhaps, the same people shirk when the public good to be provided is a cleaner public toilet!

[25] In the traditional economic approach, consumption goods and leisure are the objective of the utility function. Work is simply considered as forgone leisure and is not satisfactorily treated in this approach (see Pagano, 1985). On the other hand, it is possible to give a more general interpretation to the economic approach.

see ourselves as individuals who maximize *only* the utility obtained from traditional consumption goods.

However, this is only one particular possibility and does not seem very appealing: When we define ourselves in this way, we immediately hit the limitations due to the shortness of our life and to the relative fragility of our existence. In theory, "rational individuals" should maximize taking the constraints of their life as given.

Unfortunately, these constraints do not gently bind us; often we hit them in a very painful way. For this reason, we try to redefine ourselves in such a way that these constraints look less binding and become more acceptable. This is usually done by defining ourselves as members of something larger that does not share the same limitations. Suppose that redefining ourselves as members of a nation relaxes these constraints and makes us feel that we can overcome these limitations. In this case, utility-maximizing persons may happily and rationally die for their nation and enjoy being part of something that will never die.

This extension of the economic approach is consistent with the explanation of the origin of nationalism that is offered by Benedict Anderson (1991) in his beautiful book *Imagined Communities*. Anderson observes that "no more arresting emblems of the modern culture of nationalism exist than cenotaphs and tombs of 'Unknown Soldiers.' The public ceremonial reverence accorded these monuments precisely *because* they are deliberately empty or no one knows who lies inside them, has no true precedents in earlier times" (p. 10). Why do people feel such a sense of solidarity for somebody that they only know to have died for the national cause?[26] Why do they not express the same feeling of solidarity for people who die for other causes? Why is it so difficult to imagine a Tomb of the Unknown Marxist or a cenotaph for Fallen Liberals?

The reasons for this particular status of nationalism is that, unlike liberalism and Marxism, nationalism is much concerned with death and immortality. In this respect, nationalism has a strong affinity with religion. Like religion, nationalism transforms the contingency of human life into continuity and reduces the anguish that may come from the awareness of its fragility.

The eighteenth century did not simply see the rise of nationalism but also the crisis of a Christian vision of the world. The Enlighten-

---

[26] Ernest Gellner has pointed out to me that in "his" village in Liguria there is a shrine dedicated to the victims of *all wars*, without any restriction! However, this shows how "internationalist" feelings of solidarity adopt and generalize the symbols used by nationalists.

ment could successfully destroy paradise and salvation but not the needs that they satisfied. "Disintegration of Paradise: nothing makes fatality more arbitrary. Absurdity of salvation: nothing makes another style of continuity more necessary. What was then required was a secular transformation of fatality into continuity, contingency into meaning" (p. 13). The nation was well suited to this purpose. Even when the nation had just been invented, it was supposed to have existed since time immemorial, well before its political expression in a national state. It was also supposed to last for ever and realize its "mission" in the world. The members of the nation could believe that, in spite of their individual contingency, they shared the immortality of their imagined communities.

Religion and nationalism could be seen as alternative ways of attaining symbolic utility, and the crisis of the former favored the rise of the latter. The crisis of Marxism (and consequently of the defense of the free world) also has perhaps favored the recent reemergence of nationalism in a similar way.

The considerations made above seem to imply that an extended rational choice framework could explain the demand for alternative sources of symbolic utility and, therefore, the rise of nationalism when alternative means of getting it become less appealing.

The idea that people choose the sources of symbolic utility that best satisfy their needs is, however, somewhat contradictory. The point is that often people can attain symbolic utility only if they believe that religion or nationality constitute their identity independently of their choice. An identity that is chosen by an individual would seem to share the contingency and limitations of the individuals. In order to satisfy the need to relax the constraints of individual life, an identity must be such that individuals feel that they are not choosing their identity but rather that the identity has chosen them.

A god or a nation that is chosen to maximize our utility is meaningless and is useless to overcome the fragility and the contingency of our lives. This need can only be satisfied if we believe that the god or the nation has chosen us in order to realize its will. Only in this way can individuals believe that they are now part of something bigger that survives their bodies.

"Dying for one's country, which one does not choose, assumes a moral grandeur which dying for the Labour Party, the American Medical Association, or perhaps even Amnesty International can not rival, for these are all bodies one can join or leave at easy will" (p. 144). According to Anderson, the fact that we can choose to join these

Can economics explain nationalism? 193

associations inhibits our commitment to their goals. If we are aware of the fact that these institutions represent our interests, our actions do not acquire an aura of purity. Only this purity can make us feel part of a great cause that overcomes the limitations of our existence. "Ironically enough, it may be that to the extent that Marxist interpretations of history are felt (rather than intellected) as representation of ineluctable necessity, they also acquire an aura of purity and disinterestedness."[27]

In spite of the fact that individuals are engaged in these exercises of self-deception,[28] nationalism and other sources of symbolic utility can perhaps be seen as substitutes. If this view is correct, one way of limiting the excess of nationalism is to supply alternative means of obtaining symbolic utility in the post-1989 world. For instance, it is an open issue whether the ecological movement[29] can supply this alternative and make people feel that they have been chosen to save the world. It would be a very good outcome also for people who simply believe that they choose to save the world.

A second extension of traditional utility maximization may help to explain nationalism: to consider power and prestige, and not only wealth, as legitimate arguments of the utility function. In this way, national power and prestige can also be integrated in economic analysis.

Power and prestige have some characteristics that distinguish them from other goods. We can easily imagine a society where everyone consumes large quantities of goods such as rice, cars, and housing space. It is much harder to imagine a society where everyone con-

---

[27] Anderson (1991, 144). On the other hand, Robert Meister (1990, 24) argues that "Marx's political identification with the interests of the proletariat was a conclusion not an assumption. This makes his analytical framework especially relevant for those who may doubt his conclusion, but for whom the question of political identity remains important."

[28] On the relationship between self-deception and rational choice, see Elster (1993). Although self-deception could be a "rational" way of dealing with ourselves, this pushes the limits of rationality to a point where this concept may become an obstacle to the understanding of complex organizations. According to Simon (1991), the existence of complex organizations may be explained by the limits of human reason.

[29] An advantage of the ecological movement is that it can offer an identity that, as in the case of the great religions, is related to the role of humankind in the universe. This does not mean that a new ecological identity cannot be constructed by referring to natural sciences. In her book, *The Ecological Self,* Mathews (1991) shows that modern physics, and modern science in general, are very well suited to the construction of this identity.

sumes large quantities of power and prestige. Saying that everyone consumes power and prestige is tantamount to saying that nobody consumes these goods.

Any positive amount of power and prestige must be jointly consumed with negative quantities of it: It seems impossible to exercise power if somebody does not undergo the exercise of this power or, in other words, it is impossible for somebody to dominate if somebody is not dominated: Positive power must be jointly consumed with negative power.[30] In a similar way, it is impossible for somebody to consume prestige or "social superiority" if others do not consume some social "inferiority"; again, positive and negative amounts of the good must be jointly consumed.

Unlike traditional economic goods, power and prestige inevitably involve a particular relationship or "position" of one individual with respect to other individuals; for this reason, following Fred Hirsch's terminology, we can call goods like power and prestige "positional goods." In traditional economic theory, we usually consider two types of goods (and their intermediate combinations): private and public goods.

Private goods are characterized by the fact that other individuals consume a zero amount of what I consume: The other individuals are excluded from the consumption of my private goods. This exclusion is impossible in the case of a public good. In the case of a pure public good, another agent consumes the same positive amount that I consume. We may say that a pure positional good is a good that another agent consumes in the same, but negative amount that I consume. In this respect, positional goods define a case that is polar to the case of public goods.[31]

It is not surprising that the problems of positional goods are opposite to the problems of public goods: It is very likely that we will have overinvestment in positional goods when all the agents try to consume positive amounts of these goods. Positional competition is much harder, and sometimes more violent, than competition for private goods.

Consider the case that if all the individuals work harder they may all consume more private and public goods. Even when this is not

---

[30] Parsons (1986) disagrees but, as Aron (1986) maintains, he seems to be confusing the power over somebody with the power to do something. The former (and obviously not the latter) is a zero-sum good. On the concept of power, see also the other essays collected in Lukes (1986).

[31] This definition is given in Pagano (1990). A different definition, based on rank, is given by Frank (1985).

possible and there is a problem of natural scarcity (so that some goods are in fixed supply) the egalitarian distribution of these goods is not incompatible with their positive consumption.

The same is not true for positional goods like power and prestige: If we all work harder none of us can consume more of them. Moreover, no positive and egalitarian distribution of them is simultaneously possible: In some ways, social scarcity constrains the welfare of human kind much more than natural scarcity.

If power and prestige are positional goods, national power and prestige are simultaneously public and positional goods: They are a public good for the members of the same national community, and they are a positional good for the members of other national communities. The usual argument, based on the public good view of "national defense," implies that there is a tendency to undersupply national power and prestige; by contrast, the positional nature of national power and prestige implies that there may be a terrible tendency to overinvest in nationalistic activities – a tendency that the acquisition of wealth and consumption goods can only partially explain.

Indeed, economists like Schumpeter and Keynes were aware of the importance of something like positional goods in the explanation of nationalism. According to them the rational desire to accumulate wealth that is the characteristic of capitalist society cannot be the cause of nationalistic policies. They maintained that the desire to accumulate wealth could inhibit nationalism.

In his book, *Imperialism and Social Classes*, Schumpeter (1919) challenged the thesis of the Marxists and maintained that capitalists were not "imperialist" but rather peaceful. Peace was necessary for the expansion and the security of industry and commerce that were their most typical activities. Imperialism[32] was the expression of precapitalist social forces and ideas (such as national glory and power) that still survived in the capitalist societies. The capitalist attitude to look rationally for economic opportunities to increase wealth would have eventually attenuated nationalistic feelings.

In his *The General Theory of Employment Interest and Money*, Keynes (1936, p. 374) made a similar point, arguing that some dangerous tendencies of humankind, such as the insane passions for exercising authority and power, could be channeled into the tendency to accumulate wealth. Keynes was aware of the fact that the former can be a means to the latter, but he pointed out how it can also be an alternative to it.

---

[32] For a survey of the theories of imperialism, see Hobson (1938).

In his beautiful book, *The Passions and the Interests*, Hirschman (1977) showed that this type of argument was in fact used to support the expansion of commerce and capitalism before they spread on a massive scale; commerce and capitalism were expected to make men kinder and sweeter. According to this view, the passions of military aristocracy in search of prestige, glory, and power would have been replaced by the dull but peaceful pursuit of economic interests typical of capitalism. Market competition for goods and services with all its hardship was supposed to replace a much harder competition: that for honor, glory, power, and prestige.

Thus peaceful and reasonable capitalists may have the merit of replacing zero-sum rivalries for prestige and power with the gains from trade typical of market competition; the maximization of wealth gives us peace and freedom from nationalistic passions.

In my opinion this last view is too extreme. Rational activities intended to increase our wealth can sometimes explain nationalism and nationalist policies along the lines considered in the first two sections of this chapter.[33]

However, some extensions of the economic approach are necessary to explain some aspects of nationalism. Symbolic utility and positional goods can offer a way to make the generosities and the atrocities of nationalism compatible with rational choice types of explanations. Individuals may wish to define themselves as members of powerful nations and may wish to consume pride and superiority with respect to other national and ethnic groups. Unfortunately, if many national groups share these wishes, then an overinvestment in nationalism takes place. This overinvestment by possibly rational agents may perhaps help to explain some of the most regrettable aspects of our age.

Do nationalists and nationalism maximize their fitness?

In the preceding section, we have seen that there are possible ways of defending the thesis that nationalists "make rational choices" that explain their behavior. We have seen that this explanation has the limit that nationalism can be a source of symbolic utility only when people believe that they have not chosen to be nationalists. However, is there an alternative explanation for nationalistic behavior that can put on relatively firm ground the idea that the individuals do not

---

[33] Moreover, it is doubtful that under capitalism the desire to accumulate wealth replaces the need for power, prestige, and other positional goods: In many cases, they are not substitutes but they are instead (strictly) complementary goods.

choose to be nationalistic but may rather be "chosen" by nationalism?

In my opinion, the recent evolutionary approach can help us a great deal here. Evolutionary biology uses many of the tools that are also used by economists: Maximization, equilibrium, and stability are concepts used by both disciplines. However, one relevant difference is that, whereas evolutionary biology explains the behavior of the animals in terms of maximizing behavior, the optimizing units are not the individual animals but genes. Genes can maximize their fitness even when this is inefficient for the individuals or even for the species.

Consider a bee sacrificing its individual existence for its own "people": Biologists would not explain this behavior by referring to the maximizing behavior of the "nationalistic" bee but by referring to the maximization of the "nationalistic gene" acting in the bee. The gene is ready to sacrifice the individual bee to increase its own fitness. The bee may be irrational but, in some particular way, the gene is rational even if not intentionally rational. Bees with nationalistic genes will be better able to defend their offspring and will reproduce faster: In the long run, only bees having nationalistic genes will survive. Nationalism maximizes its fitness while many individual nationalists die.

We have used the term "nationalism" to suggest that there are mechanisms by which, in principle, the maximization of something other than utility of the individual agent could explain the emergence of some strong identification with a certain group that, as in the case of nationalism, can even lead to the extreme sacrifice of the individual.

However this analogy can be very misleading without some qualifications. In the first place, cases of extreme altruism such as that of the bee are very uncommon in the animal world. They are limited to cases like those of "social insects," where an entire population shares a single parent and a large fraction of her genes. In this case, it is in the interest of the gene to sacrifice one individual "transmitter" in order to increase its own fitness. In cases of unrelated individuals, the fitness of the selfish gene would run against this generous attitude.[34] In the second place, unlike what I have termed "bees' nationalism," human nationalism is largely a social attitude that is culturally and not (only) genetically transmitted.

---

[34] However, some cooperative behavior can evolve among animals engaged in repeated interactions; a bat can find it convenient to donate blood to other unrelated bats that are starving. The temptation of defecting is offset by the future gains of cooperation that can arise when the bat is starving (Dawkins, 1989, 231). However, unlike for bats, which donate the blood (taken from somebody else), there is no future "repeated game" for the "nationalistic bee" that sacrifices itself. In this sense, the biological implications of Axelrod (1984) do not work for the nationalistic bee.

In spite of these considerations, it is possible to apply some kind of evolutionary reasoning to the case of human societies that may offer some justification for the type of self-sacrificing "irrational" behavior that is sometimes associated with nationalism.

In his popular book, *The Selfish Gene,* Dawkins (1989) has pointed out that the validity of evolutionary models is not limited to biology but can be extended to all the cases where some "replicators" interact directly or indirectly.

Replicators are units having the property of creating copies of themselves. In biology these units are the genes. However, in different evolutionary contexts, other units share these characteristics. Units such as ways of behaving or ideas are not genetically transmitted but can be replicated by imitation and by a limited amount of learning. Especially in the first years of life, imitation can be often unconscious. However, in many cases, especially if the environment is sufficiently stable, imitation can also be a rational alternative to costly individual learning.

To emphasize the analogy with genes, Dawkins calls "memes" the "cultural" replicators that can flow from one generation to the other.[35] Even if we do not assume that culture can be encoded as discrete "particles," it is also important to emphasize that different aspects of a culture may survive better than others. Memes also maximize their fitness in a given environment.

Can the maximization of nationalistic memes explain nationalistic behavior? Is nationalism, when commonly adopted by the members of a population, a strategy that cannot be invaded by a mutant strategy or, in more technical terms, is nationalism a "culturally stable strategy?"[36]

According to Dawkins, "memes for blind faith have their own ruthless ways of propagating themselves. This is true of patriotic and political as well religious blind faith" (198).[37] However, Dawkins does

---

[35] For an application of the concept of memes to economic problems, see Hinterberger (1992).

[36] On the concept of culturally stable strategy (CSS) and its relation with evolutionary stable strategy (ESS) and developmentally stable strategy (DSS), see J. M. Smith (1982) and Boyd and Richerson (1985).

[37] Even if at a later stage nationalism becomes a way of getting symbolic utility as an alternative to universal religions, there is a close relationship between "tribal patriotism" and religion. In his *Elementary Forms of the Religious Life,* Durkheim (1947) showed that in primitive societies there was a universal tendency to believe in "tribal" gods and that the cult of god was a way of expressing the force and the unity of those societies. Primitive gods were "patriotic" gods. It is not hard to give a "mimetic" interpretation of this universal tendency. Societies that had not developed

Can economics explain nationalism?

not explain how nationalists can resist the invasions of "unpatriotic mutants" that free ride on the public good that is offered by their fellow countrymen.

An explanation of the resistance of nationalistic altruism to unpatriotic behavior is offered by Boyd and Richerson (1985) in their stimulating book, *Culture and the Evolutionary Process*.

Boyd and Richerson claim that one alternative way of explaining the evolution of altruistic cooperation is by imagining that individual selection within each group of individuals supplying a public good occurs together with selection among groups. If the marginal benefit of investing in the public good is greater than its marginal cost, then groups with a higher proportion of cooperators will enjoy a higher fitness. Selection among groups will imply that the number of cooperators will increase in the next generation. On the other hand, the selection within each group will imply that within the same group cooperators enjoy a fitness lower than free riders. Selection within groups will therefore have the opposite effect: It will imply that cooperators will decrease in the next generation.

Boyd and Richerson come to the conclusion that "co-operation will increase in the whole population only if selection among groups is a stronger force than selection within groups" (p. 230).

Boyd and Richerson observe that the theoretical arguments against group selection for the case of large groups are based on a model that assumes genetic inheritance, where selection and migration constantly erode the variation among subpopulations.[38] In the case of cultural inheritance, imitation can amplify the differentiation of the common characteristics of large subpopulations. Even in the case of large groups, group selection, based on cultural inheritance, may be a strong force.

The extinction of the groups characterized by a low level of cooperation does not entail the physical death of the individuals. The Boyd and Richerson model only requires a breakup of the group and the dispersed emigration of the individuals of the dissolved group to the other groups. If the size of the group that breaks up is not too large in relation to the entire population, the imitation mechanism will imply

---

cultural practices able to transmit patriotic feelings could not survive against those that were able to do so. In this respect, it was ironically true that primitive gods created primitive societies and that primitive societies survived only thanks to their gods.

[38] Thus biological selection cannot be used to justify the efficiency of the organizations of the species and cannot be the basis to justify the efficiency of human organizations. On this point, see Hodgson (1993).

that the immigration of the members of the dissolved group does not change the characteristics of the other groups: In each group, the few immigrants will imitate the behavior of the preexisting members. In other words, what matters for having this type of selection process is cultural extinction; physical extinction may be unnecessary.[39]

According to Boyd and Richerson, the human group that seems to satisfy the requirements of their model is the ethnic group. Ethnic groups are characterized by the fact that the flows of cultural traits within the groups are greater than those among groups. Cooperation within the ethnic group and conflicts and wars among ethnic groups are predicted by the model as interrelated consequences of a model of cultural evolution.

In an interview in *The New York Review of Books,* Isaiah Berlin has made a distinction between two concepts of nationalism: The first is not aggressive and stresses cooperation, solidarity, and familiarity with fellow countrymen whereas the other is aggressive and stresses conflict, violence, and hate for foreigners (Gardels, 1991). The Boyd and Richerson analysis implies that, even if it is possible that there are two different nationalistic "memes," their cultural fitness may have been interdependent. No cooperation and solidarity associated with the first meaning of nationalism would have evolved without the conflicts and wars associated with the second meaning of nationalism.

Can the "good nationalistic meme" be dissociated by its bad fellow meme? Can the "bad nationalistic meme" stop maximizing its fitness that, having already made so many victims, can now cause the extinction of humankind? Can we do much against the genes and memes that sometimes rule our minds with such devastating consequences? Can individual utility maximization and rational choice prevail on the replicators that maximize *their* fitness in *our* minds?

We will not even try to answer. We will simply try to get some encouragement by the words that can be found at the end of the first edition of *The Selfish Gene:* "We are built as gene machines and cultured as meme machines, but we have the power to turn against our creators. We alone on earth, can rebel against the tyranny of the selfish replicators" (Dawkins 1989, p. 201).

Can economics explain nationalism? In my opinion, the theories we have considered should not be regarded as mutually exclusive expla-

---

[39] Cultural group selection must be distinguished from the genetic selection that underlies the theories of racism. Indeed, the ease by which one culture may quickly spread among so many different individuals implies some fundamental biological unit of humankind. On the story of racism, see the beautiful collection of essays edited by Imbruglia (1992) that, unfortunately, is not available in English.

nations; each one of them can rather give some contribution to the explanation of some aspects of nationalism. Wealth creation and rent seeking, symbolic utility and positional goods, and, finally, the selfish replicators that maximize their fitness in our minds are all concepts that can help move toward the understanding of this complex phenomenon.

One may question whether some of these theories really do belong to economics. I have no answer to this question: An answer requires some agreement on the evolving boundaries of our discipline and some evaluation of the kind of fitness that is maximized by these boundaries. Both are beyond the scope of this chapter. Moreover, the relevant question may simply be: Can *we* explain nationalism and suggest what can be done against its nasty consequences?

References

Anderson, B. (1991) *Imagined Communities*. Verso, London.
Aron, R. 1986. "Macht, Power, Puissance: Democratic Prose or Demoniacal Poetry?" In Lukes, S., ed. *Power*. Oxford: Blackwell.
Axelrod, R. 1984. *The Evolution of Cooperation*. New York: Basic Books.
Babbage, C. 1832. *On the Economics of Machines and Manufactures*. Charles Knight: London.
Bateson, J. 1972. *Steps to an Ecology of Mind*. San Francisco: Chandler Publishing Company.
Boyd, R., and Richerson, J. 1985. *Culture and the Evolutionary Process*. Chicago: The University of Chicago Press.
Breton, A. 1964. "The Economics of Nationalism." *Journal of Political Economy* 72, no. 4:376–86.
Breton, A., and Wintrobe, R. 1982. *The Logic of Bureaucratic Conduct*. New York: Cambridge University Press.
Carr, E. H. 1945. *Nationalism and After*. London: Macmillan Press.
Chang, H. J. 1991. "The Political Economy of Industrial Policy." Ph.D. dissertation, University of Cambridge.
Dawkins, R. 1989. *The Selfish Gene*. New edition. New York: Oxford University Press.
Durkheim, E. 1933. *The Division of Labour in Society*. New York: Macmillan.
    1947. *The Elementary Forms of Religious Life*. New York: Free Press.
Elster, J. 1993. *Political Psychology*. New York: Cambridge University Press.
Frank, R. H. 1985. "The Demand for Unobservable and Other Non-Positional Goods." *American Economic Review* 75:101–16.
Gardels, N. 1991. "Two Concepts of Nationalism: An Interview with Isaiah Berlin." *The New York Review of Books*. November 20, 1991.
Gellner, E. 1983. *Nations and Nationalism*. Oxford: Blackwell Publisher.
    (1987) *Culture, Identity and Politics*. New York: Cambridge University Press.
Hinterberger, F. 1992. *Biological, Cultural, and Economic Evolution and the Economy-Ecology-Relationship*. Mimeo. Florence.
Hirsch, F. (1977) *Social Limits to Growth*. London: Routledge & Kegan Paul.

Hirshman, A. O. 1945. *National Power and the Structure of Foreign Trade*. Berkeley and Los Angeles: University of California Press.
1958. *The Strategy of Economic Development*. New Haven, CT: Yale University Press.
1977. *The Passions and the Interests. Political Arguments for Capitalism Before Its Triumph*. Princeton, NJ: Princeton University Press.
Hobsbawm, E. 1990. *Nations and Nationalism Since 1780*. New York: Cambridge University Press.
Hobsbawm, E., and Ranger, I. 1983. *The Invention of Traditions*. New York: Cambridge University Press.
Hobson, J. A. 1938. *Imperialism: A Study*. London: Allen & Unwin.
Hodgson, G. M. 1993. *Organisational Form and Economic Evolution: A Critique of the Williamsonian Hypothesis*. Mimeo. Cambridge.
Imbruglia, G., ed. 1992. *Il Razzismo e Le Sue Storie*. Naples: Edizioni Scientifiche Italiane.
Kennan, G. 1993. *Around the Cragged Hill: A Personal and Political Philosophy*. New York: Norton.
Keynes, J. M. 1936. *The General Theory of Employment Interest and Money*. London: Macmillan Press.
Kreps, D. 1990. "Corporate Culture and Economic Theory." In Alt, J. E., and Shepsle, K. J., eds. *Perspectives on Positive Political Economy*. New York: Cambridge University Press.
List, F. 1909. *The National System of Political Economy*. London: Longman Group.
Lukes, S., ed. 1987. *Power*. Oxford: Blackwell Publisher.
Mathews, F. 1991. *The Ecological Self*. London: Routledge & Kegan Paul.
Meister, R. 1990. *Political Identity. Thinking Through Marx*. Oxford: Blackwell Publisher.
Milgrom, P., and Roberts, J. 1990. "Bargaining Costs, Influence Costs and the Organization of Economic Activity." In Alt, J. E., and Shepsle, K. J., eds. *Perspectives on Positive Political Economy*. New York: Cambridge University Press.
Nozick, R. 1989. *The Examined Life: Philosophical Meditations*. New York: Touchstone Books.
Olson, M. L. 1982. *The Rise and Fall of Nations*. New Haven, CT: Yale University Press.
Pagano, U. 1985. *Work and Welfare in Economic Theory*. Oxford: Blackwell Publisher.
1990. *The Economics of Positional Goods*. Mimeo. Siena.
1991. "Property Rights, Asset Specificity, and the Division of Labour Under Alternative Capitalist Relations." *Cambridge Journal of Economics* 15, no. 3. Reprinted in Hodgson, G. 1993. *The Economics of Institutions*. A volume of *The International Library of Critical Writings in Economics*. Series editor: Mark Blaug. Cheltenham: Edward Elgar.
1993. "Organisational Equilibria and Institutional Stability." In Bowles, S., Gintis, H., and Gustafson, B., eds. *Markets and Democracy*. New York: Cambridge University Press.
Palma, J. G. 1978. "A Formal Theory of Underdevelopment or a Methodology for the Analysis of Concrete Situations of Underdevelopment?" *World Development* 6:881–94.

Parsons, T. 1986. "Power and the Social System." In Lukes, S., ed. 1986. *Power*. Oxford: Blackwell Publisher.
Polanyi, K. 1944. *The Great Transformation*. New York: Rinehart.
Reich, R. B. 1991. *The Work of Nations*. New York: Simon & Schuster.
Renan, E. 1882. "What is a Nation?" In Bhabha, H. K., ed. 1990. *Nation and Narration*. London: Routledge & Kegan Paul.
Schumpeter, J. 1919. *Imperialism and Social Classes*. New York: Augustus M. Kelley.
Seers, D. 1983. *The Political Economy of Nationalism*. New York: Oxford University Press.
Simon, H. A. 1991. "Organisations and Markets." *The Journal of Economic Perspectives* 5, no. 2:25–45.
Smith, Adam. [1776] 1976. *An Inquiry into the Nature and the Causes of the Wealth of Nations*. Ed. Cannan, A. Chicago: University of Chicago Press.
Smith, Anthony D. 1991. *National Identity*. Harmondsworth: Penguin Books.
Smith, J. M. 1982. *Evolution and the Theory of Games*. New York: Cambridge University Press.
Williamson, O. E. 1985. *The Economic Institutions of Capitalism*. New York: Free Press.

CHAPTER 10

The economics of socialist nationalism: Evidence and theory

Mario Ferrero

I Introduction

"Nation" and "nationality" are elusive notions. Repeated attempts by historians, sociologists, and anthropologists to identify an objective content that encompasses the myriad historical instances at hand have reportedly failed – be it territory, language, religion, race, culture, historical background, or any weighted sum thereof. As economists, we would therefore be wise to let nations and nationalities define themselves as they please.[1] If someone feels akin to someone else on whatever ground and calls this national identity or consciousness, then so be it. And if from this it follows that the two people prefer to live close together and share in the same political unit – a "nation-state" – then let them by all means do so. To an economist, tastes are not a matter for dispute. In this respect, a taste for nationality is no different than a taste for vegetarianism, and the quest for a nation-state is no different than the vegetarians' quest for a vegetarian club.

If this methodological approach is correct, however, the economist is hard-pressed to explain just why "nationalism" should exist – mean-

---

I am indebted to the participants in the 1992 Villa Colombella Seminar for extended discussion and to Alberto Cassone, Giorgio Brosio, Marco Buttino, Dinko Dubravcic, Michael Keren, and Guido Ortona for useful comments and suggestions on an earlier draft of this paper.

[1] This is the approach taken by Seton-Watson (1977, 5) in his very informative historical handbook on national problems. Anderson (1983, ch. 1) and Hobsbawm (1990, 5–8) emphatically concur with this view. As will be elaborated later in the chapter, communist theory, beginning with Stalin (1942), sharply disagrees and emphasizes territory as the distinctive mark of a nation. Rex and Mason, eds. (1986) provide an interdisciplinary assessment of the state of the art in the closely related fields of race and ethnicity; here, too, the search for objective criteria to define ethnicity has proved inconclusive.

ing active, often aggressive and violent, national or nationality-oriented policies and movements. To begin with, it is far from obvious that a "national club" should have an exclusive territory – a territorial political unit. Why not join your fellow nationals in the club next door to the other nationals' club – perhaps each with its own schools, churches, theaters, and so on? But even if one accepts that it is more practical, or safer, to have an exclusive territory for each national club, that is, a nation-state proper, what is it that in the long run of history can prevent any self-conscious nation from achieving its end? To take a current example, if Croats and Serbs want to live in separate, territorially based clubs, why fight to death for that? Why not just part company? True, national borderlines are blurred, there are Serbian enclaves within Croatia and vice versa. But if those people value nationality so highly, they ought to be ready to pay a higher price for an enclave area than that demanded by its current inhabitants, so that a mutually advantageous, peaceful exchange ought to be possible. True, people's mobility is costly and tradition plays a role, but such frictions are still a far cry from a bloodbath on the scale we are presently witnessing. True, historical processes always start from somewhere, and the legacy of past violence no doubt makes for an awkward transition. Still, when all is said, it is difficult to escape the impression that, barring the exercise of force from the outside, in the long run, "voting by the feet" should bring whatever number or variety of national clubs the people concerned desire: some homogeneous clubs or nation-states – one Croatian, another Serbian – and perhaps some mixed clubs or multinational states – comprising those Serbs and Croats who do not mind mixing up. It could be objected that problems of size, such as scale economies in production or consumption, may often stand in the way of a full-fledged separating equilibrium of voluntary associations. But then separation can always be implemented in leisure time by means of voluntary residential self-segregation or, if that is not enough, by sacrificing some potential income to satisfy the taste for nationality. What might be called the competitive national jurisdictions utopia, drawn from the economic theory of clubs,[2] seems to have no place for people spending real resources, and possibly shedding their lives, for nationalist activities.

If, on the demand side, in a frictionless world, nationalism looks "irrational," then one is driven to look to the supply side of the nationality issue: In a society in which a taste for nationality is wide-

---

[2] A comprehensive survey of results and problems in club theory may be found in Sandler and Tschirhart (1980).

spread, there might well be political entrepreneurs who gain from "selling" nationalist policies, even if at a cost in terms of social welfare. As Gellner (1964, 169) bluntly puts it, "Nationalism is not the awakening of nations to self-consciousness: It invents nations where they do not exist." That is where Albert Breton's (1964) pathbreaking contribution comes in. Focusing on the case of Quebec's French-speaking Canadians, he defines nationalism as a policy of transferring foreign assets into the ownership of nationals, with full indemnification of previous owners. Since indemnification is paid for through general taxation, whereas the chief beneficiaries of "nationalization" are the national middle classes that gain privileged access to managerial positions, Breton comes to two conclusions: First, to the extent that job allocation is distorted away from marginal productivities in favor of national affiliation, the policy reduces potential wealth and is therefore socially inefficient; second, since private ownership rights and social relations remain unchanged after nationalization, the taxpaying blue-collar workers, unlike the middle class, are net losers, and their nationalism is therefore purely ideological.

Breton's beautifully simple approach (developed and generalized by Harry Johnson [1967]) is illuminating in that it cuts through the smoke screen of nationalist propaganda, but as its stated assumptions make clear, it cannot claim to cover all possible cases. In particular, although Breton (1964, 381) does note in passing that nationalists often find their closest allies in socialists because both groups favor state intervention, the possibility that nationalization might change not just the nationality of ownership holders and managerial personnel, but also the structure of property rights, lies outside the scope of his analysis. By interpreting nationalism as an investment in public capital whose return is a flow of high-income jobs for the middle class and whose net effect is a redistribution of income from the national working class to the national middle class, Breton is correctly drawn to conclude that the working class is fooled by nationalist politicians, and indeed its support for nationalist policies is typically cooler than that of the middle class. Breton goes on to note (1964, 380, 381) that, if the working class is poor, its resistance to redistribution can be overcome only by outright confiscation, in which event (as in the case of colonialism and anticolonialist policies), a redistribution of income between national groups also takes place. This points to the possibility that, if nationalism is coupled with more fundamental change in property arrangements, that is, if nationalization is to be followed by socialization, then the nature of gains and losses, the direction of redistribution, and the support for nationalism from the various social classes might all change. This paper is devoted to extending Breton's and Johnson's analysis to the intertwining of socialism and nationalism, both before a socialist revolution and within an established, multinational socialist state. Because we will be dealing with involuntary redistributions of property rights and shifts to different politico-economic systems, issues of nationalism, decolonization, and anti-imperialist struggle will necessarily intermingle to some extent – as they always did in communist theory and practice.

Perhaps to Breton's amazement, had Joseph Stalin been alive in the 1960s, he would have wholeheartedly approved of Breton's paper as an excellent exposure of "bourgeois nationalism." In his capacity as People's Commissar for Nationality Affairs in the early years of the Soviet Russian government and later as the recognized head of Soviet and worldwide communism, Stalin (1942) never tired of warning the working classes against the trap of a nationalist movement led by the national bourgeoisie, which, if successful, would mean for them a mere change of masters. Only a firm leadership by the proletariat and its vanguard party, he urged, would ensure a successful resolution of the national question to the working-class advantage, and only membership in the brotherhood of socialist nations would shield the working classes of the world from the self-serving exploitation of nationality issues on the part of the imperialist or neocolonial bourgeoisie. I will try to show that this promise was basically fulfilled, but that its very fulfillment feeds the rebirth of aggressive nationalism in the postcommunist scenario of these days.

The focus of the paper is on the political enterprises that compete for monopoly of the market for nationalism in a society in which a national problem at least potentially exists. Following Demsetz (1968), political competition is viewed here as competition "for the field" rather than "within the field": The winner takes all. To capture this monopoly, political entrepreneurs must solve the twin problems of, first, catering to the demands of different sections and classes of the population and, second, because they trade in promises or exchange present support for future rewards, making their offers credible by appropriate commitment or enforcement mechanisms. Faced with these packages of pledges and insurances, individuals and organized groups rationally calculate which package will best serve their interests on the basis of the available information and award their support accordingly. Barring unpredictable exogenous obstacles, an enterprise's success in building up "sufficient" support will ensure its success in the pursuit of its avowed goals, whatever these may be. Because goals differ as between enterprises, however, an enterprise that succeeds in gathering sufficient following for its own goals (say, replacing the colonial officialdom with its own customers) may nevertheless be displaced by a competing enterprise that succeeds in gathering sufficient following for its own different goals (say, a revolutionary overhaul of political and economic institutions) if the latter's following is larger than the former's. Or it may be that no enterprise succeeds in gathering a significant following: Then the national problem remains dormant, and "the nation," as a political entity, literally does not come into existence. Thus, in broad agreement with the specialized literature on the subject,[3] the approach taken in this chapter is that it is supply that creates, or activates, demand; that is, it is nationalism that creates the nation, not vice versa. On the other hand, the prior existence of a national question in a latent state is what constitutes a potential market for nationalism, which gives prospective entrepreneurs the opportunity and the incentive to enter the political arena by endorsing a nationalist program and by fashioning their offers in a nationalist shape.

The market for nationalism differs from the political market in a well-established democracy in that, in the former, unlike in the latter, the rules of the game are not given, but are themselves the bone of contention. Although it is still true, here as always, that political power is a monopoly, even if one competitively acquired, political competition in the market for nationalism is not a zero-sum game because it involves the possibility of radical change in the politico-economic system itself; as a consequence, electoral politics need not always decide, and resorting to force, or revolution, is an alternative option – which is often exercised. In this sense, the market for nationalism belongs in the same category as the "markets" for social revolution or systemic change in general. This non-zero-sum property of the nationalist game explains why a nationalist party, in the example above, can be outcompeted even if successful in *its own* terms, by another party that is also successful. One important implication is that the credibility or mutual trust problem, always faced by political parties as they deal in promises, is much more severe here than in democratic politics: Because the "voters" in the market for nationalism contemplate not just a four-year term of office for the party of their choice but a more or less drastic change in the system, which will be

---

[3] Anderson (1983, 15–16), Gellner (1983, passim), and Hobsbawm (1990, 9–10) all start from the assumption that for purposes of analysis, as well as in historical sequence, nationalism comes before the nations, and they all concentrate on the supply side of the market. Surprisingly, though, none of them addresses socialist nationalism. Smith (1979) takes a more primordial approach, but deals in fact at length with nationalist (including socialist-nationalist) ideology and political entrepreneurship.

impossible or very costly to reverse if proved a delusion, and because their choice involves not just casting a ballot but intensive and costly participation in the struggle, they will ask for much stronger guarantees before awarding their support, and their temptation to free ride will be correspondingly stronger. The importance of the nationalist movements' solutions to this complex of credibility and free-rider problems will be highlighted by the story that is going to unfold in the rest of the paper.

I propose to characterize the market for nationalism as contested by two competing entrepreneurs. One is "bourgeois nationalism," which is basically nationalism as described by Breton and Johnson. The other will be labeled "socialist nationalism" for convenience: It holds that national independence and socialism cannot be achieved separately from one another and it blends nationalist goals and socialist transformation (whose exact nature is subject to change and will be clarified as we proceed) into one program, championed and implemented by a communist party or by a political or military group that turns communist or radical in the course of the struggle. For the reader's convenience, it is useful to set forth here, without proof or qualification, the two basic propositions that will be argued here. The first is that, under appropriate circumstances, socialist nationalism tends to drive out bourgeois nationalism as a solution to the national question in dependent countries. The second is that the current resurgence of nationalism in postcommunist countries is meaningfully understood not as the surfacing of primordial cleavages from precommunist times, as is so often taken for granted in the media these days, but as the direct, rational, albeit unintended, consequence of the very success of the socialist solution to the national question.

After a brief review of the communist doctrine on the national question in Section II, Section III examines the historical record as regards both the case of homogeneous nations that gained independent statehood or "national liberation" (in a sense to be explained) under communist rule and the case of "solution" of the national question within a multinational communist state. Section IV attempts to cast this material in the framework of a theoretical model of collective action. Section V uses this framework to shed light on the surge of postcommunist nationalism and its pattern.

II   The communist doctrine on the national question

Although socialist (and later, communist) ideology, with its internationalist, class-centered outlook, seems to be a world away from nationalist ideology, socialism was forced to come to grips with the national question very early in its history.[4] The idea that autonomous development of a national culture could and should be divorced from territorial autonomy or independent statehood, suggested in the previous section as a utopian exercise, was in fact forcefully argued at the beginning of the century by the Austrian socialist leaders Karl Renner and Otto Bauer. To deal with the problem of a socialist strategy for a multinational state such as the Austrian empire, they put forward a scheme of "extraterritorial national autonomy," whereby each nation, treated not as a territorial corporation but as a union of individuals, would be entered, with the names of all the citizens who chose to identify themselves as such, in a national register. The individuals thus registered would administer their cultural affairs in full autonomy, regardless of their place of residence.

The idea of extraterritorial autonomy encountered stern opposition from Russian Marxism, especially in its Bolshevik strand, on the grounds that it tended to divide the proletariat along national lines and hindered the historical tendency of capitalism to break up multinational empires into national states. This is hardly surprising: If Marxism-Leninism is a science of power in its purest form, power requires a territory to be exercised. As Stalin made clear in his much-quoted 1913 essay on the national question, the Renner-Bauer theory lacked precisely this territorial element in its political definition of a nation; thus to Stalin, the Jews of Russia were not a nation. Since 1903, the cornerstone of the program of the Russian Social-Democratic party as regards the national question was the so-called right of all nations to self-determination, which in the 1910s was increasingly interpreted and propagandized by Lenin as implying the right to secession and the formation of independent states. Lenin did not expect this right actually to be exercised within a future socialist Russia. Rather, the slogan was intended to emphasize that oppressed nations, once liberated from tsarist autocracy, had once and for all an opportunity to gain independent statehood; should they reject this option, they would hold no further claim to separate or special treatment, but would be expected to assimilate and merge into the socialist proletarian community, by its very nature "internationalist." The first purpose of the slogan was to rally around the Bolshevik party all national movements in a common struggle against autocracy, and as such it proved a very effective weapon on the way to revolution in Russia. Its

---

[4] This section is based on Pipes (1954, 21–49, 108–13, 241–86), which is the standard reference on the subject, and Carr (1950, chs. 10–14). Stalin (1942) was also found illuminating.

second purpose was to forge an alliance between the communists and the exploited masses in the colonial periphery of the world – a theme that gained increasing prominence in Lenin's theory of imperialism during World War I. To Lenin, imperialism was basically national oppression on a new basis, and the struggle for national liberation in the colonies was to go hand in hand with the struggle for social revolution.

After the Bolsheviks' seizure of power in Russia, it soon became clear that the doctrine of national self-determination required amendment. Soon after October 1917, independent republics headed by bourgeois or Menshevik forces sprang up all over the western and eastern borderlands of the former empire; and in the Central Asian lands known as Russian Turkestan, a Pan-Turkic movement began to spread, threatening to attract Turkish and other foreign intervention. Self-determination, once so expedient on the way to power, now had to be prevented from rocking the boat and jeopardizing the material basis for survival of the Soviet state. The Red Army took care of the practical side of the matter. On the theoretical side, revision was begun by Stalin, who stated in December 1917, that national self-determination could be no excuse for counter-revolution: The right to self-determination was henceforth to be granted only to the toilers and denied to the bourgeoisie. In Lenin's restatement of the doctrine, the success of socialist revolution in Russia implied that the principle of national self-determination had to evolve from a right to secession to a right to unity: The working classes of the once-oppressed nationalities could now voluntarily join in a free community of socialist nations and could count on the active solidarity of the Russian proletariat. This double standard enabled the communists, in the decades that followed, to claim the leadership of nationalist movements in the colonial and dependent countries, while at the same time giving them a free hand to put down bourgeois-nationalist opposition where they were already in power.

In the meantime, inside the Soviet Union, this right to proletarian unity for all nationalities had to be rested on a firm political foundation. It implied, in the first place, termination of traditional Great Russian chauvinism and discrimination against minorities: The latter were to be actively co-opted into the party and state apparatuses. In turn, because in the Asian territories the masses were illiterate – about the only existing culture was the mullahs' monopoly, and party membership among the local nationalities was negligible – this antidiscrimination drive implied mass schooling and promotion of a secular cultural elite in the local languages. But even this was not enough. The huge gaps in material welfare between the European and Asian parts of the country had to be overcome, and in time all nations would have to be brought up to the same level of economic development. In turn, this implied not income subsidization but industrialization and development of the potential for self-sustained growth in the backward areas, at least as a long-term goal. The reasons for this political preference for equalization of the production capacity are twofold: On the one hand, under socialism, one had to "earn" one's income by one's own labor, not just receive transfers; on the other hand, the Bolsheviks knew only too well that industrial workers and cadres, as the chief beneficiaries of the Soviet regime, could be trusted to be its most reliable supporters, whereas peasants and nomadic herders could not. But the schools, academies, factories, and bureaus that were targeted to benefit the backward nationalities had to be located somewhere. Thus the commitment to national equalization drove the Bolsheviks to adopt the federal principle: Federalism, once deemed to be a centrifugal force, was now used as a tool for unification of the restive borderlands. Importantly, the units of the federation were to be not economic regions but regions inhabited by a dominant nationality of sufficiently large size.[5] The principle of national-territorial autonomy was embodied in all successive Soviet constitutions. The 1923 constitution established nine so-called Union republics (finally to become fifteen with territorial reorganizations during the 1930s and the annexation of the Baltic states in 1940), some of which, in particular the Russian republic, contained several "autonomous" republics and provinces, also organized on a national basis, but endowed with a lesser degree of autonomy. Thus "Soviet Russia became the first modern state to place the national principle at the base of its federal structure" (Pipes 1954, 112).

To be sure, the Soviet Union was never a federal state in the Western sense of the word: Union republics never enjoyed self-rule or sovereignty in the economic domain. Two basic institutions took care that the Soviet Union remained in effect a unitary, centralized state:

[5] A historical curiosity highlights the overarching territorial bias of Soviet nationality policy. As mentioned in the text, to Lenin and Stalin the Jews, lacking a territorial domain, were not a nation. But the rising Jewish nationalism called for a "socialist" answer, if only to counter the increasing appeal of the Zionist movement. Thus, starting in the late 1920s, the Soviet leadership made a determined attempt to create a Jewish autonomous region in a remote, uninhabited area of the Soviet far east, called Biro Bidzhan, by encouraging migration of Jewish settlers from European Russia and the Ukraine. The experiment was, however, doomed to failure because the territory was hopelessly ill-suited to colonization and failed to attract immigrants in sufficient numbers to justify the proclamation of a Soviet Jewish republic. See Abramsky (1978).

the Communist party, to which Lenin and Stalin insisted that the federal and national principles should not apply, and the planning administration organized through all-Union production-branch ministries, which devolved only residual decision areas to the republican ministries. But Soviet federalism from its inception was aimed not to political and economic decentralization but to the coexistence and integration of the different nationalities into a unitary, international state. In the next section, we examine the extent to which this set of theoretical principles and goals was put into practice.

III The communist record on the national question

The Soviet empire

However much the Soviet bloc and its client states in the Third World may have been an "empire" in a political, military, and ideological sense, it differed most strikingly from all colonial empires of the past and their neocolonial remnants in that, as a rule, it involved no economic exploitation of its subject nations. Quite the contrary seems to have been the case: Although the Soviets did reap economic benefits in specific areas, sectors, and times, on balance the "external empire" seems to have been a net economic liability to the Soviet Union. This was true, at least in the 1960s and 1970s, of the East European countries (Marrese and Vanous 1983; Brada 1985); it was true throughout of Mongolia, Cuba, and Vietnam (Theriot and Matheson in Joint Economic Committee, 1979); and of the Third World countries that were recipients of Soviet economic and military aid in the 1970s and 1980s, which was selectively directed to favor "revolutionary democracies" (Albright 1991). Indeed, the total drain on Soviet resources, especially in times of economic slowdown, must have been substantial enough to be a major factor behind Gorbachev's decision to dismantle the external empire and drastically curtail foreign aid by the end of the 1980s.

As will be elaborated below, much the same picture pertains to the "internal empire" the Russians inherited from the tsarist regime and consolidated within the borders of the Soviet Union. The internal empire, in a way, served as the testing ground on which the basic policies of "socialist inter-nationalism" were first tried and found working; thus a pattern was established that could later be extended, with adjustments, to countries of the outside world.

All this in no way implies that ideological factors alone can explain the ostensibly "unselfish" nature of Soviet imperialism: No doubt military-strategic considerations were paramount in most cases; and it may well be a fate that awaits all empires, that in time the initial asset turns into a liability. Be that as it may, it must have become increasingly clear to prospective leaders of nationalist movements in the Third World that, should they opt for the socialist route to national independence, Soviet material aid (or alternatively, after the Sino-Soviet split, Chinese aid) could be trusted to be forthcoming. Added to the inherent advantages of the socialist route that will be examined below, this consideration may well have helped to tilt the balance away from bourgeois nationalism and toward socialist nationalism in a number of success stories.

Socialist-nationalist revolutions

There is no dearth of examples of successful national revolutions that achieved independent statehood and socialism in one shot. The following survey is not meant to be comprehensive in either coverage or depth, but only to highlight the prerequisites and the main features of socialist nationalism.

Although it is seldom recognized in Western accounts of communist history, the pattern was set by Outer Mongolia beginning as early as 1921.[6] Nearly three centuries of Manchu rule had resulted in a de facto monopoly of Mongolian trade and credit by Chinese merchants and usurers, and by the beginning of the twentieth century, Chinese peasant settlement of Mongol lands was being escalated by the imperial government. Manchu taxation had become a crushing burden on Mongol nomadic herders in the form of monetary tribute to the imperial treasury as well as military service and in-kind supplies exacted to man and feed the army outposts that dotted the long Russian borderline. In addition, the high clergy and the lay nobility were increasingly indebted to Chinese middlemen for extravagant ceremonial expenses and a lush life at the imperial court in Peking, and the debt burden was shifted back as ever-increasing tax levies on their Mongol subjects. The Lamaist church, by taking in at least one son in virtually every family, did provide an escape from economic pressure and was therefore cherished by the ordinary people, thus inhibiting the demand for social change; but this insurance mechanism had a disproportionate

---

[6] My principal source on Mongolia is Bawden's (1968) first-class scholarly work, which should be recommended to the uninitiated. Rupen's (1979) work is written more like a fact-finding intelligence report but is nevertheless useful. Murphy's (1966) detailed economic analysis downplays the exploitative role of the church and stresses the social conservatism of the Mongols on the eve of the revolution, but his overall picture is broadly consistent with Bawden's.

The economics of socialist nationalism

resource cost that channeled savings into unproductive uses. In such a situation, how could this same, corrupt elite possibly offer any relief, even if freed from colonial rule? The overthrow of the Manchu dynasty by the Chinese revolution of 1911 afforded the Mongols the opportunity of independent statehood under the leadership of the highest spiritual authority of the Lamaist church, the Jebtsundamba Khutuktu, and under Russian protection. The latter, however, faltered under the impact of World War I, and only limited steps were taken by the new Mongolian government to limit Chinese influence. By the early 1920s, it was clear that mere independence of the nobility and the church from foreign rule, with no change in their life styles and consumption patterns, had meant to ordinary Mongols just a change of masters. In addition, it was by no means certain that even independence could be defended against neighboring Chinese war lords. At least this much was accomplished by the communist takeover of 1921, engineered and backed by the Soviet Red Army in the process of its Siberian campaign against the Whites.

By the end of the 1920s, Chinese traders had been driven out of Mongolia and replaced by a government retail network, and the lay nobility had been liquidated as a class and its property confiscated and redistributed. The all-out attack on the powerful Lamaist church had to await the following decade, after a "leftist" interlude in which forced collectivization of livestock, hastily attempted in 1929 to 1932 on the Soviet pattern, turned into disaster, civil war, and famine. When order was restored and the livestock returned to its private owners, the church was finally expropriated, the lamaseries disbanded, and their property redistributed to low-class lamas, Mongol herdsmen, or the state treasury. The Communist party hardly had a reliable mass base: In the 1920s, its membership included representatives of such unlikely categories as progressive lamas and princes, whereas in the 1930s it was mainly made up of illiterate herdsmen who were mere passengers. Thus by 1940, only the negative side of a socialist program had been accomplished: Church, nobility, and Chinese influence had been wiped out, but Mongolia was still a nomadic, monocultural herding economy in which life continued in the age-old ways. The Communist party ruled in a void, as it were: It had no mass base but no enemy left either; all it had been doing was to preserve the country's independence in a dangerous international predicament and to introduce the beginnings of a modern national army, mass education, and Western medicine. As official ideology put it, Mongolia was taking a direct path from feudalism to socialism and entirely bypassing the capitalist stage. The positive side of the socialist program was accomplished only in the 1950s, when the Chinese communist revolution of 1949 had released pressure on the defense budget, Soviet assistance had begun to flow in, and literacy was making progress. Collectivization of livestock and settlement of the nomads were resumed and completed in 1958-9 apparently without disruptions, comprehensive central planning on the Soviet pattern was introduced, and a slow but steady diversification of production toward a mixed industrial-agrarian economy was undertaken.

What is remarkable in this process is that the Party built the social and economic base on which its power was to rest literally from scratch, thereby ensuring a lasting foundation to the country's real independence, something that the traditional ruling classes could never have done. That this is no mere propaganda can be seen by comparing it to the sorry state of the Mongol minority living in the Chinese province of Inner Mongolia, as will be detailed below. To be sure, the choice of modernization, urbanization, and industrialization as the backbones of a Mongol state had a price: the destruction of the lamaseries, the liquidation of the nomadic way of life, the westernization of culture, education, and consumption patterns. But there was hardly any real alternative. As Bawden (1968, 388-9) suggestively puts it, "the 'old life' was not at all calculated to preserve the Mongol race. . . . Every traveller noted the apathy of the people, their enslavement to a church which . . . held the people at large in ignorant dependence on itself and on its outdated and corrupt ideals. Filth, disease and ignorance marked the Mongol. . . . It is far more realistic to note what has in fact been done since the revolution of 1921 to assure the actual physical survival of the Mongols as a people." No wonder the Outer Mongols of today are proudly nationalistic in their outlook.

Albania and Vietnam represent two prototype cases in which the armed struggle for national liberation was inseparable from a socialist program. In each case, the political leadership forged in the struggle was the veterans of the partisan warfare. In a land[7] that emerged from centuries of Turkish domination at the end of World War I only to fall back under the Italian fascist economic and political protectorate in the 1930s, followed by Nazi occupation during the war, and in a land lacking a political culture, democratic political parties, or a modern

---

[7] Zavalani (1969) provides historical background to the Albanian national problem. Peters (1975) surveys the liberation war and the communist takeover. Marmullaku (1975) is a useful summary of pre- and postrevolutionary Albanian developments by a sympathetic Yugoslav, drawing judiciously on the official communist account. Schnytzer (1982) is an excellent study of the peculiar economics of Albanian communist development strategy in comparative perspective.

bourgeoisie, afflicted by hopeless destitution and 80 percent illiteracy, and in which the big landed proprietors were the cronies of a corrupt, despotic puppet monarch, the Albanian Communist party led by Enver Hoxha was the only unifying force that could mobilize the peasants and deliver the promise of real national independence. It succeeded in arousing the people to fight the foreigners by linking the liberation movement to a radical program of land redistribution, confiscation of collaborationist property, and accelerated industrialization and modernization under central planning on the pattern of a strictly Stalinist development strategy. By virtue of their pedigree of unswerving dedication to the national and socialist cause, the communist partisans acquired the authority to rule the country for over forty years and managed to preserve its independence in the midst of powerful neighbors, even if at the price of near-complete autarky and isolation from the outside world, both capitalist and communist. The Albanian experience exemplifies an extreme case in which socialist nationalism had no significant bourgeois-nationalist competitors; and in which, due to a hostile international environment, the Maoist principle of "relying on one's own forces," which in economic terms implied maximum diversification of the industrial structure and a drive for complete self-sufficiency, was carried – if one considers the tiny size and resource endowment of the country – to incredible lengths.

The Vietnamese monarchy's final surrender to the French protectorate in 1884 was followed by many years of continued armed resistance.[8] The resistance, however, lacked a democratic, mobilizing program: The proposed restoration of the feudal monarchy and Confucianism could scarcely appeal to land-hungry peasants. Under the colonial regime, the beginnings of class differentiation were introduced into traditional Vietnamese society, but the key to a successful anticolonial struggle turned out to be the agrarian question. The Communist party, founded by Ho Chi Minh in 1930, did face active competition from the beginning: Two bourgeois nationalist parties recruited followers from among the urban middle class; on the left, the Trotskyites had a following among the urban working class. None of these organizations, however, ever reached out in the countryside. The communists themselves began as an internationalist group that en-

[8] My account of the Vietnamese case follows closely Popkin's (1979) model analysis of the political economy of the Vietnamese village in the colonial and Viet Minh periods. Wolf's (1969) compact account of the revolutionary struggle is also very useful. Pike (1966) gives essentially the same picture of the Viet Cong's mobilization strategy from the standpoint of a counterinsurgency expert. Turner (1975) has much information on political history.

gaged in a few urban uprisings in the 1930s in the Bolshevik style, only to fail disastrously. Thus, like Mao Tsedong after the failed Chinese revolution of 1927, Ho Chi Minh came to realize that the path to revolution had to be a protracted revolutionary war in the countryside – a "people's war"; and that to win over the peasants' loyalty the party had to center its program around the twin watchwords of national liberation and antifeudal revolution – "the land to those who work it," so as to fuse peasant aspirations and Vietnamese nationalism into one powerful force. On this path again, the party had to face competition from rival religious sects, whose programs were also both anticolonial and antifeudal and therefore developed rural roots, especially in the south; but they eventually had to yield to the communists' superior organizational ability. The key to this superiority lay in the organization of the liberated areas: Here the peasants were mobilized to the economic and logistic support of the guerrilla units and, in exchange were delivered immediate, low-cost payoffs such as literacy campaigns, medical first aid, and the beginnings of agrarian reform and land redistribution. This effectively built up a relationship of mutual trust between communist cadres and villagers that enhanced the former's credibility as leaders and the latter's willingness to contribute, thus minimizing free-riding behavior on both sides. So it was that the Party gathered sufficient strength to endure thirty-five years of almost uninterrupted war against the Japanese, the French, and finally the Americans until complete liberation was achieved in 1975. A reading of the 1967 program of the National Liberation Front of South Vietnam (Turner 1975) bears out several revealing points for our purposes: First, all absentee and collaborationist property is to be confiscated and redistributed; second, economic and social rights and freedoms are granted to all sections of society that cooperate in the national struggle; third, reward in terms of status, educational opportunities, and political power is promised to the veterans or active supporters of the resistance; fourth, "patriotic" intellectuals, writers, artists, and the like are singled out for special favor; fifth, economic self-sufficiency and diversification is a paramount objective, as a guarantee of real independence. However deceptive the promise of freedom for all loyal social groups proved to be ex post facto, this program makes it clear that prospects for upward mobility and material reward in the postrevolutionary society were tied to previous participation in the liberation struggle, and such a commitment on the part of the leadership could be credible just because it replicated on a national scale the political exchange that had been tried and found working in the small in the liberated areas.

The economics of socialist nationalism

The Vietnamese experience[9] proved to be a prototype for the later "people's wars" that developed and succeeded in Africa, first in Algeria and then in the Portuguese colonies. In each of these cases, the national liberation movement turned radical and socialist in the course of the struggle because of the colonial power's inability or unwillingness to concede peaceful decolonization. This posture soon ruled out moderate or compromise solutions (sometimes after bitter factional struggles within the movement) and entrusted the leadership of the movement to a politically directed partisan army. The latter was able to rally widespread support among the peasantry (and, in the Algerian case, the urban laborers) and predictably emerged as the backbone of the postindependence one-party states. The challenge to unite the people against the foreigner was met in different ways, however. In Algeria[10] the key to the uncompromising attitude of the French government was the "colonial consensus" that the territory should remain part of the French state to protect the interests of the large, and politically influential, settler community. The French settlers on the eve of independence numbered about 1 million against a Muslim population of perhaps 10 million, owned fully one third of the cultivatable land (and the best land at that, on the rich coastal plains), and monopolized the ownership of, and the managerial and skilled jobs in, practically all industry. This state of affairs completely foreclosed any prospects for upward mobility in the modern sector to the natives and kept the peasantry in continuing poverty and dependence. The reverse side of this coin was, however, that the National Liberation Front could hold out to the people the prospect of large gains to be secured by simple confiscation of settler property, without setting one class

[9] Vietnam's experience with people's war and liberated areas can itself be traced back to the earlier precedent of the Chinese revolution. In a seminal study, Chalmers Johnson (1962) argued that the success of the revolution in China, and the ensuing deep links between the Communist party in power and the peasantry, are rooted in a spontaneous movement of mass peasant nationalism aroused by the social disruptions and anarchy precipitated by the invading Japanese army during 1937–45. To gain mass support among the peasantry, the communists muted their land-redistribution, collectivist programs and thus managed to outbid the competing bourgeois-nationalist party, the Kuomintang, not because they were socialists but because they turned more nationalist than the self-styled nationalists themselves. The Chinese experience, however, is something of a hybrid in terms of my typology of nationalist movements in that it is an instance of a communist-led nationalism ostensibly lacking agrarian reform or otherwise socialist programs.

[10] Smith's (1978) excellent treatment of the preindependence period informed my reading of the Algerian revolution. Wolf (1969) has an insightful analysis of the social bases of the liberation war. On postindependence policies and achievements, see Ottaway and Ottaway (1970) and Blair (1970).

against another within Muslim society. This in fact occurred in 1962 right after independence and the mass exodus of the French: Some 300,000 urban poor took over the jobs (and the apartments) formerly held by French workers, some 35,000 guerrilla veterans filled the state bureaucracy, some 220,000 peasants were employed in the former French estates turned into state farms, and the guerrilla force was turned into a professional army. This enabled the new Algerian regime to reward its constituency and to embark upon a socialist development path without immediately resorting to unpopular measures of expropriation of the peasantry.

The case of the Portuguese colonies[11] was different in that Portugal's unwillingness to grant independence was due not to settler pressure but to its inability to practice "neocolonialism," that is, to retain economic power once political control was withdrawn. Its rule relied on direct taxation or exploitation of its monopoly of local resources without either promoting Portuguese settlement (which was minimal in Angola and Mozambique and practically nonexistent in Guinea-Bissau) or providing the local populations with the indirect benefits of colonial administration in the fields of sanitation, literacy, or infrastructure. This backward, intransigent nature of Portuguese colonialism radicalized the liberation struggle by ruling out any reformist option (significantly, Mozambique's FRELIMO began as a bourgeois-nationalist group and turned Marxist-Leninist only by the early 1970s). But it also meant that, although on the one hand the colonial power was never able to build up any substantial loyal clientele in sections of the local population, on the other hand there were few direct economic gains to be reaped from the ousting of the Portuguese as such. To win over the people's active support and participation, two things were needed: a developmental program that promised to turn the local resources to the people's benefit and a principled practice that could overcome the principal divisive force in African society, namely the peasants' traditional cleavages along clan and tribal lines. Perhaps the greatest asset that ensured eventual success to Mozambique's FRELIMO, Guinea's PAIGC, and Angola's MPLA was their Marxist ideology that, in addition to being an ideology of development and modernization, was framed in terms of class and nation and denied

---

[11] For the people's wars in the Portuguese colonies, as well as in Algeria and elsewhere in Africa, see the highly sympathetic but insightful discussion by Davidson (1981). Useful in-depth studies, covering both pre- and postindependence periods, are Munslow (1983), Henriksen (1983), and Saul (1985) for Mozambique; Chabal (1983) and Galli and Jones (1987) for Guinea-Bissau; and several essays in Keller and Rothchild (1987) for all three countries.

regard or allegiance to tribe, clan, or race. This asset, owned by "a frustrated elite . . . blocked in a bid to become masters in their own house" (Henriksen 1983, 212), was put to effective use first by building a guerrilla army whose recruitment purposely cut across tribal cleavages, and second by cementing a trust relationship between peasants and party/army cadres in the liberated areas. In these areas, following the Vietnamese example, the local peasants were provided tangible benefits in exchange for feeding and supporting the fighting units: not land redistribution in this case (owing to the relatively undifferentiated class structure of the African peasantry) but literacy classes, basic medical assistance, village courts to adjudicate disputes, and mutual help in farm work. Witness to the effectiveness of this strategy of nation building is the fact that FRELIMO and PAIGC emerged from the liberation struggle as absolutely unchallenged candidates to the leadership of the independent states in 1974 and remained so afterwards (although PAIGC later split and degenerated into internecine strife between Guineans and Cape Verdians). Angola's MPLA, which had had less logistic opportunity to operate liberated areas inside the country, was less successful at independence because it faced armed opposition by splinter groups based on tribal affiliations, which precipitated the country into foreign military intervention on both sides and civil war; despite this, however, in the free election held in 1992 after the end of the fighting, the MPLA secured the overwhelming majority of voter support. In each case, after independence the leadership's side of its political contract with the peasantry, underwritten in the course of the struggle and cemented by practice in the liberated areas, was fulfilled by considering the status of guerrilla veteran or otherwise participant in the struggle as an entitlement to political and economic reward in the new state, turning the guerrillas into a professional army tightly intertwined with the party-state, the conversion of the participatory revolutionary organization into a Leninist vanguard party, and a drive toward decolonization and diversification of the sectoral structure of the economy and the development of education and other social services, all of which offered great new employment opportunities.

As a different example, consider Cuba.[12] Here the 1959 revolution was more the outcome of a lucky guerrilla coup than of a long-lasting,

---

[12] An exhaustive scholarly assessment of the economic policies and achievements of the Cuban regime is Mesa-Lago (1981). Mesa-Lago (1971) and Horowitz (1981) are useful collections of essays. The writings of Ernesto Che Guevara are unique in conveying the sense of how the revolutionaries saw their position and their task in the regime's heroic years: See the collection in Deutschmann (1987).

mass-based liberation war, and Fidel Castro's *barbudos* were not a communist party and did not have a well-defined Marxist ideology, let alone ties with the Soviet Union. Rather, ideology, party organization, and Soviet ties evolved as a response to circumstances, in the process of consolidating the revolution in the face of threats from émigré counterrevolutionary activity and American involvement in the Bay of Pigs. On the eve of the revolution, Cuba was two things: a sugar monoculture controlled by foreign capital and a holiday preserve for wealthy Americans and mafiosi. Even though formally independent, in a very real sense the Batista regime could have been said to be an American stooge. Thus "national liberation" became paramount among the new regime's goals, understood as liberation from the legacies of a dependent, monocultural economy and society. Agricultural diversification and industrialization were pushed through from the very beginning at breakneck speed, to the point of driving production to near paralysis by 1962–3. The impasse was overcome by slackening the pace of sectoral restructuring, by heavy reliance on Soviet aid, and by a reversion to sugar as a principal export crop, in a kind of "turnpike strategy" toward self-sustained multisectoral growth. Thus economic independence and diversification remained the central long-term priorities and were indeed slowly carried through, presenting the average Cuban with unprecedented opportunities for advancement in education, occupation, and income. True, the need for diversification was exacerbated by the American embargo, but here in a sense the prophecy is self-fulfilling. In any case, this "reliance on one's own forces," Cuban-style, coupled with the characteristic emphasis on mass mobilization and campaigns and the pervasive politicization and militarization of economic activities, is probably responsible for the relatively high level of popular consensus that the Cuban regime enjoyed until recently.

An interesting variation on the Cuban theme is offered by Nicaragua.[13] Here the Sandinista revolution was directed against the dictatorship of the Somoza family, which had been ruling the country for over forty years. The regime had achieved quite respectable growth rates in agricultural output in the 1960s and 1970s through the promotion of a diversified, large-scale, export-oriented agricultural sector, with a concomitant, huge concentration of wealth into its own hands and a corresponding impoverishment of the landless peasantry and the urban poor. In addition, the regime's corruption and harassment of the busi-

---

[13] My account of the Sandinista revolution and its policies is based on Booth (1982), Colburn (1986), Spalding (1987), and Close (1988).

ness sector had reached such proportions as to alienate itself from the bulk of the middle class, which eventually joined the Sandinista Front in the insurrection of 1979 that overturned what was widely labeled the Somozas" "kleptocracy." Furthermore, the armed forces were in fact not a national army but the dictator's personal guard. Thus the Sandinistas were able to claim the leadership of a "national" revolution in that it would unite all social classes and free the country from its complete dependence on foreign markets and export-led growth; conversely, it would return the country's bountiful human and natural resources to its citizens' benefit through income redistribution and changed priorities in growth promotion and government spending. The remarkable feature of the Sandinista revolution is that – much like in Algeria with the confiscation of the French settlers' property – the new regime had no need to resort to collectivization of capitalist or peasant property to start with its socialist economic program: The skewness of prerevolutionary wealth distribution was so extreme that, by sheer requisition of the abandoned property of the Somozas and their cronies, the regime found itself in possession of over 25 percent of the agricultural land and a similar proportion of all industrial and commercial firms, which raised the public sector share in the gross domestic product (GDP) from 15 percent in 1977 to over 40 percent through the 1980s. By simply turning over the confiscated land to the landless peasants, first as state or cooperative farms and then also as private family plots, by using public sector revenues to increase expenditures on basic education and health, by indirectly regulating the private commercial sector through a state monopoly of foreign trade and the banking system, and by turning the Sandinista guerrilla force into a professional army to replace the departed Somoza guard, the government was able to redistribute income and influence growth priorities to reward its supporters within the framework of a mixed economy. The mounting external pressure of the U.S. embargo and counterrevolutionary war, and the strains of the uneasy compromise between a socialist government and a private business sector, eventually did cut into the broad-based support that the regime once enjoyed. When the Sandinistas lost the free election of 1990, however, they were still able to command over 40 percent of the national vote – altogether not a bad record under the circumstances.

The upshot of this discussion is that in none of the cases surveyed here could bourgeois nationalism make offers that could even remotely compare to those of socialist nationalism: Here is the key to the latter's appeal and success.

Multinational socialist states

The Soviet Union: Over the last fifty years of existence of the Soviet Union,[14] there never was a question of who belonged to which nationality. Since the 1930s, the nationality of every citizen was registered on his or her internal passport; after a first round of more or less voluntary affiliation, the pattern of national identification was frozen once and for all, and each citizen's nationality was strictly predetermined by the parents' nationality, regardless of the place of residence. An option for choice existed only for the children of mixed marriages when they came of age. Thus national identification was institutionalized and was made the basis for political entitlement at least for the "titular" nationalities of each Union republic and, to a lesser degree, autonomous republic. No wonder that, in these conditions, children of mixed marriages typically opted for the titular nationality of their republic of residence, whenever possible (not, as one might think, for the Russian nationality when available) (Rakowska-Harmstone in Conquest, ed., 1986, 252). In addition, in former Russian Turkestan, the threat of Pan-Turkic nationalism was averted by arbitrarily "inventing" four national Union republics (Turkmenistan, Uzbekistan, Tadzhikistan, and Kirgizia) where only tribal divisions among Muslim peasants or nomadic pasturalists were known, so as to "divide and rule."

Given this institutional basis for national self-identification, two main directions to promote the equalization of nationalities and their

---

[14] The literature on nationality problems in the Soviet Union is by now very large but, in my judgement, of unequal value as it is seldom cast in a conceptual framework. The best summary introduction up to the eve of the Union's collapse is Zaslavsky (1992). This, and the insightful literature surveys by Roeder (1991) and Laitin (1991), inform my interpretation in the text. The volumes edited by Conquest (1986) and Hajda and Beissinger (1990) provide comprehensive coverage by the leading specialists in the field. Lubin (1984), focusing on Uzbekistan, is invaluable in introducing the nonspecialist to the intricacies of the problem. Very useful are also W. Fierman's and D. Carlisle's contributions in Fierman, ed. (1991). Rumer (1989) contains a wealth of material on Central Asia but completely ignores the extensive Western literature on the subject. Bahry (1987) is the basic reference on Soviet budgetary politics at the republican level. On the quantitative aspects of income differentials, development strategy, and the labor force by republic and by nationality, as well as on interrepublican transfers, a selective list includes McAuley (1979; 1985; 1991; 1992), M. Spechler's and J. Gillula's papers in Joint Economic Committee (1979), Clem (1980), Jones and Grupp (1984), Van Selm and Doelle (1992), and the contributions by G. Schroeder to the Conquest (1986) and Hajda and Beissinger (1990) volumes. Finally, Fairbanks (1978) is an illuminating analysis of the key role of nationality politics and "territorial fiefdoms" in the Stalin era.

integration into the Soviet system were pursued. The first was a policy of "nativization" of cadres, or preferential treatment of the titular nationalities within their own republics as regards access to higher education and managerial and administrative positions; this was enforced by means of an informal system of admission and hiring quotas for titular nationals, which amounted in effect to a policy of "affirmative action," Soviet-style. This reverse discrimination included even the practice of asking lower bribes to favor the titular nationals' access to sought-after educational institutions and jobs, at least in Uzbekistan (Lubin 1984, 162). Moreover, the ethnic intelligentsia – itself largely a creation of the Soviet system – was protected by the inflation of high-status positions in the republican cultural bureaucracies, academies of sciences, unions of national writers, and the like. As a result, equalization of educational levels and occupational opportunities for managerial-administrative positions was indeed by and large achieved by the 1980s, as shown by comparison of titular nationalities' shares in these positions and in total population; in the highly visible positions of the republican Party and government leaderships, the titular nationalities were in effect overrepresented. Relative rates of Communist party membership – an important ticket to upward mobility and a key indicator of political integration in the Soviet Union – showed continued increases for all titular nationalities during the 1960s and 1970s, also because of preferential recruitment policies (Jones and Grupp 1984). Thus there arose a nationality-based network of political, intellectual, and bureaucratic elites that were entirely dependent on the Soviet system for their status and income and had a vested interest in its continuation. Allegations were often heard that the Soviets enforced Russification of non-Russian nationalities. However, as one Uzbek informant put it, "in America they say that the Russians have russified our culture; that's not true. It was done by certain Uzbeks" (quoted in Lubin 1984, 227).

Besides integration of the educated national middle classes, the second avenue to national equalization was a policy of spreading the benefits of economic growth. There is no doubt that the backward Asian republics made gigantic strides under Soviet rule; nevertheless, they continued to lag behind the European republics, and the gap in official per capita personal income was widening in the 1970s and 1980s under the impact of the Asian demographic explosion. This development occurred despite the fact that the central government consistently implemented a planned subsidization of investments in the Asian republics that was billed to the European republics, while income produced in Asia was almost entirely left to local consumption; the size of these capital transfers is controversial but appears to have been substantial enough – a situation that led one writer to speak of "welfare colonialism" (Spechler in Joint Economic Committee [1979]). On the other side of the coin, Moscow implemented an interrepublican division of labor whereby Central Asia was made into a Soviet "cotton kingdom." One consequence of this industrialization strategy was that skilled industrial and technical jobs were created that could not be filled by natives, thus inducing a continuing net inflow of Russians into the Asian republics throughout the Soviet period. This was especially striking as a surplus of labor was developing among Asian nationalities, but those nationalities continued to crowd into the low-paying, low-skill jobs in the agricultural and service sectors, in the light and food industries, and in the liberal professions, or even remained in household production, that is, not gainfully employed. This state of affairs led some observers to speak of discrimination against Asian nationalities. However, Lubin (1984) presents compelling evidence that, at least in Uzbekistan and by extension in all Asian republics, this occupational and sectoral distribution by nationality was to a large extent due to a rational choice by indigenous nationalities. This had to do not just with indigenous preferences for a large family size or a slack work pace; the most sought-after jobs, although paying a low official wage, turned out to be those that offered the best opportunities for additional side incomes in the second, or underground, economy or in the taking of bribes – a set of activities that especially flourished in Central Asia. Although this pattern of occupational choice was not unknown to the Soviet Union as a whole, in Asia it was bolstered by deeply rooted "old boy networks" or mafia-type organizations, based on familism and nepotism, in which the "entrepreneur" had typically become, under Soviet conditions, the local party boss. Thus, counting official and unofficial incomes together, a Central Asia collective farmer, retail trade employee, or teacher might well earn an income many times higher than a Russian skilled worker or engineer employed in heavy industry, where opportunities for self-serving transactions involving state property were much more restricted.

Thus the Asian titular nationalities got the best of all worlds: They received a disproportionate share of investments that supported locally produced incomes at a level far above what would have been warranted by local resources; they benefited from preferential treatment in education, hiring, and political careers; and they were free to pick the best positions to develop a parallel economy for the sake of private gain. It is not surprising that this situation sparked resentment in the European republics that bore the burden of redistribution and among the European residents of the Asian republics. It is also interesting to note that growing population pressure, coupled with the voluntary self-segregation of nationalities by occupation described above, tended to increase competition *among* indigenous Central Asians for scarce jobs in the preferred traditional sectors, rather than direct competition between them and Europeans (Lubin 1984, 228–9, 231, 238). Clearly the ground was ripe for interethnic conflict when the onset of perestroika hit hard at Central Asian mafias and the further slowdown of overall Soviet growth severely curtailed the flow of investment subsidization.

We conclude from this discussion that the Soviet "solution" to the national question proved remarkably successful for over fifty years in preserving ethnic peace and promoting national consensus. However, the price for this success was that the solution, far from softening national boundaries and assimilating the different nationalities into a new, internationalist Soviet man, made nationality and ethnic awareness an all-important basis for individual advancement and political competition for resources and incomes, thereby sowing the seeds of a revival of aggressive nationalism when the Soviet Union began to collapse. In the words of a Soviet observer, "nationalities have turned into political parties" (quoted in Zaslavsky 1992, 107).

Yugoslavia: In Yugoslavia,[15] the decisive role played by the ethnically mixed League of Communists, led by Marshal Tito, in the defeat of the Nazi occupiers and their local supporters gave it a unique occasion to emerge from World War II as an arbiter and peacekeeper, ending the long-standing international conflict and offering the different nationalities the prospect to share in overall economic growth as one country. In this sense, Yugoslavia is yet another instance of a successful socialist-nationalist revolution, only that, in contrast to the cases surveyed earlier, its task in this case was not to gain independence as a separate state but to achieve unification of separate nationalities into one state. This task implied that traditional chauvinism of Greater Serbia was to be held in check and diluted into a federal union of six

---

[15] A basic reference on the Yugoslav national question and nationality policy up to the mid-1960s is Shoup (1968). This book and Johnson (1962) also thoroughly discuss the resistance war and the origins of the communists' rise to power. Lang (1974–5), Flaherty (1988), and Flakierski (1989) assess trends and policies on regional inequality, whereas Zarkovic Bookman (1990) assesses the bases for regional economic autarky. Kraft and Vodopivec (1992) and Dubravcic (1992) are my basic sources for the mechanics and measure of interrepublican redistribution.

nationally based republics. (To balance potential Serbian preponderance, Serbo-Croatian conflict over the mixed frontier area of Bosnia-Herzegovina was stalled by giving it republican status; previously unrecognized "nationalities" such as the Muslims of Bosnia and the Macedonians were given political recognition; and the two autonomous provinces of Vojvodina and Kosovo were created inside Serbia to enhance the status of non-Serbian minorities.) A crucial condition for this "social contract" to be feasible was that investment funds and development projects were to be allocated on a republican and local basis, as the outcome of continuous bargaining between local and republican representatives and the federal center. Thus the building of a communist state in Yugoslavia hinged critically on the prospects for a successful solution of the national question, to be pursued through a variant of Leninist nationality policy adapted to local institutional conditions. Redistribution toward less developed republics was effected directly through central investment planning until the early 1960s and then through a set of institutional arrangements described below. As in the Soviet Union, republican units were defined not by income levels or economic structure but were fixed once and for all on a nationality basis; and industrialization and the creation of an industrial working class were seen as a means to build consensus and "solve" the national question – especially in view of the very large income gap between the socialized sector and private agriculture. Unlike in the Soviet Union, however, the League of Communists was in time also decentralized de facto along national-republican lines. Given this, a practice of parity representation of the republics regardless of population and of decision making at the federal level by unanimous consent gradually came to prevail. As a result, republican pressures brought about wasteful duplication of projects and a near-autarkic industrial structure in every republic, especially since extensive decision-making powers were delegated to the republics in 1974, with a strong inflationary effect among other things.

Overall economic growth in Yugoslavia was remarkable over the whole communist period, and all republics shared in it. Despite this, although the ranking of republics did not change throughout the period (with Slovenia and Croatia at the top, Serbia proper and Vojvodina in the middle, and Bosnia-Herzegovina, Macedonia, Montenegro and Kosovo at the bottom), the relative position of the less developed republics began slowly but steadily to worsen, in terms of personal income per capita and most other economic indicators, after the extensive economic decentralization and increased reliance on enterprise self-management and the market introduced in the mid-1960s. This is in part explained by diverging demographic trends. However, the interrepublican differential in average wages (which was smaller than that in personal income per capita, as the latter reflected higher unemployment in the less-developed regions) was consistently narrower than the differential in labor productivity in industry; further, the productivity differential was steadily narrowing over the period. The first effect was brought about by a deliberate central policy that, despite the theoretical tenets of self-management, applied pressure on the more profitable firms, typically located in the more developed regions, to allocate a lower proportion of their net output to personal income than did the less profitable ones. In turn, these higher forced savings were channeled by various means into investment funds at the disposal of the less-developed republics, which typically exhibited a higher share of investment in total income than the more-developed ones; this explains the narrowing of the productivity differential. This redistribution of investment funds, in the postreform period, was implemented chiefly by two means: first overtly, through a special federal fund established for the purpose, and second covertly, through implicit subsidization of firms by extending loans at negative real interest rates in an inflationary environment. The extent of this investment subsidization appears to have been substantial.

Thus the political equilibrium among national republics in Yugoslavia revolved around indirect wage control and investment subsidization from the more-developed to the less-developed republics, which kept incomes higher than productivity in the latter republics while slowly narrowing the productivity differential. When inefficiency and waste brought the system to the verge of economic collapse, the more-advanced republics refused to continue to pay the bill and, relying on the nearly self-sufficient industrial base built up in the process, moved to secession. Understandably the Serbs, who had remained inbetween all along and were now threatened with diminution in their role of political intermediaries, took the lead in the attempts by the net beneficiaries of the old system to forestall secession.

The deviant cases: The record of communist nationality policy in the Soviet Union and Yugoslavia makes it difficult to disentangle political power from ideology as the motivating force behind redistribution: Raising the level of development of the backward republics was both neatly dictated by the Lenin-Stalin doctrine and serviceable to the building of the social and political foundations of a strong unitary state. However, when national self-determination and development is unnecessary to, or works at cross-purposes with, the consolidation of political power, it turns out that politics takes precedence over ideology and the Leninist nationality policy is shelved, as the examples of China and Romania will suggest.[16]

Prior to its victory in the revolutionary war in 1949, the Chinese Communist party pledged to the Leninist doctrine of self-determination, including the right of secession, to win over the allegiance of the non-Han minorities from the competing Nationalist party. Soon after 1949 the right of secession predictably gave way to a right to autonomous regions for the principal minorities, which were in fact established in Inner Mongolia, Sinkiang, and later Tibet. The underlying illusion again was that these autonomous entities would become "national in form, socialist in content," but disappointment came after hardly a decade in power with the Tibetan revolt of 1959 and the widespread defections of nationality cadres during the Great Leap. Then came the break with the Soviet Union and the massive flight of Kazakh nomads from Sinkiang to Soviet Kazakhistan in 1962. These events forced the Chinese to bring home the point that the longest border in the world was underpopulated and all but unguarded and that it was both unnecessary and unwise to entrust its defense to those unsettled, alien peoples. Thus it was external security considerations that tilted the balance toward all-out assimilation policies: These included curtailing both powers and size of the "autonomous" regions, staffing the local government officialdom with Han cadres, and above all encouraging immigration of Han settlers onto the best frontier lands. Sinification and planned peasant settlement were dramatically escalated further in the aftermath of the Cultural Revolution and the Sino-Soviet border clashes of 1969, so that by now the minorities are outnumbered by the Hans, sometimes by several times, in their very homelands. "The basic contradiction of China is that while only 6 percent of the population is non-Han, this minority makes up in fact the majority peoples of nearly 60 percent of the territory in China. Furthermore, over 90 percent of the border with her neighbors is inhabited by non-Han peoples" (Pye in Glazer and Moynihan, eds., 1976, 500). Thus, in the Chinese case, the Soviet strategy of winning over the loyalty of nationality elites through education and industrialization proved unworkable because it is a very long-term strategy, whereas external security needs, as perceived by the Chinese regime,

[16] The following interpretation of the Chinese case draws on L. Pye's essay in Glazer and Moynihan, eds. (1976). Useful detailed case studies are J. T. Dreyer's and S. Jagchid's contributions in McCagg and Silver, eds. (1979) for Sinkiang and Inner Mongolia, respectively. Background material for the Romanian case up to the mid-1970s can be found in Gilberg (1980).

could not wait that long: This left outright Sinification of the non-Han territories as the only viable option.

As in China, also in Romania small numbers provide the key to the failure to follow the Soviet nationality pattern. Non-Romanians (mainly Hungarians, followed by Germans, Gypsies, and Jews) made up only about 10 percent of total population, and they were never granted territorial or cultural autonomy; starting with the early 1960s, the leadership undertook a policy of "national communism" that increasingly emphasized ethnic Romanian nationalism in terms of language, tradition, and symbols. As the years of the Ceausescu regime wore on, outright discrimination, assimilation, and Romanianization of the minorities were implemented. Although Party recruitment at the rank-and-file level was sought among the minorities as well, Ceausescu's closest associates were all ethnic Romanians. This was a drastic departure from the practice prevailing in the early postwar years when the communist elite, here as elsewhere in Eastern Europe, was chiefly recruited from among the better-educated minorities, especially the Jews, in sharp contrast with their traditional plight of oppression and discrimination. Behind this political and ideological evolution, however, it is easy to detect a basic economic rationale. At the beginning of the communist era, the non-Romanian minorities were the most privileged groups in terms of both educational and occupational levels. The communist policies of industrialization, urbanization, and mass education dramatically raised the educational, occupational, and income status of all citizens regardless of ethnic affiliation, but in relative terms the main beneficiaries were the formerly uneducated, ethnic Romanian peasants, who gained access to the industrial working-class and white-collar jobs and became proportionately over-represented in higher-education institutions. This was perceived by the minorities, rightly enough, as a gigantic move toward leveling, whereby Romanians caught up with the privileged Hungarians, Germans, and Jews. Although this equalizing process is in itself an inevitable concomitant of modernization, it could and would have been slowed down or bent toward the interests of the minorities if they had been granted territorial autonomy and nativistic policies, Soviet-style. In other words, a Leninist nationality policy would have increased the minorities' share and correspondingly reduced the ethnic Romanians' share in the pie of economic growth, by reducing the leveling off to preserve the minorities' privileges in their homelands. Clearly, the communist leadership faced a choice of which constituency should be catered to in exchange for political support: And both numbers and relative backwardness made the ethnic Romanians, not the minorities, the most rewarding choice – as events during and after the 1989 revolution were to highlight.

IV A theoretical framework

The material on the communist theory and practice on the national question that was surveyed in the preceding sections lends itself to generalization. My task in this section is to make sense of this material in terms of the economist's paradigm of rational individual behavior.

Individuals engage in collective action, with all its attendant costs, when it pays them to do so. Individual action to achieve the same goals, when available, is less costly to the individual, if only because there is no need to police free riding. Nationalist activity is one type of utility-maximizing behavior that by definition requires collective action: It is but one form of group competition, which naturally tends to harden group boundaries (in our case, national cleavages), as opposed to individual competition in the market, which naturally tends to soften group boundaries (Banton 1983). Individuals will then choose to engage in nationalist movements, rather than seeking advances in income and status through market competition, only if expected benefits outweigh expected costs. In turn, expected benefits for any individual depend on three factors: the size of the aggregate benefits to be secured by nationalist action if successful, the sharing rule by which those aggregate benefits are to be allocated among participants, and the effectiveness of the mechanisms available to prevent free riding or defection to the enemy camp and ensure success. My hypothesis is therefore that anything that increases the size of the pie, that spreads benefits among a broader constituency rather than concentrating them on a narrow sector, or that raises the likelihood of successful completion of the struggle will make for broader participation and enhanced militancy in a nationalist struggle. In a word, nationalism is neither primordial, irrational, premodern, nor eternal: It is always ready to arise or increase if and when the prize is sufficiently appealing.[17]

The focus of analysis must thus shift to political entrepreneurs and the packages they offer potential constituencies in political markets

---

[17] This approach to nationality parallels recent developments in the related field of ethnicity. Sociologists Banton (1983) and Hechter, in Rex and Mason, eds. (1986), pioneered the application of rational choice theory, borrowed from economics, to ethnic and race relations. Earlier, Glazer and Moynihan (1976) posited the definition of an ethnic group as an interest group, which leads to the politicization of ethnicity in the modern state.

The economics of socialist nationalism

structured by a national question.[18] The chief contestants in these markets are bourgeois nationalism and socialist nationalism. The first, as we already know, is the subject of Breton's analysis. It promises no further change beyond the transfer of foreign assets to nationals, and therefore it appeals only to the burgeoning native middle class, or national bourgeoisie, which expects to replace foreigners in managerial positions; in turn, these high-paying jobs are bound to be strictly limited in number by technology and market constraints, especially if a modern capitalist sector is superimposed on a traditional subsistence sector as is typical of developing countries. Even if the foreign assets are confiscated rather than purchased, the working classes will then incur no tax costs but will still reap no benefit either. In addition, the social base of the movement is so narrow that bourgeois-nationalist elements are easily bribed to defect and become clients of the imperial or formerly colonial power, and the weapons of deterrence at the disposal of bourgeois-nationalist political parties are typically weak. As a consequence, even if the working masses should enjoy a nonmonetary or psychic reward from real national independence per se, as likely as not they would be frustrated in this aspiration, too. As communists say, the national bourgeoisie is objectively prone to sell out the national cause.[19]

Socialist nationalism[20] changes the terms of the nationalist cost–benefit calculus in a fundamental way. When leadership of the national movement is taken over by a communist vanguard, the struggle for

---

[18] Popkin (1979) is to my knowledge the only attempt explicitly to interpret a socialist-nationalist revolution (in his case, the Vietnamese experience) within Mancur Olson's paradigm for collective action. My argument in this section relies heavily on his analysis.

[19] An outstanding exception to this generalization is India's struggle for independence from British rule. At least toward the Hindu section of the country, however, Gandhi had two unique, powerful mobilizing weapons that could provide a substitute for income redistribution and Communist party discipline: a pledge for the enfranchisement of the Untouchables and the caste-system notion that the foreigners were impure and that one was "polluted" by social or commercial intercourse with them. See Moore (1966, ch. 6).

[20] Among the recent theorists of nationalism, Smith (1979, ch. 5) is the only one who deals at length with socialist (or, in his terminology, Marxist) nationalism and emphasizes its strengths (people's war, party organization, state centralization, commitment to rapid industrialization), very much in tune with my own interpretation. Smith views Marxist nationalisms as "second-wave" nationalisms, which succeed on the wake of the failure of competing ideologies (pp. 129, 137). My argument is perhaps stronger in that it implies that socialist nationalism, when the appropriate entrepreneurship is available, tends to drive out competition.

national liberation becomes one with the struggle for socialist revolution. Although this merger has important implications for communist ideology and policies both before and after the conquest of power, it is the reverse implications of communist leadership for nationalist movements that concern us here. Socialist nationalism is in a position to promise three things. First, the national bourgeoisie, at least if compromised with the foreign power, will be ousted from all managerial and administrative positions and expropriated of its assets (notably, land), thus making room for upward mobility from the ranks of the working classes. Here the armed struggle for national liberation, be it against a colonial or neocolonial power or against foreign military occupation, plays a critical role in making room for socialist nationalizations of property that are acceptable to the population. The widely observed fact that the national bourgeoisie will be likely just to side with the foreign power to put down the revolutionary movement and prevent its own ousting makes the communist prophecy self-fulfilling, with the consequence that the traditional structure of property rights is delegitimized in the public mind and the scope for sweeping changes in those rights by the new regime enhanced (incidentally, this helps to solve a legitimacy problem with the ownership structure that typically hampers communist movements in normal times). Second, the revolution will undertake a comprehensive program of industrialization and diversification of production to lessen the country's dependence on capitalist-dominated world trade and its vulnerability to the imperialist threat; an agrarian reform designed to split up large landed properties or livestock holdings among propertyless laborers; the creation of a large standing national army equipped with modern weaponry; the creation of a large bureaucracy to manage the enlarged public sector of the economy; and extensive investments in education, culture, and health. All these measures increase dramatically the number and range of relatively high-income and high-status positions that will become available to former peasants and workers, and the initial confiscation of foreign and collaborationist property may often substantially lessen the start-up costs of the development program to be borne by the laboring classes. Third, several organizational techniques substantially increase the likelihood of the movement's success. To begin with, the Communist party itself, with its centralized organization and strict discipline, provides a well-tested instrument to detect and sanction potential free riders or traitors that is normally not available to bourgeois political organizations. Further, when the national revolution is achieved through a people's war under Party guidance, the self-government of the liberated areas provides a very effective screening mechanism that links expected individual benefits from success to prior participation in the struggle, thus cementing mutual trust between leadership and masses and eliciting voluntary individual contributions. Last, the typical austerity and self-denial that sharply distinguish communist revolutionaries (and religious sects) from other politicians and that ostensibly mark the facade of communist states are a kind of insurance mechanism that guarantees the rank and file in the movement that their contribution will not be wasted and that future returns on their current investments in the struggle will be forthcoming. The same purpose is obviously served by the requirement (observed in Vietnam, Guinea, and Mozambique, as in China before) that guerrilla fighters and political leaders be involved in economic production side by side with the peasants, which would appear inefficient in terms of division of labor.

The attractiveness of this package was further bolstered by the epidemic significance of the Soviet precedent itself, skillfully propagandized to Third World countries seeking independence and backed, especially in the 1960s and 1970s, by substantial Soviet economic and (especially) military aid to those countries that undertook the socialist-nationalist path. It is small wonder that, on the whole, socialist nationalism proved remarkably successful in overcoming the disabilities of the bourgeois-nationalist path to independent statehood, and the sample of success stories surveyed above in Section III suggests that it basically fulfilled its stated promises – though at a cost, in terms of forgone alternatives, that is perhaps only lately surfacing to full light.

If communism succeeds in exploiting to its own advantage, and thereby "solving," the classic issues that confront a nationalist movement, however, it adds to the history of nationalism a new chapter that is entirely of its own making. Under a communist regime, a nationality's fate depends on whether its numbers and/or the resources or territory it controls are deemed necessary to the building of the power base of the new state. When a nationality's consensus can be dispensed with, because its size is tiny *and* its resources can most profitably be transferred under the control of the dominant nationality, as in the examples of China and Romania, then the national minorities are denied territorial autonomy and privilege and are subjected to repression and outright assimilation. In these cases, in the regime's eyes, the minorities' unrest is more than compensated for by the enhanced loyalty of the rest of the population. In contrast, when a nation of substantial size or importance achieves self-determination cum socialism not as an independent state but as a member of a federal communist state, as things turned out in the Soviet Union and

Yugoslavia (and to some extent in Czechoslovakia as well), it finds itself involved in an "implicit social contract" that dictates that, in order to uphold internal consensus and external credibility of the communist regime, in due time all member nations are to be brought up to the same level of economic development (the Lenin-Stalin nationality policy). Partly to lessen the burden of future transfers, partly to build working-class consensus, and partly because living idly on welfare runs counter to the basic work ethos of a communist regime ("to each according to his/her work"), this principle further implies that the high-income member nation must provide the low-income member nation not with income subsidies but with an industrial base and the potential for self-sustained growth. This arrangement puts a premium on individuals' identification along national lines in the backward republics or even creates nationalism where none existed before (as in Turkestan of precommunist times), in order to benefit from "affirmative-action" hiring and educational policies, income transfers, and investment subsidization. It is a peculiar kind of "nationalism," however, in that it nurtures no separatist demands: On the contrary, it feeds on, and upholds, a strong central ("federal!") state that takes care of continuing redistribution.

The pre- and postrevolutionary policies of socialist nationalism both spring from the fundamental nature of communist movements, viewed as a class of political entrepreneurs: Communism is a political enterprise and, when it succeeds in taking power, a political regime that caters to the needs and interests of the producers – indeed, one might say, a social order ruled not by consumer sovereignty but by producer sovereignty. That is the common underlying rationale for its promise of rapid industrialization with all its concomitants, during the revolutionary struggle, and for its commitment to industrialization of the backward republics, after the revolution.[21] It is this producer bias that in turn explains communism's territorial bias in nationality policy, that is, its aversion to cultural nationalism divorced from territory and its linking of federalism to nationality (as detailed in the "Communist

---

[21] This approach to communism as a brand of political entrepreneurship centered on producer constituencies is developed in Ferrero (1994), where it is used to account for the key features of communist mobilization regimes (which largely overlap with the socialist-nationalist regimes discussed here). More specifically, using the public choice model of the collectivization of private goods, I tried in another work (Ferrero, 1993) to explain formally the communist regimes' bias toward rapid industrialization and high investment rates as driven by "majority" preferences among the producer population.

doctrine on the national question" section above); because producers are more easily structured by territory or "regional fiefdoms" (Fairbanks 1978), whereas consumers need not be, and because communism's appeal is invariably directed to nationalities qua producers, whether current or prospective: peasants, herders, workers, intelligentsia, civil servants, service employees, soldiers, and so on. Johnson (1967, 6–7) observed that nationalist policies, like democratic government, tend to concentrate benefits on specific producer interests and to disperse their costs over the mass of consumers, even though their net social benefits may well be negative. Johnson's argument, formulated for what is called bourgeois nationalism in this chapter, applies to socialist nationalism as well, but with a basic difference in degree: The producers to whom socialist nationalism appeals are not just, or not at all, the educated middle classes, but virtually all the actual or potential producers – or, one might say, all the potential applicants to middle class status – listed above. Thus Breton's and Johnson's calculus of nationalism is reversed: It is no longer true that income is redistributed from the working class to the middle class. Whatever its net welfare consequences over the long run, socialist-nationalist industrialization and modernization, through a radical change in property rights and economic institutions, redistributes income from the foreigners and/or the former middle classes to the working classes – not, of course, to all of the working people, as communist ideology would like us to believe, but to those sections and individual producers that are selected and co-opted upward through a political process of consensus building presided over by the Party and its organizational devices, both before and after the conquest of power. The (selective) egalitarianism of communist ideology and practice, embraced by a radical, westernized intelligentsia, thus proves to be a powerful strategy of nation building.

Summing up, socialist nationalism appeals to a substantially broader constituency than bourgeois nationalism by holding out the prospect of unprecedented upward mobility in educational and occupational levels, by making the promise credible through the trust-building, selective commitment techniques that characterize its political leadership and by fulfilling the promise when expedient or necessary to build consensus for the new regime. Thus socialist nationalism, when the required entrepreneurship is available, proves superior to its competitor on all the three counts posited above: a larger pie, a broader spread of its slices, and an increased trustworthiness in the eyes of its followers.

238   Mario Ferrero

V   **The emergence of postcommunist nationalism**

The theoretical framework sketched out in the previous section provides a key to understanding the pattern of nationalist resurgence and ethnic strife that prevails during and after the collapse of multinational communist states.

When, due to the slowdown of overall growth, political ossification and corruption of the regime, dwindling popular consensus in the face of inefficiencies and shortages, and the ensuing pressure for radical, market-oriented economic reform, the federal status quo eventually begins to break apart, then all depends on who wields the bulk of coercive and military power. In the case of Yugoslavia, it was the most developed republics of Slovenia and Croatia, which were the net losers in the federal redistribution process, that began to secede; then the Serbs, backed by Montenegro, resorted to force to forestall secession and, since Croatian and Serbian areas are nested into one another like Chinese boxes and since Bosnia-Herzegovina, as a frontier area, was up for grabs by the highest bidder in terms of force, the ominous "ethnic cleansing" began on both sides on a grand scale, with the Serbs enjoying the advantage of controlling the federal army. Likewise, ethnic cleansing seems to be on the Serbs' agenda for the Serbian enclosure of Kosovo, now that the developed republics are no longer there to pay the bill for Kosovo's industrial development. There is no need to evoke "atavic" ethnic hatred to account for the current slaughter in former Yugoslavia: A drive for territory, resources, and subject people; a material interest in freeing oneself from the burden of redistribution in hard times; and an uneven distribution of coercive power seem sufficient to explain who's fighting whom.

Former Czechoslovakia,[22] a federal republic since 1968, with the Slovak republic encompassing one third of total population, presents a somewhat similar case in which the communist regime consistently implemented accelerated industrialization and modernization of once-backward, agricultural Slovakia, thereby substantially narrowing the income gap between republics. This industrialization, however, revolved around heavy industry mainly for military purposes, integrated in the strategic planning of the Soviet bloc. After the 1989 revolution that overthrew the communist regime, the extensive marketization and privatization program undertaken by the federal government under President Havel threatened the demise of the obsolete military-

---

[22] Background information and recent developments in former Czechoslovakia are surveyed in Steiner (1973), Klein (1975), Musil (1992), and Ulc (1992).

industrial complex that supported incomes in Slovakia, which then reawakened its slumbering nationalism and strove for independent statehood as a means of preserving a state-controlled economy. Arguably, it is only because, unlike in Yugoslavia, national-territorial contours were relatively clear-cut and because the federal army was controlled by the Czechs, whose economic interest lay in getting rid of the drag of Slovakia's backwardness, that the transition to secession in former Czechoslovakia took the "gentle" course of which the Czechs are so proud.

In the former Soviet Union, the pattern of interethnic conflict bears a close correspondence with the pattern of interrepublican redistribution flows that prevailed prior to the Union's collapse. Understandably in the light of the situation outlined above as regards the Soviet Union, it was the most advanced Baltic republics, soon joined by Georgia, that took the first steps toward secession; then the sizable Russian minorities within their borders at once became a political as well as an economic problem, though no interethnic violence is reported so far. The Asian Muslim republics, which were the chief beneficiaries of structural redistribution under Soviet rule, when faced with the prospect of having to rely on their own resources, soon realized that without further subsidization of investment from the European republics and with their breathtaking rates of demographic growth, their capital stocks and incomes per capita were bound to decline steeply; and, rationally enough, they started harassment and attempted expulsion of the "foreigners" in their midst, not so much the Russians (who were beginning to flee back to Russia anyway in anticipation of the impending economic decline) as the Asians belonging to nontitular nationalities: hence the bloody conflicts between Uzbeks and Kirghiz, Uzbeks and Kazakhs, Azeris and Armenians, and so on, since the mid-1980s. After all, an Uzbek might reason, the Tadzhiks have their "own" republic nearby, why should we let them preempt "our" scarce jobs here? As will be remembered, Asians of different nationalities tended to compete for the same occupational sectors. As a side product of all this, a revival of Great Russian nationalist feelings among Russians themselves is observable, this time not mainly with "imperial" overtones but rather of an "isolationist" character, well exemplified by Aleksandr Solzhenitsyn. However, the huge Russian republic, as it stands, contains many nationality-based autonomous republics and provinces, whose status is no longer guaranteed by the former imperial law-and-order equilibrium; hence a revival of defensive nationalism among these smaller enclosed minorities.

In all these instances of postcommunist nationalism the former beneficiaries of structural socialist redistribution – the nationalities of Serbia and Montenegro, Slovakia, and the Soviet Muslim republics – exhibit a striking similarity of behavioral patterns: They were all in favor of a centralized, redistributive state as long as feasible (regardless of whether they could avail themselves of military force to maintain the status quo); they were and are most alien to any kind of market reform and cling to types of national-communist regimes; wherever possible, they try to secure the lion's share of the material legacy of the federal state by either clearing out, or discriminating against, nonnational surplus labor or taking control of natural, territorial, or capital resources, depending on the balance of forces. The latter course is profitable precisely because socialist interrepublican redistribution took the form of the subsidized accumulation of fixed capital assets located in the republic's territory, as dictated by the producer or industrialization bias of communist regimes. Thus the legacy of communist ethnic federalism creates a strong popular demand for aggressive nationalist policies. On the other hand, the breakdown of the Communist party's monopoly of power opens up a new competitive market for independent political entrepreneurs in all fields, including the market for nationalism, now no longer frozen and channeled into factional struggle within the institutional monopoly of the Communist party. The current, plentiful supply of nationalist policies, in which each entrepreneur tries to outbid all others on the nationalist scale, is easily explained if one considers that well-established communist regimes bequeath on their successors a social landscape that, if compared to a market economy, is relatively flat in terms of income or property differentiations: The only clear-cut differentiations that stand out in this landscape are the hardened ethno-national cleavages (Linz and Stepan 1992). It is thus only natural to expect political entrepreneurs to seize eagerly upon this ready-made demand and fashion their offers accordingly. In conclusion, therefore, the observed pattern of ethnic conflict seems strongly to support my hypothesis that the revival of nationalism in former communist states is not a die-hard legacy of the precommunist past, but has an underlying economic rationale: It is the logical product of the particular type of structural redistribution that lay at the roots of the communist solution to the national question within a multinational socialist state.

As a final observation, it is interesting to note that, due to the cotton monoculture implemented by the Soviet interrepublican division of labor, the republics of Central Asia, now left to rely on their own means, will probably assign top priority to diversification of their industrial structure, by developing machine-building, textile manufacture, and other labor-intensive, water-saving sectors (Rumer 1989). Thus a key ingredient of socialist nationalism in the Western world, one which greatly contributed to its popular following and ultimately to its success, may well reappear in the former Soviet context, as if in a revenge of history ("socialism without Russians," in the phrase of Seton-Watson [1977, 319]), making for the persistence of national communist regimes in former Soviet Central Asia.

References

Abramsky, C. 1978. "The Biro-Bidzhan Project, 1927–1959." In Kochan L., ed., *The Jews in Soviet Russia Since 1917*, 64–77. 3rd ed. New York: Oxford University Press.
Albright, D. E. 1991. "Soviet Economic Development and the Third World." *Soviet Studies* 43, no. 1:27–59.
Anderson, B. 1983. *Imagined Communities. Reflections on the Origin and Spread of Nationalism.* London: Verso.
Bahry, D. 1987. *Outside Moscow. Power, Politics, and Budgetary Policy in the Soviet Republics.* New York: Columbia University Press.
Banton, M. 1983. *Racial and Ethnic Competition.* New York: Cambridge University Press.
Bawden, C. R. 1968. *The Modern History of Mongolia.* New York: Praeger.
Blair, T. L. 1970. *The Land to Those Who Work It. Algeria's Experiment in Workers' Management.* New York: Doubleday.
Booth, J. A. 1982. *The End and the Beginning: The Nicaraguan Revolution.* Boulder, CO: Westview Press.
Brada, J. C. 1985. "Soviet Subsidization of Eastern Europe: The Primacy of Economics over Politics?" *Journal of Comparative Economics* 9, no. 1:80–92.
Breton, A. 1964. "The Economics of Nationalism." *Journal of Political Economy* 72 (4):376–86.
Carr, E. H. 1950. *A History of Soviet Russia. The Bolshevik Revolution 1917–1923*, vol. 1. London: Macmillan.
Chabal, P. 1983. *Amilcar Cabral. Revolutionary Leadership and People's War.* New York: Cambridge University Press.
Clem, R. S. 1980. "Economic Development of the Russian Homeland: Regional Growth in the Soviet Union." In Allworth, E., ed. *Ethnic Russia in the USSR. The Dilemma of Dominance*, 205–13. White Plains, NY: Pergamon Press.
Close, D. 1988. *Nicaragua. Politics, Economics and Society.* London: Pinter.
Colburn, F. D. 1986. *Post-Revolutionary Nicaragua. State, Class, and the Dilemmas of Agrarian Policy.* Los Angeles and Berkeley: University of California Press.
Conquest, R., ed. 1986. *The Last Empire. Nationality and the Soviet Future.* Stanford: Hoover Institution Press.
Davidson, B. 1981. *The People's Cause. A History of Guerrillas in Africa.* London: Longman.

Demsetz, H. 1968. "Why Regulate Utilities?" *Journal of Law and Economics* 11:55–5.
Deutschmann, D., ed. 1987. *Che Guevara and the Cuban Revolution. Writings and Speeches of Ernesto Che Guevara.* Sydney: Pathfinder/Pacific and Asia.
Dubravcic, D. 1992. "Economic Causes and the Political Context of the Dissolution of a Multinational Federal State: The Case of Yugoslavia." Paper presented at the Second EACES Conference, Groningen, September 24–6.
Fairbanks, Jr., C. H. 1978. "National Cadres As a Force in the Soviet System: The Evidence of Beria's Career, 1949–53." In Azrael J. R., ed. *Soviet Nationality Policies and Practices,* 144–86. New York: Praeger.
Ferrero, M. 1993. "Why Were Investment Ratios So High in Soviet-Type Economies? A Public Choice Approach." *Eastern Economic Journal* 19, no. 1:1–14.
———. 1994. "Bureaucrats vs. Red Guards." In Campbell, R. W., and A. Brzeski, eds. *Issues in the Transformation of Centrally Planned Economies.* Boulder, CO: Westview Press.
Fierman, W., ed. 1991. *Soviet Central Asia. The Failed Transformation.* Boulder, CO: Westview Press.
Flaherty, D. 1988. "Plan, Market and Unequal Regional Development in Yugoslavia." *Soviet Studies* 40, no. 1:100–24.
Flakierski, H. 1989. "Economic Reform and Income Distribution in Yugoslavia." *Comparative Economic Studies* 31, no. 1:67–102.
Galli, R. E., and Jones, J. 1987. *Guinea-Bissau. Politics, Economics and Society.* London: Pinter.
Gellner, E. 1964. *Thought and Change.* London: Weidenfeld & Nicholson.
———. 1983. *Nations and Nationalism.* Oxford: Basil Blackwell.
Gilberg, T. 1980. "State Policy, Ethnic Persistence and Nationality Formation in Eastern Europe." In Sugar, P. F., ed. *Ethnic Diversity and Conflict in Eastern Europe,* 185–235. Santa Barbara, CA: ABC-Clio.
Glazer, N., and Moynihan, D. P., eds. 1976. *Ethnicity. Theory and Experience.* Cambridge: Harvard University Press.
Hajda, L., and Beissinger, M., eds. 1990. *The Nationalities Factor in Soviet Politics and Society.* Boulder, CO: Westview Press.
Henriksen, T. H. 1983. *Revolution and Counterrevolution. Mozambique's War of Independence, 1964–74.* Westport, CT: Greenwood Press.
Hobsbawm, E. J. 1990. *Nations and Nationalism Since 1780.* New York: Cambridge University Press.
Horowitz, I. L., ed. 1981. *Cuban Communism.* 4th ed. New Brunswick, NY: Transaction Books.
Johnson, C. A. 1962. *Peasant Nationalism and Communist Power. The Emergence of Revolutionary China 1937–1945.* Stanford, CA: Stanford University Press.
Johnson, H. G. 1967. "A Theoretical Model of Economic Nationalism in New and Developing States." In Johnson, H. G., ed. *Economic Nationalism in Old and New States,* 1–16. Chicago: University of Chicago Press.
Joint Economic Committee. U.S. Congress 1979. *Soviet Economy in a Time of Change.* Washington D.C.: U.S. Government Printing Office.
Jones, E., and Grupp, F. W. 1984. "Modernisation and Ethnic Equalisation in the USSR." *Soviet Studies* 36, no. 2:159–84.

Keller, E. J., and Rothchild, D., eds. 1987. *Afro-Marxist Regimes. Ideology and Public Policy.* Boulder, CO: Lynne Rienner.
Klein, G. 1975. "The Role of Ethnic Politics in the Czechoslovak Crisis of 1968 and the Yugoslav Crisis of 1971." *Studies in Comparative Communism* 8, no. 4:339–69.
Kraft, E., and Vodopivec, M. 1992. "How Soft Is the Budget Constraint for Yugoslav Firms?" *Journal of Comparative Economics* 16:432–55.
Laitin, D. D. 1991. "The National Uprisings in the Soviet Union." *World Politics* 44:139–77.
Lang, N. 1974–5. "The Dialectics of Decentralization: Economic Reform and Regional Inequality in Yugoslavia." *World Politics* 27:310–35.
Linz, J. J., and Stepan, A. 1992. "Political Identities and Electoral Sequences: Spain, the Soviet Union, and Yugoslavia." *Daedalus* (Spring):123–39.
Lubin, N. 1984. *Labour and Nationality in Soviet Central Asia. An Uneasy Compromise.* London: Macmillan.
Marmullaku, R. 1975. *Albania and the Albanians.* London: Hurst & Co.
Marrese, M., and Vanous, J. 1983. *Soviet Subsidization of Trade with Eastern Europe: A Soviet Perspective.* Berkeley: University of California Institute of International Studies.
McAuley, A. 1979. *Economic Welfare in the Soviet Union. Poverty, Living Standards, and Inequality.* Madison: University of Wisconsin Press.
  1985. "Soviet Development Policy in Central Asia." In Cassen, R., ed. *Soviet Interests in the Third World,* 299–318. London: Sage.
  1991. "Costs and Benefits of De-integration in the USSR." *Moct-Most* 2:51–65.
  1992. "The Central Asian Economy in Comparative Perspective." In Ellman M., and Kontorovich V., eds. *The Disintegration of the Soviet Economic System,* 137–56. London: Routledge.
McCagg Jr., W. O., and Silver B. D., eds. 1979. *Soviet Asian Ethnic Frontiers.* New York: Pergamon Press.
Mesa-Lago, C. 1981. *The Economy of Socialist Cuba. A Two-Decade Appraisal.* Albuquerque: University of New Mexico Press.
  1971. *Revolutionary Change in Cuba.* Pittsburgh: University of Pittsburgh Press.
Moore, B. 1966. *Social Origins of Dictatorship and Democracy.* Boston: Beacon Press.
Munslow, B. 1983. *Mozambique: The Revolution and its Origins.* London: Longman.
Murphy, G. 1966. *Soviet Mongolia. A Study of the Oldest Political Satellite.* Berkeley and Los Angeles: University of California Press.
Musil, J. 1992. "Czechoslovakia in the Middle of Transition." *Daedalus.* (Spring):175–95.
Ottaway, D., and Ottaway, M. 1970. *Algeria: The Politics of a Socialist Revolution.* Berkeley and Los Angeles: University of California Press.
Peters, S. 1975. "Ingredients of the Communist Takeover in Albania." In Hammond, T., ed. *The Anatomy of Communist Takeovers,* 273–92. New Haven, CT: Yale University Press.
Pike, D. 1966. *Viet Cong. The Organization and Techniques of the National Liberation Front of South Vietnam.* Cambridge, MA: The M.I.T. Press.
Pipes, R. 1954. *The Formation of the Soviet Union. Communism and Nationalism 1917–1923.* Cambridge: Harvard University Press.

Popkin, S. L. 1979. *The Rational Peasant. The Political Economy of Rural Society in Vietnam.* Berkeley and Los Angeles: University of California Press.
Rex, J., and Mason, D., eds. 1986. *Theories of Race and Ethnic Relations.* New York: Cambridge University Press.
Roeder, P. G. 1991. "Soviet Federalism and Ethnic Mobilization." *World Politics* 43:196–232.
Rumer, B. Z. 1989. *Soviet Central Asia. A Tragic Experiment.* Boston: Unwin Hyman.
Rupen, R. 1979. *How Mongolia Is Really Ruled. A Political History of the Mongolian People's Republic 1900–1978.* Stanford: Hoover Institution Press.
Sandler, T., and Tschirhart, J. T. 1980. "The Economic Theory of Clubs: An Evaluative Survey." *Journal of Economic Literature* 18, no. 4:1481–1521.
Saul, J. S., ed. 1985. *A Difficult Road. The Transition to Socialism in Mozambique.* New York: Monthly Review Press.
Schnytzer, A. 1982. *Stalinist Economic Strategy in Practice. The Case of Albania.* New York: Oxford University Press.
Seton-Watson, H. 1977. *Nations and States. An Enquiry into the Origins of Nations and the Politics of Nationalism.* London: Methuen.
Shoup, P. 1968. *Communism and the Yugoslav National Question.* New York: Columbia University Press.
Smith, A. D. S. 1979. *Nationalism in the Twentieth Century.* New York: New York University Press.
Smith, T. 1978. *The French Stake in Algeria, 1945–1962.* Ithaca, NY: Cornell University Press.
Spalding, R. J., ed. 1987. *The Political Economy of Revolutionary Nicaragua.* London: Allen & Unwin.
Stalin, J. 1942. *Marxism and the National Question.* New York: International Press.
Steiner, E. 1973. *The Slovak Dilemma.* New York: Cambridge University Press.
Turner, R. F. 1975. *Vietnamese Communism. Its Origins and Development.* Stanford: Hoover Institution Press.
Ulc, O. 1992. "The Bumpy Road of Czechoslovakia's Velvet Revolution." *Problems of Communism* 41, no. 3:19–33.
Van Selm, G., and Doelle E. 1992. "Soviet Interrepublican Capital Transfers and the Republics' Level of Development, 1966–91." Paper presented at the Second EACES Conference, Groningen, September 24–6.
Wolf, E. R. 1969. *Peasant Wars of the Twentieth Century.* New York: Harper & Row.
Zarkovic Bookman, M. 1990. "The Economic Basis of Regional Autarchy in Yugoslavia." *Soviet Studies* 42 no. 1:93–109.
Zaslavsky, V. 1992. "Nationalism and Democratic Transition in Postcommunist Societies." *Daedalus* (Spring):97–121.
Zavalani, T. 1969. "Albanian Nationalism." In Sugar, P. F., and Lederer, I. J., eds. *Nationalism in Eastern Europe,* 55–92. Seattle, WA: University of Washington Press.

CHAPTER 11

Regulating nations and ethnic communities

Brendan O'Leary and John McGarry[1]

National and ethnic conflict is a persistent feature of modernity and will continue to be so despite intermittently fashionable theories that assert otherwise.

The last decade has seen seismic changes in the relations between national and ethnic communities around the world. Most spectacularly the disintegrations of the Soviet Union and Yugoslavia burst asunder the borders of the communist empires – and what was Ethiopia will probably imitate them. Much of the conventional political wisdom about nationality and ethnicity collapsed with these empires. For instance, it had been widely maintained that the international (for which read the interstate) system had stabilized the borders of the world's states, so that secessions and the redrawing of territorial frontiers through conquest or partitions were phenomena of previous ages (see Mayall 1990). The aftermath of World War II and the decolonization of Europe's empires had allegedly carved states' borders in stone, and many concurred with the verdict that "the twentieth-century bias against political divorce, that is, secession, is just about as strong as the nineteenth-century bias against marital divorce" (Huntingdon 1972). The forging of the states of Israel and Bangladesh through war and insurrection, Indonesia's conquests of East Timor and West Irian, and India's invasion of Goa were merely exceptions that proved the rule.

Today we all should know that the stability of state borders after 1945 (or 1960) owed more to the geopolitics of the Cold War than to

---

[1] The authors thank Brian Barry, Alan Beattie, Patrick Dunleavy, Christopher Hood, Tom Nossiter, David Schiff, and all the participants in the Villa Colombella Group, especially Ronald Finlay, Russell Hardin, Paul Seabright, and Ron Wintrobe for their critical commentary. They are individually and severally liable for the remaining errors.

the triumph of particular norms of "international law." While it remains to be seen whether the "new international order" proclaimed over the rubble of the cities of Kuwait and Baghdad presages a new stabilization of the world's territorial frontiers, the sages of "international relations" and the prophets of postmodernity have had their wings clipped. The urge of nations to be states and the capacities of states to create nations, intentionally or otherwise, are not diminishing. Saddam Hussein's adventurism may have been the first and least successful of a new round of state-and nation-building projects that will owe more to conquest than consent. Many Serbians at least appear to have made this calculation.

The renewed instability of state frontiers is merely one symptom of the global political power of national and ethnic consciousness. The last two decades have seen the final collapse of white settler regimes in Africa (in Angola, Guinea-Bissau, Mozambique, Namibia, and Zimbabwe), and the South African system of apartheid, the last bastion of European settler domination in Africa, hovers on the verge of negotiated extinction. Yet during the same period new systems of ethnic domination have been established around the world, by native Melanesians in Fiji, by Morocco in the Western Sahara, by Israelis in what was Palestine; and attempts to establish such regimes have led to protracted "civil" wars, notably in Uganda and Sudan. And the fear (or pretext) that open, multiparty democracies would degenerate into ethnic contests for state power, put much of postcolonial Africa and considerable portions of Asia and Latin America under one-party dictatorships or military rule. Other parts of the world appear trapped in deadlocked ethnic wars, where no faction is sufficiently powerful to control or crush completely its opponent(s): for example, Burma/Myanmar (Smith 1991) and Peru.

National and ethnic conflict have not been confined to areas of the world characterized by economic underdevelopment. To the contrary: Since the 1960s separatist and autonomist movements have flourished in Corsica, Scotland, Northern Ireland, Catalonia, and Quebec, that is, in regions of the "advanced West." In happier Western zones ethnic communities have been able to negotiate agreed changes to their political systems, notably in Belgium, Switzerland, and the South Tyrol; and some proclaim the European Community is a successful case of the transcendence of national conflicts. There remains nevertheless a twilight world of nations and ethnic communities alternating between deadlocked war and permanent negotiation: Cyprus, Northern Ireland, and Sri Lanka fit this description. The Balkans are joining them, again. As this chapter was composed, Bosnia, Canada, Cyprus, Israel/

Palestine, Northern Ireland, and South Africa were the subjects and objects of inter-ethnic and international (in both senses) negotiations about their governmental futures.

Do all these national and ethnic phenomena have common causes and connections? Can we understand both their genesis and their consequences? These questions can be answered in the affirmative, but they are not our concern here. Instead we concentrate on the macropolitical methods used to manage or eliminate national and ethnic conflict.

Scientific endeavors, as conventionally understood, are built upon theories and hypotheses, evidence and experiments. Scientific development is conventionally measured by successful precision in prediction and postdiction[2] and by the development of quantified indicators of the phenomena being examined or explained. The study of national and ethnic conflict and conflict management have not always met these positivist ideals of social science,[3] and we cannot hope to make good these deficiencies here. Instead we attempt a humbler task, that of classification, the necessary precursor of scientific theory and empirical verification and falsification.

This chapter nevertheless has positive and normative functions. The taxonomy of eight modes of ethnic-conflict resolution, developed below, should facilitate research on whether there are "laws of motion" that govern the forms of national and ethnic-conflict regulation: regularities that enable the "postdiction" (if not the prediction) of the circumstances under which particular strategies for managing conflict will be attempted, and successfully implemented. Normative concerns are also present: We evaluate the merits of the different forms of conflict regulation to establish whether multinational and multiethnic states can be stabilized in ways that are compatible with liberal democratic values and institutions.

We present below a taxonomy of the macropolitical[4] forms of ethnic-conflict regulation, leaving its further refinement to future work

---

[2] The discipline of economics may be an exception: Its practitioners thrive on the failure of forecasts.
[3] Pioneering works have been carried out by Walker Connor (1973) and Donald Horowitz (1985), and most notably by Arend Lijphart (1977, 1984).
[4] Micropolitical forms of conflict-regulation are smaller scale and include inter alia discrimination and segregation, public demographic policies, immigration policies, equal opportunities policies, affirmative action programs, community relations and cultural encounter-promotions, specific forms of electoral representation, and so on. Micropolitical policies are the tools of macropolitical objectives.

(McGarry and O'Leary, forthcoming). The term "regulation" is inclusive, covering both conflict termination and conflict management. Eight distinct macro methods of national- and ethnic-conflict regulation can be distinguished, to wit:

Methods for elimination of differences
   genocide
   forced mass population transfers
   partition and/or secession (self-determination)
   integration and/or assimilation
Methods for managing differences
   hegemonic control
   arbitration (third-party intervention)
   cantonization/federalism
   consociation or power sharing

This is a taxonomy, and not a typology: the classification of entities by logical types.[5] It was arrived at simply through researching cases of ethnic-conflict termination and regulation, and putting together "likes with likes."[6]

This taxonomy does not suggest Linnaeus-like discreteness or exhaustiveness. Often the eight modes are found in combination and targeted at the same national or ethnic group(s), or, alternatively, different strategies are aimed at different ethnic groups within the same state. Thus the Nazis practiced genocide, mass population transfers and hegemonic control of Jews. Stalin executed genocide, mass population transfers, and hegemonic control of multiple ethnic groups. Yugoslavia under Tito employed elements of control, arbitration, and consociation. Oliver Cromwell offered Irish Catholics a choice between genocide and forced mass population transfer. They could go "To Hell or Connaught!" The United States practiced genocide on Native Americans, integration of immigrant Europeans, and control of

---

[5] Typologies are heuristics used to codify existing knowledge. Good typologies are simple, constructed through the use of logical antonyms rather than empirical observations, and provide a fruitful basis for further theoretical development and empirical investigation. Taxonomy by contrast is the classification of organisms and originated with the Swedish scientist Linnaeus. Taxonomists aim to place all organisms in a hierarchical classification scheme in which, to put it very crudely, "likes" are classified with "likes." Taxonomies, unlike typologies, are empirical rather than ideal-typical, a posteriori rather than a priori categories.

[6] Although the eight methods were arrived at taxonomically, two of them are typologically related, namely consociationalism and control (Lustick 1979), and arbitration (or third-party intervention) can be typologically contrasted with them (McGarry and O'Leary, forthcoming).

black Americans in the Deep South. Contemporary Israel practices consociationalism among Jews of different ethnic origins but control over Palestinians; it executed forced mass population transfers in the past and may do so again. Settler colonialists often permit some combination of genocide, mass population transfers, assimilation, and hegemonic control. Belgium has practiced consociationalism to regulate divisions between its "spiritual families" and federalism to resolve tensions between its linguistic communities.

However, this taxonomy is logically divisible between modes of conflict regulation that seek to eliminate or terminate national or ethnic differences, and those that seek to manage the consequences of differences. Thus genocide, mass population transfers, partition/secession, and integration/assimilation are political strategies that seek to eliminate (or radically reduce) differences, at least within a given state. By contrast strategies that manage differences include control, arbitration, federalism/cantonization, and consociationalism.[7]

It is possible to rank the eight methods in the taxonomy normatively, but not to construct a simple or lexicographic moral hierarchy (unless one adopts Kantian cosmopolitanism). We do not think it is justifiable to say that either difference-eliminating or difference-managing methods are inherently ethically superior.

Of the difference-eliminating strategies there are moral justifications for partition/secession (e.g., Barry 1991c; Beran 1987; Buchanan 1991) and arguments for integration (assimilation) (Buchanan 1991) that have been advanced by generations of liberals and socialists. But there is no obvious moral hierarchy that enables people to claim that integration is better than partition (or vice versa), unless there is widespread consent for one option rather than the other – where widespread consent refers to substantial majorities within all the relevant ethnic communities. The merits of partition/secession as against integration/assimilation must be decided by political argument and pragmatic considerations, such as feasibility and estimates about long-run efficacy. There is nothing morally weighty to be said in favor of genocide or forced mass-population transfers, the other difference-eliminating strategies, although "ethical" arguments have usually accompanied the implementation of these gruesome projects.

Of the difference-managing strategies one, hegemonic control, should be morally unacceptable to liberals. The rest (arbitration, can-

---

[7] Eliminating and managing differences are mutually exclusive strategies from the perspective of the target community. However, states may seek to eliminate differences between some communities while seeking to manage differences between others.

tonization/federalism, and consociationalism) are compatible with democratic norms, although there are critics of the democratic quality of consociational practices (e.g., Barry 1991a, b; Lustick 1979; Glazer 1987). Advocacy of the merits of federalism/cantonization, consociation, and arbitration must, however, be tempered by empirical judgments about their feasibility and long-term efficacy.

Methods for eliminating differences

Genocide

The first two extreme and terminal "solutions" to national and ethnic conflict are the most abhorrent: genocide and forced mass population transfers. They often go together. Genocide literally means the killing of a race or kind. There is some controversy as to how the concept should be used, either legally or by social scientists (e.g., Chalk and Jonassohn 1990; Kuper 1981).[8] We believe it should be employed only in cases where the victims share (real or alleged) national or ascriptive traits, whereas Harff's useful term *politicide* should be employed for the systematic mass killing of people who may or may not share ascriptive traits (Harff 1992).[9]

Genocide then is the systematic mass killing of a national or ethnic collectivity (however defined), or the indirect destruction of such a community through the deliberate termination of the conditions that permit its biological and social reproduction. On this definition appalling genocides were perpetrated by the Nazis in the 1930s and 1940s and within the communist bloc in Eurasia. The European colonizers of the Americas, and Russians and Turks in the czarist and Ottoman empires also perpetrated genocides by this definition.

Genocide is still practiced; indeed, in absolute terms the twentieth century has been more genocidal than its predecessors. Only confident optimists believe that genocide has become outmoded because of the

---

[8] "Genocide" was coined to describe the systematic destruction of Jews, Gypsies, and Slavs by the Nazis (Lemkin 1944).
[9] The UN *Convention on the Prevention and Punishment of the Crime of Genocide* (1948) defines it as "acts committed with intent to destroy, in whole or in part, a national, ethnic, racial or religious group, as such" (Article II). The article's sub-clauses include "(a) killing members of the group; (b) causing serious bodily or mental harm to members of the group; (c) deliberately inflicting on the group conditions of life calculated to bring about its physical destruction in whole or in part; (d) imposing measures intended to prevent births within the group; (e) forcibly transferring children of the group to another group." There is much debate over whether subclause (b) is too inclusive.

triumph of universal norms in what some sociologists are pleased to call "late modernity." The infamy won by Hitler and Stalin notwithstanding genocide has not become unthinkable.[10] Since 1945 there have been genocides perpetrated in the Soviet Union (of the Chechens, the Ingushi, the Karachai, the Balkars, the Meskhetians, and the Crimean Tartars[11]); in Burundi (of Hutu); in Iraq (of the Kurds); in Paraguay (of the Ache Indians); in Indonesia (of the Chinese[12] and the indigenous population of East Timor); in Nigeria (of Ibo residents in the North); in Equatorial Guinea (of the Bubi); in Uganda (of the Karamojong, the Acholi, the Lango, Nilotic tribes, and the Bagandans); in Pakistan (of the Bengalis in what became Bangladesh); in Burma (of Muslims in border regions); in Iran (of Kurds and Baha' is); and it appears in Bosnia (of Muslims).

Genocides are usually one-sided – indeed some would say this is one of their defining features (Jonassohn 1992, 19) – and they are intended to terminate national or ethnic conflict. Do they have an economic function? In the construction of many empires it can be said that genocides "worked" instrumentally: They secured the relevant territories for imperial rulers and colonial settlers. In other cases the instrumental rationality of genocides is not at all obvious: European Jews were the victims of the most atrocious genocide in World War II, and the Armenians and others suffered grievously in World War I. In both cases the perpetrators resolved on final solutions, believing it would "purify" their national cultures and stabilize their empires.[13]

---

[10] Recently McNeill (1986, 71) argued that Hitler's genocides of Jews, Gypsies, and Slavs had decisively tainted advocacy of the ideal of ethnic unity within an existing state.

[11] Some believe that these were cases of forced transfers rather than genocide because Stalin's express intention was to remove these peoples from militarily sensitive areas and not to kill them. However, by the "indirect destruction" element in our definition (and that of the UN), they count as genocides.

[12] The Chinese were (conveniently) treated as coterminous with communists: So it is difficult to distinguish genocide from politicide in Indonesia. Estimates of the number of victims during 1965 to 1966 range from 500,000 to 1,000,000.

[13] That the Armenians were the victims of Turkish genocide has been challenged by Turks and others who maintain that "those who question the 'Armenian genocide' are very different from those who question the genocide of the Jews by Hitler and his Nazis" and include "the foremost experts on the history of Turkey in the United States" (McCarthy 1989, 97). But, sadly, it is normal for genocides to be denied by the perpetrators or their descendants. Modern Turks cannot bear to think their ancestors behaved in a an extremely brutal fashion in 1916; and their historical apologists concentrate on the (accurate) claim that the Armenians were preparing to seek autonomy and to use violence, as if these arguments excuse genocide. For discussions of the genocide of Armenians, see inter alia Hovannisian, ed. (1986; 1992), and the Permanent People's Tribunal (1985).

Genocides often fail to achieve their objectives. Naturally they create explosive and historically entrenched bitterness and fear among survivors and the descendants of victims. Serb–Croat relations in what was Yugoslavia are inflamed by memories of wartime genocide during World War II. If Russians and indigenous groups in the Baltic states, Ukraine, and Kazakhstan are to coexist peacefully lots of skeletons have to remain buried. The state of Israel's "siege mentality" owes its existence to a reaction against the Nazi genocide of Jews.[14] Moreover, one of the consequences in a community that has undergone genocide is a high birthrate, which shifts a political conflict downstream to the next generation.

Although it is not something we can examine at length here, it is possible to identify circumstances under which genocide is likely to be contemplated.

State genocide is more likely to occur when:

- An empire is being constructed and maintained (when genocide is used as a deliberate policy of land acquisition and mass terrorization).
- An ethnic community lacks geopolitical resources (its own state or a powerful diaspora).
- A subordinate ethnic community is left vulnerable within a disintegrating system of control (whether organized by an empire or a party dictatorship).
- A given ethnic community (e.g., Jews, Ibos, Armenians, overseas Chinese) possesses economic superiority and cultural identifiability in conditions of industrialization, but lacks military and political power (Gellner 1983, 105).
- A given ethnic community is convinced that its position is one of "kill or be killed";
- The relevant state is not democratic.[15]

Frontier genocide is a concomitant of colonization and conquest, but by contrast may not be directly implemented by state officials. It is likely to occur when settlers, possessed of technologically superior resources, displace natives from their access to land and have few incentives to make natives into dependent laborers: Indeed to protect

---

[14] The Israeli state was founded through the mass expulsion of Palestinian Arabs, and their systematic maltreatment has radicalized them, making conflict resolution even more problematic. In response to the Israeli-organized Palestinian catastrophe, some Palestinians wish to execute full-scale retribution, by driving Israelis "into the sea."

[15] However, frontier genocides occurred in all the parliamentary colonies of the British empire. Indeed, one definition of a "white dominion" is that it was where settlers practiced genocide against indigenous peoples.

their position as free farmers they may have every reason to eliminate potential competition.

These conditions are facilitative, not necessary. A necessary condition for genocide appears to be the presence of a racial, ethnic, or religious ideology that sanctions a nonuniversalist conception of the human species and makes mass murder easier to accomplish. These belief systems may be more important than technological capacities for managing mass killings, as it is the discipline of the killers, rather than their instruments, that may best account for the scale of genocides. The Old Testament God of the Jews (and subsequently of the Christians and Muslims) could be used to sanction the extermination of peoples long before Nazi racism. Some have argued that ideological (as opposed to imperial) genocides are modern: Beginning in the religious wars of the Middle Ages they have been carried further by the spread of nationalist and Marxist-Leninist doctrines. We do not agree. Genocide is not "modern," although it occurs in modern times.[16] Genocides can be instrumental and "preemptive" as well as being ideological: Indigenous peoples were killed by European colonizers on the supposition that their circumstances were those of "kill or be killed." The same beliefs seem to have been important in motivating Tutsi genocides of Hutu in Burundi.

Forced mass population transfers

Forced mass population transfers occur where one (or more) national or ethnic community is physically transplanted from its homeland and compelled to live elsewhere: The contemporary Serbian expression is "ethnic cleansing," although the term has its roots in the Nazi era. A population subject to forced mass population transfers can also be forcibly "repatriated" and pushed back toward its alleged "homeland," as occurred during the high tide of apartheid in South Africa.

Forced mass population transfers must be distinguished from agreed "population exchanges," that is, the transfers that accompany agreed partitions or secessions (such as those between Greece and Turkey after the end of World War I). The population transfers in Cyprus in 1974–5 were in no sense agreed. They were the result of frightened populations moving under the threat of military coercion. Populations that move after agreed exchanges never consider such

---

[16] Nationalism and racism should be carefully distinguished. Nationalism recognizes the equality of nations and is not genocidal, though racism, which ranks races in a hierarchy, is dispositionally genocidal. Totalitarianism, of all brands, has encouraged fearsome politicides (e.g., of so-called kulaks), but such killings should be conceptually distinguished from genocides, even if they overlapped in practice.

moves to be voluntary, but their fate must be distinguished from those unilaterally compelled to move.

Forced mass population transfers may displace rather than terminate ethnic conflict. The turmoil in what was the Soviet Union is partly an outcome of forced mass population transfers executed by Lenin and Stalin and their successors. Violence in the contemporary Caucasus is, in part, the result of similar policies pursued by both czarist and Ottoman emperors. Palestinians were expelled from Israel during the insurrectionary war that founded the state of Israel, and many Palestinians fear that the settlement of the West Bank by Israeli colonizers is merely the prelude to a further set of expulsions. In turn the creation of a Palestinian diaspora helped precipitate the destabilization of Jordan, Lebanon, and even Kuwait. Some have predicted that Bosnian Muslims face the fate of becoming the "Palestinians of Europe": dispossessed, uprooted, and stateless. In what may soon be described as the former state of Ethiopia, forced resettlement policies exacerbated the civil war and famine-proneness of the country during the mid–1980s. In the last decade the states of Nigeria, Vietnam, and Burma have expelled large numbers of residents on plainly ethnic criteria, and India has promised to expel Bengali immigrants (from Bangladesh) from the state of Assam, although this decision has not yet been implemented.

Forced mass population transfers, like genocides, are often advocated as integral components of imperial consolidation strategies. They are usually implemented after or during wars and civil wars – consider Oliver Cromwell's "transplantation" program in Ireland, czarist and Turkish policies in the Caucasus in the nineteenth century, or Stalin's movement of the Volga Germans, Cossacks, and others. They may have economic dimensions: the expropriation of land and property, the removal of competitors, the denial of citizenship entitlements. Forced mass population transfers are likely to be advocated in response to the perceived threat of "ethnic swamping," as seen in the Assamese demonstrations against illegal Bengali immigration or in response to economic depressions, when the call for "repatriation" of "guest workers" may be extended to include all those who are not "sons and daughters of the soil." The call for ethnic cleansing by Serbian irregulars in Bosnia demonstrates that forced mass population transfers can be politically instrumental: to establish "facts" that might make possible territorial adjustments "impossible."[17]

---

[17] There is a variation on forced transfers, that is, "induced population transfers" that dilute a compact minority. In this case settlers are moved into a given territory and threaten the minority (e.g., Italians were sent to the Alto Adige under Mussolini in

There are no moral merits to forced mass population transfers, especially as they facilitate genocidal assaults on vulnerable populations and/or encourage the likelihood that the victims will suffer famine. Forced mass population transfers violate any minimalist conceptions of human rights and any egalitarian political philosophies. Nevertheless, where peoples believe that their homelands have been stolen from them by settler peoples, it becomes thinkable if not justifiable to argue that historic retribution is in order.

Partition and/or secession (self-determination)

Genocide and forced mass population transfers are obnoxious from the perspective of democratic liberalism or socialism and violate Article 27 of the United Nations' *International Covenant on Civil and Political Rights:* "In those states in which ethnic, religious or linguistic minorities exist, persons belonging to such minorities shall not be denied the right, in community with the other members of their group to enjoy their own culture, to profess and practise their own religion, or to use their own language."[18]

Partitioning territories to permit self-determination or secession, by contrast with genocide and mass population transfers, can, in principle, respect the rights of national and ethnic communities. Partition and secession are compatible with liberal democratic institutions (universal, periodic, and competitive elections; alternations in power; and civic freedoms of expression, assembly, and organization), in that such states can, in principle, permit secessions and preserve democratic institutions.

Partition resolves national and ethnic conflict, if it works, by divorcing communities that do not wish to live together in the same state. It can be executed in at least three different ways. Partition can be implemented by the core of the relevant state, which chooses how much of the periphery may secede: as when the United Kingdom government in effect decided how much of Ireland would be permitted to secede in 1921. Alternatively it can be carried out democratically, through consensus, that is, by allowing the relevant communities the right to exercise self-determination, to vote on whether they wish to be part of one state or another, and to draw boundaries and partition territories accordingly. The breakup of Czecho-Slovakia in 1992–3 is a

---

order to break up German areas). This strategy, however, is really a subset of settler colonialism, which we primarily associate with hegemonic control (see below).

[18] In 1992 a text inspired by Article 27 was adopted in the UN: *A Draft Declaration on the Rights of Persons Belonging to National or Ethnic, or Religious and Linguistic Minorities.*

case in point. Finally, partition can be externally imposed, by outside power(s): Consider the partition of Palestine or the dismemberments of Poland in the eighteenth century and Germany in the twentieth century.

In the years between 1948 and 1991 only one new state, Bangladesh, was carved out of an existing state – *if* we exclude the very numerous cases of decolonization of European- and United States-controlled territories in Asia, Africa, and Latin America. However, since the collapse of the communist empires of Ethiopia, Yugoslavia and the Soviet Union secession has become a growth-industry, the in-vogue method of ethnic conflict-resolution. Kurdistan will be next if Iraqi Kurds are allowed to have their way. The Quebecois and Eritreans are also in the queue. There are secessionist or semisecessionist[19] movements in Europe (e.g., among the Basque, Corsican, Northern Irish nationalist, Scottish, Slovak, and Welsh peoples), in Africa (e.g., the Polisario movement in the Moroccan-controlled western Sahara, the Dinkas of the southern Sudan, and a bewildering variety of communities in the Horn of Africa); in the new republics of the Commonwealth of Independent States (e.g., Nagorno-Karabakh wishes to secede from Azerbaijan, South Ossetia from Georgia, Crimea from the Ukraine, and the "Dniester Republic" from Moravia); and in central and south Asia (the Khalistan movement for a Sikh homeland, the Kashmiri independence movement, Tibetans in communist China, and the multiple secessionists of Burma).[20]

The normative idea behind principled partitions and secessions is the idea of self-determination.[21] However, the key problem with self-determination as a means of eliminating conflict is that it begs four questions: (1) Who are the people? (2) What is the relevant territorial unit in which they should exercise self-determination? (3) What constitutes a majority? and (4) Does secession produce a domino effect in which minorities within seceding territories seek self-determination for themselves?

---

[19] We use the term semisecessionist movements to cover those seeking to leave one state to unite or reunite with another. Strict secessionists seek to create an independent state and are wrongly called irredentist. States that seek to expand to complete their nation-stateness are properly irredentist. Naturally irredentist states and semisecessionist movements often go together. To avoid the prejudicial nature of the term irredentist perhaps we should call such states "unificationist."

[20] Although the occupied territories of the West Bank and the Gaza Strip are not legally part of the Israeli state, the Palestinian population there wants to secede from Israeli political control.

[21] Self-determination can in principle be exercised to agree to integration, assimilation, or cantonization (autonomy). However, full self-determination is understood as isomorphic with secession.

In what were Yugoslavia and the Soviet Union these questions were not academic. Whereas there was little dispute as to "Who are the Slovenes?" and everybody knew the answer to the question "Where is Slovenia?" the same was not true of Croatia, Serbia, or Bosnia. In what was the Soviet Union it was eventually accepted that the citizens of each of the former republics had the right to self-determination, but there was no such agreement about peoples trapped in republics that they would rather not be in. Most of the former Soviet republics are in fact ethnic mine fields. There are large Russian populations (at least 20 percent of the population) in Ukraine, Latvia, Estonia, Kazakhstan, and Kirgizia, and a smaller but militant one in Moldavia (12.8 percent). Russia itself is fending off secessionist bids from Checheno-Ingush and Tatarstan.

There are many other hard cases in seeking to apply the doctrine of self-determination. In Transylvania there are two major populations (Hungarians and Romanians) mixed together in the same region along with other smaller communities, and the potential territorial units for plebiscites would be strongly disputed by the relevant minorities. In Northern Ireland each ethnic community claims that it is part of another nation and wishes the putative boundaries of that nation to be the relevant jurisdiction for decision making (O'Leary and McGarry 1993).[22] In Quebec native Canadians, who occupy a huge proportion of the province's land mass, are unwilling to secede from Canada with the Francophone majority. In the Punjab and Kashmir Hindus vehemently oppose the very idea of secession. In Slovakia the Hungarian minority fears that the secession of the Slovaks from Czechoslovakia will be detrimental to their interests.

A majority for secession begs the question of a majority in what region? In moderately complex cases the principle of self-determination seems indeterminate. As Ivor Jennings remarked: "On the surface [the principle of self-determination] seem[s] reasonable: let the people decide. It [i]s in fact ridiculous because the people cannot decide until somebody decides who are the people" (1956, 56). Exercising self-determination is only straightforward where there is no large or disgruntled minority within the relevant region affected by the proposed secession *and* when the seceding area includes the great majority of those who wish to leave.

There have been some ingenious proposals for a normative liberal theory of secession that can answer Jennings's question about who

---

[22] However, Northern Ireland unionists are ambiguous about whether they believe the boundaries of the UK or of Northern Ireland should be the ultimate jurisdiction for constitutional decision making.

decides who are the people (e.g., Beran 1984; 1987). Beran advances the argument that every (self-defined) area within a liberal democratic state should be given the right to secede, provided the same right is extended to every subarea within the proposed secessionist territory. This argument answers the serious accusation that self-determination creates a dangerous domino effect by saying two different things: There is nothing wrong with allowing a state to fragment on the principle of self-determination; and (b) the fact that the seceding units themselves should grant the right of secession within their boundaries should put a prudential check on the aspiration to seek secession in territorially problematic zones.

Unfortunately it is difficult to think of instances where the optimal conditions for self-determination leading to full independence have applied. Norway's secession from Sweden was an exemplary case. So was the case of Swiss Jura, which illustrates that Beran's conditions can be fulfilled (although it is an example from a substate region). Here, in an "internal secession" plebiscites were held commune by commune to produce a result that split the new canton into two, along religious rather than ethnic lines (Protestants voted to stay with Bern canton).

Usually, however, partitions are very messy. The partitions of Ireland and India left significant minorities behind in Northern Ireland and Kashmir. And those who celebrated the exercise of self-determination in Yugoslavia and the Soviet Union have tempered their enthusiasm in the light of the time bombs left in the debris. Even when secessions seem straightforward and the seceding areas appear reasonably homogeneous, new conflicts can emerge fairly rapidly. The Ukraine is a possible future example. Most commentators have focused on the dangers posed by the sizeable Russian minority, but less attention has been paid to the deep historical, cultural, and geographical divisions between Catholic westerners (who were annexed by Stalin) and the Orthodox (who have been linked to Russia for some three centuries). After the glow of national liberation fades, so might Ukrainian national unity.

A fundamental problem with partition is that many communities identify a national territory as sacred and indivisible. Until 1988 the Palestine Liberation Organization (PLO) refused to consider the partition of Palestine (calling the idea "filastinian"). The Likud and other right-wing parties in Israel refuse to consider the partition of "Eretz Israel." The very idea of the partition of Ireland, rather than the particular partition imposed in 1920, continues to outrage Irish nationalists. The African National Congress (ANC) is wedded to the concept

Regulating nations and ethnic communities 259

of a united South Africa and refuses to consider white or Inkatha proposals for partition.

Some argue that the right of secession should be built into the South African constitution to reduce the fears of the Zulu-based Inkatha and white extremists that a democratic South Africa will become a vehicle of ANC/non-Zulu hegemony, believing that the inclusion of a secession clause in the new constitution will create incentives to accommodate ethnic minorities (for a contrary argument see Buchanan 1991, 159–61). However, the right of secession seems unlikely to be entrenched in many modern liberal democratic constitutions, although the Canadians may pioneer the implementation of the principle,[23] and secession is likely to continue to have a bad press among liberals and socialists.[24] Yet, with the collapse of the global Cold War, there is now much greater room for successful secession and the alteration of borders artificially frozen by the strategic interests of the superpowers – as the reunification of Germany suggests. The Cold War had elevated the stability of boundaries into a necessity: Rather than face nuclear confrontation each superpower respected the boundaries of the other's client-states, at least in Europe. "Globalization" and the increasing power of suprastate organizations may also make some international boundaries less inviolate.

However, secession remains an option very likely to produce vio-

---

[23] The one liberal democracy to have granted the right of secession is the United Kingdom. In 1949 it granted the right of secession to the Northern Ireland parliament, and in 1985 it granted the right of the people of Northern Ireland to become part of the Republic of Ireland. However, this right, Irish nationalist critics point out, was not one that the local majority of unionists were likely to choose.

The right of secession was fictionally embodied in successive Soviet constitutions, even though the Bolsheviks had ruthlessly reconquered the territories of the Czarist Russian empire. It will now be more difficult for western political elites who recognized the breakaway republics of the Soviet Union and Yugoslavia to deny the right of secession to their own communities. Thus the Canadian government, pandering to its large Ukrainian minority, was the first western state to recognize the Ukraine after its December 1991 referendum. Refusal to recognize Quebec's right to self-determination would be glaring hypocrisy.

[24] It is a nice irony that liberals and socialists favour lax divorce laws rather than indissoluble marriage, whereas their arguments against secession have a remarkable isomorphism with the arguments deployed against the legalization of divorce. Thus the dangers posed to children by divorce are analogous to the dangers posed to minorities; the reduced incentives to work out differences between marriage partners are analogous to the reduced incentives to establish a workable accommodation between communities; and the likelihood that one partner will benefit more than another from divorce is analogous to the argument that the better-off group should not be allowed to secede in order to obtain material advantages.

lence and problems (initially) as bad as the ones it is intended to solve. Partitions can lead to population movements, often involuntary ones, and mobile populations are highly vulnerable to massacre, as happened during and after the partition of the Indian subcontinent (Khoshla 1950). Who does the partitioning matters, and the principles under which they carry it out may determine the future pattern of conflict. Consider the British-managed partitions in Ireland, India, and Palestine (Fraser 1984); but, conversely, consider where the British decided not to partition: Sri Lanka and Cyprus.

Whether implementing secession is straightforward, along Beran's lines or not, the proposal of any community to secede from any state is likely to encourage key "unionist" elites in the affected states to behave in chauvinistic and warlike ways: The peaceful secessions of Iceland from Denmark or Norway from Sweden were exceptional in modern history.[25] The secessions from the Soviet Union have been surprisingly less violent than those from Yugoslavia. Normally, however, secessionist movements provoke unionist movements against traitors.

What can be said about the circumstances under which secession/partitions are likely to be carried out? Three external phenomena matter most and need to be studied closely: (1) the nature of the interstate (international) system (is it permissive or restrictive?); (2) the aftermath of wars (which often lead to territorial transfers/partitions, often without any considerations of consent); and (3) the disintegration of empires (although this observation is almost tautological).

What, if anything, can be said about the economics of self-determination? People seek full self-determination, in the form of independent statehood, for a variety of reasons, of which strictly economic ones are but a subset, and which sometimes supersede narrowly economic "rationality." The urge for self-government may be motivated by a reaction against ethnic discrimination and humiliation, by the pragmatic expectation that the new nation-state will have greater political freedom, by the wish to have a state in which different public policies will be pursued, by the desire for power and prestige among nationalist elites, or to protect an ethnic culture from extinction.

Not much of a very general nature can be successfully sustained about the economic circumstances or motivations of full-scale ethnic secessionist movements (Connor 1973; 1984). One lucid observer

---

[25] It was ironic to watch U.S. commentators warning the Soviet Union during 1990–1 to allow its republics the right to self-determination. As Gorbachev observed, the heirs of Lincoln have short memories.

notes that secessions are demanded both by economically advanced groups (e.g., Basques, Catalans, Ibos, Lombards, Sikhs, Tamils) and by economically backward communities (East Bengalis, Karens, Kurds, Slovaks) and that secessionist communities can be located in either backward or advanced regional economies (Horowitz 1985, 229ff). Although the (absolute and relative) economic circumstances of communities matter there are good arguments for rejecting "direct causal relationships between regional economic disparity and ethnic secession" (p. 235). One tentative generalization Horowitz offers is that backward communities in backward regions are the most likely to be early secessionists, whereas advanced communities have to suffer considerably before their cost–benefit calculus shifts in favor of secessionism. Yet even this thesis needs to be revised in the light of the breakup of the Soviet Union and Yugoslavia – in which the economically advanced nations of the west and north, respectively, were in the vanguard of secession.[26]

Enthusiasm for self-determination flows primarily from the democratization of the world. Democratization means that the people are to rule, however indirectly. But the question is: Who are the people? The ethnic nationalist declares that they are the nation, whereas the civic nationalist declares they are all those who are resident in a given state or political unit's boundaries. In a few happy cases – Iceland – these two answers approximately coincide. However, in most cases they do not. In the general case the definition *and* championing of the people are up for grabs. The possibility of partition/secession threatens any state where ethnic and civic nationalisms point to different definitions of the nation.

Democratization poses a clustered and linked set of issues: the most important being the definition of citizenship, the possession of the franchise, the state's boundaries, and the organizational structure of the state. These issues facilitate political entrepreneurs who seek to build parties on national or ethnic cleavages, whether at the foundation of the state or afterwards. Politicians in multinational and multi-ethnic states have multiple incentives to play national or ethnic cards: whether it be Churchill playing the Orange card in the United Kingdom in the 1880s, Le Pen playing the Algerian card in France in the 1980s, or Advani fanning Hindu chauvinism in India in the early 1990s.

---

[26] Economic explanations may have more potency in accounting for decisions by imperial elites to accept the dismemberment of their empires. When the costs of empire or redistribution outweigh geopolitical benefits, secession on the periphery may be countenanced.

It seems impossible to immunize the democratic process to exclude potentially explosive civic and ethnic issues – although constitutional protections can, in principle, be established. They are always there for mobilization by the oppressed or the opportunist or both. Those who lose out politically under existing state arrangements and policies, whoever they may be, may always choose to redefine the rules of the game by playing the national or ethnic card in the arena of party politics.

If there are any economic differences between communities in a liberal democratic state,[27] these reinforcing cleavages are more likely to result in the formation of ethnic parties. Where political parties are representative of all ethnic communities, party competition raises no immediate threat of destabilization. However, this case is unusual. Contemporary India is the more predictable outcome of the mobilization of both ethnic and economic inequalities into the party system. Now the dominant Congress party is primarily mobilized around the dominant community, in competition with a more extreme chauvinist party of the same community, the Bharatiya Janata Party (BJP), while facing an array of opposition parties that are either autonomist or secessionist.

The reason national and ethnic questions are potentially explosive and raise the possibility that some people(s) will be tempted to exercise self-determination through secession is simple. National and ethnic questions raise relatively nontradable issues. Nationality, language, territorial homelands, and culture are not easily bargained over. They are not easily divisible public goods in the language of economists. They create zero-sum conflicts and provide ideal materials for political entrepreneurs interested in creating or dividing political constituencies.

Having suggested why democratization increases the likelihood that communities will seek self-determination and thereby destabilize multiethnic and multinational states, we must make two qualifications. First, destabilization is likely to be contained if the relevant state exists in a milieu of liberal democratic states. Thus far in the twentieth century, liberal democracies have never gone to war against one another. Whether the avoidance of wars is a systemic feature of liberal democratic interstate relations is not something upon which we wish to pronounce, although there may be some grounds for "thinkful wish-

---

[27] There will almost inevitably be such differences, whether or not they flow from discrimination, historic advantages/disadvantages, or differing cultural traits or preferences that give some groups an advantage in the relevant division of labor.

ing." Second, there are circumstances under which the destabilizing effects of democratization upon multiethnic states can be muted and inhibit the impetus to consider secession. These factors include: internal territorial segregation that permits self-government ("good fences make good neighbors"); demographic dominance (where the largest community is sufficiently secure not to fear the minority [or minorities] and behaves in a generous way); demographic stability (where one or more communities are not outgrowing or "outfalling" one another); and a history of predemocratic cooperation among ethnic political elites that gives the postauthoritarian state a reasonable chance of promoting accommodation.

Integration and/or assimilation

A fourth method of macropolitical-conflict regulation is built upon the idea of trying to eliminate differences by seeking to integrate or assimilate the relevant communities into a new transcendent identity. Integration and assimilation can be considered as end points of a continuum. Whereas civic integration has the more modest object of creating a common civic, national, or patriotic identity,[28] assimilation aims to create a common cultural identity through the merging of differences (the melting pot). Proponents of integration or assimilation can find implicit support in John Stuart Mill's declaration that "free institutions are next to impossible in a country made up of different nationalities. Among a people without fellow feeling . . . the united public opinion necessary to the working of representative government cannot exist" (Mill 1988, 392).

Integration has been the official aspiration of civil rights leaders in the United States, the ANC in South Africa, unionist "integrationists" and the integrated education lobby in Northern Ireland, and the democratic left and right in those European countries striving to cope with the Fourth World: the new immigrant communities of western Europe.[29] Though inconceivable a few years ago integration has been embraced by pragmatists in South Africa's National party who believe that capitalism can be secured and improved under liberal integration better than under apartheid.

Advocates of integration policies usually favor reducing the differences between communities, ensuring that the children of the (poten-

---

[28] Horowitz (1985, 567) calls civic integration "inter-ethnic nationalism."
[29] The term "fourth world" is also claimed by the movements aiming to unite all the aboriginal peoples of the world.

tially rival) communities go to the same schools, socializing them in the same language and conventions, encouraging public and private housing policies that prevent segregation, and ensuring that the workplace is integrated through outlawing discrimination. Liberal integrationists promote bills of rights with equal rights for individuals (rather than communities).

Assimilationists go further. They favor merging ethnic identities, either into one already established (e.g., a Soviet or Yugoslav identity). The ultimate proof of successful assimilation is large-scale intermarriage across the former ethnic boundaries that leads first to their blurring and then to their eradication.

Integrationists and assimilationists, whatever their differences, support "catchall" political parties, argue against ethnic political parties, and aim to shun all policies that might show up differences between communities.[30]

Integration/assimilation strategies are very characteristic of two types of states: those engaged in nation building, that is, states that are seeking to forge a common national identity when they know that such an identity does not exist or is at best precarious; and those that have very numerically small minorities.

Integration and assimilation are driven by both high-minded and instrumental motives. Liberals and socialists, with the best of intentions, associate ethnic pluralism with sectarianism, parochialism, narrow-mindedness, and chauvinist bigotry. They maintain that those opposed to integration either want or risk societal disintegration. Canadian integrationists demanded a Charter of Rights after 1945 to prevent a repeat of the war-time internment of ethnic minorities (Japanese, Italians, and Ukrainians). White liberals in the United States funded court cases promoting black integration. Other liberals in North America sincerely advocate the assimilation of aboriginal minorities as the best way to end atrocious conditions on reservations (e.g., Gibson 1992). Likewise the European left and center generally espouses the integration of immigrants because it abhors racism and discrimination. Economic instrumentalism may also suggest integration or assimilation: A linguistically and culturally homogenized national community is functional for industrial civilization (Gellner 1983).

However, sometimes integrationism is not so high-minded or liberal

---

[30] Integrationists/assimilationists are especially skeptical about consociational arrangements that they believe entrench ethnic divisions and reward divisive political leaders.

in its instrumentalism. Integration or assimilation may mask the imposition of a core or dominant culture. In Northern Ireland those who advocate integration of all as either British or Irish citizens are often scoring ethnic points; whereas in South Africa some of those who advocate integration are either interested in preserving their economic privileges (whites) or see it as a way of establishing majority control (blacks). Sometimes integrationism is not even accompanied by formal generosity – consider white Canadians or white Britons who rail against Sikhs being allowed to wear their turbans where others would not be permitted to do so.

Integration/assimilationist projects may also aim at uniting (moderately) different communities against a common foe. The Anglican ascendancy in early modern Ireland promoted pan-Protestant unity against an insurgent native/Catholic threat. The South African government ensured that all whites (English, Greeks, Italians, European Jews) and not just Afrikaners benefited from apartheid to create pan-white unity against blacks. Israeli governments downplay Sephardic–Askenazi differences in the interest of presenting a united front against Palestinians. During the nineteenth century the dominant English minority in Quebec welcomed Irish and other English-speaking immigrants as allies against French Canadians, and contemporary Quebecois, troubled by the low birth rate among Francophones, have recently turned to nonwhite but French-speaking immigrants (from Haiti, Senegal, and former French colonies) to bolster their linguistic community.

The targets of integration/assimilation policies respond in various ways – partly as a function of their perceptions of the motives lying behind the policies. Integration/assimilation policies are often targeted at migrants in liberal democratic states. These policies are more overtly liberal than the form of quasi-control associated with *metic,* or guest-worker, policies. In Canada immigrant communities have acquired a Canadian civic identity on top of their original ethnic identity. The United States has proved a melting pot in which some ethnic assimilation has taken place,[31] although it would be better to say that white Protestants have assimilated (Swedes, Norwegians, and Germans) and that white Catholics (Irish, Italians, and Poles) have gradually assimilated.[32] After 1945 both Canada and the United States

[31] American assimilationism is built on the concept of the "melting pot," whereas Canadian assimilationism is based on the idea of "the cultural mosaic." In theory the latter is more tolerant of multiculturalism under a common civic identity.

[32] It was not until 1960 that the Americans elected their first Irish Catholic president. They have never elected a Pole or an Italian.

have had some success in integrating Asian immigrants. Similarly, "New Australians" have emerged in the wake of postwar continental European migrations. These cases of moderately successful integration/assimilation involved migrations to a "new" country, where the migrants, in principle, were willing to adapt their cultures to their new host country and accept a new civic identity.

However, where national or ethnic communities insist on autonomy or self-government, or where no external threat can compel pancommunity unity, integration/assimilation policies fall on stonier ground. Integrations/assimilations occurring within and across historic homelands, as opposed to new societies, are much more difficult to find in modern history.[33] Communities living in their putative ancestral territories are less willing than individual migrants to shed their culture or accept some new overarching identity. In the United States and Canada, Native Americans resist assimilation and hold out for varying degrees of self-government (or what we call cantonization below). They call themselves "first nations" to stress the moral superiority of their claims to cultural protection.[34]

Assimilation on contested homeland, however high-minded, cannot work consensually where it involves assimilation on one community's terms: If one community's language, culture, religion, and national myths are given precedence then we are not talking of assimilation or integration but of annexation; in such cases people complain of *ethnocide,* the destruction of a people's culture as opposed to physical liquidation of its members. This complaint is the standard one raised by the indigenous peoples of the world.

Some forms of integration and assimilation appear to require coercion: Compulsory educational homogenization and the imposition of standard cultural codes are preconditions of full industrial and welfare-state citizenship. Making peasants into French people in the nineteenth century, the schooling of black South Africans in Afrikaans, the Russification practiced by the czars and the CPSU, the periodic attempts at Anglicization of French Canada in the eighteenth and

---

[33] The integration of immigrants in "new states" – in the Americas and elsewhere – often took place after the genocide or expulsion of indigenous peoples.

[34] There are, however, some examples of assimilation within and across historic homelands. Substantial numbers of Slavs were assimilated as Germans and Austrians (see Vienna's telephone directory). Likewise Germans and Slavs were assimilated by Hungarians; Ukrainians and Germans were assimilated by Poles; and some Poles were assimilated by Russians. Where urbanization is occurring, and the assimilating group is relatively open and prestigious, the assimilands may not care to preserve their ethnic identity.

nineteenth centuries, and the Romanization implemented by Ceausescu in Transylvania are policies cut from the same cloth: In the extreme, ethnocidal assimilation looks indistinguishable from milder forms of genocide. But even arguably more neutral strategies of integration/assimilation have encountered significant resistance, as with Nehruvian secularism in India or Yugoslav and Soviet communism. These efforts to establish transcendent or panethnic identities were seen by minorities as disguised forms of cultural annexation, although the same policies were often rejected by the relevant dominant communities who saw the new identities as detrimental to their Hindu, Serbian, or Russian cultures.

Those who regard assimilation/integration strategies as benign forms of ethnic-conflict regulation in contested homelands are sometimes naive. Optimistic observers of South Africa need to be counseled that it will be some time before representative Afrikaners and blacks embrace the ANC and the National party, respectively. The Hutu in Burundi are not likely to abandon their distinct identity or their ethnic organizations just because such actions would fit the agenda of the Tutsi-dominated government. In the foreseeable future Northern Ireland Catholics, Basques, and Croats are unlikely to be integrated or assimilated with their ethnic enemies. In fact resistance to unwanted assimilation or integration projects is likely to be very high and can provoke ethnic revivals and secessionism in response, as has occurred in Burma, Ghana, Iraq, Sudan, and Uganda (Horowitz 1985, 567–8).

Modern minority ethnic identities can only be significantly sustained through educational and neighborhood segregation of some kind, because these conditions are necessary to preserve a cultural critical mass in the relevant communities. Some go further and claim that such communities require broadcasting media and control over access to landed property to sustain their identities. Such arguments explain why policies designed to compel people to be schooled together and to be neighbors or indeed simply to promote the rules of free-market capitalism are provocative and possibly productive of violence.

In short, unless assimilation/integration projects are targeted at people willing to acquire a new civic identity (like voluntary migrants) and to modify their national or ethnic identity, they produce rather than provoke conflict (Nordlinger 1972, 36–9).

For these reasons, among others, many liberal democracies that are managing large-scale immigrations or multiple recently established ethnic communities, have realized that multicultural policies may make greater sense than straightforward integration or assimilation strategies. They are abandoning the spirit of classical liberalism to manage the Fourth world. In England and France, at least in previous generations, liberals had a general bias toward integration/assimilation as macropolitical forms of ethnic-conflict resolution – at least within the metropolitan cores of their empires. This strategy sought to resolve ethnic conflict by eliminating ethnic differences. But often the relevant problem is the desire of members of ethnic communities to maintain differences that liberals committed to the right of individuals to choose their own conceptions of the good find it hard to argue against. This difficulty leads to a normative division of opinion between liberal integrationists (who are accused of intolerance) and liberal multiculturalists (who are accused of surrendering liberalism to a cultural relativism that tolerates illiberalism, e.g., in the form of Muslim schools).[35]

Political engineers seeking to resolve national or ethnic conflict frequently recommend the development of catchall political parties to break down ethnic cleavages, that is, they advocate electoral integration/assimilation. For example, the absence of British political parties in Northern Ireland before 1989 led one enthusiast to argue that the British party boycott was "the fundamental reason" for continuing conflict in the region (Roberts 1991, 132). Those persuaded of the merits of engineering electoral integration include the military framers of Nigeria's second constitution, which forced political parties nominating presidential candidates to develop some support in all regions of the state.

Such electoral integrationist projects may be well-intentioned ways of regulating ethnic conflict, but they are mostly based on wishful thinking. If there are parties that already mobilize across ethnic divisions then political stability is likely to be greater, and that is all to the good; but the belief that one can generate parties with such effects through heroic acts of will or engineering is fundamentally utopian, especially if the relevant ethnic communities have already been mobilized behind different conceptions of nationalism.[36] As one astute observer generalizes:

[35] Liberal multiculturalists have abandoned integrationism in favor of macropolitical ways of managing differences rather than eliminating them (e.g., Kymlicka, 1991, and see below).

[36] When one of us had more hair he held such foolishly optimistic beliefs about Northern Ireland (O'Leary 1987). Reading of failed panaceas elsewhere is a salutary experience for those inclined to offer political prescriptions based on a narrow range of political experience.

Regulating nations and ethnic communities 269

It is sometimes possible to maintain a system of party alignments cutting across a line of communal cleavage. It is usually possible to shift from this to a system where parties articulate the communal cleavage. But it is extremely difficult if not impossible to move in the reverse direction, because of the primitive psychological strength of communal identification and the effects of social reinforcement on maintaining the political salience of communal identification. (Barry 1991b, 146)[37]

In addition to the agreed and coercive forms of integration/assimilation discussed above there are cases where the dominated community has sought assimilation/integration, but has been denied it by the dominant community. America's melting pot has not successfully extended (if it was ever so intended) to blacks or Afro-Americans, whose ancestors were not voluntary immigrants to the United States. Until the 1950s the local white majorities in the Deep South worked a system of control and sought to prevent any kind of integration, let alone assimilation. While blacks, with some exceptions,[38] support integration and won formal victories to establish this goal in public policy in the 1950s and the 1960s, American cities and schools remain segregated and racial life chances are still dramatically unequal.[39] In Northern Ireland the unionist government and party blocked the integrationist ambitions of at least some Catholics in the 1960s, precipitating the current long wave of political violence. If, as one academic anticipates, the Palestinians switch their demands from separate nationhood to demanding civil rights within the Israeli state, we might expect a similar pattern (Nusseibeh 1990).

Although some liberal and bourgeois elites within dominant communities might favor integration/assimilation of the dominated, as a way of broadening the legitimacy of their regimes, they often find that such

---

[37] Barry (1991a) cites the case of Sri Lanka as an illustration. After Sinhalese politicians exploited antagonisms toward Tamils in the 1956 elections, they found that the potent communal tensions they had provoked could not be reversed (Rabushka and Shepsle 1972, 135–6).

[38] Some blacks (e.g., Malcolm X and Louis Farakhan) have rejected the American way, preaching separatism, black consciousness, self-reliance, and, on occasions, secession.

[39] The undeclared goal of American public policy in major conurbations appears to be that of controlling rather than integrating blacks. The Reagan and Bush administrations have effectively quarantined blacks and controlled them through increased spending on police and prisons: leading to more young blacks being in prison than in higher education by the end of the 1980s. Although control works reasonably well, from the perspective of whites, it can lead to sudden breakdowns – as in Los Angeles in April 1992.

ambitions provoke a furious backlash from their coethnics in less privileged positions. In Northern Ireland in the late 1960s moderate integrationist Protestant unionists lost all influence over their "followers." The current South African government is gambling that it can integrate blacks into a new political system before it has to face the white electorate again: If it fails it will go the way of all flesh.

Methods for managing differences

Hegemonic control

The most common system of managing as opposed to eliminating ethnic conflict practiced in multi- or biethnic states is that of "hegemonic control," a concept first developed by Ian Lustick (1979; 1987), although we use the term slightly differently (O'Leary and Arthur 1991; O'Leary and McGarry 1993, chs. 3, 4). Hegemonic control has been the most common mode through which multiethnic societies have been stabilized in world history. Imperial or authoritarian regimes controlled multiple cultures within their territories through coercive domination and elite co-option.[40] They suppressed latent divisions between ethnic communities that might otherwise have been manifested, especially in conditions of modernization. The control was "hegemonic" if it made an overtly violent ethnic contest for state power either "unthinkable" or "unworkable" on the part of the subordinated communities: Ethnically based slave systems were exemplary cases of authoritarian hegemonic control, so also were colonial settler systems that made native revolts unworkable. Hegemonic control in imperial or authoritarian regimes need not have rested, although it often did, on the support of the largest or most powerful ethnic community.[41] What was necessary was control of the relevant coercive apparatuses: Thus minorities in Burundi, Fiji (after 1987), Liberia (before 1980), and South Africa (until 1990–1) were able to sustain hegemonic control because of their sovereignty over security and policing systems.

Hegemonic control is therefore coercive and/or co-optive rule that

---

[40] Co-opting elites as a technique for monopolizing power should be distinguished from offering to share power: The former is characteristic of control, the latter of consociationalism. Some leaders of the ANC believe that the South African government is offering them the former under the guise of offering them the latter.

[41] The Soviet Union and Yugoslavia were good examples of modern authoritarian regimes in which ethnic contests for state power were made "unworkable" under communist hegemony. In several respects they were indistinguishable from empires.

successfully manages to make unworkable an ethnic challenge to the state order. In authoritarian empires there was usually no grand objective pursued to eliminate ethnic difference, although one might argue that the world religions were propagated to confer transcendent identities. By contrast, in communist hegemonic systems, a new transcendent identity was consistently proclaimed: one which would eventually eliminate ethnic differences as irrelevant to people's civic identities as citizens. However, after initial postrevolutionary fervor it was rare for this vision to be articulated as one that would utterly eradicate ethnic difference, and the policies of Communist parties primarily focused on suppressing the politicization of ethnic differences.

In liberal democracies, or "open regimes" (to use Nordlinger's expression [1972]), hegemonic control appears infeasible. Liberal democracies permit, indeed facilitate, ethnic organization and mobilization; and ethnic contests for state power become eminently thinkable and workable within liberal democratic or open institutions. Think of how Irish nationalism was facilitated by the democratization of the United Kingdom or of how nationalism was encouraged by *glasnost* in the Soviet Union. Similarly, the breakdown of the Franco regime in Spain after 1975 facilitated challenges to the Spanish state. The liberal optimist might conclude that democratization spells doom to systems of hegemonic control.

However, systems of hegemonic control, or ethnic domination, can be constructed in liberal democratic states. The most obvious method is when liberal democratic institutions are monopolized by a minority of the state's population. Thus white South Africans and Rhodesians established settler control over other ethnic communities, while governing themselves through liberal democratic rules. Citizenship and representative government were confined to the *Herrenvolk*. Minority control within a given region is very common: Consider Serbia's ruthless domination of Albanians in Kosovo after 1987 or the treatment of the majority Bengalis in what was East Pakistan. In Fiji the native minority, frightened by electoral returns that threatened their participation in government, supported a coup in 1987 that led to minority hegemonic control. They hope, however, that demographic trends and increased Indian emigration will reconvert natives into a majority.[42]

---

[42] Unlike Northern Ireland, Rhodesia, and South Africa, all of which are, or have been, forms of settler control, Fiji and Malaysia are – or are becoming – forms of native control. Native hegemonic control over settlers may also be experimented with in the former Soviet Union – if the Latvian proposal to exclude Russian immigrants from citizenship sets a trend.

But hegemonic control can occur in states in which the majority or entirety of the relevant state's adult population have formal access to citizenship. Democracy in its most primitive meaning is understood as "majority rule." Where political "majorities" constantly fluctuate, as people change their minds on the key policy or political issues of the day, then majority rule is a sensible decision rule, infinitely preferable to the kind of minority rule practiced by emperors, military dictators, or one-party regimes. However, where there are two or more deeply established national or ethnic communities and where the members of these communities do not agree on the basic institutions and policies the regime should pursue, or where the relevant communities are not internally fragmented on key policy preferences in ways that crosscut each other, then majority rule can become an instrument of hegemonic control.

When simple majoritarianism is implemented in multiethnic or bicommunal societies it usually either leads to hegemonic control (e.g., postindependence Sri Lanka) or, over the longer run, promotes state fragmentation through the development of civil war and secessionist movements (e.g., contemporary Sri Lanka). Many of the postcolonial states of Africa and south Asia, after the British abandoned their imperial commitments, were built on the Westminster model of liberal democracy. They soon became vehicles for ethnic domination and, with the notable exception of India, almost invariably became straightforward dictatorships. Northern Ireland (1920–72), and the Deep South of the United States (c. 1870–c. 1964), are examples of regions in liberal democratic states where formal majoritarianism coexisted with hegemonic control over the relevant minority. The relevant majority monopolized the police and judicial systems, manipulated the franchise to consolidate their domination, practiced economic discrimination in employment and the allocation of public housing and institutional discrimination against the minority's cultural and educational system(s), and ruthlessly repressed minority discontent. The Canadian state practiced control over aboriginal peoples: Natives were policed through the white judicial system, denied certain privileges if they left reservations, and denied the (federal) franchise if they remained on them (until 1961). In India, the demands of Sikhs for an autonomous Punjab partly arose from their fear that Nehruvian tolerance had increasingly given way to Hindu chauvinism, presaging a move toward control as the preferred Hindu method of governing India.

The normative lesson is obvious: A majoritarian system of liberal democratic government, designed to create strong powers for the governing party, is no guarantee of liberty for minorities. A "winner takes all" system in the presence of ethnic parties ensures that ethnic competition will be regarded as a zero-sum conflict. Where two or more communities wish to belong to different external nation-states the potential instability of majoritarian liberal democracy is even more obvious, and the temptations to establish a system of control by the majority are correspondingly greater (consider Northern Ireland unionists' treatment of Irish nationalists after 1920). However, majoritarianism on the Westminster (or Paris) model is not the only form of democratic institution poorly designed for conflict regulation, merely the worst.[43]

Some maintain that systems of hegemonic control can be normatively defensible. Lustick (1979) argues that control is often the only alternative to continuous war – he had in mind Lebanon after 1976. However, this quasi-Hobbesian reasoning (any state is better than none) is suspect. Consider the consequences of universalizing Lustick's argument. It would lead one to maintain, as *some* now do, that the dictatorial Communist Party of the Soviet Union (CPSU) and the Yugoslav League of Communists were morally justified precisely because they suppressed national and ethnic conflict in the Soviet Union and Yugoslavia,[44] that one-party states in Africa and Asia are similarly defensible, and that the reimposition of Ba'thist control over the Kurds is preferable to continuous civil war in Iraq.

There are further difficulties. The options in any given national or ethnic conflict are rarely simply between those of control and continuous war – although there will always be plenty of politicians and paramilitaries seeking to advance precisely this argument. Some of the alternative options to control (federalism/cantonization, arbitration, and consociationalism) have some record of success in stabilizing democracy in deeply divided societies, whereas any system of control is easily convertible into a system for the execution of genocide, ethnocide, forced mass population transfers, and other violations of human rights. Partitionist or secessionist options are almost invariably more desirable than the imposition of control. If the relevant partition

---

[43] O'Leary was interviewed by a Serbian television crew in 1988 about the merits of the British system of government. The interviewer, an admirer of Slobodan Milosevic, brought the interview to a halt when O'Leary said the introduction of plurality rule (the British voting system) into Yugoslavia would be disastrous.

The present Serb and Croat leaderships (Milosevic in Serbia and Tudjman in Croatia) were elected under plurality rule and their parties are dramatically over-represented in their respective legislatures.

[44] Wiseacres will soon speak of the "golden age of Brezhnev" or the "halcyon days of Tito."

or secession is even moderately well executed it should ensure that more people can enjoy legitimate self-government than would otherwise be the case. Also, under systems of control the subordinated minority will always seek to "internationalize" their plight under the relevant hegemonic group or party/dictator and thereby threaten the stability of the relevant regime as well as the international order. Therefore one can use stability arguments that are the converse of Lustick's.[45] Finally, if a system of control eventually breaks down, its practices will simply have added to the accumulated stock of grievances. Continual repression sidelines moderates, bolsters extremists, and obstructs prospects for future accommodation: Consider the Punjab, Northern Ireland, and the West Bank and Gaza strip.

Arbitration (third-party intervention)

Arbitration of biethnic or multiethnic states is the least recognized mode of conflict regulation, except perhaps in the literature of international relations and peace studies (Hoffman 1992). The main classification problems with arbitration are deciding whether or not it includes: both internal and external arbitration; what one of this book's authors has elsewhere called "co-operative internationalization" (O'Leary 1989); and forceful intervention by a self-appointed umpire concerned with establishing stability in a given region. These classification problems share one feature. One must decide whether to classify any conflict-regulating activity that is the outcome of third-party intervention as arbitration or to confine arbitration to cases where the third-party intervention is characterized by procedural neutrality of some kind. Our preference is for the latter, more exclusive usage[46] – especially because many third-party interventions are indistinguishable from efforts to establish control of a given region.

Arbitration, on our construal, entails the intervention of a neutral, bipartisan or multipartisan authority. It differs from other methods used to stabilize antagonistic societies because it involves conflict regulation by agents other than the contending parties. Integral to the

---

[45] One might even argue in a realist fashion, although the evidence would need careful appraisal, that wars may sort matters out more successfully than exercising hegemonic control and create incentives for postwar cooperative behavior (as some believe to be true of Nigeria).

[46] In legal literature adjudication is the term usually used to refer to neutral third-party intervention (coupled with an imposed decision), whereas arbitration can often involve nonneutral third parties (e.g., commercial arbitrations) pushing the parties toward compromise (my thanks to David Schiff).

concept of arbitration is that the disinterestedness of the arbiter makes it possible for this person (or institution or state) to win the acquiescence, if not the enthusiastic support, of the contending ethnic segments; and thereby dampen the violence that would otherwise occur. An arbiter provides governmental effectiveness where war or anarchy might otherwise prevail. Arbitration is distinguishable from *mediation* because the arbiter makes the relevant decisions, whereas mediators merely facilitate them. Thus from 1991 the European Community has primarily been mediating rather than arbitrating in what was "Yugoslavia."

The role of the arbiter is portrayed like that of a conciliator presiding over a family quarrel. The arbiter pursues the common interests of the rival segments in the relevant society as she/he perceives them; regulates the political exchanges between the segments as an umpire (to prevent a further and more dramatic breakdown in state order); and presides over elites who have varying incentives to engage in responsible and cooperative behavior.

Arbitration, in principle, can establish the conditions for longer-term conflict resolution: secessions, partitions, power sharing, or even the peaceful integration or assimilation of the rival communities. But third-party interventionists can play the role of self-appointed arbiters and act to reconstruct the old system of ethnic control – as for example occurred when a Russian czar handed back Hungary to Hapsburg control in 1849 or when the British empire handed Northern Ireland to the Ulster Unionist party in 1920–1. Alternatively self-appointed arbiters can presage the creation of a new system of control by handing power to a different ethnic segment, as some maintain Syria will eventually do in the Lebanon.

The prerequisite for agreed arbitration is that the arbiter's claim to neutrality be broadly accepted by the major contending ethnic segments.[47] Not all professed arbiters pass this test. Since "neutrality" is rhetorically superior to "partisanship" and useful for domestic and international consumption, the self-presentations of arbiters must be treated with scepticism: Few observers credited Syria's intervention in Lebanon or Soviet federal intervention in Nagorno Karabakh with impartiality, and the disinterestedness of U.S. arbitration in the Middle East is widely questioned. Irish nationalists in Northern Ireland

---

[47] Within any ethnic community there are likely to be activists who will challenge the neutrality of any arbiter, and there will always be those who are so co-opted that they will proclaim the benign impartiality of even the most blatantly partisan interventionist. Observers and reporters of ethnic conflicts have to ensure that spokespersons of ethnic communities are representative.

did not regard the British government as a neutral arbiter after 1972 (O'Leary and McGarry 1993, ch. 5); and the British government appeared to acknowledge this fact when it signed the Anglo-Irish Agreement in 1985, providing a role for the Irish government as guardian of the Irish nationalist minority (ch. 6).

Arbitration of ethnic conflicts is of two broad types, the internal and the external, each of which can be performed by different kinds of agents. *Internal arbitration* can be executed by an individual who is not a member of the main antagonistic communities: for example Julius Nyrere in postindependence Tanzania. It can be fulfilled by statesmen with the moral authority to transcend their ethnic origins: for example Mahatma Gandhi in the Indian subcontinent or President Tito in Yugoslavia. It can also be managed by someone who can claim a connection with all the major ethnic groups: for example Siaka Stevens in Sierra Leone. Internal arbitration can also be performed by institutions. The monarchy in pre-1965 Burundi arbitrated between Tutsi and Hutu. The U.S. Supreme Court, under the leadership of Justice Warren, arbitrated conflicts between blacks and whites in the 1950s and 1960s. Federal governments, like supreme courts, can arbitrate ethnic conflict within the constituent units of their federation, as occurs regularly in Canada, where the Ottawa government has constitutional responsibility for indigenous minorities in the provinces. Although few U.S. blacks or Canadian natives regarded the federal government as their institutions, they clearly thought them more impartial than state or provincial governments.[48] Finally, internal arbitration can be performed by a political party. One-party states claim to absorb key members of rival ethnic communities and to regulate their rival aspirations. This argument was advanced by Nkrumah in Ghana in the 1960s, Nimeiri in Sudan in the 1970s, and Mugabe in Zimbabwe in the 1980s. However, it is difficult to distinguish this (alleged) form of arbitration from hegemonic control. In a competitive political system, by contrast, internal arbitration can be performed by a pivotal political party, one judged to be sufficiently disinterested by the other contending factions to be able to chair a cross-ethnic coalition. The Alliance party has long sought to perform this function, without success, in Northern Ireland; and the Indian Congress party has continually claimed to be a reasonable arbiter of conflicts in India's regions, a

---

[48] Blacks in the United States welcomed the intervention of federal troops to replace Arkansas state troopers at Little Rock in 1957, just as native Canadians welcomed the intervention of federal troops to replace Quebec provincial police at Oka in 1990.

claim that has become steadily more threadbare in the years since Nehru's death.

External arbitration by contrast suggests that conflict cannot be successfully managed within the relevant political system. It is a potentially useful conflict-regulating device during processes of decolonization, when an external power still possesses authority, but is less effective when the conflict zone is a strong sovereign state. External arbitration can be performed by a single external agent or state, a bipartisan authority, or a multipartisan force. Multipartisan arbitration or cooperative internationalization, as originally envisaged for the United Nations' peacekeeping (and peacemaking) forces, has been performed with intermittent success in Cyprus and in parts of the Middle East and Africa, for example in Namibia. Except in cases of decolonization (like Namibia) UN arbitration is usually a sign that the relevant ethnic conflict is seen as insoluble and as a dangerous threat to the security of an entire set of states. There is truth in the cynical observation that "when the UN comes you know that your problems are with you for ever".[49] However, adjudication of international law by the International Court of Justice shows that there are instruments for multipartisan arbitration of ethnic conflicts, should we choose to develop them.

Bipartisan arbitration in its fullest form involves two states sharing sovereignty over a disputed territory[50] – in the form of a condominium – but it can also involve an agreement by a state that maintains sovereignty over the relevant region to consult with another interested state over how that region's government is conducted and to grant the external government a role as guardian of an ethnic minority within the relevant region. One example is the Anglo-Irish Agreement between the British and Irish governments, signed in 1985 (O'Leary and McGarry 1992, ch. 6). The Italian and Austrian governments in 1946 came to a similar agreement over South Tyrol, consolidated in 1992, ensuring the German-speaking community "complete equality of rights with the Italian-speaking inhabitants within the framework of special provisions to safeguard the ethnic character and the cultural and economic development of the German-speaking element" (Alcock 1970; Hannum 1990, 432–40). The Finnish and Swedish governments also

---

[49] Churchill is said to have observed of the Balkans that it produces more violence than it can consume domestically, which is one reason why it has often been the site of external intervention (cited by Buchanan 1991, 2).

[50] We have argued for the merits of this way of regulating ethnic conflict in Northern Ireland (O'Leary and McGarry 1993, ch. 8).

developed an agreement over the Åland islands – although this agreement in effect set up a Swedish canton within Finland, a canton with the right to prevent Finnish citizens from settling on the islands (Ålands landsting 1988). Other bilateral agreements between states over contested regions and national minorities existed in interwar Europe (Hannum 1990, ch. 17).

Cantonization/federalization

There are two territorial principles of macropolitical conflict regulation, cantonization and federalization, both of which can be used to manage national and ethnic differences in liberal democratic ways.

Cantonization might more accurately be designated as "communization" after the communes that operate beneath the cantons in Switzerland. Cantonization might also be considered synonymous with devolution organized on an ethnoterritorial basis. However, we prefer the term cantonization because unlike communization or devolution it is a term distinctively associated with the regional management of ethnic differences.

Under cantonization the relevant multiethnic state is subjected to a micropartition in which political power is devolved to (conceivably very small) political units, each of which enjoys minisovereignty. Although it is usual to discuss cantonization in the context of federalism – as the Swiss paradigm might suggest – the principle of cantonization is separable, in principle, from formally federal forms of government. Cantonization must be distinguished from mere administrative decentralization, common in unitary states: It is built upon the recognition of ethnic difference and allows for asymmetrical relations between different cantons and the central government. The democratic Spanish state, erected after the fall of Franco, which is formally speaking an asymmetrical form of decentralized unitary state, can be considered an example of relatively successful cantonization, with the notable exception of the protracted conflict in the Basque country.

Cantonization is an application of the fashionable idea of subsidiarity to ethnic relations: Decision-making power is managed at the lowest appropriate level of a political hierarchy. Cantons must be designed to create culturally homogeneous units where majority rule is practically coterminous with the self-government of all the relevant communities.[51] Where ethnic conflict is high the partitioning of ex-

---

[51] Cantons could be designed to achieve a very local form of power-sharing government between the rival ethnic communities, especially where communities are so intermin-

isting governmental units to create ethnic homogeneity is the operating administrative principle, as happened in the case of the Bernese Jura.

Cantonization decomposes the arena of ethnic conflict and competition into smaller more manageable units: It involves a negotiable form of "internal secession." Under "rolling cantonization" policing and judicial powers can be gradually devolved to those areas where the population expresses a wish to exercise such powers and where it is judged that the experiment had some prospects of success. In the newly independent state of Bosnia a carefully designed and agreed-upon form of cantonization might have made a great deal of sense and prevented the possibility of extensive bloodletting between Serbs, Croats, and Muslims. However, cantonization is fraught with potential difficulties, notably the drawing and policing of appropriate units of government, winning consent for them, and the ever-present threat that the cantonization of policing and judicial powers might be used by paramilitary organizations to seize control of parts of the relevant territories and treat them as "liberated zones." This danger might explain why the Bosnian foreign minister told a seminar that his government would not consider cantonization.[52] Yet cantonization is often as realistic, as pushing full-blooded nationalist positions, whether these be integrationist, secessionist, or irredentist. Cantonization is more gradualist in its implications than drastic repartition of state boundaries because it permits governments the freedom to reverse any experiments that go badly wrong. The Canadian government seems to be moving in the direction of cantonization after its recent recognition of the "inherent right" of native peoples to self-government "within the Canadian federation."

"Pseudocantonization" is also a possible political strategy, where territorial decentralization of ethnic conflict is used to facilitate or disguise control, and merits the condemnation of liberals and socialists. For example the South African government established a number of barren "homelands" for blacks in an unsuccessful attempt to delegitimise their demands for power at the center. Successive Likud governments in Israel (1977–92) refused to partition "Eretz Israel," instead offering a form of autonomy for the occupied territories that no genuinely representative Palestinian could embrace.

gled as to prevent neat partitioning: However, the logic of this system is really that of local consociationalism (see below).

[52] Address by Bosnian foreign minister at the London School of Economics, March 1992. In light of the European Community's ill-thought-out cantonization plan for Bosnia, which gave Bosnian Serbs what they regarded as a casus belli, the Bosnian foreign minister's skepticism has been justified.

Overlapping cantonization and federalism there exists a gray area of territorial management of ethnic differences that is often found in conjunction with external arbitration. International agreements between states can entrench the territorial autonomy of certain ethnic communities, even though the "host state" does not generally organize itself along either cantonist or federalist principles: for example the agreement between Italy and Austria guaranteeing the autonomy of South Tyrol or the agreement between Finland and Sweden guaranteeing the autonomy of the Åland islands.

Federalism is similar but not coterminous with cantonization as a device for regulating multiethnic states: The states, provinces, or *Länder* are usually much larger than cantons.[53] By federalism we do not mean the kind of pseudofederalism used to characterize the Soviet Union. In a genuine federation the central government and the provincial governments both enjoy separate domains of authority, although they may also have concurrent powers. The central government cannot unilaterally alter the constitution, which requires the consent of both levels of government. Federations automatically imply codified and written constitutions and bicameral legislatures. In the federal as opposed to the popular chamber the smallest component units are usually disproportionally represented, that is, overrepresented.

Federalists maintain that if the boundaries between the components of the federation match the boundaries between the relevant ethnic, religious, or linguistic communities, that is, if there is a "federal society" (Stein 1968), federalism is an effective conflict-regulating device because it has the effect of making a heterogeneous society less heterogeneous through the creation of more homogeneous subunits. However, of the seven genuine federations in long-term liberal democracies, only three achieve this effect: those of Belgium, Canada, and Switzerland. The federations of Australia, Austria, Germany, and the United States do not achieve this effect, and therefore federalism cannot be used to explain the relative ethnic tranquillity of Australia and postwar Austria and Germany (where past genocides are more important). In the cases of Belgium, Canada, and Switzerland the success of federalism in conflict regulation, such as it is, is based upon the historic accident that the relevant communities are sharply segregated geographically. Federalism is less successful for communi-

---

[53] Indeed the constituent units of federations can be subdivided into cantons to manage ethnic conflict. The current proposals of the Canadian government for the management of the Northwest territories envisage "cantonizing" the area to allow the various peoples of the Dene nation and nonnatives to exercise limited self-government.

ties that, because of their geographical dispersal or paucity of numbers, cannot control federal units, as with Quebec Anglophones, Francophones outside Quebec, Flemish speakers in Wallonia, Francophones in Flanders, blacks in the United States, and indigenous peoples in Australia and North America. One reason why federalism proved totally insufficient as a conflict-regulating device in Yugoslavia was because there was insufficient geographical clustering of the relevant ethnic communities.

Geographically clustered communities accept federations for a variety of reasons. Federations have often evolved out of multiethnic colonies, where secession might have provoked conflict with those who wanted to keep the polity unified. Even if a history of common colonial government did not promote overarching cultural loyalties, for example through what Anderson (1983, ch. 4) calls "administrative pilgrimages," it usually creates elites (soldiers, bureaucrats, and capitalists) with an interest in sustaining the existing regime's territory. Federal states can often be sold economically – they promise a larger single market, a single currency, economies of scale, reductions in transactions' costs, and fiscal equalization. Large federal states can also be marketed as geopolitically wise, offering greater security and protection than small states. Finally, the personal philosophies and dispositions of federation builders matter: The MacDonald–Cartier alliance in Canada and Nehru's leadership in India were critical in establishing and sustaining their federations.

Unfortunately federalism thus far has a poor track record as a conflict-regulating device in multiethnic states, even where it allows a degree of minority self-government. Democratic federations have broken down throughout Asia and Africa, with the possible exception of India – whose survival is partly accounted for by the degree of central control possible in its quasifederal system. Federal failures primarily occur because minorities continue to be outnumbered at the federal level of government. The resulting frustrations, combined with an already defined boundary and the significant institutional resources flowing from control of their own province/"state," provide considerable incentives to attempt secession, which in turn can invite harsh responses from the rest of the federation: The disintegration of the Nigerian federation was halted only through two million deaths. Because the ingenious federal engineering of the Nigerian second republic went down before a military coup the jury must remain out on the success or otherwise of democratic federalism in resolving Nigeria's ethnic dilemmas. India, the most successful postcolonial federation, faces secessionist movements in Kashmir and Punjab, and Canada is perennially threatened with the secession of Quebec (although this, like Godot, never comes). Even the sham federations of Yugoslavia and the Soviet Union provided various nationalist movements with the resources to launch successful secessions during 1991–2. The threat of secession in federations is such that Nordlinger (1972, 32) excludes federalism from his list of normatively defensible conflict-regulating practices. Integrationist nation builders in Africa have distrusted federalism precisely for this reason.

Federations have been especially fragile in biethnic societies. With the possible exception of Belgium there is not a single case of successful federalism based upon dyadic or two-unit structures (Vile 1982). Even the Belgian federation technically has four subunits, although it is built around a dualist ethnic division, and the European Community has helped sustain the unity of Belgium.

Even relatively successful multiethnic federations appear to be in permanent constitutional crises. Not only does the division of powers need to be constantly renegotiated as a result of technological advances, economic transformations, and judicial interventions, but to maintain stability, supplemental consociational practices are often required at the federal and subcentral levels of government.

However, despite the difficulties associated with it, genuine democratic federalism is clearly an attractive way to regulate ethnic conflict, with obvious moral advantages over control. The argument that it should be condemned because it gives rise to secession and civil war can be sustained only under two circumstances. First, if in the absence of federalism, there would be no secessionist bid and if it can be shown that ethnic conflict can be more justly managed by alternative democratic means; and second, if the potential secessionist unit would be likely to exercise hegemonic control (or worse) over its indigenous minorities.

Consociation or power sharing

Political relationships can be organized between communities to prevent conflict according to *power-sharing* or *consociational* principles. These principles can operate at the level of an entire state or within a region of a state characterized by ethnic conflict: They are relevant to both central and local governments. Consociational principles were invented or reinvented by Dutch politicians from 1917 until the 1960s and by Lebanese politicians between 1943 and 1975. Malaysian politicians experimented with consociationalism between 1955 and 1969;

Fijians, on and off between 1970 and 1987; and Northern Irish politicians, for a brief spell in 1974.

Consociational democracies usually have four features (Lijphart 1977):

- A grand coalition government incorporates the political parties representing the main segments of the divided society or there is *government by more than a simple majority* that guarantees representation for ethnic minorities;
- *Proportionality rules* apply throughout the public sector; that is, each community is proportionally represented in the legislature(s), the executive, the judiciary, the civil service, and the police: that is, in the core institutions of the liberal democratic state. Proportionality applies both to public employment and public expenditure – each community gets its fair share of public expenditure, for example to fund its educational and broadcasting needs. Proportionality might also apply to private sector employment, requiring employers to have balanced workforces to prevent or correct ethnic discrimination in employment.
- *Community autonomy* norms operate in consociational systems. Each community is given self-government over those matters of most profound concern to them. In most cases these issues revolve around language, education, religion, culture, and expression of national identity. Ideally community autonomy differs from autonomy under federal systems because members of each community have their autonomy respected irrespective of where they live and work. One can think of it as "community federalism," or "corporate federalism," in contrast to territorial federalism. The most obvious examples of the principle are denominationally or linguistically organized education systems.
- They entrench constitutional *vetoes* for minorities. These vetoes can take various forms. For example, in Belgium weighted majorities are required before some legislation becomes law. Vetoes can also be legally entrenched.[54] Bills of rights are established, with supreme courts to uphold them, and if these bills entrench individual as well as communal

[54] In Canada, before the adoption of its new constitution in 1982, Quebec had an informal veto over constitutional change. Quebec's loss of this veto is one of the factors underlying Canada's current constitutional crisis.

rights, they can provide an effective way of entrenching minority rights.[55]

Consociational principles are based upon the acceptance of ethnic pluralism. They aim to secure the rights, identities, freedoms, and opportunities of all communities and to create political and other social institutions that enable them to enjoy the benefits of equality without forced assimilation. They do not oblige people to be schooled or housed together, although they do imply a commitment to proportionality in political and legal institutions and possibly to proportionality in economic work organizations because these arenas are the ones in which ethnic differences are likely to produce violence, instability, and perpetuation of conflict. In some zones of conflict the relevant populations effectively have a simple choice between creating consociational democratic institutions or having no meaningful democratic institutions at all. A case in point is Lebanon, whose delicate consociational compromise was destabilized by Israel and Syria in 1975–6 and by the impact of the Palestinian diaspora.

Consociational arrangements do not require academic experts or consociational engineers to come into being: They are constantly reinvented by politicians. The key thing, according to Lijphart, is that politicians have the autonomy, imagination, and incentives to construct such compromises and the appropriate external environment. By no means all consociational experiments have proven successful – as the cases of Cyprus, Lebanon, and Northern Ireland indicate – but some have. The best normative case for consociational arrangements is that they involve the self-government of the relevant communities and they are often better than the alternatives: majority domination, bloody partition, secessionist warfare, and the unthinkable options of forced population transfers and genocide.

However, consociational systems are easily destabilized. To work, consociational systems require at least three fundamental conditions.[56] First, the rival communities must not be unreservedly committed to immediate or medium-term integration or assimilation of others into

---

[55] A controversial but interesting example of this phenomenon in the English-speaking world is the Canadian Charter of Rights and Freedoms (1982). It protects both individual and communal rights. From the perspective of Quebec Francophones the problem is that the Charter protects the individual rights of English and French speakers throughout Canada: preventing the Quebec government from protecting the French language in ways seen as discriminatory toward English speakers.

[56] Detailed discussions of the circumstances under which consociationalism is likely to succeed can be found in Barry (1991), Lijphart (1977, 1985), McGarry (1990), McGarry and Noel (1989), O'Leary (1989), and Pappalardo (1981).

"their" nation or to the creation of their own exclusive nation-state. Nationality conflicts, based on the explicit embrace of integral nationalism, appear to have an irreducibly zero-sum character; people kill for the proposition that "one nation = one state." Preventing communities from developing full-scale, "integral" or exclusive national consciousness requires political elites either to downplay the state's national identity in a world in which the pressures to the opposite are very powerful or to develop an artificial and transcendent national identity, which may prove very difficult. Second, successive generations of political leaders must have the appropriate motivations to engage in conflict regulation. The leaders of the rival communities must fear the consequences of war and desire to preserve economic and political stability. They must, for example, believe they are incapable of governing on their own (or establishing hegemonic control). The motivations may be self-interested or high-minded, but without them there is no prospect of producing a consociational arrangement. The moment rival elites believe that the benefits of war exceed the costs of peace a consociational system is doomed. Third, the political leaders of the relevant communities must enjoy some political autonomy, so they can make compromises without being accused of treachery. If they lack confidence – for example because they are outbid by external irredentists or by rival leaders – they will not be prepared to engage in hard bargaining. This condition not only requires restraint on the part of external elites outside the affected area but also within the relevant communities. In addition to no majority ethnic party believing it can govern on its own, a consociational settlement requires that each community must be internally stable politically in a way that promotes compromise. This condition is most exacting and is made more excruciating by a fundamental dilemma in the constitutional design of democratic systems. Proportional representation systems, which go with consociational practices, create incentives for extremist ethnic leaders to compete for office, confident that they will not lower the overall support for their bloc, but then each minority's extremists will lack the incentive to moderate their demands. The dangerous phenomenon of outflanking – of Sharon outflanking Shamir or of Ian Paisley's Democratic Unionist party outflanking the Ulster Unionist party – is latent in all proportional representation-based consociational systems. But by contrast in plurality-rule systems, which dovetail neatly with control practices, a dominant party may have no obvious incentive to appeal to minorities – unless very special circumstances make a cross-ethnic ("catchall") dominant party possible.

If these demanding conditions are not present, as in Lebanon,

Northern Ireland, Malaysia, Cyprus, and Fiji, consociational experiments break down. An even more depressing conclusion is also possible. Consociational practices may work to calm ideological, religious, linguistic, or ethnic conflicts, but only if these conflicts have not become the bases of separate national identities. In other words consociationalism may only be practicable in moderately, rather than deeply, divided societies (Horowitz 1985, 571-2). This conclusion is not appetizing for enthusiasts of consociationalism in Burundi, Fiji, Northern Ireland, Malaysia, and Lebanon, and detailed consideration of the South African case provides solid grounds for being pessimistic about a consociational settlement, even if it were to be negotiated (McGarry and Noel 1989).

The taxonomy presented above is merely the first stage of a wider project. We believe it provides a clear map of the possible macropolitical forms of national- and ethnic-conflict regulation. The harder task is to see whether regularities in the genesis, stabilization, and breakdown of these forms can be successfully established. Even if they cannot we hope this framework can be developed to assist in appraising the morality, feasibility, and consequences of macropolitical strategies. The comparative evaluation of national- and ethnic-conflict regulation matters because we are all nationals or ethnics of one kind or another, even when we want not to be, and because our community relations are too important to be left to chauvinists.

References

Ålands landsting. 1988. *Aland in brief*. Marie-Hamn: Ålands landskapysstrelse.
Alcock, A. 1970. *The History of the South Tyrol Question*. London: Michael Joseph.
Anderson, B. 1983. *Imagined Communities: Reflections on the Origins and Spread of Nationalism*. London: Verso.
Barry, B. 1991a. "Political Accommodation and Consociational Democracy." In Barry, B., ed. *Democracy and Power: Essays in Political Theory 1*, 100–35. New York: Oxford University Press.
―――. 1991b. "The Consociational Model and Its Dangers." In Barry, B., ed. *Democracy and Power: Essays in Political Theory 1*, 136–55. New York: Oxford University Press.
―――. 1991c. "Self-Government Revisited." In his *Democracy and Power: Essays in Political Theory 1*, 165–86. New York: Oxford University Press.
Beran, H. 1984. "A Liberal theory of secession." *Political Studies*. 32:1. 1988. "More theory of secession: reply to Birch." *Political Studies*. 32:316-23.
―――. 1987. *The Consent Theory of Political Obligation*. London: Croom Helm.

Buchanan, A. 1991. *Secession: The Morality of Political Divorce from Fort Sumter to Lithuania and Quebec*. (Oxford: Westview Press).
Chalk, F., and Jonassohn, K. 1990. *The History and Sociology of Genocide: Analyses and Case Studies*. New Haven, CT: Yale University Press.
Connor, W. 1973. "The Politics of Ethno-nationalism." *Journal of International Affairs*. 27, no. 1:1-21.
1984. "Eco- or ethno-nationalism?" *Ethnic and Racial Studies* 7:342-59.
Fraser, T. G. 1984. *Partition in Ireland, India and Palestine: Theory and Practise*. London: Macmillan.
Freeman, M. 1984. "Genocide in World Historical Perspective." Essex Papers in Government.
Gellner, E. 1983. *Nations and Nationalism*. Oxford: Blackwell Publisher.
Gibson, G. 1992. "Self-government: Isolating Aboriginal People from the Mainstream is a Mistake." Toronto *Globe and Mail*. 1 June.
Glazer, N. 1987. *Affirmative Discrimination: Ethnic Inequality and Public Policy*. Cambridge: Harvard University Press.
Hannum, H. 1990. *Autonomy, Sovereignty, and Self-Determination: The Accommodation of Conflicting Rights*. Philadelphia: University of Pennsylvania Press.
Harff, B. 1992. "Recognising Genocides and Politicides." In Fein, H., ed. *Genocide Watch*, 27-41. New Haven, CT: Yale University Press.
Hoffman, M. 1992. "Third Party Mediation and Conflict Resolution in the Post-Cold War World." In Baylis, J., and Rengger, N., eds. *Dilemmas in World Politics*. New York: Oxford University Press.
Horowitz, D. 1985. *Ethnic Groups in Conflict*. Berkeley and Los Angeles: University of California Press.
Hovannisian, R. G., ed. 1986. *The Armenian Genocide in Perspective*. Oxford: Transaction Books.
ed. 1992. *The Armenian Genocide: History, Politics, Ethics*. London: Macmillan.
Huntingdon, S. 1972. Foreword to Nordlinger, E. A. *Conflict Regulation in Divided Societies*,
Jennings, I. 1956. *The Approach to Self Government*. New York: Cambridge University Press.
Jonassohn, K. 1992. "What is Genocide?" In Fein, H., ed. *Genocide Watch*, 17-26. New Haven, CT: Yale University Press.
Khoshla, G. D. 1950. *Stern Reckoning: A Survey of Events Leading Up to and Following the Partition of India*. New Delhi: Bhawnani.
Kuper, L. 1981. *Genocide: Its Political Use in the Twentieth Century*. New Haven, CT: Yale University Press.
Kymlicka, W. 1991. *Liberalism, Community and Culture*. New York: Oxford University Press.
Lemkin, R. 1944. *Axis Rule in Occupied Europe*. Washington DC: Carnegie Endowment for International Peace.
Lijphart, A. 1977. *Democracy in Plural Societies*. New Haven, CT: Yale University Press.
1984. *Democracies*. New Haven, CT: Yale University Press.
1985. *Power-Sharing in South Africa*. Berkeley and Los Angeles: University of California Press.

Lustick, I. 1979. "Stability in deeply divided societies: consociationalism versus control." *World Politics* 31:325–44.
 1985. *State-Building Failure in British Ireland and French Algeria*. Berkeley, CA: Institute of International Studies.
 1987. "Israeli State-Building in the West Bank and Gaza Strip: Theory and Practice" *International Organization* 41, no. 1:151–71.
Mayall, J. 1990. *Nationalism and International Society*. New York: Cambridge University Press.
McCarthy, J. 1989. *Turks and Armenians: A Manual on the Armenian Question*. Washington, DC: Committee on Education, Assembly of Turkish American Associations.
McGarry, J. 1990. "A Consociational Settlement for Northern Ireland?" *Plural Societies* 20, no. 1:1–21.
McGarry, J., and O'Leary, B. Forthcoming. *Resolving Ethnic Conflict*. London: Macmillan.
McGarry, J., and Noel, S. J. R. 1989. "The Prospects for Consociational Democracy in South Africa." *Journal of Commonwealth and Comparative Studies* 27, no. 1:3–22.
McNeill, W. 1986. *Polyethnicity and World History*. Toronto: Toronto University Press.
Mill, J. S. 1988. *Utilitarianism, On Liberty and Considerations on Representative Government*, ed. Acton, H. B. London: Dent.
Nordlinger, E. 1972. *Conflict Regulation in Divided Societies*. Cambridge: Harvard University Centre for International Affairs.
Nusseibeih, S. 1990. "A Palestinian View of the Occupied Territories." In Giliomee, H., and Gagiano, J., eds. *The Elusive Search for Peace: South Africa, Israel and Northern Ireland*, 132–5. Oxford University Press.
O'Leary, B. 1987. "The Anglo-Irish Agreement: Meanings, Explanations, Results and a Defence." In Teague, P., ed. *Beyond the Rhetoric: Politics, the Economy and Social Policy in Northern Ireland*. London: Lawrence & Wishart.
 1989. "The Limits to Coercive Consociationalism in Northern Ireland' *Political Studies* 34, no. 4:562–88.
O'Leary, B., and Arthur, P. 1990. "Introduction. Northern Ireland as a Site of State- and Nation-building Failures." In McGarry, J., and O'Leary, B., eds. *The Future of Northern Ireland*, 1–47. New York: Oxford University Press.
O'Leary, B., and McGarry, J. 1993. *The Politics of Antagonism: Understanding Northern Ireland*. London: Athlone Press.
Pappalardo, A. 1981. "The Conditions for Consociational Democracy: A Logical and Empirical Critique." *European Journal of Political Research* 9:365–90.
Permanent People's Tribunal, ed. 1985. *A Crime of Silence: The Armenian Genocide*. London: Zed Books.
Rabushka, A., and Shepsle, K. A. 1972. *Politics in Plural Societies: A Theory of Democratic Instability*. Westerville, OH: Merrill.
Roberts, H. 1990. "Sound Stupidity: The British Party System and the Northern Ireland Question." In McGarry and O'Leary, eds. *The Future of Northern Ireland*, 100–36. New York: Oxford University Press.

Smith, M. 1991. *Burma: Insurgence and the Politics of Ethnicity*. London, Zed Press.
Stein, M. 1968. "Federal Political Systems and Federal Societies." *World Politics* 20, no. 4:721–47.
Vile, M. 1982. "Federation and Confederation: The Experience of the United States and the British Commonwealth." In Rea, D., ed. *Political Cooperation in Divided Societies,* 216–28. Dublin: Gill & Macmillan.

CHAPTER 12

Nations conspiring against themselves: An interpretation of European integration

Pierre Salmon

I Introduction

Nationalists are prone to suspect conspiracies where there are none. But in the case of Europe their suspicion is not completely unfounded. The process of integration appears as incremental, insidious, endless. The question of where it will lead to ultimately is left to the appreciation or rhetoric of each sector of opinion or politician. Public discourse smacks of deception or self-deception. Each particular step forward is defended on its own merits, in utilitarian terms, generally of a purely economic kind. Its predicted positive effects – increased growth, reduced unemployment, diminished uncertainty or transaction costs, for instance – seem often highly debatable or exaggerated. Alternative arrangements which could fill the same avowed needs are not discussed seriously. Important turning points in the integration process are obfuscated. Far-reaching decisions are taken that remain unnoticed. Discussions about whether the next step will or will not allow national sovereignty to remain unimpaired hides the fact that a lot of sovereignty has already been abandoned in practice. Europe is more advanced in the direction of supranationality or even federalism than appears or has been agreed on on paper.[1]

If, thus, observers of integration who detect in it conspiratorial characteristics (Cohen-Tanugi 1992, e.g.) seem to have a point, the intriguing question is: Who are the conspirators? The "Commission" is the typical scapegoat of conspiracy stories and, it is true, a natural

---

I am grateful to the participants in the Fifth Villa Colombella Seminar (especially my discussant, Manfred Holler), the participants in the Public Economics Workshop of the University of Toronto, and Alain Wolfelsperger for helpful comments and suggestions.

[1] The Brussels system should be viewed as a hybrid, neither purely federal nor purely intergovernmental.

candidate for that role. Although it pays lip service to the principle of "subsidiarity," it seizes (deviously, some would say) every occasion to enlarge its powers or, more generally, to push for increased integration. This behavior is perfectly consistent both with the public choice theory of bureaucracy and, if "Brussels" is seen as an embryonic government, with Albert Breton's theory of vertical intergovernmental competition (1987). The Commission's responsibilities can increase mainly at the expense of national governments and bureaucracies. How could its relationship with these governments and bureaucracies not be fundamentally adversary?[2] Yet, from the Schuman Declaration and the Coal and Steel Community to the Treaty of Maastricht, through the European Defense Community, the Treaty of Rome, the European Monetary System, and the Single Act, the major integrative steps have typically been not only authorized but initiated by national governments. The part played by the Commission has rarely been the leading one.[3] Anyhow, even if it had had such a role, the fact would remain that it is a creature of governments in its ambition to extend its powers as in all its other characteristics, and, in practice, can seldom move forward without at least their tacit consent.[4] Thus, the Commission is not such a plausible conspirator after all and we must turn to the national governments themselves as the main suspects.

But this is certainly a major puzzle, for are not the governments and their bureaucracies also the main victims of the conspiracy? Why and how can governments conspire to deprive themselves of a growing part of their powers or responsibilities? In a recent paper, Roland Vaubel (1992) addresses this problem and seeks a solution inspired

---

[2] Stressing this basically adversary relationship is compatible with completely different views about the desirability of integration or the preferences of the "peoples." Federalists feel that the peoples are on their and the Commission's side, and they see in the resistance of self-seeking governments the main cause of what they consider as the excessively slow pace of integration. Anti-Europeans claim that the peoples are even more opposed to integration than their governments. For them, the integration process reflects a conspiracy engineered by a coalition of "Eurocrats" in Brussels and networks or lobbies such as the European movement in each country. This interpretation can claim some support from the early history of European integration at a time when, under the influence of Jean Monnet notably, the role of elites and networks was stressed by the promoters of European construction. Whether networks have been important or not in the distant past, I think that their role has been marginal now for a long time.

[3] The European Court of Justice is another matter (see Mancini 1992).

[4] Indeed, close scrutiny of the way the Council of Ministers (representing the governments) and the Commission cooperate in Brussels shows that national governments do much more in favor of increased integration than acquiescing (see, e.g., Ludlow 1992; Wessels 1992).

by the theory of bureaucracy. My interpretation is different. Behind democratic governments, there are voters or – to use a term whose meaning is unclear but which is convenient in the present context – nations. As a rule, democratic governments cannot depart over extended periods of time and on essential issues from the wishes of a majority of voters. Thus, inasmuch as European integration is a conspiracy of national governments against themselves, that conspiracy, at a deeper level, must be one of nations against themselves. I attempt in Section II to justify this hypothesis by the way of five propositions. In Section III, I present a model which captures, I hope, a particular aspect of the phenomenon.

II   Five propositions about European integration

A major objective of integration consists in tying together the member countries.

That tying together the European countries was the main objective of the founding fathers in the late forties and early fifties is indisputable (see, e.g., Schuman 1963, or the recollections of Altiero Spinelli, Denis de Rougemont and others in Ionescu 1972, and Hodges 1972). The two world wars had started as European wars and it was felt that everything had to be done to avoid the possibility of a rivalry between the nation–states of Western Europe, especially France and Germany, leading again to a situation which might evolve into open conflict. That concern became much less important as the East–West divide and the North Atlantic alliance came to provide the dominant perspective. Still, the long-term concern with building up ties, so to say, for ties's sake never left completely the minds of the political personnel and of many citizens in the original six countries (see, e.g., Taylor 1983). The end of the East–West conflict, the collapse of communism in Eastern Europe and the unification of Germany have brought it back to the fore. War between Western European countries is still hard to imagine, but a return to some form of balance of power or alliance politics is not unconceivable anymore, and, given the relative size and geographical position of the countries involved, it is as potentially dangerous as ever.

Admittedly, member countries other than the original six are less concerned with the issue. I feel entitled, however, to gloss over these differences. In most cases, unconcerned members have been fearful of being excluded from the "core" and this fear has allowed the "core countries" to impose their perspective in the end. Indeed, the main effect of the reluctance of countries such as Britain to share the political goals of integration has been to increase the ambiguity of public discourse or the phrasing of agreements, and, therefore, the conspiratory aspect of the whole process.[5]

In addition to what I think is fairly direct evidence in support of the centrality of the concern with "tying," indirect evidence is provided by the fact that many other displayed objectives are questionable. This has always been a major problem for the determination of functions which should be transferred to the Community according to the theory of fiscal federalism, public goods, or externalities. Sometimes, the claimed objectives could have been achieved most economically by arrangements between a few countries only, not all of them necessarily members of the Community. More often, the optimal agreement would have involved all the members of more encompassing organizations such as the Council of Europe, OECD, NATO, or GATT. As to the objective consisting in the European countries as a whole having a bigger influence in world affairs, even admitting that it is a worthwhile objective (which is not obvious), it would not necessarily be enhanced by Europe becoming a unitary actor.[6] In sum, it is often difficult to understand the drive to pursue integration in the framework and along the lines of the European Community if one does not acknowledge the prominence of the desire to strengthen ties.[7]

Cultural, economic, and constitutional ties are not likely to be sufficiently binding.

When defined narrowly (e.g., in terms of language, literature, television, music, food habits), cultural ties between member countries are unlikely to become sufficiently strong for the purpose of binding these

---

[5] An example is the way Britain succeeded in preventing the words "federal perspective" from being included in the Treaty of Maastricht.

[6] In many matters, the fact that there is no common foreign policy means that it is difficult, say, for third world countries to disentangle themselves from tight relations with one European country or another. If the relation of a particular country with, say, France becomes strained, that particular country typically turns to another European country, say, Italy or Germany, instead of turning necessarily to non-European countries as it would have done if it had faced Europe as a unitary actor and if its relationship with that unitary actor had been strained. As Ronald Findlay (1992) says, in another setting: "Divided we stand, united we fall."

[7] In a previous paper (Salmon 1991), I argue that the Single Act of 1985 can be interpreted as a roundabout way chosen by governments to eliminate or mitigate aspects of the welfare state that prevented adaptation and growth in the context of increased external competition. But this is a minor qualification to the argument defended here. In this particular case, Britain played a substantial role (cf. Moravscik 1991). The more politically oriented members saw in it, in addition to the effect noted here, an important step toward integration in general.

countries together. The main reason for their ineffectiveness is the variety of languages spoken in Europe and the strength of cultural ties between member countries and countries outside Europe, the United States in particular. Defined more broadly, in terms of way of life or something of the kind, the idea of a European culture is on a somewhat firmer ground. There is an element of truth in the idea of a "European model" (cf. Schnapper and Mendras 1990). On the whole, however, I think that we should share Anthony Smith's skepticism (1992) about a European identity based on purely cultural aspects.

Reliance on economic ties encounters three main problems. First, history shows that, being purely utilitarian, they are prone to yield when most needed, that is, when challenged by strong nonutilitarian sentiments.[8] Second, purely EC ties suffer from being embedded in the larger systems of world trade or trade between industrialized countries, both largely liberalized. Even if investments specific to European integration have been made, the cost of secession for a member country of the European Community – or, for that matter, for the province of any developed country (e.g., Canada) – is very much reduced by the existence of the efficient and powerful international regimes that regulate trade, direct investment and finance. Third, even if at one point of time economic motives may provide a strong justification for remaining a member, this may change rapidly. Figure 12.1, which applies to member country X, illustrates what I have in mind here. The vertical axis measures "welfare," W, which, I assume for the moment, is the sole determinant of electoral support. The horizontal axis measures European integration, E. Curve TV represents the initial relationship between the two, as perceived in X. Maximum welfare and, hence, electoral support obtains at point A, corresponding to a degree of integration E_A and a welfare level W_A. I assume that the actual degree of integration is E_A. Then, perspectives change. For example, as a result of new opportunities, curve TV shifts to T'V'. Maximum welfare and support now obtain at point B, with degree of integration E_B and welfare W_B (whether W_B is greater or smaller than W_A does not matter, what counts is that E_B is smaller than E_A).

At this stage, constitutional ties must be brought in. Given present rules, enforced by the European Court of Justice (see Mancini 1992),

---

[8] Income distribution considerations are disregarded in this paper. If they were taken into account, it would appear in some cases that different categories of the population have conflicting interests with regard to integration and secession. For a theoretical discussion of the relationship between income distribution and nationalism, see Breton (1964). For some factual studies on the same relationship, see, e.g., Coakley (1992).

Nations conspiring against themselves

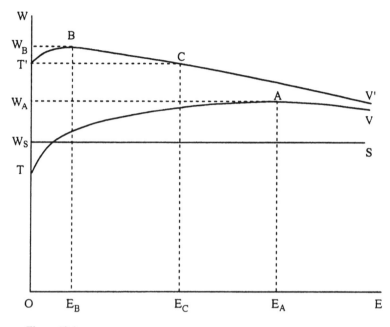

Figure 12.1

a single member country could not move from E_A to E_B without the consent of the other countries. However, it could always move to level of integration 0. I have argued elsewhere (Salmon 1992) that it is hardly conceivable in democratic settings that even a province would seriously be prevented from seceding from a federal or a unitary state if the majority of its population consistently asked for it. In any case, although it is nowhere said that the member countries may leave the European Community, it is clear to all, I think, that they can. Thus, if the other members do not accept a departure from E_A, country X may prefer to secede completely, that is, to pick point T′ on the vertical axis. If the other members are willing to compromise, the equilibrium level of integration may obtain somewhere between O and E_C. I have assumed so far that the system of redistribution between member countries is fixed. If it can be changed, and if the other member countries want at all cost to safeguard the level of integration E_A, they will have to compensate country X in such a way that X will prefer E_A to secession. But this is a very simplified story. As a result of more complicated strategic interaction between the members a collapse of integration agreements may be caused by changes in economic perspectives of a smaller magnitude than that depicted in Figure 12.1.

Attachment of citizens to their nation–states is productive but must be brought under control.

By attachment to one's country, I mean what is usually called "patriotism" or "national sentiment." A sentiment, according to dictionaries, is "an affective state related to representations." The word "representation" is particularly relevant here. According to Benedict Anderson (1983), a nation (identical with a country for our purpose) is an "imagined community." As such, it is often treated in individual minds on the same footing as a real community such as the family. Like the latter, it can be loved, and Anderson provides striking examples of patriotic discourse expressing love. For the purpose of later discussion, we can go further than Anderson does and observe that love for one's family and love for one's country share a distinctive characteristic: an individual who notices that he experiences no love typically feels guilty (or is expected by others to feel guilty). According to philosophers such as Allan Gibbard (1990), feeling guilty – or, rather, being expected by others to feel guilty (I simplify somewhat Gibbard's subtle analysis) – signals the existence of a moral norm. Patriotism or attachment to one's country often leads to actions and attitudes which are (in a sense) disinterested or self-sacrificing, help solve free-riding problems, or, more generally, reduce the costs of policy making. But this implies that an individual who is not patriotic may consider himself and be considered by others as free-riding, actually or potentially, on the patriotism of others. This may explain the feeling of guilt – and, in others, of resentment.

I will return in the next section to the productive aspects of patriotism or attachment to one's country. But at this stage let me stress that the existence and importance of these productive aspects implies that patriotism is an asset that, collectively, the European countries cannot dispense with, at least for the time being. At the same time, patriotism (or nationalism) certainly leads to undesired social outcomes in some circumstances. That extreme national sentiments can be a collective liability hardly needs illustrating. But even patriotism of a very moderate kind can be detrimental. In the context of international relations, with the national states as unitary actors, it has been shown that very small differences in payoffs can change completely the game played by nation-states in a particular setting, for example from a game whose equilibrium is "good" to one (e.g., a prisoner's dilemma) whose equilibrium is "bad" – that is, possibly, from peace to war (see Oye 1986, e.g.). Since patriotism affects payoffs, it is quite possible, then, that a given level of patriotism generates payoffs whose consequence is a "bad" equilibrium, while, with less patriotism, different payoffs would have obtained that would have led to a "better" equilibrium. The game-theoretic context is typically assumed in this literature to be a purely international one in the sense that all citizens in a given country are considered as identical and perfectly represented by their government. Nation–states are then considered as unitary actors and the degree to which their objectives are influenced by patriotism or nationalism reflects the beliefs and sentiments which prevail at the level of citizens. But in many cases the international interaction is influenced by domestic circumstances that distort the relationship between the real or dominant preferences of the electorate and the objectives of the government. Let me give three examples of these circumstances. First, although the majority of voters may be only moderately patriotic, the building up of a governing coalition in a multidimensional setting (without a Condorcet winner) can require accommodation of the bellicist views of a minority. Second, in a context of probabilistic voting, in which "non-issue" characteristics of candidates count, a populist leader who is more inclined to nationalism than the majority of voters can nonetheless be elected. Third, because patriotism is well-regarded socially, it may be in the interest of each individual to display sentiments that are more patriotic than they really are,[9] and this may induce or allow policies that are more nationalistic than voters would really wish them to be.

It is tempting to argue that the lower the average level of patriotism, the less likely the occurrence of democratic mechanisms having perverse effects of the kind just described. An objection to this line of reasoning is that it takes no heed of the benefits of patriotism stressed above. More seriously, perhaps, a low average level of patriotism provides no safeguard against at least some of the democratic interactions suggested above. What really reduces the likelihood of perverse effects is the existence of other positive forces that may counter patriotism or nationalism when it goes too far – or, better still (to account for the pluridimensionality of this sentiment), the existence of forces that oppose its undesirable forms or manifestations. Thus, rather than citizens not being very patriotic or bellicist on average it is a majority of voters being strongly attached to peace, individual rights or humanistic values which may prevent a bellicist government from going to war or moderate voters from allying with extremists. This is a general point. In the context of this paper, patriotism or nationalism is

---

[9] For a discussion of this kind of mechanism, based on a distinction between what he calls public and private preferences, see the work of Timur Kuran (1991, e.g.).

dangerous inasmuch as it may lead to the disintegration of the European Community (and to what could happen after such disintegration). What can make this process unlikely is less diminished average patriotism than the existence of forces which would counter patriotism insofar as it could produce that effect. The main force which could play that role is another sentiment: attachment of citizens to the European Community.

Ties of the kind integration seeks require attachment to Europe.

Under the name of "affine agency," James Coleman (1990) analyzes a mechanism which, although it refers to the notion of identification rather than to that of attachment or sentiment, is very close in practice to the mechanism underlying Anderson's "imagined communities." But, for Coleman, "identification with the nation," although important, is only an instance of a more general phenomenon. In other words, countries or nations are not the only relevant "imagined communities." Social classes, churches, political parties, unions, and large firms often arouse feelings of the same kind and magnitude that patriotism does.

Can the European Community also arouse such feelings? Let me make the following points. First, we observe that individuals can have multiple attachments (e.g., Scotland and Britain, Catalogna and Spain). This opens the possibility of Europeans being attached both to their countries and to Europe. Second, although attachments or sentiments cannot be generated or eliminated at will, they can be influenced deliberately or manipulated. Thus, if attachment to Europe cannot be created by fiat or exhortation, it can be generated in the course of time by more roundabout methods. I return to that below. Third, attachment can concern not only "imagined communities" (that is, ultimately, people), but also material objects (such as territories and landscapes) or abstract ideas (such as revolution, freedom, constitutions, pluralism, diversity). This opens the possibility that attachment to Europe may differ in kind from attachment to nations – attachment to nations being anyhow different across countries and across individuals within countries.[10] Taken together, these three points provide some support for the view that attachment to Europe can become very significant and yet coexist with attachment of indi-

---

[10] Switzerland is a highly instructive case to study in this perspective (see Carol Schmid 1981).

viduals to their nation-state remaining a strong and widely-shared sentiment. I think that this is a necessary assumption since the perspective of Europe becoming a nation–state itself remains remote.[11]

What would be achieved by strong attachment to the European Community if it existed? A major concern underlying the integration process is the possibility that anti-European politicians would come in power in some member-countries. Let me compare two situations. In the first situation, there is no particular attachment to Europe in the electorate while electoral competition is not so compelling that it leaves no discretionary power to office-holders. Returning to Figure 12.1, and assuming that the initial situation corresponds to point A, this means for example that politicians must reach a "minimum support" line $W_S S$ which lies below $W_A A$. An anti-European government in one country would move leftwards – that is reduce the level of integration – as much as possible given the constraints represented or imposed by $W_S S$, TV, and EC rules. If $W_S S$ were to cut the vertical axis below T, that government would engage the country into a process of secession. Even if this did not happen, a nationalist government in a single country would probably make itself such a nuisance for the other member countries that nationalism would spread to these other countries, which may well lead to disintegration.

Now, assume that individual citizens in the member countries are attached to the European Community in the sense that they are reluctant to depart from a particular division of powers E_A between "Brussels" and the national states. Graphically, this corresponds in Figure 12.2 to a minimum support curve taking the form of the kinked line gsk. Assume also that Figure 12.2 illustrates the situation in all the member-countries and that nationalist politicians come into power (for some unknown reason) in each of them. Then, given economic conditions corresponding to curve TV, the nationalist governments can reduce the level of integration only to E_d. If, in addition to the coming into power of nationalists, there is a change in economic conditions favouring reduced integration – depicted, as discussed previously, by a shift of line TV to T'V' – the politicians could move only to point d', with level of integration $E_{d'}$. Clearly, compared to the first situation, the capacity of governments to achieve disintegration, if that became their objective, would now be much more limited.

[11] This is remote but not ultimately unlikely. One can sympathize with Jean-Marc Ferry's idea of "a post-national identity" (1990) but note that in a world in which the United-States, Japan, Russia, China, and other important countries are not likely to cease being nation–states, there may be inducements for Europe at a later stage to become a nation–state also.

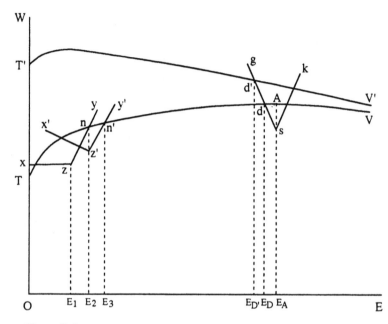

Figure 12.2

So far, I have tried to show that the main objective of European integration is to establish ties between the member countries which are solid enough to resist unforeseeable, but not wholly implausible, changes in economic and political conditions, and that, for that purpose, attachment of Europeans to Europe is essential. How is such attachment to come about?

Creating attachment to Europe is a roundabout and conspiratory process.

I argued previously that attachment to Europe is consistent with the continuing attachment of individuals to their own countries. This, however, does not imply that attachment to one's own country can remain exactly the same as when it does not have, so to say, to be "shared" with attachment to Europe. There are many reasons for the attachment to one's country to be affected. There may exist, in many individuals, a limited capacity for attachment in general, which means that, for these individuals, investment in attachment of one kind will require disinvestment in attachments of other kinds. Conflicts of interest between Europe and their own country may create in the citizens of a country a psychological phenomenon of "divided loyalties" whose consequences are uncertain. Attachment to one's own country may be related to an image of that country (sovereignty or "grandeur", e.g.) which is inconsistent both with integration and with attachment to another entity.

These phenomena do not have to be actual to influence the response of individuals to a perspective of increased attachment to Europe. What counts is that they are perceived as plausible anticipations of things to come. For example, it is enough for affecting their present attitude that people think that increased attachment to Europe will require less attachment to their own country. If, as argued above, patriotism, although a sentiment, is controlled by a norm – that is, if not experiencing patriotism creates a feeling of guilt – it is logical that the vivid or lucid anticipation of a decrease in one's patriotism also creates, by itself, a painful feeling of guilt. Thus, if individuals feel, even mistakenly, that they will become attached to another entity and that this will affect negatively their current attachment, this may be enough for generating a psychological cost. This mechanism explains to a large extent, I submit, the conspiratory character of the process of integration, although social and political mechanisms such as conformism and demagogy should also be considered and given a role in a more complete explanation. Even for a single individual, undertaking to change his or her sentiments or emotions (or, for that matter, habits, tastes, or beliefs) – for instance, to love person A less and person B more – is a process which looks very much like a conspiracy. It usually involves roundabout methods and self-deception (see Elster 1979). For a whole society, changing norms about feelings (Gibbard 1990) is a collective process which is likely to require these characteristics to an even greater degree.

Here, of course, the politicians define the roundabout methods and concur in the self-deception. But this does not necessarily mean that voters do not acquiesce in the process. I have argued elsewhere (Salmon 1993b) that voters wish politicians to engage in unpopular policies when necessary. This means that we do not have to interpret the conspiracy to change the attachments of voters as a conspiracy by politicians against voters. We can interpret it as a conspiracy by voters against themselves, that is, against their present distribution of attachments. Trusted politicians take the initiative but with the tacit consent of voters. Voters are not opposed to the policy but – because knowledge in this case is painful (and, let us note in passing, may be exploited by demagogues) – they prefer to be kept ignorant of it as much as possible.

To illustrate the way this may happen in practice, let me return to Figure 12.2 and assume that the initial level of integration is E_1. Politicians have sufficient support at point z. Voters are not attached to E_1, which means that they would accept a lower level of integration provided welfare is not reduced, hence the (horizontal) branch zx of the support curve. Their attachment to national sovereignty, or something of the kind, makes increased integration psychologically costly. Thus, they accept it only if sweetened by an increase in welfare. Hence the branch zy of the minimal support curve. Politicians use that possibility to move to n, on curves zy and TV, that is, they implement level of integration E_2. After some time, voters discover that they are satisfied with E_2. Minimal support moves to z'. There is now some attachment to the Community, hence the slope of the branch z'x' of the support curve. The slope of the other branch, z'y', reveals however that voters are reluctant to accept integration beyond E_2 if not compensated by a new increase in welfare. Politicians use their discretion to move to n', that is, to level of integration E_3; and so on.[12]

This is a mere illustration of verbal reasoning. I have no model available for the process discussed here. But there is one aspect of growing attachment to Europe which seems easier to model. I noted above that, as a rule, national sentiments are a valuable asset for the government of the country. They help the collection of taxes, the implementation of rules, the acceptance of redistribution. Still, the productivity of attachments played a part only indirectly in the story told so far. Since it is the basis of a major argument against the transfer of responsibilities to Brussels, it is time now to consider it more directly. Given the present state of attachments, the argument goes, substantial and rapid transfers of responsibilities would reduce the efficiency of policy making in the areas concerned. For example, given the strength of patriotic sentiments and the weakness of attachment to Europe, a European army would be much less effective than the armies which now exist at the level of countries. In the next section, I present a model which purports to capture this phenomenon. Although it is based on assumptions that are not perfectly consistent with the ones underlying the foregoing discussion, it leads to an image of the process of integration which is quite similar.

---

[12] TV being positively sloped in this range is not necessary for the process to take place. It could be horizontal or even decreasing.

III A model of integration with productive attachments

The model is inspired by a well-known short-run model of international trade, the specific-factor model, or, more exactly, by the modeling of its relationship with long-run equilibrium (see, e.g., Caves and Jones 1985). Instead of two sectors, I assume two levels of government, the national level and the "Brussels" level. Such borrowing is natural if we interpret attachment as a factor of production, if we assume that it has the dimension of a capital stock, and if we assume that it is specific to existing usages in the short run but ceases to be specific and can move across levels of government in the longer run.[13]

The basic framework

The assumptions which define this framework are the following:

(1) There are two levels of jurisdiction: nation–states (N) and "Brussels" (B); nation–states are identical; they behave in the same way;
(2) Nation–states and "Brussels" produce 2 "goods" (Q_N and Q_B), which are perfect substitutes;[14]
(3) The production functions of the two goods are the same; they are homogeneous of degree 1 in terms of two "factors," which are the powers given to the jurisdiction (P_N or P_B), and the attachment of citizens to the two "imagined communities" (attachment to their nation–state, A_N, or attachment to Europe, A_B);
(4) The sum of the powers ($P_T = P_N + P_B$) given to the two levels of jurisdiction is fixed; the distribution is decided upon by the national governments;
(5) The sum of the attachments of citizens to the two levels of jurisdiction ($A_N + A_B$) is fixed; the distribution is also fixed in the short run.

---

[13] Attachment is one component of what I have called in another paper "the social capital" available to the governments of collectivities such as Europe, countries, regions, or towns (see Salmon 1993a). The other components of that social capital could also contribute to explaining the characteristics of a process of transfer of powers such as European integration.

[14] This assumption is not indispensable but it allows us to concentrate on the phenomenon addressed. It can be interpreted as an extreme implication of Breton's vertical competition, already referred to.

304   Pierre Salmon

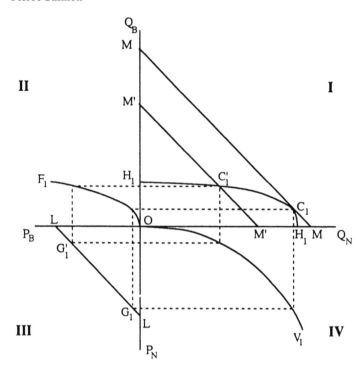

Figure 12.3

In quadrant II of Figure 12.3, OF_1 relates the production of Q_B to the powers assigned to B (i.e., to P_B), for a given level of attachment to B (i.e., A_{B1}). Now, if A_B (attachment to B) is given, so is A_N (attachment to N) – assumption (v). Curve OV_1 in quadrant IV relates the production of Q_N to the powers assigned to N for that given value of A_N (i.e., A_{N1}). Since the production functions of Q_B and Q_N are homogeneous of degree 1, the curves OF_1 and OV_1 show diminishing returns to increases in P_B and P_N, respectively. In quadrant III, curve LL expresses the assumption that $P_B + P_N$ is constant. From the three curves in quadrant II, IV and III, we can derive the production frontier H_1H_1 in quadrant I, which is thus drawn on the assumption of a particular distribution of attachments. To each point on LL corresponds a point on H_1H_1. Since the two goods are perfect substitutes, production is maximized at point C_1, where H_1H_1 is tangent with a line MM whose slope is -1. To this point in quadrant I corresponds point G_1 on line LL in quadrant III. The meaning of point G_1 is clear: given attachments A_{B1} and A_{N1}, and if they want to maximize aggregate

Nations conspiring against themselves

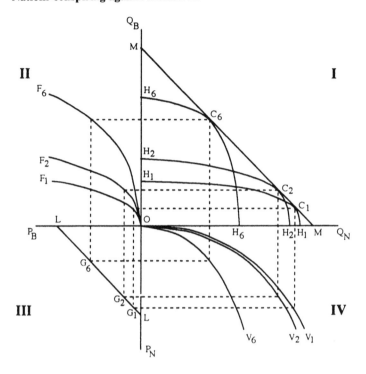

Figure 12.4

production, the national governments must assign powers to the two levels of jurisdiction according to G_1. If instead of choosing G_1, they distribute powers according to G_1', for instance, production then will correspond to point C_1', lying on a line $M'M'$, parallel to MM but situated below it.

Figure 12.4 shows what happens when the distribution of attachments changes (the sum remaining constant). The equilibrium depicted on Figure 12.3 corresponded to attachments A_{B1} and A_{N1}. If A_B increases and A_N decreases to A_{B2} and A_{N2}, respectively, curves OF_1 and OV_1 move to OF_2 and to OV_2. Curve H_1H_1 moves to H_2H_2. Maximum aggregate production is now C_2, which corresponds to the distribution of power G_2. Similarly, if A_B and A_N become equal to A_{B6} and A_{N6}, OF and OV become OF_6 and OV_6, HH becomes H_6H_6 and maximum production becomes C_6 with distribution of powers G_6. Line LL is fixed by assumption, but we notice that line MM remains unchanged. This is a consequence of our assumptions (fixed sums of powers and attachments, identical and homogenous production functions, and goods being perfect substitutes). Whatever the ratio k that A_B/A_N is equal to, the other two ratios (Q_B/Q_N and P_B/P_N) must also be equal to that ratio k for total production to be maximized, and changes in k do not affect the maximum production. Hence, the stability of MM and also the fact that, when production is maximized, k can be read directly on both line LL and line MM (for instance, at C_6 and G_6, k = 3/2).

To go further, we must make assumptions about the way attachments change and about the behavior of politicians and voters. I shall present two submodels.

Submodel 1

This submodel is based on three additional assumptions: (A) the support given by the voters of each country to the politicians in office in their own country is a function of total production ($Q_B + Q_N$); (B) electoral competition compels office-holders to maximize support; (C) the distribution of attachment changes autonomously and slowly in the direction of more attachment to Europe (up to some point, of no practical importance here).

It is clear, then, that politicians are compelled to choose a distribution of powers such that production is maximized, that is, they must make sure that they remain on MM. But this implies that the distribution of powers (on LL) must reflect exactly the distribution of attachment. With the slow change taking place in the distribution of attachment, there is a slow movement upward on curves LL and MM.

This submodel captures some views often found among those Euro-skeptics who do not reject European contruction as a matter of principle. They stress the strength of national attachments and their importance for efficient policy making. They consider European sentiments as comparatively weak. They perceive the growth of these sentiments as slow and largely autonomous. Thus, transfers of powers to Brussels, which should follow rather than precede this growth, must remain limited. Trying to accelerate these transfers would serve no purpose. If we relax assumption (b) above and borrow to the next submodel the assumption that governments do not have to maximize production exactly, this does allow, to some limited extent, transfers of powers to Brussels beyond what is authorized by the change in attachments. The essential characteristic of the first submodel remains, however: the trend of European construction is still constrained by the autonomous change in attachments.

Moderate Euro-skeptics often adopt a variant of this position which we can analyse with the help of a fairly popular distinction between "negative" (largely "market") integration and "positive" integration (see, e.g., Pinder 1968). Attachments or sentiments are now perceived as an essential consideration for positive integration only. This has two consequences. First, negative integration can be pushed as far as one wishes; it is not constrained by the distribution of attachments. Second, and more importantly for our purpose, negative integration, resulting in more transactions within Europe, may eventually enhance European sentiments (for a critical discussion of this widely held view, see Cohen-Tanugi 1992). To account for that position, we can reinterpret the submodel as referring excusively to positive integration. But then its main message is more limited: only positive integration does not affect attachments and must follow rather than precede their evolution. The door remains open for governments to influence attachments by the way of negative integration.

Submodel 2

All the assumptions hold except assumptions (B) and (C) of submodel 1, which are replaced by the following: (B') electoral competition compels office holders to reach a "sufficient" level of support (rather than a maximum level); (C') the distribution of attachments adjusts with a time lag to the distribution of powers.

Politicians in office need not maximize production any more. They must only make sure that they reach a level of production which gives them "sufficient" support. This level of production is represented by line SS in quadrant I of Figure 12.5. Let us start from an equilibrium situation with maximum production corresponding to point C_2, with attachments A_{B2} and A_{N2}, and with a distribution of powers corresponding to point G_2. If the politicians in office in member-countries want to maximize transfers of powers to Brussels, they choose a point G_3, on line LL, yielding point C_2^* on curve H_2H_2 and line SS. After some time, the distribution of attachments adjusts to the distribution of powers, which means that curves OF_2, OV_2 and H_2H_2 move to curves OF_3, OV_3 and H_3H_3 (not depicted) and that production moves from C_2^* to C_3 on line MM. If the national politicians wanted instead to recover powers from Brussels and reduce attachments to Europe, they would choose on line LL a point G_1 (not depicted) such that production is measured by point C_2' on curve H_2H_2 and line SS. After some time, production would move rightward from C_2' to C_1 (not indicated) on MM.

I have argued in the previous section that a major objective of

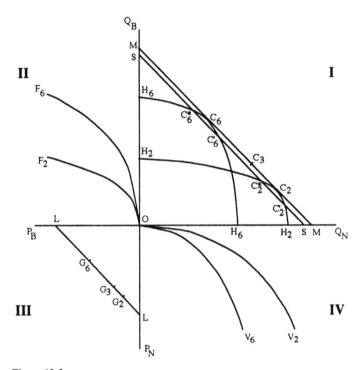

Figure 12.5

European integration is binding together the member countries, which requires, I have also argued, building up European sentiments. In that section, the story, illustrated by Figure 12.2, referred to attachment to a particular division of powers between the two levels of jurisdiction. In this section, however, voters are assumed to be unconcerned by this division of powers. The objective of politicians is to change the A_B/A_N ratio. Changing the distribution of powers, P_B/P_N is now only an instrument toward that end. It has no binding capacity by itself.

Presumably, at some point, the politicians would consider that attachment to Europe is sufficient. Let us assume that this corresponds to attachments equal to A_{B6} and A_{N6}, reflected by curves OF_6, OV_6 and H_6H_6, and by points C_6 and G_6. Against what can such a distribution of attachments protect Europe? Within the limits of the submodel, it can only mean protection against anti-European politicians coming into power in the member countries some time in the future. Such politicians would be constrained by line SS and curve H_6H_6. In the short run, they would have to make sure that the point they choose on

LL does not lead to an aggregate production below C_6' on H_6H_6. In the light of this submodel, integration is a process by which, through a roundabout action on attachments, the politicians who are in office now want to bind the politicians who will come into power in the future. By relaxing a number of assumptions of the model, such as the two goods being perfect substitutes or their production functions being identical, we could also account, however, for a desire by politicians to protect the Community from disintegration-inducing changes in economic conditions as discussed in the previous section. Of course, the remarks made there about voters acquiescing in the strategy implemented by politicians apply here also.

IV Conclusion

Irrevocable binding is a dream. I do not want to argue that secession or disintegration can be made impossible. What can be hoped for, if such tendencies appear, is that ties will impose disintegration to be as gradual as integration itself. In the model of the previous section, as in the discussion of Section II, the whole process is logically reversible but it is not reversible at a single stroke. Since (sentimental) ties will have been created by a process of conspiracy extended over a long period of time, it can be hoped that only a similar process could succeed in destroying them. I do not want to argue either that European integration, in fact, has followed the best path according to my hypothesis or in general. At most, this hypothesis suggests that widespread criticism about the "lack of transparency" or "conspiratorial aspects" of integration may be mistaken.

References

Anderson, Benedict. 1983. *Imagined Communities: Reflections on the origin and spread of nationalism*. Revised and extended edition 1991. London: Verso.
Breton, Albert. 1964. "The economics of nationalism." *Journal of Political Economy* 72, No. 4 (August), pp. 376–86.
  1987. "Towards a theory of competitive federalism." *European Journal of Political Economy* 3, No. 1–2.
Caves, Richard E., and Jones, Ronald W. 1985. *World trade and payments: An introduction*. 4th ed. Boston: Little, Brown and Co.
Coakley, John (ed.). 1992. *The social origins of nationalist movements: The contemporary West European experience*. London: Sage.
Cohen-Tanugi, Laurent. 1992. *L'Europe en danger*. Paris: Fayard.
Coleman, James S. 1990. *Foundations of social theory*. Cambridge, Mass.: The Belknap Press of Harvard University Press.

Elster, Jon. 1979. *Ulysses and the sirens: Studies in rationality and irrationality*. Cambridge and Paris: Cambridge University Press and Editions de la Maison des Sciences de l'Homme.
Ferry, Jean-Marc. 1990. "Vers une identité postnationale?", *Esprit* 162, September.
Findlay, Ronald. 1992. "The roots of divergence: Western economic history in comparative perspective." *American Economic Review*. 82, No. 2 (May), pp. 158–61.
Gibbard, Allan. 1990. *Wise choices, apt feelings: A theory of normative judgment*. Cambridge, Mass.: Harvard University Press.
Hodges, Michael (ed.). 1972. *European integration*. Harmondsworth: Penguin.
Ionescu, Ghita (ed.). 1972. *The new politics of European integration*. London: Macmillan.
Kuran, Timur. 1991. "The role of deception in political competition," in A. Breton et al. (eds.). *The competitive state*. Dordrecht: Kluwer, pp. 71–95.
Ludlow, Peter. 1992. "The European Commission", in R. O. Keohane and S. Hoffman (eds.). *The new European Community: Decisionmaking and institutional change*. Boulder: Westview Press.
Mancini, G. Federico (1992). "The making of a Constitution for Europe," in R. O. Keohane and S. Hoffman (eds.). *The new European Community: Decisionmaking and institutional change*. Boulder: Westview Press.
Moravscik, Andrew. 1991. "Negotiating the Single European Act: National interests and conventional statecraft in the European Community." *International Organization* 45, No. 1, pp. 651–88.
Oye, Kenneth A. (1986). "Explaining cooperation under anarchy: Hypotheses and strategies," in K. A. Oye (ed.), *Cooperation under anarchy*. Princeton: Princeton University Press, pp. 1–24.
Pinder, John. 1968. "Positive integration and negative integration: Some problems of economic union in the EEC," *World Today* 24, pp. 88–110. Reprinted in Hodges (1972).
Salmon, Pierre. 1991. "Checks and balances and international openness," in A. Breton et al. (eds.). *The competitive state*. Dordrecht: Kluwer, pp. 169–84.
 (1992). "Leadership and integration", in G. Bertin and A. Raynauld (eds.), *L'intégration économique en Europe et en Amérique du Nord/Economic integration in Europe and North America*. Paris: Editions Clément Juglar, pp. 367–85.
 1993a. "Transfert de compétences et réallocation du capital social à la disposition des collectivités territoriales". *Revue Economique* 44, No. 4 (July), pp. 821–34.
 1993b. "Unpopular policies and the theory of representative democracy", in A. Breton et al. (eds.). *Preferences and democracy*. Dordrecht and Boston: Kluwer, pp. 13–39.
Schmid, Carol L. 1981. *Conflict and consensus in Switzerland*. Berkeley: University of California Press.
Schnapper, Dominique, and Mendras, Henri (eds.). 1990. *Six manières d'être européen*. Paris: Gallimard.
Schuman, Robert. 1963. *Pour l'Europe*. Paris: Nathan.

Smith, Anthony D. 1992. "National identity and the idea of European unity." *International Affairs* 68, No. 1 (January), pp. 55-76.
Taylor, Paul. 1983. *The limits of European integration.* New York: Columbia University Press.
Vaubel, Roland. 1992. "The political economy of centralization and the European Community," paper prepared for the Interlaken Seminar on Analysis and Ideology, June 8-12, 1992, mimeo.
Wessels, Wolfgang. 1992. "The EC Council: The Community's decisionmaking center," in R. O. Keohane and S. Hoffman (eds.). *The new European Community: Decisionmaking and institutional change.* Boulder: Westview Press.

Index

Acton, John (lord), 157
Adorno, Theodor W., 45, 62
Africa
    See also colonialism
    Algeria, 219-20
    Algerian National Liberation Front, 219-20
    Angola, 220-1
    Mozambique, 220-1
    Portuguese colonies, 219-21
Ajami, Faoud, 32
Ajzenstat, Janet, 136
Akerlof, George A., 44
Ålands landsting, 278
Albania, 216-17
Albright, D. E., 213
Alchian, Armen A., 62
Alcock, A., 277
Alexander Nevsky (1938), 39
Allair Report, Canada, 119, 120, 138
Allen, Douglas, 109-10
Alter, Peter, 146
altruism, 56-7
Anderson, Benedict, 191-3, 281, 296
Anglophone population
    Canada, 135
    compared to Francophones, 138-9
Anglophone population
    Quebec, 121-6
arbitration
    bipartisan, 277-8
    concept of, xiv, 274-5
    external and internal, 276-7, 280
    as method to manage differences, 248, 274-8
Arendt, Hannah, 65
Arrow, Kenneth J., 54
Arthur, P., 270

assimilation
    See also integration
    Chinese communist policy, 230
    coercive, 266-7
    conditions for, xii, 72
    examples of, 265-6
    as method to eliminate differences, xiv, 248-9
    policy of, 264
    resistance to, 266-70
    state strategy for, 264-5
Auster, R. D., 171
authoritarianism
    personality, 62-4, 68
    in societies with social welfare programs, 64
authority
    defined, 3
authority
    effect of diminished system of, 8-10
    rights in hierarchal system of, 3-10
autonomy
    Bolshevik idea of, 210-13
    of community in consociational systems, 283
    federal structure of Soviet Union, 152
    government response to separatism, 162
    integrations or assimilation with ethnic or national, 266
    movements for, 246
Axelrod, Robert, 21

Babbage, Charles, 175-6, 179, 181
Bandaranaike, S. W. R. D., 156
Banting, Keith G., 130
Banton, M., 232

314 Index

barriers to entry and exit
  in ethnic networks and groups, 49–50, 52–5, 68
  xenophobic exclusion, 110–11
Barry, B., 161, 249, 250, 269
Bashevkin, Sylvia, 138
Bauer, Otto, 210
Bawden, C. R., 216
Beaud, Jean-Pierre, 127
Becker, Gary S., 28, 56–7, 91
Bélanger, André J., 127
Bélanger-Campeau Commission, 120, 138
beliefs, nationalist, 33
benefits
  expected from nationalist movements, 232
  expected under conservative and other forms of nationalism, 161
  of investment in nationalism, x, 107–10
bequests, 56–8
Beran, H., 249, 258
Bercuson, David Jay, 131
Berlin, Isaiah, 39, 200
Bernheim, B. Douglas, 57
Blais, André, 127, 128, 135, 136, 138
Blake, Donald E., 138
Bloc Québécois, 120
Borjas, George, 54
Bouchard, Lucien, 120
Bourassa, Robert, 119–20, 125, 132–4
Boyd, R., 199–200
Bracher, Karl, 102
Brada, J. C., 213
Breton, Albert, xiv, 46, 51, 98, 100, 101, 103, 105–6, 108, 113, 148, 169, 182, 187, 206, 291
Buchanan, A., 249, 259
Buchanan, J. M., 74, 106
Bulow, Jeremy, 46
Bush, George, 154

Canada
  See also Meech Lake Accord; Quebec
  accord without Quebec, 133–4
  decentralization in, 128
cantonization, xiv, 248, 278–82
  See also pseudocantonization
capital
  See also ethnic capital; social capital
  cultural, 165
  investment in cultural nationalism, 102
  trust relationships as, 46
Carr, E. H., 184–6
Castro, Fidel, 222
Cauley, J., 162

Caves, Richard, 108
centralization
  effect of breakdown of Soviet, 153–4
  in Quebec, 128
  of Soviet Union federal structure, 152, 212–13
Chalk, P., 250
children
  bequests to, 56–8
  factors in adherence to ethnic norms, 55–9
  pressure from parents, 44–5
China, 230–1
choice of group identity, 16
Clarkson, Stephen, 132
Clift, Dominique, 119
Cloutier, Edouard, 119, 125, 128
Coase, Ronald, 106–7
codes of conduct enforcement, 79
Cohen-Tanugi, Laurent, 290, 307
Cold War
  collapse of, 259
  geopolitics of, 245–6
Coleman, James S., 44, 46, 298
collective action
  in ethnic groups, 50–1
  free riding with, 9
  as utility-maximizing behavior, 232
colonialism
  decolonization, 144–5, 154–6
  nationalism within, 154–5
  Portuguese, 220–1
communism
  aversion to cultural nationalism, 236
  ethnic loyalty under, 112–13
  nationality policy under, 229–30, 235
  as political enterprise, 236–7
competition
  as determinant of authority of ethnic elites, 111–12
  ethnic conflict effect on, 30
  ethnic group barriers to entry and exit, xi, 49–50, 52–5, 68, 110–11
  in market for nationalism, 208–9
  multiethnic states, 84
  nationalist activity as form of group, 22, 232
  political, 207
Comte, Auguste, 165
conflict
  See also ethnic conflict
  conditions for producing, 267
  conditions for violence with, 29–34
  with coordination, 38–9
  former Yugoslavia, 30–2, 34–6
  from group coordination, 24–9

Index

post-World War II states, 145
between republics in Soviet Union, 153
Romania and Hungary, 32–3
Connor, Walker, 11, 33–4, 260
consciousness, national, 146
consociation
  conditions for success, 284–6
  examples of, 248–9
  as method to manage differences, xiv, 248, 282–6
Constitutional Act (1982), Canada, 131–5
constitutions
  allocation of rights by, 7–8
  of federations, 280
  Meech Lake Accord, Canada, 119, 131–7
Cooper, Barry, 131
coordination, group
  in achievement of group identification, 17–21
  conflict from, 24–9
  information through, 21–4, 41
  for political power, 38–9, 41
  power in population coordination, 38–9
coordination game
  of group identification, 17–20
  state/club enforcement of codes of conduct, 79–84
Corbeil, Michel, 130
Cornes, R., 74, 162
Courchene, Thomas J., 129
Crawford, Robert, 62
Cuba, 221–2
cultural capital, 165
culture
  See also nationalism, cultural
  advantages of sharing common, 178
  idea of European, 293–4
  protection of, 184
culture, national
  development and acquisition of, 146–7
  two-culture model, 147
Culture and the Evolutionary Process (Boyd and Richerson), 199–200
Curtis, James E., 122
Cyprus, 253
Czechoslovakia, 238–40

Dahl, R. A., 159n
Daly, Donald, 108
Darmesteter, J., 36–7
Dawkins, R., 198–99, 200
decentralization
  in Canada, 128
  in communist Yugoslavia, 228
  distinct from cantonization, 278
  as government response to separatism, 162
decolonizations, post-World War II, 144–5
De Juvenel, Bertrand, 166
democracies
  consociational, 283
  criticism of representative, 164–5
  demand for nationalism in, 167–71
  federations in liberal, 280
  hegemonic control in, 271–3
  nationalist view of, 163–4
democratization, 261–3
Demsetz, H., 207
Dernberger, Robert, 102
deterrence, ethnic group, 40–1
de Tocqueville, Alexis, 138
Dion, Stéphane, 117, 128, 130–1, 138
di Palma, Giuseppe, 66–7
Director, Aaron, 99
discrimination, ethnic
  based on group identity, 28
  conditions for, 28–9
division of labor
  limitations, 179–80
  mobility with nationalism, 180–1
  risks associated with, 178
  specialization principles, 175–6
Djilas, Milovan, 29–30
Durkheim, E., 181

economic issues
  in conflict, 33
  in European integration, 294–5
  rationale of postcommunist nationalism, 240–1
  of self-determination, 260–2
Edwards, John, 121
Eisenstein, Sergei, 39
Elster, Jon, 116, 301
Enelow, J. M., 170
enforcement
  of codes of conduct by ethnic group and state, 79–84
  in multinational states, 84–5
  of parents' contracts with children, 56–61
  self-enforcement, 59–60
ethnic capital
  advantages of investment in, 48–51
  determination of returns to, 65–7
  disadvantages of investment in, 51–5
  investment in, 44, 48–55
  managers of, 52

ethnic capital (*cont.*)
  parental investment in children's, 55–9
  self-enforcement of investment in, 59–60
  unequal returns to, 52–5
ethnic cleansing, 253, 254
ethnic clubs
  membership in and enforcement, 74–84
  services of, x, xi–xii, 75–9, 93
ethnic conflict
  competition within, 30
  ideas to regulate, 267–70
  influence of state institutions on, 93–4
  internal and external arbitration of, 276–7
  intra- and inter-group, 55–64
  in multinational state, 84–93
  resources committed to, 93–4
  in societies with social welfare programs, 64
  violence with, 29–34
  with cantonization, 279
ethnic-conflict regulation
  micropolitical forms, 247n
  taxonomy of macropolitical forms, 247–9
ethnic domination. *See* hegemonic control
ethnic groups
  See also identity, ethnic; identity, group; minorities, ethnic
  barriers to entry and exit, 49–50
  coordination of, 38–9
  deterrence strategies, 40–1
  factors in seeking independence, 93–5
  guilt as form of pressure to comply, 59
  as interest groups, 85
  membership in, 74–5
  participation in, 75–9
  provision of services, 79–84
  rent-seeking activities, 85–90
  role in state policy making, 85
  sanctions by, 59
  services of, 90
  strategies to eliminate or manage differences, 247–86
ethnic hatred, 33, 34–8
ethnicity
  in defining a nation, 12
  institutionalization under Soviet regime, 65–7
  in Soviet federal structure, 152–4
  territorial divisions in Soviet Union according to, 152

ethnic leaders
  See also political entrepreneurs
  in former Soviet bloc, 68
  as managers of ethnic capital, 52
ethnic nationalism
  See also independence movements
  factors in determination of extent of, 71–9, 93
  factors in reemergence of, 83–4
ethnic networks
  See also ethnic capital
  entry and exit barriers to, 54–5, 68
  investment in, 44
  multipurpose function of, 48–51
  under Soviet system, 66–7
ethnic norms, 56
ethnic pluralism, 284
ethnic politics. *See* interest groups; political entrepreneurs; political parties
ethnocentrism, 64
ethnocide, 266–7
exchange, social and economic, 1
extra-rational action, 14–15

Fairbanks, C. H., Jr., 237
Falardeau, Louis, 121
Faucher, Philippe, 136
favoritism, government, 95
federalism
  community, 283
  conditions for success of, xiv, 280–2
  idea in Canada of renewed, 131–2
  as method to manage differences, 248, 278–82
  Soviet Union, 212–13
Fichte, Johann, 102
Forbes, H. D., 122
forced mass population transfers
  circumstances for advocacy of, xiv, 254
  examples and effect of, 253–4
  as method to eliminate differences, 248, 253
Fortin, Pierre, 126
former Soviet Union
  post communist nationalism, 239–41
  reemergence of nationalism, 65–7
Fournier, Pierre, 132
Francophones
  beliefs of Canadian, 138
  compared to Anglophones, 138–9
  in Quebec, 121–7
Frank, Robert H., 44, 56
Fraser, Graham, 123
Fraser, T. G., 260

Index

free riding
  problems in collective action, 9
  resolution of public good incentives for, 106–7
  in secession movements, 152
Free Trade Agreement, U.S./Canadian, 129, 137
Freud, Sigmund, 58
frontier genocide, 252–3

Gardels, N., 200
Geertz, Clifford, 116, 145
Gellner, Ernest, 116, 146–9, 150–1, 177, 206, 252, 264
genocide
  circumstances for undertaking, xiv, 252–3
  defined, 250
  examples of, 248–53
  incidence and effectiveness of, 250–1
Germany, 8, 102
Gerschenkron, Alexander, 148
Gibbard, Allan, 296, 301
Gibson, G., 264
Glazer, N., 250
Glenny, Misha, 147
Globerman, Stanley, 108
Goebbels, Joseph, 102
goods
  See also public goods
  distributional, 25–8
  positional, 25–8
Gorbachev, Mikhail, 213
government
  in consociational democracies, 283
  favoritism of, 95
  nationalist social objectives, 163–4
  Quebec's attacks on Canada's federal, 129
government role
  Canadian federal and provincial, 128–9
  in Quebec, 128
Gow, James Iain, 130–1
Gray, Gwendolyn, 128
Guay, Jean H., 119, 125, 128, 130
guilt
  ethnic group pressure in formation of, 59
  as substitute for legal enforcement of ethnic norms, 56, 58
Guinea-Bissau, 220–1

Hamilton, Richard, 118, 127
Hannum, H., 277, 278
Harff, B., 250

Hassner, P., 162
hatred, ethnic, 34–8
Hechter, Michael, 61, 65
hegemonic control
  arguments for and alternatives to, 273–4
  coercive and/or co-optive rule, 270–1
  examples of, 270–2
  to manage differences, 248, 270–4
Henriksen, T. H., 221
Herder, Johann Gottfried, 39
Herskovits, Melville, 39–40
Hinich, M. J., 170
Hirschman, A. O., 183, 196
Hirshleifer, Jack, 56–7, 104
Hitler, Adolph, 102
Hobbes, Thomas, 21, 30–2
Hobsbawm, E. J., 55, 154
Ho Chi Minh, 217–18
Hodges, Michael, 292
Hoffman, M., 274
homesteading, 109–10
homogeneity, ethnic
  creation of, 278–9
  examples of, 144
Horowitz, Donald, 261, 267, 286
Howitt, Peter, 51
Hoxha, Enver, 217
Huizinga, Johan, 146
Hume, David, 40
Hunter, A. A., 138
Huntingdon, S., 245

Iannaccone, Laurence R., 51
identity
  political, 121–6
  state-generated, 12
identity, cultural
  as aim of assimilation, 263
  in Scottish nationalism, 151–2
identity, ethnic, 15–16
  as aim of assimilation policy, 264
  in former Soviet bloc, 65–8
  sustaining minority, 267
  theoretic nature of, 37
  under totalitarian government, 65–8
identity, group
  association with self-interest, xi, 17–21
  congruence with self-interest, 15
  discrimination based on, 28–9
  from coordination, 17–21
  means to strengthen, 9–11
  rational, 21–2, 41
  reinforcement of or defection from, 10–11

318   Index

identity, national
   of conservative nationalism, 160-3
   factors in shaping, 149-50
   medieval sense of, 146
   in Soviet Union, 224-7
immigration
   conditions for and effect of restrictions on, 184-7
   management of large-scale, 267-8
independence
   of Albania under socialist nationalism, 217
   confidence of Quebec population for, xii, 126-31
   Portuguese colonies after, 221
independence movements
   conditions for engagement in, 232
   factors in ethnic group, 74, 93-5
   post-world War II, 145, 155-6
industrialization
   in communist Yugoslavia, 228
   strategy in Soviet Union, 225-7
information
   protection of ethnic groups from, 110-11
   through coordination, 21-4
institutions
   of hegemonic control, 271
   of nationalism, 181
   Soviet Union, 212-3
integration
   See also assimilation
   coercive, 266-7
   examples of, 265-6
   as method to eliminate differences, 248, 263-70
   policy of, xiv, 263-4
integration
   state strategy of, 264-5
integration, European
   creation of binding ties, 293-5
   model of, 303-9
   process of, xv, 290-1
   tying of member countries, 292-3
interest groups
   model of ethnic political activities, 86-90
   Mouvement Québec Français, 125
   in multinational states, 85
   opposition to Meech Lake Accord, 135
International Court of Justice, 277, 294
investment
   of parents in ethnic capital, 61-4
   self-enforcement of ethnic, 44-5

Ionescu, Ghita, 292
irrational action, 14

Jennings, Ivor, 257
Johnson, Harry, 108, 206, 237
Johnson, Pierre-Marc, 119
Johnston, Richard, 138
Jonassohn, K., 250, 251
Jones, E., 225
Jones, Ronald, 303

Kandell, Eugene, 58
Kaplan, Robert D., 34-5
Keynes, John Maynard, 195
Khoshla, G. D., 260
Kirkpatrick, Jeane, 65
Klein, Benjamin, 43, 45, 62
Kuper, L., 250
Kuran, Timur, 170, 171

labor markets
   contract enforceability in, 46-7
   distortions with nationalism, 168-9
Laforest, Guy, 132
Laitin, David, 65, 66
Lambert, Ronald D., 122
Landa, Janet, 46
Landry, Bernard, 129
language
   French language in North America, 121-6
   as issue in European integration, 294
   as issue in political identity, 121-6
language policy, 28-9
language policy
   in bilingual region, 137
   Quebec, 121-6, 137
Laponce, Jean, 137
Latouche, Daniel, 119, 125, 128
Lazear, Edward, 58
Le Bon, Gustave, 165
Leffler, Keith B., 43, 45
legitimacy (of an action), 3
Lenin, V. I., 210-11
Lessard, Denis, 120
Lévesque, René, 132
Liberal party, Canada, 119, 131
Lijphart, A., 283, 284
linguistic policy
   Canada, 125-6, 135
   Quebec, 125-6, 265
Linz, J. J., 240
List, Friedrich, 183
loyalty, ethnic
   under communism, 112-13

Index

investment in, xi, 102–12
Lubin, N., 225, 226, 227
Lustick, Ian, 250, 270, 273

McCallum, John, 130
McCall, Christina, 132
McGarry, John, 248, 257, 270, 276, 277, 286
McRae, Kenneth, 137
McRoberts, Kenneth, 124
majority rule, 272
Mancini, G. Federico, 294
markets
 See also competition; political markets
 for nationalism, 208–9
 regulation absent in ethnic networks, 52–5
Marrese, M., 213
Martin, Pierre, 129
Marx, Karl, 2
Mastnak, Tomaz, 154
Mayall, J., 245
Meadwell, Hudson, 128, 130
mediation, 275
Meech Lake Accord, 119, 131, 132–5, 138
Mendras, Henri, 294
Merton, Robert K., 111
Mill, John Stuart, 156, 263
Minogue, Kenneth, 146
minorities, ethnic
 under communist regime, 235
 in consociational democracies, 283–4
 in former Soviet republics, 144
 under Soviet regime, 65–7, 153
 sustaining ethnic identity, 267
mobilization
 ethnic, 153
 nationalism as force for, 38–40
Mongolia, Inner and Outer, 214–16
morality
 to eliminate or manage ethnic differences, 249–50
 of forced mass population transfers, 255
Morin, 138
motivation (rational, irrational, and extra-rational), 14–15
Mouvement Québec Français, 125
Mulroney, Brian, 132
Murphy, Kevin, 57

Nadeau, Richard, 123, 127, 128, 135
nation
 created by nationalism, 208
 defined, 11–12, 143
 equilibrium condition with state, 143–4
 as imagined community, xiii, 143, 173, 296
 political equilibrium in, 160–3
national capital region, Canada, 131
national differences, 247–9
national groups
 as actors, 8–10
 in common defense, 10–11
nationalism
 See also identity, national; secession; separatism
 as argument for mobilization, 38–40
 beneficiaries of investment in, 107–10
 characterization of, 191–2
 defined, 65
 determinants of demand for, 167–71
 differences in nineteenth- and twentieth-century, 184–8
 emergence of, 149–50
 expansionist type of, 161–2
 as force for mobilization, x, 38–40
 Gellner's theory of, xiii, 146–51
 as ideology, 145–9, 159
 in less-developed countries, 154–6
 of Liberal party, Canada, 119–20
 negative attitude toward, 153–4
 Northern Ireland, 151
 phenomena involving war, 3
 postcommunist, 238–41
 present problems, 150
 pure, 39
 in Quebec, 118–20, 123, 127, 138, 148, 151–2
 reemergence in former Soviet bloc, 65–8, 71
 remergence, 112–13, 188
 resource allocation model (1964), 98–100, 108, 206
 resource allocation model reformulated, 101–14
 role in war, 39
 in Scotland, 151–2
nationalism, bourgeois, xiv, 206–7, 209–13, 233, 237
nationalism, conservative
 criticism of democracy, 164–5
 defined, 159
 levels of demand for, 170–1
 logic of, 160–3
 social objectives of, 163–4
nationalism, cultural, 101–6
 communism's aversion to, 236

nationalism, cultural (*cont.*)
  effect of xenophobia on investment in, 111
  investment in, 102
  yield on investment in, 103-5
nationalism, political, 101-2
  investment in, 103-5, 107
  yield on investment in, 104-5
nationalism, postcommunist, 238-41
nationalism, socialist
  appeal of, 237
  as competitor for bourgeois nationalism, xiv, 209-13
  in Cuba, 221-2
  in political market for nationalism, 233-7
  in Portuguese colonies, 220-1
  revolutions, 214-23
  in Yugoslavia, 227-9
nationalist conflicts
  rights related to, 7-8
  without system of authority, 8-10
nationalist feelings
  Quebec's confidence, xii, 126-31
  Quebec's linguistic insecurity, 121-6
  Quebec's rejection, xii, 131-7
  of secessionist ethnic groups, 16-18
nationality
  as basis for identity, 11-12
  Bolshevik doctrine of national self-determination for, 210-12
  under communist regime, 235
  definition under conservative nationalism, 165-7
  economic reasons for claim to, 9-10
  equalization strategy in Soviet Union, 224-7
  integration in Soviet Union, 212-13
  in Soviet Union, 224-7
  in states created by European expansion, 145
  unification under socialist regime in Yugoslavia, 227-9
nationality policy
  communist, 229-30
  of Soviet Union, 152-3
national sentiment, 296, 302
nation building
  assimilation and integration strategies, 264-5
  by conquest, 246
Nazism, 102
neutrality, 275-6
Nicaragua, 222-3
Niemi, Richard G., 123
Noël, Alain, 127

Noel, S. J. R., 286
Nordlinger, E., 267, 271, 282
Nozick, Robert, 190
Nusseibeh, S., 269

Oates, Wallace, 84
O'Leary, Brendan, 248, 257, 270, 274, 276, 277
Olson, Mancur, Jr., 19, 106
Orwell, George, 150
Oye, Kenneth A., 296

Pagano, Ugo, 187
Palma, J. G., 183
Paquet, Gilles, 99
parents
  ethnic capital investments of, 55-60
  pressure on children, 44-5
Parizeau, Jacques, 119, 130
Parti Québécois, 118-26, 129-32
partition
  See also secession
  circumstances for implementation, xiv, 260
  effect of, 260
  examples of, 255-6, 258
  with high ethnic conflict, 278-9
  as method to eliminate differences, 248, 255-63; 255
patriotism
  as danger to European integration, 297-8
  emotion of, 146
  as European country asset, 296-7
Peacock, Alan, 106-7
Pinard, Maurice, 116, 118, 119, 126, 127, 128, 131
Pinder, John, 307
Pipes, R., 212
Plamenatz, John, 148
Poggi, Gianfranco, 67
policy
  circumstances for multicultural, 267-8
  determinants of multinational state, 85
political entrepreneurs
  bourgeois and socialist nationalism as, 209-13
  in competition, xiv, 207
  in former Soviet Union, 240
  offerings to potential constituencies, 22-3
  selling nationalist policies, 206
  use of democratization issues, 261-2
political markets
  contract enforceability in, 47

Index

demand for and supply of nationalism in, 167–71
nationalism offerings to potential constituencies, 22–3
political parties
  formation of ethnic, 262
  model of activity in ethnic, 86–9
  politicians in consociational societies, 284, 285
Popkin, S. L., 217n
population transfers. *See* forced mass population transfers
power-sharing, 248, 282–6
primordialism, 36–7
prisoner's dilemma
  national or ethnic commitment, 17–18, 20
  in state/club enforcement game, 79–84
privatization, post-revolution Czechoslovakia, 238
property rights, 1
  costless, 143–4
  in former Soviet bloc, 67
  homesteading to insure, 109
  with nationalization, 206
  to social capital, 165–6
  when enforcement is lacking, 8, 45–7
proportional representation, 283, 284, 285
protectionism
  cultural, 184
  ethnic group barriers to entry and exit, 49–50, 52–5, 68
  with nationalism, 168, 182–4
  xenophobia as form of, 110–12
Proulx, Pierre-Paul, 126
pseudocantonization, 279
public goods
  bargaining over divisibility, 262
  cultural and political nationalism as, 106
public goods
  information to understand supply of and demand for, 107

Quebec
  See also Canada
  decline of English speakers in, 121–6
  economy of, 127, 130
  fear of losing French language, xii, 121–6
  perception of Meech Lake Accord, 135–6
  public debt, 130
  response to Canadian accord without Quebec, 133–4
  special status in Canada of, 136
Quebec Inc, 129

Ramet, Sabrina P., 50
rationality
  definition of rational action, 14–15
  of group identity, 21–2, 41
  of individuals, 45
Raynaud, André, 130
redistribution (with nationalism), 168–9
Rees-Mogg, William, 20
religion, 12
Renner, Karl, 210
rents
  conditions for existence of, 46–8
  as determining returns to ethnic capital, 65–7
  ethnic rent seeking, xii, 73, 85–90
  in highly politicized state, 86
resource allocation, 85–90
revolutions, socialist-nationalist, 214–23
Ricardo, David, 175
Richerson, J., 199–20
rights
  See also property rights
  allocation by constitutions, xi, 7–8
  allocation with diminished authority, xi, 8–10
  in Basque region, 5–8
  concept of, 1
  effect of system collapse, 9
  in hierarchal system of authority, 3–6
  under Russian Social-Democratic party, 210–11
  of secession, 259
  sources of, 4, 6–8
  winning group, 9–10
Riker, W. H., 163
Roberts, H., 268
Rocher, François, 133
Roeder, Phillip G., 66, 68
Rogowski, Ronald, 65
Romania, 231–2
Rumer, B. Z., 241

Salmon, Pierre, 111, 295, 301
Samuelson, Paul, 106
sanctions
  of clubs, 75–7
  cost of ethnic group or government, 83
  in non-enforcement of ethnic norms, 59
  payoffs with club or government sanctions, 80–3
Sandinista revolution, Nicaragua, 222–3

Index

Sandler, T., 74, 162
Schnapper, Dominique, 294
Schuman, Robert, 292
Schumpeter, Joseph, 149, 195
secession
   Czech Republic and Slovakia, 239
   free riding in movements for, 152
   idea in Quebec, 118–21, 129
   implementation of, 260
   movement in Quebec, 118
   objections to, 162–3
   problems of post-colonial states, 145
   proposals for theory of, xiv, 257–8
segregation
   to diminish destabilization, 263
   to preserve minority ethnic identity, 267
self-determination
   Bolshevik doctrine of national, 210–11
   with democratization, 261–3
   economics of, 260
   as idea in partitions and secessions, 256–7
   Leninist policy, 230
self-enforcement, 59–60
self-government, consociational democracies, 284
self-identification
   bases for individual, 9–10
   in Soviet Union, 224–7
self-interest
   association of group identity with, 17–21
   in choice of group identity, 16
   as rational action, 14–15
The Selfish Gene (Dawkins), 198–200
separatism, 162
services, ethnic groups and clubs, x, xi–xii, 75–84, 93–5
services, government
   effect of decline in, 94–5
   effect on demand and supply of ethnic services, 84–93
   in highly politicized state, 86–8
   relation to independence movements, 93–4
   as substitute for or complement of club services, 79, 85–93
Seton-Watson, Hugh, 146, 155, 241
shame, 56, 58
Shapiro, Carl, 43, 45
Shleifer, Andrei, 57
Silver, M., 171
Simeon, Richard, 138
Sipos, Peter, 71

Smith, Adam, 175–76, 179, 181
Smith, Anthony D., 116, 146, 294
Smith, M., 246
Sniderman, Paul M., 138
social capital, 165–6
socialism, 209–10
   See also nationalism, socialist
societies
   cultural development, 146–7
   effect of majoritarianism in multiethnic, 272–3
sovereignty
   idea in Quebec, 119–21, 126, 129
   profitability of, 131
   support in Quebec for, 127–8
Soviet Union
   See also former Soviet Union
   ethnic networks, 65–7, 153
   federal structure, 152, 212–13
   national identity in, 224–7
   nationality policy, 152–3
specialization, 177–8
Stalin, Joseph, 39, 210–11
Stark, Andrew, 136
state, multinational or multiethnic
   properties of, 84
   Soviet Union, 224–7
state, the
   defined, 143
   equilibrium condition with nation, 143–4
states
   created by European expansion, 145
   creation of new independent post-colonial, 144–5
   European colonial, 145
   genocide by, 252
   newly independent post-World War II, 144–5, 155–6
states, multiethnic or multinational
   under cantonization, 278
   destabilizing factors, 262–3
   federalism as conflict regulator, 281–2
   Yugoslavia, 227–9
Stein, M., 280
Stepan, A., 240
Stigler, George J., 99
Stroup, Richard, 110
subsidiarity
   cantonization as application of, 278
   in European integration process, 291
subsidies, 51
Summers, Lawrence, 46, 57
symbols
   Quebec–Canada question, 138
   symbolic utility, 190–2, 196

Index

Tambiah, Stanley, 156
Taylor, Charles, 136, 138
Taylor, Paul, 292
territory
  Soviet tying of minorities through, 65–6
  in Soviet Union according to ethnicity, 152
Tito, Josip Broz, 227
totalitarian governments, 65–8
Tremblay, Rodrigue, 126
Trudeau, Pierre Elliott, 123, 131
trust, 56
trust relationships
  capital formation in, 45–8
  investment in, 46–8
Tullock, Gordon, 99
Turner, R. F., 218

United Nations, 277
Urquhart, Ian, 136
utility maximization, 190–6

Vaillancourt, François, 127
Vanous, J., 213
Vaubel, Roland, 291
vetoes, constitutional, 283–4
Vietnam, 216–19
Vietnamese Communist party, 217–18
Vile, M., 282
violence, 29–34

voters
  in market for nationalism, 208–9
  voting behavior theory, 167–9

Wallerstein, Immanuel, 149
war, 38–41
Ward, Barbara, 44
Waring, Stephen P., 117
Watkins, Mel, 99–100
wealth accumulation, 178
Weaver, R. Kent, 133
Weber, Eugen, 11
Weisbrod, Burton, 106
Wells, Clyde, 131
Wilson, Woodrow, 39
Wintrobe, Ronald, 43, 46, 51, 65, 67, 187

xenophobia
  description of, 110–11
  examples of, 112
  relation to nationalism, xiii, 111–12
  Sri Lanka, 156

Young, Robert, 125, 136
Yugoslavia
  under communism, 228
  federalism in, 281
  post-communist nationalism, 238, 240
  socialist nationalism in, 227–9

Zaslavsky, Victor, 65–6, 153, 227

For EU product safety concerns, contact us at Calle de José Abascal, 56–1°, 28003 Madrid, Spain or eugpsr@cambridge.org.

www.ingramcontent.com/pod-product-compliance
Ingram Content Group UK Ltd.
Pitfield, Milton Keynes, MK11 3LW, UK
UKHW040609070825
461487UK00005BA/324